# Instant Vortex Air Fryer Cookbook:

600+ Flavorful and Quick Air Fryer Recipes for Beginners and advanced Users, to Make Everyday Cooking Easier and Tastier

Written by
**Rachel Dash**

This document is geared towards providing exact and reliable information in regards to the topic and issue covered. The publication is sold with the idea that the publisher is not required to render accounting, officially permitted, or otherwise, qualified services. If advice is necessary, legal or professional, a practiced individual in the profession should be ordered.

From a Declaration of Principles which was accepted and approved equally by a Committee of the American Bar Association and a Committee of Publishers and Associations.

In no way is it legal to reproduce, duplicate, or transmit any part of this document in either electronic means or in printed format. Recording of this publication is strictly prohibited and any storage of this document is not allowed unless with written permission from the publisher. All rights reserved.

The information provided herein is stated to be truthful and consistent, in that any liability, in terms of inattention or otherwise, by any usage or abuse of any policies, processes, or directions contained within is the solitary and utter responsibility of the recipient reader. Under no circumstances will any legal responsibility or blame be held against the publisher for any reparation, damages, or monetary loss due to the information herein, either directly or indirectly.

Respective authors own all copyrights not held by the publisher.

The information herein is offered for informational purposes solely, and is universal as so. The presentation of the information is without a contract or any type of guarantee assurance.

The trademarks that are used are without any consent, and the publication of the trademark is without permission or backing by the trademark owner. All trademarks and brands within this book are for clarifying purposes only and are owned by the owners themselves, not affiliated with this document.

# Table of Contents

An Air Fryer is a modern kitchen device that cooks food by blowing extremely hot air around it instead of using oil. It provides a low-fat variant of food that in a deep fryer will usually be fried. Consequently, fatty foods such as French fries, fried chicken, and onion rings are usually prepared with no oil or up to 80% less fat relative to traditional cooking techniques.

The Air Fryer offers fried foods and nutritious meals, helping you eliminate the calories that come with fried foods and providing you the crunchiness, taste, and flavor you love. This household appliance works by blowing very hot air (up to 400°F) uniformly and rapidly around a food ingredient. The heat renders the food part on the outside crispy and brittle, but it is warm and moist on the inside. You can use an Air Fryer on pretty much everything. You should barbecue, bake, and roast in addition to frying. Its cooking choices allow you to eat any food at any time of the day in a simpler way.

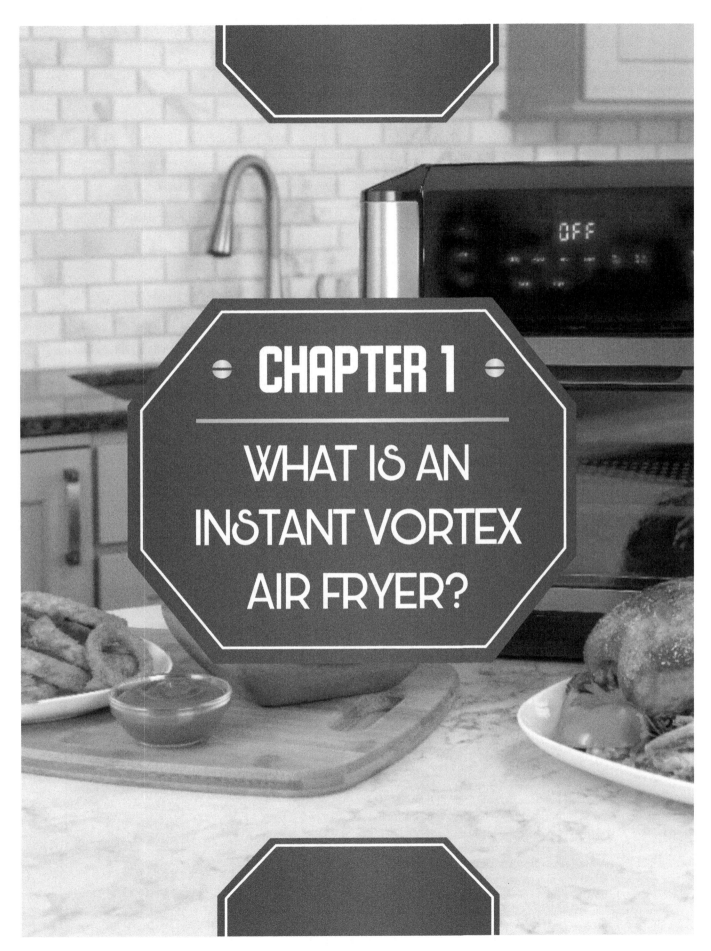

# CHAPTER 1

## WHAT IS AN INSTANT VORTEX AIR FRYER?

The Instant Vortex Air Fryer allows you to make healthy variations of all of your beloved fast foods, from natural to frozen, cooked to excellence and guilt-free. Get the deep-fried flavor and feel by using up to 95% less oil, and enjoy quick cleanup since less oil implies less mess.

Air frying uses super-heated cooling air instead of hot oil to provide the same chewy flavor and feel deep-fried cuisine. It also traps juices within the crispy coating without adding more oil: it's faster, safer, better, and a ton less work.
Air fry, grill, toast, and reheat in a flash with the pre-programmed Smart Services. Juicy buffalo wings, chewy potatoes, hash browns, and more can all be air fried, like cabbage bites roasted in the oven, garlicky peas, shrimp skewers, and corn dogs.

Meatball subs or small pizzas, soft cinnamon rolls, and chewy brownie bits, all baked in the oven. Alternatively, for dinner, reheat last night's meal.

### Advantages of the Air Fryer
Next are some of the advantages of using this cooking method

## Using an Air Fryer May Help Cut Fat Content

Deep-fried foods are typically richer in calories than foods cooked with other cooking techniques. A fried turkey breast, for instance, has around 30% greater fat than just a roasted turkey breast. According to certain suppliers, using an Air Fryer will reduce fatty foods' fat content by close to 75%. This is because Air Fryers use a lot less fat than standard deep fryers. Most deep-fried recipes call for up to 3 c. (750 ml.) of oil, but air-fried items need around 1 tbsp. (15 ml.). Deep fryers use up to 50 times more oil than Air Fryers, and although not any of that oil is consumed by the cooking, utilizing an Air Fryer will greatly reduce the food's total fat level. Air frying yielded a substance of somewhat less fat but comparable color and moisture content. This may have a significant effect on your well-being, as consuming more fat from plant oils has been linked to an elevated risk of heart failure and swelling.

## Transitioning to an Air Fryer Might Help You Lose Weight

Deep-fried items are rich in sugar, but they're still high in calories, leading to weight gain. Fried food consumption was linked to an increased risk of overweight. Change from deep-fried foods to air-fried foods may be a healthy way to begin if you're trying to lose weight. Nutritional fat provides about twice as much energy per serving as the other macro and micronutrients, including complex carbohydrates, with 9 calories per g. This can be a convenient way to reduce calories and encourage weight reduction since air-fried foods have less fat than deep-fried foods.

## The Production of Hazardous Substances May Be Reduced by Using Air Fryers

Frying food can produce possibly hazardous substances like acrylamide, in contrast to becoming rich in fat and calories. Acrylamide is a carbohydrate-rich food compound produced through a high-heat cooking technique such as frying. Acrylamide is listed as a "human carcinogen" by the International Agency for Testing on Cancer, which means that any evidence suggests that it could be related to cancer growth.

While the evidence is contradictory, several reports have linked nutritional acrylamide to an elevated risk of renal, endometrial, and ovarian cancers.
Using an Air Fryer rather than a deep fryer will help reduce the amount of acrylamide in your fried foods.

In reality, compared to conventional deep frying, one study showed that air frying decreased acrylamide by 90%. It's worth noting, though, that other potentially hazardous compounds can develop during the air-frying phase.

Other possibly harmful chemicals produced by high-heat cooking include heterocyclic amines, aldehydes, and polycyclic aromatic hydrocarbons, linked to increased cancer risk. To find out how air frying affects the production of these substances, further study is required.

## Cleaning and Upkeep

- After every use, wipe your Air Fryer.
- When washing, disconnect the Air Fryer and allow it to cool to room temperature.
- For all of the pieces, do not use harmful chemicals cleaning products, scouring sheets, or pigments.

## Part/Accessory Cleaning

Basket for Air Frying
- Using a towel or rag, scrub the Air Fryer container with some warm water and liquid soap mixture.
- Be sure the oil and food residue are out.
- The basket should not be submerged in water or some other material.
- Must not use an electric dishwasher to rinse the container.

## Cooking Tray

- Clean your cooking tray with a washcloth and some warm water and dish soap mixture, or run it through an electric dishwasher.

- The cooking tray is made of nonstick material.
- Do not use steel washing utensils to prevent damaging the nonstick surface.

## Cooking Chamber

- Using a towel or rag, wash the cooking area with some warm water and dish soap mixture.
- Spray the cooking area with a combination of baking soda and vinegar and scrub clean using a wet cloth to prevent baked-on oil and food debris. Enable the solution to settle on the contaminated region for a few minutes before brushing clean for persistent stains.
- Check for oil splotches and food residue on the heating coil. If necessary, clean the heating coil with a wet towel. Before using it again, make sure the heating coil is fully dry.

## Exterior

- Wash and dry with a soft, moist cloth or sponge.

# CHAPTER 2

## BREAKFAST AND BRUNCH RECIPES

## 1. Easy Granola Recipe

Ready in: 50 minutes | Servings: 6 | Difficulty: Hard

**Ingredients**

- 3/4 c. dried fruit (optional)
- 1/3 c. extra-virgin olive oil
- 1/3 c. maple syrup
- ½ c. light brown sugar
- 1 tbsp. sea salt
- 1/3 c. pumpkin seeds
- 1 c. unsweetened coconut chips
- 1 c. nuts, pistachios, almonds, etc.
- 2 ¾ c. rolled oats

**Directions**

1. Dehydrate at about 165°F in your Air Fryer. The rack would be at the bottom level.

2. In a big mixing pot, combine the coconut, nuts, pumpkin seeds, oats, and salt.

3. Heat the oil, sugar, and syrup in a saucepan until the sugar dissolves completely. Microwaving appears to fit as well (60–90 seconds and mix after every 30 seconds).

4. Stir the mixture into the oats until they are evenly covered.

5. In your Air Fryer, use Pyrex or a bowl that would work. Make sure to spray it thoroughly and without sticking.

6. Combine the oats and water in a mixing bowl. Spread out the oats as far as feasible; however, overlapping is appropriate.

7. Allow 30–40 minutes for dehydration. At 10 minutes, stir.

8. If required, add dried fruit after it's done.

9. This recipe yields approximately 6 bowls. Please keep it in an airtight container to store.

Nutrition: **Calories: 335 | Protein: 11 g | Carbohydrates: 34 g | Fat: 5 g | Sugar: 34 g**

## 2. Baked Eggs

Ready in: 34 minutes | Servings: 5 | Difficulty: Hard

**Ingredients**

- Cooking spray
- 2 tbsps. olive oil
- 6 tbsps. milk
- 8 oz. ham, chopped
- 2 lbs. baby spinach, torn
- 5 eggs
- Salt and black pepper according to your taste

**Directions**

1. Heat the oil in a pan on a medium-high flame, add some baby spinach, cook for a few minutes and switch off the flame.

2. Butter 4 trays with some cooking spray and split your baby spinach and ham among the trays.

3. In each ramekin, break an egg, split some milk, season using pepper and salt, put the ramekins at 350°F in the preheated Air Fryer, and cook for around 20 minutes.

4. Serve your fried eggs for a healthy breakfast and enjoy!

Nutrition: **Calories: 310 | Sodium: 365 mg | Protein: 11 g | Carbohydrates: 42 g | Fiber: 6 g | Fat: 9 g**

## 3. Sweet Casserole

Ready in: 47 minutes | Servings: 5 | Difficulty: Hard

**Ingredients**

- ½ c flour
- 1 ½ tsp cinnamon powder
- 2 tbsps. white sugar
- 4 tbsps. butter
- 3 tbsps. brown sugar

**For The Casserole:**

- 2 2/3 c blueberries
- Zest from 1 lemon, grated
- 4 tbsps. butter
- 3 c buttermilk
- 1 c milk
- 2 eggs
- 2 tsps. baking powder
- 2 tsps. baking soda
- 2 ½ c white flour
- 3 tbsps. white sugar
- 3 eggs

**Directions**

1. Mix your eggs in a bowl with tablespoons of white sugar, baking powder, 2 ½ c white flour, baking soda, buttermilk, milk, lemon zest, 4 tablespoons of butter, and blueberries.

2. Add tablespoons of brown sugar in a separate bowl with tablespoons of butter, 2 tablespoons of white sugar, cinnamon, and ½ cup of flour, stir until crumbled, and sprinkle over the blueberry mixture.

3. Put it in a preheated Air Fryer and cook for about 30 minutes at around 300°F.

4. Split them into plates and serve them for breakfast Enjoy!

Nutrition: **Calories:143 | Fat: 35 g | Sodium: 159 mg | Carbohydrates: 19 g | Fiber: 0 g | Protein: 18 g**

## 4. Delicious Potato Hash

Ready in: 42 minutes | Servings: 5 | Difficulty: Hard

**Ingredients**

- 2 ½ potatoes, cubed
- 2 yellow onion, chopped
- 3 tsps. olive oil
- 2 green bell pepper, chopped
- Salt and black pepper according to your taste
- 1 tsp thyme, dried
- 3 eggs

**Directions**

1. Heat the Air Fryer to about 350°F, add some oil, warm it, add the bell pepper, onion, pepper, salt, mix, and cook for about 5 minutes.

2. Add the thyme, potatoes, eggs, mix, cover, and simmer for about 20 minutes at around 360°F.

3. Split them into plates and eat them for brunch Enjoy!

Nutrition: **Calories: 310 | Sodium: 365 mg | Protein: 11 g | Carbohydrates: 42 g | Fiber: 6 g | Fat: 9 g**

## 5. Tasty Cinnamon Toast

Ready in: 21 minutes | Servings: 8 | Difficulty: Normal

**Ingredients**
- 2 ½ tsp cinnamon powder
- 2 ½ tsp vanilla extract
- 1 c sugar
- 16 bread slices
- 2 stick butter, soft

**Directions**

1. Add the soft butter with vanilla, sugar, and cinnamon in a bowl and stir together well.
2. Put this over your bread slices, put them in the Air Fryer, and cook for about 5 minutes at 400°F.
3. Split them into plates and serve them for brunch Enjoy!

Nutrition: **Calories: 484 | Fat: 21 g | Sodium: 402 mg | Potassium: 56 mg**

## 6. Delicious Potatoes

Ready in: 55 minutes | Servings: 5 | Difficulty: Hard

**Ingredients**
- 2 tsps. onion powder
- 2 tsps. sweet paprika
- 2 tsps. garlic powder
- Salt and black pepper according to your taste
- 2 red bell pepper, chopped
- 2 yellow onions, chopped
- 4 potatoes, cubed
- 3 tbsps. olive oil

**Directions**

1. Oil your Air Fryer basket with some olive oil; add your potatoes, toss, and season using pepper and salt.
2. Add the garlic powder, onion, paprika, bell pepper, and onion powder Mix properly, cover the pot, and cook it for about 30 minutes at around 370°F.
3. Split the mixed potatoes into bowls and eat them for brunch Enjoy!

Nutririon: **Calories: 231 | Fat: 4 g | Sodium: 270 mg | Protein: 8 mg | Calcium: 5 mg**

## 7. Polenta Bites

Ready in: 37 minutes | Servings: 6 | Difficulty: Hard

**Ingredients**
For the polenta:
- 4 c water
- 2 c cornmeal
- 2 tbsps. butter
- Salt and black pepper according to your taste
For the polenta bites:
- Cooking spray
- 2 tbsps. powdered sugar

**Directions**

1. Add butter, cornmeal, pepper, and salt with water in a saucepan, whisk, bring to a simmer on medium-high heat, steam for about 10 minutes, and remove from flame, mix again and hold in the refrigerator until it cools.
2. Scoop 1 tbsp. polenta, place on a working board and form a sphere.
3. Repeat the same procedure with the remaining polenta; place all the balls in your Air Fryer's cooking basket, spray with some cooking spray, cover and cook for about 8 minutes at around 380°F.
4. Arrange bites of polenta on bowls dust all over with sugar and enjoy for brunch.

Nutrition: **Calories: 192 | Fat: 8 g | Cholesterol: 8 mg | Protein: 14 g**

## 8. Egg Muffins

Ready in: 30 minutes | Servings: 5 | Difficulty: Hard

**Ingredients**
- 1 splash of Worcestershire sauce
- 3 egg
- 3 oz. Parmesan, grated
- 2 tbsps. baking powder
- 4 ½ oz. white flour
- 4–5 tbsps. milk
- 3 tbsps. olive oil

**Directions**

1. Add eggs with your oil, flour, milk, baking powder, Parmesan, and Worcestershire in a bowl, mix well, and split into 5 silicone muffin molds.
2. Organize the molds in the baking basket of the Air Fryer, cover, and steam for about 15 minutes at around 392°F
3. For brunch, serve warmly Enjoy!

Nutrition: **Calories: 346 | Carbohydrates: 47 g | Sugar: 8 g | Protein: 28 g**

## 9. Rustic Breakfast

Ready in: 27 minutes | Servings: 5 | Difficulty: Normal

**Ingredients**
- Cooking spray
- 5 eggs
- 5 bacon slices, chopped
- 5 chipolatas
- 2 garlic cloves, minced
- Salt and black pepper according to your taste
- 10 tomatoes, halved
- 10 chestnuts mushrooms, halved
- 8 oz. baby spinach

**Directions**

1. Oil your cooking pan with some butter or oil and add some garlic, tomatoes, and mushrooms to your cooking pan.
2. Add chipolatas and bacon, now add spinach and finish with cracked eggs.
3. Season using pepper and salt, put your pan in your Air Fryer cooking basket, and bake at about 350°F for around 15 minutes

4. Split them into plates and serve them for some breakfast Enjoy!

Nutrition: **Calories: 261 | Fat: 10 g | Carbohydrates: 63 g | Sugar: 9 g | Protein: 7 g**

## 10. Air-Fried Sandwich

Ready in: 20 minutes | Servings: 3 | Difficulty: Normal

**Ingredients**
• 3 English muffins, halved
• 3 eggs
• 3 bacon strips
• Salt and black pepper according to your taste

**Directions**
1. In your Air Fryer, break and add the eggs, put bacon on top, cover, and cook for about 6 minutes at around 392°F .
2. In your oven, warm your English muffin halves for a few seconds, split the eggs into 2 halves, top with bacon, add some salt and pepper, top with the other half of your English muffins and enjoy for brunch.

Nutrition: **Calories: 377 | Fat: 16 g | Carbohydrates: 73 g | Protein: 13 g**

## 11. Delicious Breakfast Soufflé

Ready in: 25 minutes | Servings: 5 | Difficulty: Normal

**Ingredients**
• 3 tbsps. chives, chopped
• 3 tbsps. parsley, chopped
• 1 pinch of red chili pepper, crushed
• 5 tbsps. heavy cream
• 5 eggs, whisked
• Salt and black pepper according to your taste

**Directions**
1. Mix the salt, eggs, heavy cream, pepper, red chili pepper, chives, and parsley in a big bowl, blend well, and split into 4 soufflé bowls.
2. Organize the pots into your Air Fryer and cook the soufflés for around 8 minutes at about 350°F.
3. Serve them warm And enjoy!

Nutrition: **Calories: 270 | Fat: 4 g | Carbohydrates: 60 g | Sugar: 7 g | Protein: 23 g**

## 12. Breakfast Egg Bowls

Ready in: 40 minutes | Servings: 5 | Difficulty: Hard

**Ingredients**
• 5 tbsps. Parmesan, grated
• Salt and black pepper according to your taste
• 5 tbsps. mixed parsley and chives
• 5 eggs
• 5 tbsps. heavy cream
• 5 dinner rolls, tops sliced off and insides scooped out

**Directions**
1. On a baking tray, place your dinner rolls and break 1 egg into each one.
2. Split the heavy cream in all rolls with the mixed herbs and season using some pepper and salt.
3. Toss some Parmesan on top of the rolls, put them into your Air Fryer, and fry for about 25 minutes at around 350°F.
4. Add the bread bowls to plates and eat them for breakfast And enjoy!

Nutrition: **Calories: 262 | Fat: 11 g | Sodium: 6 mg | Carbohydrates: 52 g | Sugar: 12 g | Protein: 6 g**

## 13. Tomato and Bacon Breakfast

Ready in: 47 minutes | Servings: 7 | Difficulty: Hard

**Ingredients**
• 2 lbs. white bread, cubed
• 2 lbs. smoked bacon, cooked and chopped
• ½ c olive oil
• 2 yellow onions, chopped
• 30 oz. canned tomatoes, chopped
• 1 tsp red pepper, crushed
• 1 lb. Cheddar, shredded
• 3 tbsps. chives, chopped
• 1 lb. Monterey Jack, shredded
• 3 tbsps. stock
• Salt and black pepper according to your taste
• 10 eggs, whisked

**Directions**
1. Into your Air Fryer, add some oil and warm it to about 350°F.
2. Add and stir in the bacon, bread, tomatoes, onion, red pepper, and stock.
3. Put the Cheddar, eggs, and Monterey Jack together and simmer for about 20 minutes Season with salt and black pepper.
4. Split into bowls, dust with chives, and eat Enjoy!

Nutrition: **Calories: 476 | Fat: 17 g | Carbohydrates: 70 g | Sugar: 7 g | Protein: 14 g**

## 14. Ham Breakfast

Ready in: 33 minutes | Servings: 8 | Difficulty: Hard

**Ingredients**
• Cooking spray
• Salt and black pepper according to your taste
• 2 tbsps. mustard
• 8 eggs
• 3 c milk
• 6 oz. Cheddar cheese, shredded
• 12 oz. ham, cubed
• 6 oz. green chilies, chopped
• 8 c French bread, cubed

**Directions**
1. Heat up the Air Fryer to about 350°F and oil it with some cooking spray.
2. Mix the cheese, milk, salt, mustard, and pepper with the eggs in a bowl and stir.

3. In an Air Fryer, place the bread cubes and combine them with the ham and chilies.

4. Add the mixture of eggs, spread evenly, and simmer for about 15 minutes.

5. Split and serve between plates Enjoy!

Nutrition: **Calories: 388 | Fat: 212 g | Carbohydrates: 41 g**

## 15. Oatmeal Casserole

Ready in: 37 minutes | Servings: 8 | Difficulty: Hard

### Ingredients

- Cooking spray
- 2 tsps. vanilla extract
- 3 tbsps. butter
- 2 eggs
- 3 c milk
- 2 bananas, peeled and mashed
- 1 c blueberries
- 1 c chocolate chips
- 2 tsps. cinnamon powder
- 2/3 c brown sugar
- 2 tsps. baking powder
- 3 c rolled oats

### Directions

1. Mix the cinnamon, sugar, baking powder, blueberries, chocolate chips, bananas in a container, and stir.

2. Mix the eggs with vanilla essence, milk, and butter in a different bowl and stir.

3. Warm your Air Fryer to about 320°F, oil with some cooking spray, and add some oats to the base.

4. Transfer the mixture of eggs and cinnamon, mix, and simmer for about 20 minutes.

5. Mix again, split into bowls, and eat with some tea Enjoy!

Nutrition: **Calories: 337 | Fat: 12 g | Carbohydrates: 48 g | Sugar: 11 g | Protein: 25 g**

## 16. Tofu Scramble

Ready in: 45 minutes | Servings: 6 | Difficulty: Hard

### Ingredients

- Salt and black pepper according to your taste
- 1 c yellow onion, chopped
- 3 ½ c red potatoes, cubed
- 1 tsp garlic powder
- 1 tsp onion powder
- 6 c broccoli florets
- 3 tbsps. extra-virgin olive oil
- 2 tsps. turmeric, ground
- 2 tofu blocks, cubed
- 4 tbsps. soy sauce

### Directions

1. In a container, mix the tofu and salt, 1 tbsp. oil, pepper, garlic powder, soy sauce, onion powder, onion, and turmeric, stir and set aside.

2. Mix the potatoes with a pinch of salt, the remainder of the oil, and pepper in a small bowl and toss to coat completely.

3. Set the potatoes into your Air Fryer at about 350°F, and cook for about 15 minutes, turning once.

4. Now add tofu into your Air Fryer and its marinade, and cook for about 15 minutes.

5. In the fryer, add some broccoli and bake it for about 5 more minutes.

6. Serve immediately Enjoy!

Nutrition: **Calories: 286 | Fat: 12 g | Carbohydrates: 27 g | Sugar: 01 g | Protein: 20 g**

## 17. Turkey Burrito

Ready in: 24 minutes | Servings: 4 | Difficulty: Normal

### Ingredients

- 2/3 c Mozzarella cheese, grated
- Salt and black pepper according to your taste
- 6 tbsps. salsa
- 2 small avocados, peeled, pitted, and sliced
- 4 eggs
- 1 red bell pepper, sliced
- 6 slices turkey breast already cooked
- Tortillas for serving

### Directions

1. Mix the eggs in a bowl with some pepper and salt according to taste, put them in a pan, and place them in the basket of your Air Fryer.

2. Cook for about 5 minutes at around 400°F, take out the pan from the Air Fryer, and shift the eggs to a dish.

3. On a working board, place tortillas, split eggs on them, split turkey meat, cheese, bell pepper, avocado, and salsa.

4. Once you've packed it with some tin foil, wrap your burritos and put them in the Air Fryer.

5. Warm the burritos for about 3 minutes at around 300°F, split them into plates, and eat Enjoy!

Nutrition: **Calories: 493 | Fat: 41 g | Carbohydrates: 6 g | Sugar: 0 g | Protein: 29 g**

## 18. Biscuits Casserole

Ready in: 35 minutes | Servings: 10 | Difficulty: Hard

### Ingredients

- Cooking spray
- 3 ½ c milk
- 1 pinch of salt and black pepper
- 1 lb. sausage, chopped
- 5 tbsps. flour
- 14 oz. biscuits, quartered

### Directions

1. Apply cooking oil to your Air Fryer and warm it at around 350°F.

2. Add some biscuits at the bottom, and then blend with the sausage.

3. Add some milk, flour, pepper, salt and simmer for about 15 minutes, mix a little and simmer.

4. Split them into plates and serve them for brunch Enjoy!

Nutrition: **Calories: 197 | Fat: 14 g | Carbohydrates: 6 g | Sugar: 2 g | Protein: 14 g**

## 19. Air-Fried Bake Cheese

Ready in: 40 minutes | Servings: 6 | Difficulty: Hard

**Ingredients**

• Cooking spray
• 5 tbsps. parsley, chopped
• Salt and black pepper according to your taste
• 1 tsp onion powder
• 3 eggs
• 2 lbs. breakfast sausage, casings removed and chopped
• 3 ½ c Cheddar cheese, shredded
• 3 c milk
• 6 bacon slices, cooked and crumbled

**Directions**

1. Mix the milk, eggs, onion powder, cheese, pepper, salt, and parsley in a bowl and mix thoroughly.
2. Use cooking spray to oil your Air Fryer, heat it to 320°F now add bacon and sausage.
3. Add the mixture of eggs, scatter, and simmer for about 20 minutes.
4. Split and serve between plates Enjoy!

Nutrition: **Calories: 424 | Fat: 37 g | Carbohydrates: 5 g | Sugar: 1 g | Protein: 21 g**

## 20. Sausage, Eggs, and Cheese Mix

Ready in: 37 minutes | Servings: 6 | Difficulty: Hard

**Ingredients**

• Cooking spray
• Salt and black pepper according to your taste
• 2 c milk
• 10 eggs, whisked
• 2 c Mozzarella cheese, shredded
• 2 c Cheddar cheese, shredded
• 12 oz. sausages, cooked and crumbled

**Directions**

1. Mix the Mozzarella, Cheddar cheese, milk, eggs, pepper, and salt with the sausages into a bowl and stir well.
2. Warm the Air Fryer to about 380°F, spray the cooking oil, add the sausage mixture and eggs, and simmer for around 20 minutes.
3. Split and serve between plates Enjoy!

Nutrition: **Calories: 279 | Fat: 20 g | Carbohydrates: 6 g | Sugar: 08 g | Protein: 20 g**

## 21. Eggs Casserole

Ready in: 42 minutes | Servings: 8 | Difficulty: Hard

**Ingredients**

• 3 tomatoes, chopped for serving
• Salt and black pepper according to your taste
• 2 c baby spinach
• 2 sweet potato, cubed
• 14 eggs
• 1 tsp chili powder
• 2 tbsps. olive oil
• 2 lbs. turkey, ground

**Directions**

1. Mix the eggs with the pepper, salt, tomatoes, chili powder, spinach, sweet potato, and turkey in a bowl and stir together well.
2. Heat your Air Fryer to about 350°F, add the oil, and heat it.
3. Add the mixture of eggs, scatter over the Air Fryer, cap, and simmer for about 25 minutes.
4. Split them into dishes and serve them for brunch Enjoy!

Nutrition: **Calories: 312 | Protein: 9 g | Carbohydrates: 60 g | Fat: 75 g | Sugar: 23 g**

## 22. Loaded Cauliflower Breakfast Bake

Ready in: 35 minutes | Servings: 4 | Difficulty: Hard

**Ingredients**

• 12 slices sugar-free bacon, cooked and crumbled
• 2 scallions, sliced on the bias
• 8 tbsps. full-fat sour cream
• 1 medium avocado, peeled and pitted
• 1 c shredded medium Cheddar cheese
• 1 ½ c chopped cauliflower
• ¼ c heavy whipping cream
• 6 large eggs

**Directions**

1. Mix the eggs and whipping cream in a medium dish Pour it into a circular 4-cup baking tray.
2. Add and blend the cauliflower, and cover it with Cheddar Put your dish in the Air Fryer bowl.
3. Change the temperature and set the timer to about 320°F for around 20 minutes.
4. The eggs will be solid once fully baked, and the cheese will be golden brown Slice it into 4 bits.
5. Cut the avocado and split the bits equally Put 2 tablespoons of sliced scallions, sour cream, and crumbled bacon on top of each plate.

Nutrition: **Calories: 145 | Sodium: 77 mg | Protein: 85 g | Carbohydrates: 19 g | Fat: 45 g**

## 23. Scrambled Eggs

Ready in: 24 minutes | Servings: 4 | Difficulty: Normal

**Ingredients**

• ½ c shredded sharp Cheddar cheese
• 2 tbsps. unsalted butter, melted
• 4 large eggs

**Directions**

1. Crack the eggs into a round 2-cup baking pan and whisk them Put the tray in the Air Fryer container.
2. Change the temperature settings and set the timer to about 400°F for around 10 minutes.
3. Mix the eggs after about 5 minutes and add some cheese and butter Let it cook for another 3 minutes and mix again.
4. Give an extra 2 minutes to finish frying or remove the eggs from flame if they are to your preferred taste.
5. For fluffing, use a fork Serve it hot.

Nutrition: **Calories: 235 | Sodium: 64 mg | Protein: 5 g | Carbohydrates: 56 g | Fat: 15 g | Sugar: 37 g**

## 24. Hard-Boiled Eggs

Ready in: 22 minutes | Servings: 4 | Difficulty: Easy

### Ingredients
• 1 c water
• 4 large eggs

### Directions
1. Put the eggs in a heat-proof 4-cup round baking tray and pour some water over your eggs Put the tray in the Air Fryer basket
2. Set the Air Fryer's temperature to about 300°F and set the clock for about 18 minutes.
3. In the fridge, store boiled eggs before ready to consume or peel and serve warmly.

Nutrition: Calories: 190 | Sodium: 118 mg | Protein: 4 g | Carbohydrates: 40 g | Fat: 1 g

## 25. Breakfast Stuffed Poblanos

Ready in: 32 minutes | Servings: 5 | Difficulty: Easy

### Ingredients
• ½ c full-fat sour cream
• 8 tbsps. shredded Pepper Jack cheese
• 4 large poblano peppers
• ¼ c canned diced tomatoes and green chilies, drained
• 4 oz. full-fat cream cheese, softened
• 4 large eggs
• ½ lb. spicy ground pork breakfast sausage

### Directions
1. Crumble and brown the cooked sausage in a large skillet over medium-low heat until no red exists Take the sausage from the skillet and clean the oil Crack your eggs in the skillet, scramble, and simmer until they are no longer watery.
2. In a wide bowl, add the fried sausage and add in cream cheese Mix the sliced tomatoes and chilies Gently fold the eggs together
3. Cut a 4–5-inch gap at the top of each poblano, separating the white layer and seeds with a tiny knife In 4 portions, divide the filling and gently scoop into each pepper Cover each with tablespoons of cheese from the Pepper Jack.
4. Drop each pepper into the container of the Air Fryer.
5. Change the temperature and set the timer to about 350°F for around 15 minutes.
6. The peppers will be tender, and when prepared, the cheese will be golden brown Serve instantly with sour cream on top.

Nutrition: Calories: 150 | Sodium: 360 mg | Protein: 66 g | Carbohydrates: 32 g | Fat: 2 g

## 26. Cheesy Cauliflower Hash Browns

Ready in: 22 minutes | Servings: 4 | Difficulty: Easy

### Ingredients
• 1 c shredded sharp Cheddar cheese
• 1 large egg
• 1 (12 oz.) steamer bag cauliflower

### Directions
1. Put the bag in the oven and cook as per the directions in the box To extract excess moisture, leave to cool fully and place cauliflower in a cheesecloth or paper towel and squeeze
2. Add the cheese and eggs and mash the cauliflower using a fork
3. Cut a slice of parchment to match the frame of your Air Fryer Take ¼ of the paste and make it into a hash-brown patty shape and mold it Put it on the parchment and, into your Air Fryer basket, if required, running in groups
4. Change the temperature and set the clock to about 400°F for around 12 minutes
5. Halfway into the cooking process, turn your hash browns They will be nicely browned when fully baked Instantly serve

Nutrition: Calories: 145 | Sodium: 62 mg | Protein: 3 g | Carbohydrates: 25 g | Fat: 4 g

## 27. Egg, Cheese, and Bacon Roll-Ups

Ready in: 40 minutes | Servings: 4 | Difficulty: Hard

### Ingredients
• ½ c mild salsa for dipping
• 1 c shredded sharp Cheddar cheese
• 12 slices sugar-free bacon
• 6 large eggs
• ½ medium green bell pepper, seeded and chopped
• ¼ c chopped onion
• 2 tbsps. unsalted butter

### Directions
1. Melt the butter in a small skillet over medium flame Add the pepper and onion to the skillet and sauté until aromatic, around 3 minutes, and your onions are transparent.
2. In a shallow pot, whisk the eggs and put them into a skillet Scramble the pepper and onion with the eggs once fluffy and fully fried after 5 minutes Remove from the flame and set aside.
3. Put 3 strips of bacon beside each other on the cutting board, overlapping about ¼ Place ¼ c scrambled eggs on the side nearest to you in a pile and scatter ¼ c cheese on top of your eggs.
4. Wrap the bacon around the eggs securely and, if needed, protect the seam using a toothpick Put each wrap into the container of the Air Fryer.
5. Switch the temperature to about 350°F and set the clock for around 15 minutes Midway through the cooking time, turn the rolls.
6. When fully fried, the bacon would be brown and tender For frying, serve immediately with some salsa.

Nutrition: Calories: 166 | Protein: 21 g | Carbohydrates: 17 g | Fat: 2 g | Fiber: 2 g

## 28. Pancake

Ready in: 17 minutes | Servings: 4 | Difficulty: Easy

### Ingredients
• ½ tsp ground cinnamon
• ½ tsp vanilla extract
• ½ tsp unflavored gelatin
• 1 large egg
• 2 tbsps. unsalted butter, softened
• ½ tsp baking powder
• ¼ c powdered Erythritol
• ½ c blanched finely ground almond flour

**Directions**

1. Combine the Erythritol, almond flour, and baking powder in a wide pot Add some egg, butter, cinnamon, gelatin, and vanilla Place into a rectangular 6-inch baking tray.

2. Place the tray in the container of your Air Fryer.

3. Change the temperature to about 300°F and set the clock for 7 minutes.

4. A toothpick can pop out dry when the dessert is fully baked Split the cake into 4 servings and eat.

**Nutrition:** Calories: 167 | Protein: 9 g | Carbohydrates: 27 g | Fiber: 3 g | Cholesterol: 4 mg

## 29. Lemon Poppy Seed Cake

Ready in: 24 minutes | Servings: 6 | Difficulty: Easy

**Ingredients**

- 1 tsp poppy seeds
- 1 medium lemon
- 1 tsp vanilla extract
- 2 large eggs
- ¼ c unsweetened almond milk
- ¼ c unsalted butter, melted
- ½ tsp baking powder
- ½ c powdered Erythritol
- 1 c blanched finely ground almond flour

**Directions**

1. Mix the Erythritol, almond flour, butter, baking powder, eggs, almond milk, and vanilla in a big bowl.

2. Halve the lime and strain the liquid into a little pot, then transfer it to the mixture.

3. Zest the lemon with a fine grinder and transfer 1 tbsp. zest to the mixture and blend Add the poppy seeds to your batter.

4. In the nonstick 6-inch circular cake tin, add your batter Put the pan in the container of your Air Fryer.

5. Change the temperature and set the clock to about 300°F for around 14 minutes.

6. Insert a wooden skewer in the middle; if it comes out completely clean, means it's thoroughly fried The cake will stop cooking and crisp up when it cools Serve at room temperature.

**Nutrition:** Calories: 167 | Protein: 9 g | Carbohydrates: 27 g | Fiber: 3 g | Cholesterol: 4 mg

## 30. Banana Nut Cake

Ready in: 50 minutes | Servings: 6 | Difficulty: Hard

**Ingredients**

- ¼ c chopped walnuts
- 2 large eggs
- ¼ c full-fat sour cream
- 1 tsp vanilla extract
- 2 ½ tsps. banana extract
- ¼ c unsalted butter, melted
- ½ tsp ground cinnamon
- 2 tsps. baking powder
- 2 tbsps. ground golden flaxseed
- ½ c powdered Erythritol
- 1 c blanched finely ground almond flour

**Directions**

1. Mix the Erythritol, almond flour, baking powder, flaxseed, and cinnamon in a big dish.

2. Add vanilla extract, banana extract, butter, and sour cream and mix well.

3. Add your eggs to the combination and whisk until they are fully mixed Mix in your walnuts.

4. Pour into a 6-inch nonstick cake pan and put in the bowl of your Air Fryer.

5. Change the temperature and set the clock to about 300°F for around 25 minutes.

6. When fully baked, the cake will be lightly golden, and a toothpick inserted in the middle will come out clean To prevent cracking, allow it to cool entirely.

**Nutrition:** Calories: 145 | Protein: 18 g | Carbohydrates: 5 g | Fat: 4 g | Fiber: 1 g

## 31. Bacon Strips

Ready in: 17 minutes | Servings: 5 | Difficulty: Easy

**Ingredients**

- 10 slices sugar-free bacon

**Directions**

1. Put slices of bacon into the bucket of your Air Fryer.

2. Change the temperature and set the timer to about 400°F for around 12 minutes.

3. Turn the bacon after 6 minutes and proceed to cook Serve hot.

**Nutrition:** Calories: 165 | Protein: 3 g | Carbohydrates: 35 g | Fat: 25 g | Fiber: 3 g | Cholesterol: 0 mg

## 32. Pumpkin Spice Muffins

Ready in: 25 minutes | Servings: 6 | Difficulty: Easy

**Ingredients**

- 2 large eggs
- 1 tsp vanilla extract
- ¼ tsp ground nutmeg
- ½ tsp ground cinnamon
- ¼ c pure pumpkin purée
- ¼ c unsalted butter, softened
- ½ tsp baking powder
- ½ c granular Erythritol
- 1 c blanched finely ground almond flour

**Directions**

1. Mix the Erythritol, almond flour, butter, baking powder, nutmeg, cinnamon, pumpkin purée, and vanilla in a big dish.

2. Stir in the eggs softly.

3. Add the batter into about 6 or more silicone muffin molds equally Put muffin molds in the Air Fryer basket If required, make them in groups.

4. Change the temperature and set the clock to about 300°F for around 15 minutes.

5. A wooden skewer inserted in the middle will come out completely clean if thoroughly cooked Serve hot.

**Nutrition:** Calories: 190 | Protein: 5 g | Carbohydrates: 39 g | Fat: 25 g

## 33. Veggie Frittata

Ready in: 22 minutes | Servings: 4 | Difficulty: Easy

**Ingredients**
- ¼ c chopped green bell pepper
- ¼ c chopped yellow onion
- ½ c chopped broccoli
- ¼ c heavy whipping cream
- 6 large eggs

**Directions**

1. Whisk the heavy whipping cream and eggs in a big bowl Add in the onion, broccoli, and bell pepper.

2. Load into a 6-inch circular baking dish that is oven-safe Put the baking tray in the basket of an Air Fryer.

3. Switch the temperature to about 350°F and set the clock for around 12 minutes.

4. When the frittata is finished, eggs must be solid and thoroughly cooked Serve it hot.

Nutrition: **Calories: 267 | Protein: 8 g | Carbohydrates: 45 g | Fat: 7 g | Fiber: 3 g**

## 34. Buffalo Egg Cups

Ready in: 24 minutes | Servings: 3 | Difficulty: Easy

**Ingredients**
- ½ c shredded sharp Cheddar cheese
- 2 tbsps. buffalo sauce
- 2 oz. full-fat cream cheese
- 4 large eggs

**Directions**

1. In 2 4-inch ramekins, add the eggs.

2. Mix the buffalo sauce, cream cheese, and Cheddar in a little, microwave-safe container For about 20 seconds, microwave and then mix Put a spoonful on top of each egg within each ramekin

3. Put the ramekins in the container of an Air Fryer.

4. Change the temperature and set the timer to about 320°F for around 15 minutes.

5. Serve it hot.

Nutrition: **Calories: 233 | Protein: 9 g | Carbohydrates: 38 g | Fat: 5 g | Fiber: 2 g**

## 35. Crispy Southwestern Ham Egg Cups

Ready in: 20 minutes | Servings: 4 | Difficulty: Easy

**Ingredients**
- ½ c shredded medium Cheddar cheese
- 2 tbsps. diced white onion
- 2 tbsps. diced red bell pepper
- ¼ c diced of green bell pepper
- 2 tbsps. full-fat sour cream
- 4 large eggs
- 4 (1 oz.) of slices deli ham

**Directions**

1. Put a piece of ham at the bottom of 4 or more baking cups.

2. Whisk the eggs along with the sour cream in a big bowl Add the red pepper, green pepper, and onion and mix well.

3. Add the mixture of eggs into baking cups that are ham-lined Top them with some Cheddar cheese Put the cups in the container of your Air Fryer.

4. Set the clock for around 12 minutes or until the peaks are golden browned, cook at a temperature of about 320°F.

5. Serve it hot.

Nutrition: **Calories: 233 | Protein: 9 g | Carbohydrates: 38 g | Fat: 5 g | Fiber: 2 g**

## 36. Jalapeño Popper Egg Cups

Ready in: 22 minutes | Servings: 3 | Difficulty: Easy

**Ingredients**
- ½ c shredded sharp Cheddar cheese
- 2 oz. full-fat cream cheese
- ¼ c chopped pickled jalapeños
- 4 large eggs

**Directions**

1. Add the eggs to a medium container, and then put them into 4 silicone muffin molds.

2. Place the cream cheese, jalapeños, and Cheddar in a wide, microwave-safe dish Heat in the microwave for about 30 seconds and mix well Take a full spoon and put it in the middle of one of the egg cups, around ¼ of the paste Repeat for the mixture left

3. Put the egg cups in the container of your Air Fryer.

4. Change the temperature and set the clock for around 10 minutes to about 320°F.

5. Serve it hot.

Nutrition: **Calories: 180 | Protein: 8 g | Carbohydrates: 33 g | Fat: 2 g | Fiber: 3 g**

## 37. Crunchy Granola

Ready in: 15 minutes | Servings: 6 | Difficulty: Easy

**Ingredients**
- 1 tsp ground cinnamon
- 2 tbsps. unsalted butter
- ¼ c granular Erythritol
- ¼ c low-carb, sugar-free chocolate chips
- ¼ c golden flaxseed
- 1/3 c sunflower seeds
- 1 c almond slivers
- 1 c unsweetened coconut flakes
- 2 c pecans, chopped

**Directions**

1. Blend all the ingredients in a big bowl

2. In a 4-cup circular baking tray, put the mixture into it

3. Place the tray in the Air Fryer container

4. Change the temperature and set the clock to about 320°F for around 5 minutes

5. Let it cool absolutely before serving

Nutrition: **Calories: 180 | Protein: 8 g | Carbohydrates: 33 g | Fat: 2 g | Fiber: 3 g**

## 38. Toasted French toast

Ready in: 7 minutes | Servings: 1 | Difficulty: Easy

### Ingredients

- ½ c unsweetened shredded coconut
- 1 tsp baking powder
- ½ c lite culinary coconut milk
- 2 slices of gluten-free bread (use your favorite)

### Directions

1. Stir together the baking powder and coconut milk in a large rimmed pot.

2. On a tray, layout your ground coconut.

3. Pick each loaf of your bread and dip it in your coconut milk for the very first time, and then pass it to the ground coconut, let it sit for a few minutes, then cover the slice entirely with the coconut.

4. Place the covered bread loaves in your Air Fryer, cover it, adjust the temperature to about 350°F, and set the clock for around 4 minutes.

5. Take them out from your Air Fryer until done, and finish with some maple syrup of your choice French toast is done Enjoy!

Nutrition: Calories: 250 | Protein: 13 g | Carbohydrates: 31 g | Fat: 11 g | Fiber: 5 g

## 39. Vegan Casserole

Ready in: 32 minutes | Servings: 3 | Difficulty: Normal

### Ingredients

- ½ c cooked quinoa
- 1 tbsp. lemon juice
- 2 tbsps. water
- 2 tbsps. plain soy yogurt
- 2 tbsps. nutritional yeast
- 7 oz. extra-firm tofu about ½ block, drained but not pressed
- ½ tsp ground cumin
- ½ tsp red pepper flakes
- ½ tsp freeze-dried dill
- ½ tsp black pepper
- ½ tsp salt
- 1 tsp dried oregano
- ½ c diced shiitake mushrooms
- ½ c diced bell pepper (I used a combination of red and green)
- 2 small celery stalks, chopped
- 1 large carrot, chopped
- 1 tsp minced, garlic
- 1 small onion, diced
- 1 tsp olive oil

### Directions

1. Warm the olive oil over medium-low heat in a big skillet Add your onion and garlic and simmer till the onion is transparent (for about 3–6 minutes) Add your bell pepper, carrot, and celery and simmer for another 3 minutes Mix the oregano, mushrooms, pepper, salt, cumin, dill, and red pepper powder Mix completely and lower the heat to low If the vegetables tend to cling, stir regularly and add about a tablespoon of water.

2. Pulse the nutritional yeast, tofu, water, yogurt, and some lemon juice in a food mixer until fluffy To your skillet, add your tofu mixture Add in ½ c cooked quinoa Mix thoroughly.

3. Move to a microwave-proof plate or tray that works for your Air Fryer basket.

4. Cook for around 15 minutes at about 350°F (or 18–20 minutes at about 330°F, till it turns golden brown).

5. Please take out your plate or tray from your Air Fryer and let it rest for at least 5 minutes before eating.

Nutrition: Calories: 171 | Protein: 5 g | Carbohydrates: 19 g | Fat: 10 g | Fiber: 5 g

## 40. Vegan Omelet

Ready in: 40 minutes | Servings: 4 | Difficulty: Normal

### Ingredients

- ½ c grated vegan cheese
- 1 tbsp. water
- 1 tbsp. brags
- 3 tbsps. nutritional yeast
- ¼ tsp basil
- ¼ tsp garlic powder
- ¼ tsp onion powder
- ¼ tsp pepper
- ½ tsp cumin
- ½ tsp turmeric
- ¼ tsp salt
- ¼ c chickpea flour (or you may use any bean flour)
- ½ c finely diced veggies (like chard, kale, dried mushrooms, spinach, watermelon radish, etc.)
- ½ piece of tofu (organic high in protein kind)

### Directions

1. Blend all your ingredients in a food blender or mixer, excluding the vegetables and cheese.

2. Move the batter from the blender to a container and combine the vegetables and cheese in it Since it's faster, you could use both hands to combine it.

3. Brush the base of your Air Fryer bucket with some oil.

4. Put a couple of parchment papers on your counter On the top of your parchment paper, place a cookie cutter of your desire.

5. In your cookie cutter, push ⅙ of the paste Then raise and put the cookie cutter on a different section of your parchment paper.

6. Redo the process till you have about 6 pieces using the remainder of the paste.

7. Put 2–3 of your omelets at the base of your Air Fryer container Using some oil, brush the topsides of the omelets.

8. Cook for around 5 minutes at about 370°F, turn and bake for another 4 minutes or more if needed And redo with the omelets that remain.

9. Offer with sriracha mayo or whatever kind of dipping sauce you prefer Or use them for a sandwich at breakfast.

Nutrition: Calories: 235 | Protein: 13 g | Carbohydrates: 47 g | Fat: 1 g | Fiber: 3 g

## 41. Vegan Waffles with Chicken

Ready in: 25 minutes | Servings: 2 | Difficulty: Normal

### Ingredients

**For the fried vegan chicken:**
- ¼–½ tsp black pepper
- ½ tsp paprika
- ½ tsp onion powder
- ½ tsp garlic powder
- 2 tsps. dried parsley
- 2 c gluten-free panko
- ¼ c cornstarch
- 1 c unsweetened non-dairy milk
- 1 small head of cauliflower

**For the yummy cornmeal waffles:**
- ½ tsp pure vanilla extract
- ¼ c unsweetened applesauce
- ½ c unsweetened non-dairy milk
- 1–2 tbsps. Erythritol (or preferred sweetener)
- 1 tsp baking powder
- ¼ c stoneground cornmeal
- 2/3 c gluten-free all-purpose flour

**For the toppings:**
- Vegan butter
- Hot sauce
- Pure maple syrup

## Directions

**For the vegan fried chicken:**

1. Dice the cauliflower (you wouldn't have to be careful in this) into big florets and put it aside.

2. Mix the cornstarch and milk in a tiny pot.

3. Throw the herbs, panko, and spices together in a big bowl or dish.

4. In the thick milk mixture, soak your cauliflower florets, then cover the soaked bits in the prepared panko mix before putting the wrapped floret into your Air Fryer bucket.

5. For the remaining of your cauliflower, redo the same process

6. Set your Air Fryer clock for around 15 minutes to about 400°F and let the cauliflower air fry.

**For the waffles:**

7. Oil a regular waffle iron and warm it up.

8. Mix all your dry ingredients in a pot, and then blend in your wet ingredients until you have a thick mixture.

9. To create a big waffle, utilize ½ of the mixture and redo the process to create another waffle for a maximum of 2 peoples

**For the serving:**

10. Put on dishes your waffles, place each with ½ of the cooked cauliflower, now drizzle with the hot sauce, syrup, and any extra toppings that you want Serve warm!

**Nutrition: Calories: 158 | Protein: 8 g | Carbohydrates: 26 g | Fat: 3 g | Fiber: 2 g**

## 42. Tempeh Bacon

Ready in: 2 hours and 25 minutes | Servings: 4 | Difficulty: Normal

### Ingredients

- ½ tsp freshly grated black pepper
- ½ tsp onion powder
- ½ tsp garlic powder
- 1 ½ tsp smoked paprika
- 1 tsp apple cider vinegar
- 1 tbsp. olive oil (plus some more for oiling your Air Fryer)
- 3 tbsps. pure maple syrup
- ¼ c gluten-free, reduced-sodium tamari
- 8 oz. gluten-free tempeh

### Directions

1. Break your tempeh cube into 2 parts and boil for about 10 minutes, some more if required Add 1 c warm water to the rice cooker bowl Then, put the pieces of tempeh into the steamer basket of the unit Close the cover, push the button for heat or steam cooking (based on your rice cooker's type or brand), and adjust the steaming timer for around 10 minutes.

2. Let the tempeh cool completely before taking it out of the rice cooker or your steamer basket for around 5 minutes.

3. Now make the sauce while cooking the tempeh In a 9x13-inch baking tray, combine all the rest of your ingredients and mix them using a fork Then set it aside and ready the tempeh.

4. Put the tempeh steamed before and cooled on a chopping board, and slice into strips around ¼-inch wide Put each slice gently in the sauce Then roll over each slice gently Seal and put in the fridge for 2–3 hours or even overnight, rotating once or twice during the time.

5. Turn the bits gently one more time until you are about to create the tempeh bacon And if you would like, you may spoon over any leftover sauce.

6. Put your crisper plate/tray into the Air Fryer if yours came with one instead of a built-in one Oil the base of your crisper tray or your Air Fryer basket slightly with some olive oil or using an olive oil spray that is anti-aerosol.

7. Put the tempeh slices in a thin layer gently in your Air Fryer bucket If you have a tiny Air Fryer, you will have to air fry it in 2 or multiple rounds Air fry for around 10–15 minutes at about 325°F before the slices are lightly golden but not burnt You may detach your Air Fryer container to inspect it and make sure it's not burnt It normally takes about 10 minutes.

**Nutrition: Calories: 135 | Protein: 10 g | Carbohydrates: 17 g | Fat: 2 g | Fiber: 0 g**

## 43. Delicious Potato Pancakes

Ready in: 24 minutes | Servings: 4 | Difficulty: Normal

### Ingredients

- Potatoes
- 3 tbsps. flour
- ¼ tsp black pepper
- ¼ tsp salt
- ½ tsp garlic powder
- 2 tbsps. unsalted butter
- ¼ c milk
- 1 beaten egg
- 1 medium onion, chopped

### Directions

1. Preheat the fryer to about 390°F and combine the potatoes, garlic powder, eggs, milk, onion, pepper, butter, and salt in a small bowl; add in the flour and make a batter.

2. Shape around ¼ c your batter into a cake.

3. In the fryer's cooking basket, put the cakes and cook for a couple of minutes.

4. Serve and enjoy your treat!

**Nutrition: Calories: 2 | Protein: 0 g | Carbohydrates: 1 g | Fat: 0 g | Fiber: 0 g**

## 44. Pumpkin Spice Muffins II

Ready in: 22 minutes | Servings: 2 | Difficulty: Normal

### Ingredients

- 3 tbsps. oil
- ¼ c milk
- 1 egg
- 1/3 c pumpkin puree
- 1 tbsp. pumpkin spice
- 1 tbsp. vanilla extract
- 1/3 c sugar
- 1 tbsp. baking powder
- 1 c flour

### Directions

1. In a muffin tray, put muffin liners Set it aside.

2. Mix baking powder, flour, and sugar in a mixing dish.

3. Add the pumpkin spice, vanilla extract, egg, pumpkin puree, oil, and milk in a separate dish.

4. Slowly whisk in the wet ingredients into your dry ingredients until all is well combined and no lumps remain.

5. Fill the muffin tins halfway with the batter Place in the bowl of your Air Fryer Preheat the fryer to about 360°F and air fry for around 10–12 minutes

6. Put your brace in the center of the space

**Nutrition: Calories: 2 | Protein: 0 g | Carbohydrates: 1 g | Fat: 0 g | Fiber: 0 g**

## 45. Potato, Sausage, and Bell Pepper Hash
Ready in: 2 hours | Servings: 2 | Difficulty: Hard

**Ingredients**
- ½ tsp Cajun seasoning
- ¼ tsp garlic powder
- ½ green bell pepper seeded and diced
- ½ onion diced
- ½ tbsp. extra-virgin olive oil
- 1 link sausage (we like Bradley's Country Sausage)
- 2 potatoes peeled and cubed
- Salt and freshly ground black pepper

**Directions**
1. Preheat your Air Fryer to about 350°F.
2. Place the potatoes in a pot, sliced Season with 1 tsp olive oil and a pinch of salt and black pepper.
3. Cook for around 5 minutes, tossing the potatoes once in the process.
4. Dice the remainder of the vegetables and sausage as they're frying Place the vegetables in a mixing dish Season with 1 tsp olive oil, Cajun seasoning, garlic powder, and a pinch of salt and black pepper.
5. Place the remaining ingredients on a rack just above potatoes in your Air Fryer for 5 minutes in the oven.
6. Cook for another 5 minutes after combining all of the vegetables on one rack Be cautious when combining them because the rack would be hot.

Nutrition: Calories: 2 | Protein: 0 g | Carbohydrates: 1 g | Fat: 0 g | Fiber: 0 g

## 46. Garlic Mix
Ready in: 2 minutes | Servings: 1 | Difficulty: Easy

**Ingredients**
- 1 pinch of salt and pepper to taste
- 1 tbs. parsley
- 2 cloves of minced garlic or
- 2 tbsps. garlic powder
- 1 stick of butter softened best if left out at room temperature about ½ hour before making

**Directions**
1. Mix all of the items.
2. Put your leftovers in the fridge for up to 7 days or store them in the freezer for up to 3 months in an enclosed container.

Nutrition: Calories: 122 | Protein: 57 g | Carbohydrates: 211 g | Fat: 22 g | Fiber: 2 g | Cholesterol: 28 mg | Sodium: 34 mg | Potassium: 216 mg

## 47. Breakfast Sausage
Ready in: 5 minutes | Servings: 1 | Difficulty: Easy

**Ingredients**
- Sausages

**Directions**
1. Preheat the Air Fryer to about 165°F
2. Crumbled into small pieces
3. Cook for around 4–5 minutes by placing on the lowest rack of your Air Fryer

Nutrition: Calories: 212 | Fat: 3 g | Fiber: 6 g | Carbohydrates: 14 g | Protein: 6 g

## 48. Breakfast Biscuits
Ready in: 25 minutes | Servings: 18 | Difficulty: Normal

**Ingredients**
- Vegetable shortening to oil the muffin tins
- 2 eggs
- 4 tbsps. butter melted
- 2 oz. cream cheese melted
- 4 c shredded Mozzarella cheese melted
- ½ c 1:1 Stevia powder
- ½ tsp salt
- 4 tsps. baking powder
- 2 c almond flour

**Directions**
1. Mix the salt, baking powder, almond flour, and Stevia powder in a mixing pot Using a whisk, combine all components, so they are uniformly mixed.
2. Add the cream cheese, Mozzarella cheese, and butter in an oven-safe cup, cover, and heat on high for around 2 minutes or longer to soften the components far enough to be able to mix them along using a fork before thoroughly combined.
3. Add the butter and cheese combination into the dry ingredients with a stiff spoon and stir to combine.
4. Add in the eggs and blend the flour until it is combined or till the combination is soft but not sticky to the touch.
5. Preheat the Air Fryer to about 350°F on the "Bake" setting Vegetable shortening can be used to coat any of the interior surfaces of the muffin molds.
6. Fill each cup with golf ball-sized pieces of dough This recipe yields 18 standard muffins or 36 small muffins.
7. Bake the muffins for around 10–15 minutes at about 350°F, just until the muffin tops' tops and sides tend to tan.
8. It would take around 20 minutes to make full-size muffins.
9. It's likely to roast these muffins if you leave them in for too long, so be careful.
10. Put the muffin tins on a cooling rack to cool until they're finished.
11. When the muffins are cold enough to handle, loop a butter knife blade along the sides to help cut them out from the tins.
12. To crack the muffin loose from the tin's base, we softly force from the side to the middle with the knife's tip.
13. Serve with some butter and sugar-free jams and marmalades, if desired.
14. It's a delicious complement to breakfast or as a treat at any time of the day.

Nutrition: Calories: 211 | Fat: 2 g | Fiber: 4 g | Carbohydrates: 14 g | Protein: 6 g

## 49. Refrigerated Cinnamon Rolls
Ready in: 9 minutes | Servings: 8 | Difficulty: Easy

**Ingredients**
- 1 can of cinnamon rolls

**Directions**
1. Preheat the Air Fryer to about 350°F on the "Bake" setting.
2. Remove the contents of the box Position equally spaced apart on the shelf.

3. Wrap the rack and position it on the lowest floor Place a second rack on top of the first Cook for around 7 minutes in the fryer .

4. If the roll mixture isn't solid to touch, cook for an extra minute or so.

5. If wanted, ice the cake.

Nutrition: **Calories: 283 | Fat: 12 g | Fiber: 3 g | Carbohydrates: 13 g | Protein: 8 g**

## 50. Egg, Ham, and Cheese Breakfast Biscuits

Ready in: 10 minutes | Servings: 4 | Difficulty: Easy

**Ingredients**
- 1 slice cheese quartered
- ½ tsp salt and pepper
- 2 slices of ham, halved, or 4 small slices of bacon, sausage, etc. will work too
- 1 tbsp. milk
- ¼ can biscuits 4 biscuits
- 2 eggs

**Directions**

1. Preheat your Vortex Air Fryer to about 350°F Put the rack in the center of the space.

2. Cook 4 cookies on the rack for around 8 minutes, tossing midway through.

3. Cook the egg in the microwave, or you may use your Air Fryer.

4. Arrange the sandwiches until the cookies are done: biscuit, cheese, egg, and ham.

Nutrition: **Calories: 182 | Fat: 2 g | Fiber: 4 g | Carbohydrates: 12 g | Protein: 6 g**

## 51. Cinnamon Rolls from Pizza Dough

Ready in: 15 minutes | Servings: 8 | Difficulty: Easy

**Ingredients**
- 2 tsps. powdered sugar
- ¼ c brown sugar
- 2 tsps. cinnamon
- 1 pizza dough can or use 1 can of refrigerated pizza dough

**Directions**

1. On a smooth surface, roll out the pizza dough It's easier if you roll it into a square, but we went for a circle for this one.

2. You'll wind up with strange-looking end rolls if you do circles.

3. Rectangles are more efficient!.

4. Melt ¼ c brown sugar and 2 tablespoons of cinnamon in the oven for around 20 seconds or until fully melted.

5. Preheat your Vortex Air Fryer to about 400°F using the "Bake" setting Roll up the pizza dough until coating it with the brown sugar mixture.

6. After that, split the roll into 1 ½-inch sections and put them on a shelf Approximately 8 rolls must be obtained using the dough.

7. Cook, occasionally stirring, for around 7 minutes or until it's golden brown.

8. Finish with a dusting of powdered sugar!

9. Sprinkle with icing sugar and serve.

Nutrition: **Calories: 281 | Fat: 12 g | Fiber: 3 g | Carbohydrates: 14 g | Protein: 6 g**

## 52. Eggs Mini Waffles

Ready in: 20 minutes | Servings: 4 | Difficulty: Normal

**Ingredients**
- ½ tsp vanilla extract
- ¼ tsp salt
- 4 tsps. baking powder
- 1 tbsp. white sugar
- ½ c vegetable oil
- 1 ¾ c milk
- 2 c all-purpose flour
- 2 eggs

**Directions**

1. Preheated your Air Fryer to about 300°F.

2. In a big mixing cup, whisk the eggs with a hand mixer until smooth.

3. Only until smooth, combine milk, flour, sugar, vegetable oil, salt, baking powder, and vanilla.

4. Spray a nonstick cooking pan with some spray oil.

5. Pour the batter into the pan add your pan to the preheated fryer.

6. Cook until golden brown on all sides.

7. Rep for the entire mixture and serve.

Nutrition: **Calories: 211 | Fat: 2 g | Fiber: 4 g | Carbohydrates: 12 g | Protein: 6 g**

## 53. Breakfast Pizza

Ready in: 10 minutes | Servings: 4 | Difficulty: Easy

**Ingredients**
- 4 tbsps. gravy (I used homemade sausage gravy) (optional)
- 2 egg
- ¼ c sausage; I used Bradley's Smoked Sausage
- ¼ c Mexican cheese
- ½ can biscuits rolled flat

**Directions**

1. Preheat your Air Fryer to about 390°F

2. Place your rack in the center section of the Air Fryer

3. Take 2 eggs and microwave them

4. Flatten your biscuits, put the ingredients on them, and cook them in the Air Fryer for around 5 minutes

5. Cook for an extra minute to melt the toppings

Nutrition: **Calories: 221 | Fat: 3 g | Fiber: 6 g | Carbohydrates: 12 g | Protein: 6 g**

Note: If you have some remaining gravy, proceed with that It's not required, but it makes these even more delicious!

## 54. Scotch Eggs with Smoked Sausage

Ready in: 15 minutes | Servings: 10 | Difficulty: Easy

**Ingredients**

• ½ c pork rinds ground (you could use breadcrumbs if you don't want a low-carb option)
• ½ lb. smoked sausage (we use Bradley's)
• 12 eggs

**Directions**

1. In your Instant Pot, cook 11 eggs for around 10 minutes on high pressure with a fast release.
2. Place the smoked sausage in a fast-food mixer after it has been opened.
3. Preheat your Air Fryer to about 390°F.
4. Place the rack in the center space.
5. Mix in 1 egg and breadcrumbs.
6. Allow the eggs to cool after they've been cooked.
7. Wrap the eggs in the bacon mixture.
8. Cook for around 6 minutes in the Vortex Air Fryer, turning halfway through.
9. If required, cook for a few minutes longer until golden.
10. To eat, cut in half and top with Easy Hollandaise Sauce if needed.

Nutrition: **Calories: 221 | Fat: 4 g | Fiber: 4 g | Carbohydrates: 13 g | Protein: 7 g**

## 55. Easy Peach Bread with Cinnamon

Ready in: 45 minutes | Servings: 6 | Difficulty: Normal

**Ingredients**

• 1 peach skin on, finely diced
• 1/3 c vegetable oil
• 3 eggs
• ½ c sugar
• ¼ tsp salt
• 1 tsp cinnamon
• 1 tsp baking powder
• 1 tsp baking soda
• 1 ½ c flour

**For the glaze:**
• Powdered sugar
• Milk

**Directions**

1. Preheat your Vortex Air Fryer to 350°F and put it on "Bake" mode.
2. Combine the flour, baking soda, baking powder, cinnamon, and salt in a big mixing cup.
3. Mix, and blend well.
4. Cream together the eggs, sugar, and vegetable oil in a separate cup.
5. Combine the wet and dry ingredients in a mixing bowl and stir until a batter emerges.
6. Mix with the chopped peaches.
7. Bake for 35 minutes at 350°in an oiled loaf tin.
8. Cover a part of the top with tin foil if it begins to tan.
9. Enable to cool entirely before adding the glaze.
10. To create the glaze, mix powdered sugar and milk in a small bowl until the powdered sugar is completely dissolved.
11. Using a brush or a pour, coat the loaf.
12. Split and eat!

Nutrition: **Calories: 211 | Fat: 3 g | Fiber: 6 g | Carbohydrates: 14 g | Protein: 8 g**

## 56. Perfect Banana Muffins

Ready in: 22 minutes | Servings: 12 | Difficulty: Normal

**Ingredients**

• 1/3 c butter melted
• 1 egg
• 1 tsp cinnamon
• ¾ c white sugar
• 3 large bananas mashed
• ½ tsp salt
• 1 tsp baking soda
• 1 tsp baking powder
• 1 ½ c all-purpose flour

**Directions**

1. Allow the butter to soften in the open air.
2. Preheat the Air Fryer to 350°F Place the rack in the center of the bed.
3. Combine all ingredients in a mixer or a mixing cup Mix, so it is well blended It's supposed to be fluffy.
4. Place muffin molds on a rack and cook half of the muffins at a time.
5. Fill the cups with the mixture and cover with the bottom drip tray.
6. Leave for 5 minutes in the oven and cook for another 5 minutes after uncovering.
7. Cook for another 5 minutes if not completed This is dependent on how crowded they are.

Nutrition: **Calories: 221 | Fat: 3 g | Fiber: 3 g | Carbohydrates: 14 g | Protein: 7 g**

# CHAPTER 3

## LUNCH RECIPES

## 57. Pasta Salad

Ready in: 30 minutes | Servings: 8 | Difficulty: Normal

**Ingredients**

• 4 tbsps. basil, chopped
• 4 tbsps. balsamic vinegar
• ½ c olive oil
• 1 c kalamata olive, pitted and halved
• 1 ½ c cherry tomatoes, halved
• 1 ½ lb. penne rigate, already cooked
• 2 tsps. Italian seasoning
• Salt and black pepper according to your taste
• 6 oz. brown mushrooms, halved
• 2 red onion, roughly chopped
• 2 green bell pepper, roughly chopped
• 2 orange bell pepper, roughly chopped
• 2 zucchinis, sliced in half and roughly chopped

**Directions**

1. Add the zucchinis with mushrooms, the green bell pepper, the orange bell pepper, the salt, the red onion, the Italian seasoning, the pepper, and the oil in a dish, mix properly, move to the preheated Air Fryer at about 380°F and cook for around 12 minutes.
2. Blend the pasta with the cooked vegetables, olives, cherry tomatoes, vinegar, and basil in a broad salad bowl, mix and serve it for lunch.
3. Enjoy!

Nutrition: **Calories: 199 | Fat: 3 g | Fiber: 4 g |**
**Carbohydrates: 14 g | Protein: 6 g**

## 58. Delicious Beef Cubes

Ready in: 30 minutes | Servings: 6 | Difficulty: Normal

**Ingredients**

• 1 ½ lb. sirloin, cubed
• 18 oz. jarred pasta sauce
• 2 ½ c breadcrumbs
• 3 tbsps. olive oil
• 1 tsp marjoram, dried
• White rice, already prepared for serving

**Directions**

1. Mix the pieces of meat with the pasta sauce in a dish and toss properly.
2. In another dish, combine the marjoram and oil with some breadcrumbs and mix well.
3. In this mixture, dip the pieces of meat, position them into your Air Fryer and bake for about 12 minutes at around 360°F.
4. Split into dishes and serve with some white rice as a side dish Enjoy!

Nutrition: **Calories: 235 | Fat: 4 g | Fiber: 7 g |**
**Carbohydrates: 14 g | Protein: 7 g**

## 59. Hash Brown Toasts

Ready in: 30 minutes | Servings: 6 | Difficulty: Normal

**Ingredients**

• 2 tbsps. basil, chopped
• 2 tbsps. balsamic vinegar
• 3 tbsps. Parmesan, grated
• 5 tbsps. Mozzarella, shredded
• ¼ c cherry tomatoes, chopped
• 2 tbsps. olive oil
• 6 hash brown patties, frozen

**Directions**

1. Place the hash brown patties into your Air Fryer, drizzle them with the oil and bake them for about 7 minutes at around 400°F.
2. Mix the Mozzarella, tomatoes, vinegar, Parmesan, and basil in a bowl and stir thoroughly.
3. Break brown hash patties on bowls, cover each with a combination of vegetables and eat for lunch Enjoy!

Nutrition: **Calories: 147 | Fat: 5 g | Fiber: 5 g |**
**Carbohydrates: 11 g | Protein: 6 g**

## 60. Fish and Chips

Ready in: 30 minutes | Servings: 4 | Difficulty: Normal

**Ingredients**

• 4 c kettle chips, cooked
• ¼ c buttermilk
• Salt and black pepper according to your taste
• 4 medium cod fillets, skinless and boneless

**Directions**

1. Mix the fish with the pepper, salt, and buttermilk in a dish, toss and allow settling for about 5 minutes.
2. In your food mixer, put chips, crumble them and scatter them on a tray.
3. Add your fish and cover on both sides, press good.
4. Transfer the fish to the Air Fryer's basket and cook for about 12 minutes at around 400°F.
5. Serve it warm for lunch Enjoy!

Nutrition: **Calories: 179 | Fat: 2 g | Fiber: 4 g | Protein: 7 g**

## 61. Lunch Chicken Salad

Ready in: 40 minutes | Servings: 6 | Difficulty: Hard

**Ingredients**

• 6 tbsps. BBQ sauce
• ½ c ranch dressing
• 16 cherry tomatoes, sliced
• 6 green onions, chopped
• 4 tbsps. cilantro, chopped
• 2 c Cheddar cheese, shredded
• 2 c canned black beans, drained
• 1 ½ romaine lettuce head, cut into medium strips
• 1 ½ iceberg lettuce head, cut into medium strips
• 1 ½ tsp garlic powder
• 2 tbsps. brown sugar
• 2 tsps. sweet paprika
• Salt and black pepper according to your taste
• Olive oil as required
• 2 lbs. chicken tenders, boneless
• 4 ears of corn, hulled

## Directions

1. Add some corn into your Air Fryer, drizzle with some oil, mix, cook for about 10 minutes at around 400°F, place it on a plate and leave for now.

2. Place the chicken in the basket of your Air Fryer, add some pepper, salt, paprika, brown sugar, and garlic powder, mix, drizzle with more oil, cook for about 10 minutes at around 400°F, turn midway, place tenders to the chopping board and chop.

3. Move the corn to a dish, add in the chicken, romaine lettuce, iceberg lettuce, cheese, black beans, tomatoes, cilantro, BBQ sauce, onions, and ranch dressing, mix well and serve for lunch Enjoy!

Nutrition: **Calories: 177 | Fat: 2 g | Fiber: 4 g | Carbohydrates: 9 g | Protein: 8 g**

## 62. Lunch Fajitas

Ready in: 30 minutes | Servings: 6 | Difficulty: Normal
### Ingredients

• 1 c lettuce leaves, torn for serving
• Sour cream for serving
• Salsa for serving
• 6 tortillas, warmed up
• Cooking spray
• 2 tbsps. lime juice
• 2 yellow onion, chopped
• 2 green bell pepper, sliced

• 2 red bell pepper, sliced
• 2 lbs. chicken breasts, cut into strips
• ½ tsp cilantro, ground
• Salt and black pepper according to your taste
• ½ tsp chili powder
• ½ tsp cumin, ground
• 2 tsps. garlic powder

### Directions

1. Mix the chicken with the garlic powder, the chili, the cumin, the cinnamon, the cilantro, the salt, the pepper, the lime juice, the green bell pepper, the red bell pepper, and the onion in a bowl, mix, set it aside for 10 minutes, transfer it to the Air Fryer and drizzle all over using some cooking spray.

2. Mix and simmer for about 10 minutes at around 400°F.

3. On a chopping board, place tortillas, split chicken mix evenly, mix in the sauce, lettuce, and sour cream, cover and eat for lunch Enjoy!

Nutrition: **Calories: 177 | Fat: 2 g | Fiber: 4 g | Carbohydrates: 9 g | Protein: 8 g**

## 63. Macaroni and Cheese

Ready in: 45 minutes | Servings: 4 | Difficulty: Hard
### Ingredients

• Salt and black pepper according to your taste
• Cooking spray
• 1 c Parmesan, shredded
• 1 c Mozzarella cheese, shredded

• 1 c Cheddar cheese, shredded
• 1 c chicken stock
• 1 c heavy cream
• 2 ½ c favorite macaroni

### Directions

1. Spray your cooking pan with some cooking spray, add heavy cream, macaroni, stock, Mozzarella, Cheddar cheese, Parmesan, and also some salt and black pepper, mix gently, put the pan in

the basket of your Air Fryer, and cook for about 30 minutes.

2. Split into dishes and eat for lunch Enjoy!

Nutrition: **Calories: 211 | Fat: 3 g | Fiber: 4 g | Carbohydrates: 8 g | Protein: 4 g**

## 64. Chicken Pie

Ready in: 35 minutes | Servings: 6 | Difficulty: Hard
### Ingredients

• 4 chicken thighs, boneless, skinless, and cubed
• 2 carrot, chopped
• 2 yellow onion, chopped
• 3 potatoes, chopped
• 3 mushrooms, chopped
• 3 tsps. soy sauce
• Salt and black pepper according to your taste

• 2 tsps. Italian seasoning
• 1 tsp garlic powder
• 1 ½ tsp Worcestershire sauce
• 1 ½ tbsp. flour
• 1 ½ tbsp. milk
• 4 puff pastry sheets
• 2 tbsps. butter, melted

### Directions

1. Over a medium-high flame, heat a saucepan, add carrots, potatoes, and onion, mix and simmer for about 2 minutes.

2. Add soy sauce, salt, Italian seasoning, pepper, Worcestershire sauce, garlic powder, flour, and milk, add chicken and mushrooms, mix very well and take off the fire.

3. Put 1 puff pastry sheet on the bottom of the pan of your Air Fryer and cut the surplus edge.

4. Add your chicken mix, top with the other puff pastry layer, cut the surplus, and sprinkle some butter on the pie.

5. Put it in your Air Fryer and cook for about 6 minutes at around 360°F.

6. Slice and eat for tea Leave the pie to cool off Enjoy!

Nutrition : **Calories: 200 | Fat: 3 g | Fiber: 4 g | Carbohydrates: 14 g | Protein: 7 g**

## 65. Buttermilk Chicken

Ready in: 35 minutes | Servings: 5 | Difficulty: Hard
### Ingredients

• 2 tbsps. garlic powder
• 2 tbsps. sweet paprika
• 2 tbsps. baking powder
• 3 c white flour

• 1 pinch of cayenne pepper
• Salt and black pepper according to your taste
• 3 c buttermilk
• 2 lbs. chicken thighs

### Directions

1. Mix the salt, buttermilk, pepper, and cayenne with the chicken thighs in a bowl, blend and set aside for at least 6 hours.

2. Mix the flour with the paprika, baking powder, and garlic powder in a different bowl and stir.

3. Wash the chicken thighs, dredge them in the flour mixture, place them in your fryer, and sear for about 8 minutes at around 360°F.

4. Turn the pieces of chicken, steam them for about 10 more minutes, place them on a plate and serve them for lunch Enjoy!

Nutrition: **Calories: 191 | Fat: 3 g | Fiber: 8 g | Carbohydrates: 14 g | Protein: 7 g**

## 66. Hot Bacon Sandwiches

Ready in: 25 minutes | Servings: 6 | Difficulty: Normal

**Ingredients**

- 3 tomatoes, sliced
- 4 pita pockets, halved
- 2 yellow bell pepper, sliced
- 2 red bell pepper, sliced
- 10 bacon slices, cooked and cut into thirds
- 3 tbsps. honey
- 2 ¼ c butter lettuce leaves, torn
- 2/3 c BBQ sauce

**Directions**

1. Mix the BBQ sauce with the honey in a container and shake well.

2. Brush your bacon with some of this mixture and all of the bell peppers, put them in your Air Fryer, and steam for about 4 minutes at around 350°F.

3. Turn the fryer and allow it to steam for another 2 minutes.

4. Pour the remainder of the BBQ sauce and eat for lunch with pita pockets of bacon blend, even filled with lettuce and tomatoes Enjoy!

Nutrition: Calories: 182 | Fat: 4 g | Fiber: 4 g | Carbohydrates: 13 g | Protein: 11 g

## 67. Fresh Chicken Mix

Ready in: 45 minutes | Servings: 6 | Difficulty: Hard

**Ingredients**

- 4 tbsps. butter, soft
- 8 bread slices
- 12 oz. Alfredo sauce
- 1 tsp thyme, dried
- 2 tbsps. olive oil
- 2 red bell pepper, chopped
- 10 button mushrooms, sliced
- 3 chicken breasts, skinless, boneless, and cubed

**Directions**

1. Mix the chicken with the bell pepper, mushrooms, and oil in your Air Fryer, shake well to coat, and steam for about 15 minutes at around 350°F.

2. Transfer the chicken mixture to a bowl, whisk in the Alfredo sauce and thyme, turn, move to the fryer, and steam for about 4 more minutes at around 350°F.

3. Put butter on slices of toast, transfer to the fryer, butter side up, and steam for another 4 minutes.

4. Arrange baked slices of bread on a plate cover each with a blend of chicken and eat for lunch Enjoy!

Nutrition: Calories: 201 | Fat: 2 g | Fiber: 4 g | Carbohydrates: 12 g | Protein: 7 g

## 68. Chicken Sandwiches

Ready in: 30 minutes | Servings: 5 | Difficulty: Normal

**Ingredients**

- 2 tbsps. olive oil
- 2 c cherry tomatoes, halved
- 5 pita pockets
- 3 c butter lettuce, torn
- 1 tsp thyme, dried
- 1 c Italian seasoning
- 2 red bell pepper, sliced
- 2 red onion, chopped
- 4 chicken breasts, skinless, boneless, and cubed

**Directions**

1. Mix the chicken with the bell pepper, onion, Italian seasoning, and oil in your Air Fryer, mix, and sear for about 10 minutes at around 380°F.

2. Move the chicken mix to a dish, add the cherry tomatoes, thyme, and butter lettuce, combine gently, add the pita pockets and serve for lunch.

3. Enjoy!

Nutrition: Calories: 221 | Fat: 7 g | Fiber: 2 g | Carbohydrates: 13 g | Protein: 14 g

## 69. Scallops and Dill

Ready in: 25 minutes | Servings: 5 | Difficulty: Normal

**Ingredients**

- Salt and black pepper according to your taste
- 4 tsps. olive oil
- 2 tsps. dill, chopped
- 2 tbsps. lemon juice
- 1 ½ lb. sea scallops, debearded

**Directions**

1. Mix the scallops with the oil, dill, pepper, salt, and lemon juice in your Air Fryer, cover, and cook for about 5 minutes at around 360°F.

2. Toss away unopened ones, break on plates with scallops and dill sauce and eat for lunch.

3. Enjoy!

Nutrition: Calories: 221 | Fat: 7 g | Fiber: 2 g | Carbohydrates: 13 g | Protein: 14 g

## 70. Lunch Special Pancake

Ready in: 30 minutes | Servings: 4 | Difficulty: Normal

**Ingredients**

- 2 c small shrimp, peeled and deveined
- 2 c salsa
- 1 c milk
- 1 c flour
- 6 eggs, whisked
- 2 tbsps. butter

**Directions**

1. Preheat the Air Fryer to around 400°F, transfer the tray to the fryer, add 1 tbsp. butter, and melt.

2. Mix the eggs with the flour and milk in a bowl, mix genteelly and put into the Air Fryer's tray, scatter, cook for about 12 minutes at around 350°F and move to a tray.

3. Place the shrimp with the salsa in a bowl, blend and eat the pancake with this as aside Enjoy!

Nutrition: Calories: 211 | Fat: 2 g | Fiber: 6 g | Carbohydrates: 14 g| Protein: 8 g

## 71. Lunch Shrimp Croquettes

Ready in: 25 minutes | Servings: 5 | Difficulty: Normal

**Ingredients**

- 4 tbsps. olive oil
- Salt and black pepper according to your taste

- 1 tsp basil, dried
- 4 green onions, chopped
- 2 ½ tbsps. lemon juice
- 2 egg, whisked
- 1 c breadcrumbs
- 1 lb. shrimp, cooked, peeled, deveined, and chopped

**Directions**

1. Mix half the breadcrumbs with the lemon juice and egg in a bowl and stir thoroughly.
2. Add the basil, green onions, shrimp, salt, and pepper and mix quite well.
3. Mix the remainder of the breadcrumbs with the oil in a different bowl and toss well.
4. Use shrimp mix to form circular balls, dredge them in your breadcrumbs, put them in the preheated Air Fryer, and cook at about 400°F for around 8 minutes.
5. Serve them for lunch with a sauce Enjoy!

Nutrition: **Calories: 172 | Fat: 4 g | Protein: 7 g | Carbohydrates: 14 g | Protein: 8 g**

## 72. Squash Fritters

Ready in: 24 minutes | Servings: 5 | Difficulty: Normal

**Ingredients**
- 4 tbsps. olive oil
- 1 c breadcrumbs
- 2/3 c carrot, grated
- 2 yellow summer squash, grated
- 1 pinch of salt and black pepper
- 1 tsp oregano, dried
- 2 egg, whisked
- 5 oz. cream cheese

**Directions**

1. Mix the pepper, salt, egg, oregano, carrot, breadcrumbs, and squash with the cream cheese in a bowl and stir properly.
2. From this blend, form small patties and spray them with the oil.
3. Put the squash patties into your Air Fryer and cook them for about 7 minutes at around 400°F.
4. For lunch, serve them hot Enjoy!

Nutrition: **Calories: 177 | Fat: 3 g | Fiber: 6 g | Carbohydrates: 14 g | Protein: 6 g**

## 73. Tuna and Zucchini Tortillas

Ready in: 30 minutes | Servings: 5 | Difficulty: Normal

**Ingredients**
- 2 c Cheddar cheese, grated
- 4 tbsps. mustard
- 2/3 c mayonnaise
- 2 c zucchini, shredded
- 8 oz. canned tuna, drained
- 6 tbsps. butter, soft
- 6 corn tortillas

**Directions**

1. Rub the butter on the tortillas, put them in the bucket of your Air Fryer, and bake for about 3 minutes at around 400°F.
2. In the meantime, combine the tuna with the zucchini, mayonnaise, and mustard in a dish and stir.

3. On each tortilla, split this blend, top with cheese, roll tortillas, put them in the basket of your Air Fryer again, and cook for about 4 minutes more at around 400°F.
4. For lunch, eat Enjoy!

Nutrition: **Calories: 190 | Fat: 4 g | Fiber: 8 g | Carbohydrates: 11 g | Protein: 5 g**

## 74. Lunch Gnocchi

Ready in: 25 minutes | Servings: 5 | Difficulty: Normal

**Ingredients**
- 10 oz. spinach pesto
- ½ c Parmesan, grated
- 18 oz. gnocchi
- 4 garlic cloves, minced
- 2 tbsps. olive oil
- 2 yellow onion, chopped

**Directions**

1. Oil the fryer pan with olive oil, add the onion, gnocchi, and garlic, mix, place the pan in the Air Fryer and cook for about 10 minutes at around 400°F.
2. Add the pesto, toss it well, and simmer at around 350°F for another 7 minutes.
3. Split into dishes and serve with cheese for lunch Enjoy!

Nutrition: **Calories: 224 | Fat: 8 g | Fiber: 9 g | Carbohydrates: 16 g | Protein: 15 g**

## 75. Quick Lunch Pizzas

Ready in: 24 minutes | Servings: 5 | Difficulty: Normal

**Ingredients**
- 2 c grape tomatoes, sliced
- 4 c Mozzarella, grated
- 4 green onions, chopped
- 1 tsp basil, dried
- 5 oz. jarred mushrooms, sliced
- 1 c pizza sauce
- 2 tbsps. olive oil
- 5 pitas

**Directions**

1. Cover each pita bread with some pizza sauce Scatter with green basil and onions, split the mushrooms, and top up with cheese and oil.
2. Organize the Air Fryer with pita pizzas and cook them for about 7 minutes at around 400°F.
3. Cover each pizza with slices of tomato, split between plates, and serve Enjoy!

Nutrition: **Calories: 176 | Fat: 3 g | Fiber: 6 g | Carbohydrates: 14 g | Protein: 9 g**

## 76. Stuffed Mushrooms

Ready in: 40 minutes | Servings: 5 | Difficulty: Hard

**Ingredients**
- ½ tsp rosemary, chopped
- 2/3 c breadcrumbs
- 2 c spinach, torn
- 7 tbsps. Parmesan, grated
- ½ c Ricotta cheese
- 2 tbsps. olive oil
- 5 big Portobello mushroom caps

## Directions

1. Brush the caps of the mushrooms with some oil, put them in the basket of your Air Fryer, and cook for about 2 minutes at around 350°F.
2. In the meantime, blend half of the Parmesan cheese with Ricotta, spinach, breadcrumbs, and rosemary in a bowl and mix well.
3. With this mixture, fill the mushrooms, add the rest of the Parmesan on top; bring them back in your Air Fryer's basket and cook for about 10 minutes at around 350°F.
4. Split them into plates and offer them for lunch with your choice of side salad Enjoy!

Nutrition: **Calories: 176 | Fat: 3 g | Fiber: 6 g | Carbohydrates: 14 g | Protein: 9 g**

## 77. Veggie Toast

Ready in: **24 minutes** | Servings: **5** | Difficulty: **Normal**

### Ingredients

- 1 c goat cheese, crumbled
- 4 tbsps. butter, soft
- 5 bread slices
- 2 tbsps. olive oil
- 4 green onions, sliced
- 2 yellow squash, chopped
- 2 c crème mushrooms, sliced
- 2 red bell pepper, cut into thin strips

### Directions

1. Add the red bell pepper with the mushrooms, the green onions, the squash, and the oil in a bowl, toss, move to your Air Fryer, cook for about 10 minutes at around 350°F, shake the fryer once and switch to a bowl.
2. Put the butter on the slices of bread, position them in an Air Fryer, and cook for about 5 minutes at around 350°F.
3. On each bread slice, split the veggie mix, cover it with crumbled cheese and eat it for lunch Enjoy!

Nutrition: **Calories: 188 | Fat: 4 g | Fiber: 7 g | Carbohydrates: 14 g | Protein: 8 g**

## 78. Lunch Egg Rolls

Ready in: **34 minutes** | Servings: **5** | Difficulty: **Normal**

### Ingredients

- 2 tbsps. cornstarch
- 2 eggs, whisked
- 10 egg roll wrappers
- 4 tbsps. soy sauce
- 4 green onions, chopped
- 1 c zucchini, grated
- 1 c carrots, grated
- 1 c mushrooms, chopped

### Directions

1. Mix the mushrooms, carrots, green onions, zucchini, and soy sauce in a bowl and mix well.
2. On a cutting board, place egg roll wrappers, cut veggie mix on each, and roll tight.
3. Place the cornstarch and egg in a cup, stir properly, and brush the egg rolls with this combination.

4. Seal the sides; position all the rolls in your preheated Air Fryer and cook for about 15 minutes at around 370°F.
5. Assemble them and serve them for lunch on a large plate Enjoy!

Nutrition: **Calories: 188 | Fat: 4 g | Fiber: 7 g | Carbohydrates: 14 g | Protein: 7 g**

## 79. Air-Fried Japanese Duck Breasts

Ready in: **40 minutes** | Servings: **8** | Difficulty: **Hard**

### Ingredients

- 2 tsps. sesame oil
- 6 tbsps. hoisin sauce
- 6 ginger slices
- 25 oz. chicken stock
- Salt and black pepper according to your taste
- 4 tbsps. honey
- 2 ½ tsp 5-spice powder
- 6 tbsps. soy sauce
- 8 duck breasts, boneless

### Directions

1. Mix your soy sauce, 5-spice powder, pepper, salt, and honey in a small bowl, mix, add your duck breasts, shake to cover, and set aside for the time being.
2. Warm a pan over a medium-high flame with the stock, ginger, hoisin sauce, and sesame oil, mix well, cook for about 2–3 more minutes, turn off the heat and set it aside.
3. Place the duck breasts in your Air Fryer and cook them for about 15 minutes at around 400°F.
4. Split and serve between dishes Drizzle some more hoisin on top, and pour some ginger sauce all over them.
5. Enjoy!

Nutrition: **Calories: 188 | Fat: 4 g | Fiber: 7 g | Carbohydrates: 14 g | Protein: 7 g**

## 80. Duck and Plum Sauce

Ready in: **55 minutes** | Servings: **4** | Difficulty: **Hard**

### Ingredients

- 2 c beef stock
- 4 tbsps. red wine
- 4 tbsps. sugar
- 14 oz. red plumps, stoned, cut into small wedges
- 2 shallots, chopped
- 2 tbsps. olive oil
- 2-star anise
- 2 tbsps. butter, melted
- 4 duck breasts
- Salt and black pepper to taste

### Directions

1. Over medium flame, warm the pan with some olive oil, add the shallot, mix well and simmer for about 5 minutes.
2. Stir in the sugar and plums, blend and simmer until the sugar is dissolved.
3. For now, add some stock and wine, whisk, simmer for another 15 minutes, take off the flame and keep it warm.
4. Season the duck with some salt and black pepper, brush with melted butter, switch to a heat-proof dish that suits your Air Fryer Add star anise and plum sauce, place it in the Air Fryer, and cook for about 12 minutes at around 360°F.
5. Split and serve all on dishes Enjoy!

Nutrition: **Calories: 200 | Fat: 4 g | Fiber: 6 g | Carbohydrates: 12 g | Protein: 7 g**

## 81. Chicken and Creamy Mushrooms

Ready in: 45 minutes | Servings: 10 | Difficulty: Hard

**Ingredients**

- ½ c Parmesan, grated
- 2 tbsps. mustard
- 1 tsp oregano, dried
- 1 tsp thyme, dried
- 1 tsp basil, dried
- ½ c heavy cream
- 2 c chicken stock
- 6 tbsps. butter, melted
- 6 garlic cloves, minced
- 10 oz. criminal mushrooms, halved
- Salt and black pepper according to your taste
- 10 chicken thighs

**Directions**

1. Rub the chicken bits with 2 tbsps. butter, season with some salt and black pepper, place in the basket of your Air Fryer, cook for about 5 minutes at around 370°F, and leave in a bowl for now.
2. In the meantime, over medium-high flame, prepare, heat a skillet with the remainder of the butter, including the mushrooms and garlic, mix and simmer for about 5 minutes.
3. Add pepper, salt, thyme, oregano, stock, and basil, mix well, and move to a heat-proof bowl.
4. Add the chicken, toss it, bring the Air Fryer in, and cook for about 20 minutes at around 370°F.
5. Add the Parmesan, mustard, and heavy cream, toss it all over again, simmer for an additional 5 minutes, split between plates, and eat Enjoy!

Nutrition : **Calories: 200 | Fat: 4 g | Fiber: 6 g | Carbohydrates: 12 g | Protein: 7 g**

## 82. Chicken and Capers

Ready in: 45 minutes | Servings: 4 | Difficulty: Hard

**Ingredients**

- 6 green onions, chopped
- 2 lemon, sliced
- 1 c chicken stock
- Salt and black pepper according to your taste
- 3 tbsps. butter, melted
- 5 garlic cloves, minced
- 3 tbsps. capers
- 5 chicken thighs

**Directions**

1. Rub the butter on the meat, sprinkle the salt and black pepper to taste, and put them in a baking pan that's perfect for your Air Fryer
2. Add chicken stock, garlic, capers, and lemon slices as well, toss to cover, put in your Air Fryer and cook for about 20 minutes at around 370°F, turning midway
3. Sprinkle with green onions, split between dishes, and eat Enjoy!

Nutrition: **Calories: 188 | Fat: 3 g | Fiber: 7 g | Carbohydrates: 14 g | Protein: 8 g**

## 83. Easy Chicken Thighs and Baby Potatoes

Ready in: 45 minutes | Servings: 5 | Difficulty: Hard

**Ingredients**

- 4 tsps. thyme, chopped
- 2 red onion, chopped
- 3 garlic cloves, minced
- Salt and black pepper according to your taste
- 1 tsp sweet paprika
- 4 tsps. rosemary, dried
- 4 tsps. oregano, dried
- 2 lbs. baby potatoes halved
- 3 tbsps. olive oil
- 10 chicken thighs

**Directions**

1. Mix the chicken thighs, pepper, salt, paprika, thyme, rosemary, onion, oregano, garlic, baby potatoes, and oil in a small bowl.
2. Toss to cover, scatter everything in a heat-proof pan that suits your Air Fryer, and cook for about 30 minutes at around 400°F, rotating midway.
3. Split and serve between dishes Enjoy!

Nutrition: **Calories: 275 | Fat: 3 g | Fiber: 4 g | Carbohydrates: 16 g | Protein: 6 g**

## 84. Chinese Stuffed Chicken

Ready in: 75 minutes | Servings: 10 | Difficulty: Hard

**Ingredients**

- 5 tsps. sesame oil
- Salt and black pepper according to your taste
- 2 tsps. soy sauce
- 2 yams, cubed
- 6 ginger slices
- 4 red chilies, chopped
- 20 wolfberries
- 2 whole chicken

**Directions**

1. Season the chicken with some salt, black pepper, sesame oil, soy sauce, yam cubes, wolfberries, chilies, and ginger to taste.
2. Put it in your Air Fryer, cook for about 20 minutes at around 400°F, then for another 15 minutes at around 360°F.
3. Carve the chicken, split it between bowls, and eat Enjoy!

Nutrition: **Calories: 275 | Fat: 3 g | Fiber: 4 g | Carbohydrates: 16 g | Protein: 6 g**

## 85. Chinese Duck Legs

Ready in: 55 minutes | Servings: 4 | Difficulty: Hard

**Ingredients**

- 2 tbsps. rice wine
- 18 oz. water
- 2 tsps. sesame oil
- 2 tbsps. soy sauce
- 2 tbsps. oyster sauce
- 4 ginger slices
- 2 bunch spring onions, chopped
- 4-star anise
- 2 tbsps. olive oil
- 4 dried chilies, chopped
- 4 duck legs

**Directions**

1. Heat the pan over medium-high heat with the oil, mix in the chili, star anise, rice wine, sesame oil, soy sauce, oyster sauce, ginger, water, and simmer for 6 minutes.
2. Add the spring onions and the legs of the duck, toss to cover, move to a pan that suits your Air Fryer Bring the Air Fryer in and cook for about 30 minutes at around 370°F.
3. Split and serve between dishes Enjoy!

Nutrition: **Calories: 235 | Fat: 4 g | Fiber: 4 g | Carbohydrates: 10 g | Protein: 6 g**

## 86. Honey Duck Breasts

Ready in: 45 minutes | Servings: 3 | Difficulty: Hard

**Ingredients**

- 1 tsp apple vinegar
- 2 tbsps. mustard
- 2 tsps. tomato paste
- 2 tsps. honey
- 2 smoked duck breasts, halved

**Directions**

1. Mix honey with some mustard, tomato paste, and vinegar in a small bowl, whisk good, adds pieces of duck breast, mix to cover well, move to your Air Fryer and cook for about 15 minutes at around 370°F.

2. Take the duck breast out of your fryer, apply it to the honey blend, toss it again, return it to the Air Fryer, and steam for another 6 more minutes at around 370°F.

3. Split it into dishes and serve it with a side salad Enjoy!

Nutrition: **Calories: 235 | Fat: 4 g | Fiber: 4 g | Carbohydrates: 10 g | Protein: 6 g**

## 87. Italian Chicken

Ready in: 32 minutes | Servings: 5 | Difficulty: Normal

**Ingredients**

- 4 tbsps. basil, chopped
- 1 c sun-dried tomatoes
- ½ c Parmesan, grated
- 2 tsps. red pepper flakes, crushed
- 1 c chicken stock
- 1 c heavy cream
- 2 tbsps. thyme, chopped
- 4 garlic cloves, minced
- 2 tbsps. olive oil
- 5 chicken thighs
- Salt and black pepper according to your taste

**Directions**

1. Add salt and pepper to the meat, brush with half of the oil, put in your preheated 350°F Air Fryer, and cook for about 4 minutes.

2. In the meantime, over medium-high heat, heat a pan with the rest of the oil, add garlic, thyme, pepper flakes, heavy cream, sun-dried tomatoes, Parmesan, salt, stock, and pepper, mix, bring to a boil, take off flame and switch to an air-fryer-friendly dish.

3. Add the top of the chicken thighs, place them in your Air Fryer and cook for about 12 minutes at around 320°F.

4. Split between dishes and serve with the top sprinkled with basil Enjoy!

Nutrition: **Calories: 188 | Fat: 4 g | Fiber: 5 g | Carbohydrates: 14 g | Protein: 6 g**

## 88. Creamy Chicken, Rice, and Peas

Ready in: 55 minutes | Servings: 6 | Difficulty: Hard

**Ingredients**

- 2 ½ c Parmesan, grated
- 4 c peas, frozen
- ½ c parsley, chopped
- 2 c chicken stock
- ½ c heavy cream
- 1 c white wine
- 2 yellow onion, chopped
- 4 garlic cloves, minced
- 2 tbsps. olive oil
- Salt and black pepper to the taste
- 2 c white rice, already cooked
- 2 lbs. chicken breasts, skinless, boneless, and cut into quarters

**Directions**

1. Season the chicken breasts with some salt and black pepper, drizzle half the oil over them, rub gently, place them in the basket of your Air Fryer and cook them for about 6 minutes at around 360°F.

2. Heat the pan over a medium-high flame with the remainder of the oil, add the onion, pepper, garlic, stock, wine, salt, and heavy cream, mix, bring to boil, and cook for another 9 minutes.

3. Move the chicken breasts to a heat-proof tray that suits your Air Fryer Cover them with peas, rice, and cream blend Mix some Parmesan and parsley and scatter all over Put in your Air Fryer, and cook for about 10 minutes at around 420°F.

4. Split between plates and serve once heated Enjoy!

Nutrition: **Calories: 100 | Fat: 2 g | Fiber: 3 g | Carbohydrates: 14 g | Protein: 4 g**

## 89. Mexican Chicken

Ready in: 35 minutes | Servings: 5 | Difficulty: Normal

**Ingredients**

- 2 tsps. garlic powder
- ½ c cilantro, chopped
- 2 ½ c Monterey Jack cheese, grated
- 2 lbs. chicken breast, boneless and skinless
- Salt and black pepper according to your taste
- 2 tbsps. olive oil
- 18 oz. Salsa Verde

**Directions**

1. Season the chicken with salt, garlic powder, cilantro, pepper, spray with olive oil, and put it over your Salsa Verde Pour the Salsa Verde into a baking dish that suits your Air Fryer.

2. Put it in an Air Fryer and cook for about 20 minutes at around 380°F.

3. Sprinkle on top of cheese and roast for an additional 2 minutes

4. Split between plates and serve once heated Enjoy!

Nutrition: **Calories: 100 | Fat: 2 g | Fiber: 3 g | Carbohydrates: 14 g | Protein: 4 g**

## 90. Chicken Parmesan

Ready in: 35 minutes | Servings: 5 | Difficulty: Normal

**Ingredients**

- 5 tbsps. basil, chopped
- 4 c tomato sauce
- 2 c Mozzarella, grated
- Salt and black pepper according to your taste
- 2 ½ lbs. chicken cutlets, skinless and boneless
- 2 egg, whisked
- 4 c white flour
- 1 tsp garlic powder
- ½ c Parmesan, grated
- 4 c panko breadcrumbs

**Directions**

1. Mix the panko with the Parmesan and garlic powder in a small bowl, then stir.

2. Placed the flour in a small bowl and a third of the egg.

3. Add salt and pepper to the meat, dip in the flour, then mix in the egg mixture and panko.

4. Put the chicken parts in your fryer and cook each side for about 3 minutes at around 360°F.

5. Move the chicken to an air-fryer-friendly baking dish, apply tomato sauce, and top with Mozzarella, put it in your Air Fryer, and cook for about 7 minutes at around 375°F.

6. Split between bowls, scatter on top with basil, and serve Enjoy!

Nutrition: **Calories: 100 | Fat: 2 g | Fiber: 3 g | Carbohydrates: 14 g | Protein: 4 g**

## 91. Herbed Chicken

Ready in: 80 minutes | Servings: 6 | Difficulty: Hard

**Ingredients**

- 4 tbsps. olive oil
- 2 tbsps. lemon juice
- 2 tsps. rosemary, dried
- 1 tsp thyme, dried
- 2 tsps. onion powder
- 2 tsps. garlic powder
- Salt and black pepper according to your taste
- 2 whole chicken

**Directions**

1. Add salt and pepper to the chicken, combine with rosemary, thyme, garlic powder, and onion powder, cook with lemon juice and olive oil and let stand for at least 30 minutes.

2. Put your chicken in an Air Fryer and cook each side for about 20 minutes at around 360°F.

3. Leave the chicken aside, carve, and serve to cool off Enjoy!

Nutrition: **Calories: 100 | Fat: 2 g | Fiber: 3 g | Carbohydrates: 14 g | Protein: 4 g**

## 92. Chinese Chicken Wings

Ready in: 2 hours and 55 minutes | Servings: 6 | Difficulty: Hard

**Ingredients**

- 6 tbsps. lime juice
- ½ tsp white pepper
- Salt and black pepper according to your taste
- 4 tbsps. soy sauce
- 4 tbsps. honey
- 18 chicken wings

**Directions**

1. Mix honey with some salt, soy sauce, black and white pepper, and some lime juice in a tiny bowl, mix well, add pieces of meat, cover, and refrigerate for at least 2 hours.

2. Move the chicken to your fryer, cook on each side for about 6 minutes at around 370°F, and raise the fire to 400°F, and cook for another 3 minutes.

3. Serve it warm Enjoy!

Nutrition: **Calories: 188 | Fat: 4 g | Fiber: 4 g | Carbohydrates: 14 g | Protein: 4 g**

## 93. Creamy Coconut Chicken

Ready in: 3 hours 40 minutes | Servings: 6 | Difficulty: Hard

**Ingredients**

- 6 tbsps. coconut cream
- Salt and black pepper according to your taste
- 4 tbsps. ginger, grated
- 6 tsps. turmeric powder
- 6 big chicken legs

**Directions**

1. Mix the cream with the ginger, salt, turmeric, and pepper in a small bowl, whisk, add some meat pieces, mix well and leave for at least 2 hours.

2. Move the chicken to your preheated Air Fryer, cook for about 25 minutes at around 370°F, split between plates, and serve with a side salad.

3. Enjoy!

Nutrition: **Calories: 188 | Fat: 4 g | Fiber: 4 g | Carbohydrates: 14 g | Protein: 4 g**

## 94. Chicken Fajitas

Ready in: 25 minutes | Servings: 2 | Difficulty: Normal

**Ingredients**

- ½ medium red bell pepper, seeded and sliced
- ½ medium green bell pepper, seeded and sliced
- ¼ medium onion, peeled and sliced
- ½ tsp garlic powder
- ½ tsp paprika
- ½ tsp cumin
- 1 tbsp. chili powder
- 2 tbsps. coconut oil, melted
- 10 oz. boneless, skinless chicken breast, sliced into ¼-inch strips

**Directions**

1. In a big bowl, mix the chicken and coconut oil and scatter with the paprika, cumin, chili powder, and garlic powder Toss the chicken with spices until well mixed Put the chicken in the basket of an Air Fryer.

2. Set the temperature and adjust the clock to about 350°F for around 15 minutes.

3. When your clock has 7 minutes left, throw in the peppers and onion into the fryer bucket.

4. When frying, flip the chicken at least 2–3 times Veggies should be soft; when done, the chicken should be thoroughly cooked to at least 165°F internal temperature Serve it hot.

Nutrition: **Calories: 231 | Fat: 4 g | Fiber: 8 g | Carbohydrates: 16 g | Protein: 6 g**

## 95. Pepperoni and Chicken Pizza Bake

Ready in: 25 minutes | Servings: 5 | Difficulty: Normal

**Ingredients**

- ¼ c grated Parmesan cheese
- 1 c shredded Mozzarella cheese
- 1 c low-carb, sugar-free pizza sauce
- 20 slices pepperoni
- 2 c cubed cooked chicken

**Directions**

1. Add the pepperoni, chicken, and pizza sauce into a 4-cup rectangular baking tray Stir such that the chicken is coated fully in the sauce.

2. Cover with grated Mozzarella and Parmesan Put your dish in the Air Fryer bucket.

3. Set the temperature and adjust the clock to about 375°F for around 15 minutes.

4. When served, the dish would be brown and bubbly Instantly serve.

Nutrition: Calories: 175 | Fat: 12 g | Fiber: 4 g | Carbohydrates: 13 g | Protein: 6 g

## 96. Almond-Crusted Chicken
Ready in: 40 minutes | Servings: 6 | Difficulty: Hard

**Ingredients**

• 1 tbsp. Dijon mustard
• 2 tbsps. full-fat mayonnaise
• 2 (6 oz.) boneless, skinless chicken breasts
• ¼ c slivered almonds

**Directions**

1. In a food processor, pulse your almonds or cut until finely diced Put the almonds equally and put them aside on a tray.

2. Completely split each chicken breast lengthwise in part.

3. In a shallow pot, combine the mustard and mayonnaise now, cover the entire chicken with the mixture.

4. Place each piece of chicken completely coated in the diced almonds Transfer the chicken gently into the bucket of your Air Fryer.

5. Set the temperature and adjust the clock to about 350°F for around 25 minutes.

6. When it has hit an interior temperature of about 165°F or more, the chicken will be cooked Serve it hot.

Nutrition: Calories: 175 | Fat: 12 g | Fiber: 4 g | Carbohydrates: 13 g | Protein: 6 g

## 97. Southern "Fried" Chicken
Ready in: 40 minutes | Servings: 4 | Difficulty: Hard

**Ingredients**

• 2 oz. pork rinds, finely ground
• ¼ tsp ground black pepper
• ¼ tsp onion powder
• ½ tsp cumin
• 1 tbsp. chili powder
• 2 tbsps. hot sauce
• 2 (6 oz.) boneless, skinless chicken breasts

**Directions**

1. Longitudinally, split each chicken breast in half Put the chicken in a big pot and add some hot sauce to coat the chicken completely.

2. Mix the onion powder, cumin, chili powder, and pepper in a shallow container Sprinkle the mix over your chicken.

3. In a wide bowl, put the seasoned pork rinds and dunk each chicken piece into the container, covering as much as necessary Put the chicken in the bucket of the Air Fryer.

4. Set the temperature and adjust the clock to about 350°F for around 25 minutes.

5. Turn the chicken gently midway through the cooking process.

6. The internal temperature will be at most 165°F when finished, and the coating of the pork rind will be rich golden brown Serve it hot.

Nutrition: Calories: 200 | Fat: 4 g | Fiber: 5 g | Carbohydrates: 14 g | Protein: 8 g

## 98. Spinach and Feta-Stuffed Chicken Breast
Ready in: 40 minutes | Servings: 2 | Difficulty: Hard

**Ingredients**

• 1 tbsp. coconut oil
• 2 (6 oz.) boneless, skinless chicken breasts
• ¼ c crumbled Feta
• ¼ c chopped yellow onion
• ½ tsp salt, divided
• ½ tsp garlic powder, divided
• 5 oz. frozen spinach, thawed and drained
• 1 tbsp. unsalted butter

**Directions**

1. Add some butter to your pan and sauté the spinach for around 3 minutes in a medium-sized skillet over a medium-high flame Sprinkle the spinach with ¼ tsp salt, ¼ tsp garlic powder Now, add your onion to the plate.

2. Sauté for another 3 minutes, then turn off the flame and put it in a medium-sized dish Fold the Feta mixture into the spinach.

3. Lengthwise, carve a nearly 4-inch cut through the side of each chicken breast Scoop half of the mix into each portion and seal with a pair of toothpicks shut Dust with leftover salt and garlic powder outside of your chicken Drizzle some coconut oil Put the chicken breasts in the bucket of your Air Fryer.

4. Set the temperature and adjust the clock to about 350°F for around 25 minutes.

5. The chicken must be golden brown and have an internal temperature of at least 165°F when fully cooked Cut and serve hot.

Nutrition: Calories: 200 | Fat: 4 g | Fiber: 5 g | Carbohydrates: 14 g | Protein: 6 g

## 99. Blackened Cajun Chicken Tenders
Ready in: 28 minutes | Servings: 6 | Difficulty: Normal

**Ingredients**

• ¼ c full-fat ranch dressing
• 1 lb. boneless, skinless chicken tenders
• 2 tbsps. coconut oil
• ⅛ tsp ground cayenne pepper
• ¼ tsp onion powder
• ½ tsp dried thyme
• ½ tsp garlic powder
• 1 tsp chili powder
• 2 tsps. paprika

**Directions**

1. Mix all the seasonings in a shallow container.

2. Drizzle oil over chicken wings and then cover each tender thoroughly in the mixture of spices Put tenders in the bucket of your Air Fryer.

3. Set the temperature and adjust the clock to about 375°F for around 17 minutes.

4. Tenders, when completely baked, will have a temperature of 165°F centrally.

5. For dipping, use some ranch dressing and enjoy.

Nutrition: Calories: 117 | Fat: 4 g | Fiber: 5 g | Carbohydrates: 14 g | Protein: 4 g

## 100. Chicken Pizza Crust

Ready in: 32 minutes | Servings: 4 | Difficulty: Normal

**Ingredients**

• 1 lb. ground chicken thigh meat
• ¼ c grated Parmesan cheese
• ½ c shredded Mozzarella

**Directions**

1. Combine all the ingredients in a wide bowl Split equally into 4 portions.
2. Slice out 4 (6-inch) parchment paper circles and push down the chicken mixture on each one of the circles Put into the bucket of your Air Fryer, working as required in groups or individually.
3. Set the temperature and adjust the clock to about 375°F for around 25 minutes.
4. Midway into the cooking process, turn the crust.
5. You can cover it with some cheese and your choice of toppings until completely baked, and cook for 5 extra minutes Or, you can place the crust in the fridge or freezer and top it later when you are ready to consume.

Nutrition: **Calories: 117 | Fat: 4 g | Fiber: 5 g | Carbohydrates: 14 g | Protein: 4 g**

## 101. Chicken Enchiladas

Ready in: 30 minutes | Servings: 4 | Difficulty: Normal

**Ingredients**

• 1 medium avocado, peeled, pitted, and sliced
• ½ c full-fat sour cream
• ½ c shredded Monterey Jack cheese
• 1 c shredded medium Cheddar cheese
• ½ lb. medium-sliced deli chicken
• 1/3 c low-carb enchilada sauce, divided
• 1 ½ c shredded cooked chicken

**Directions**

1. Combine the shredded chicken and at least half of the enchilada sauce in a big dish On a cutting surface, lay pieces of deli chicken and pour 2 tablespoons of the shredded chicken mixture on each of your slices.
2. Sprinkle each roll with 2 tsps. Cheddar cheese Roll softly to close it completely.
3. Put each roll, seam side down, in a 4-cup circular baking tray Over the rolls, pour the leftover sauce and top with the Monterey Jack Put the dish in the Air Fryer basket.
4. Set the temperature and adjust the clock to about 370°F for around 10 minutes.
5. Enchiladas, when baked, would be golden on top and bubbling With some sour cream and diced avocado, serve hot.

Nutrition: **Calories: 198 | Fat: 4 g | Fiber: 4 g | Carbohydrates: 14 g | Protein: 5 g**

## 102. Jalapeño Popper Hassel Back Chicken

Ready in: 40 minutes | Servings: 4 | Difficulty: Hard

**Ingredients**

• 2 (6 oz.) boneless, skinless chicken breasts
• ¼ c sliced pickled jalapeños
• ½ c shredded sharp Cheddar cheese, divided
• 2 oz. full-fat cream cheese, softened
• 4 slices sugar-free bacon, cooked and crumbled

**Directions**

1. Put the fried bacon in a medium-sized dish; add in half of the Cheddar, cream cheese, and the jalapeño strips.
2. Using a sharp knife to build slits around ¾-inch of the way across the chicken in each of the chicken thighs, being cautious not to go all the way through You would typically get 6–8 per breast, cuts based on the chicken breast's length.
3. Spoon the premade cream cheese mix onto the chicken strips Toss the leftover shredded cheese over your chicken breasts and put it in the Air Fryer basket.
4. Set the temperature and adjust the clock to about 350°F for around 20 minutes.
5. Serve it hot.

Nutrition: **Calories: 164 | Fat: 12 g | Fiber: 3 g | Carbohydrates: 10 g | Protein: 7 g**

## 103. Chicken Cordon Bleu Casserole

Ready in: 32 minutes | Servings: 5 | Difficulty: Normal

**Ingredients**

• 1 oz. pork rinds, crushed
• 2 tsps. Dijon mustard
• 2 tbsps. unsalted butter, melted
• 1 tbsp. heavy cream
• 4 oz. full-fat cream cheese, softened
• 2 oz. Swiss cheese, cubed
• ½ c cubed cooked ham
• 2 c cubed cooked chicken thigh meat

**Directions**

1. Put the chicken and ham in a 6-inch circular baking pan and toss to blend the meat uniformly Scatter on top of the meat some cheese cubes.
2. Add butter, heavy cream, cream cheese, and mustard in a big bowl, and then spill the mix over your meat and cheese Cover with rinds of pork Put the pan in the bucket of your Air Fryer.
3. Set the temperature and adjust the clock to about 350°F for around 15 minutes.
4. When finished, the saucepan will be caramelized and bubbling Serve hot.

Nutrition: **Calories: 2 | Protein: 0 g | Carbohydrates: 1 g | Fat: 0 g | Fiber: 0 g**

## 104. Chicken Parmesan II

Ready in: 32 minutes | Servings: 4 | Difficulty: Normal

**Ingredients**

• 1 oz. pork rinds, crushed
• ½ tsp garlic powder
• 1 c low-carb, no-sugar-added pasta sauce
• ½ c grated Parmesan cheese, divided
• 2 (6 oz.) boneless, skinless chicken breasts
• 1 c shredded Mozzarella cheese, divided
• 4 tbsps. full-fat mayonnaise, divided
• ½ tsp dried parsley
• ¼ tsp dried oregano

**Directions**

1. Cut each chicken breast longitudinally in half and hammer it to lb. out a thickness of about ¾-inch Sprinkle with parsley, garlic powder, and oregano.

2. On top of each slice of chicken, scatter 1 tbsp. mayonnaise, then cover each piece with ¼ c Mozzarella.

3. Mix the shredded Parmesan and pork rinds in a shallow bowl Sprinkle the surface of the Mozzarella with the paste.

4. In a 6-inch circular baking tray, transfer the sauce and put the chicken on top Place the pan in the bucket of your Air Fryer.

5. Set the temperature and adjust the clock to about 320°F for around 25 minutes.

6. The cheese will be light browned, and when completely baked, the chicken's internal temperature will be at about 165°F Serve hot.

Nutrition: Calories: 251 | Fat: 12 g | Fiber: 4 g | Carbohydrates: 13 g | Protein: 6 g

## 105. Fajita-Stuffed Chicken Breast

Ready in: 40 minutes | Servings: 4 | Difficulty: Hard

**Ingredients**

- ½ tsp garlic powder
- 1 tsp ground cumin
- 2 tsps. chili powder
- 1 tbsp. coconut oil
- 1 medium green bell pepper, seeded and sliced
- ¼ medium white onion,} peeled and sliced
- 2 (6 oz.) boneless, skinless chicken breasts

**Directions**

1. Slice each chicken breast into 2 equal parts entirely in half longitudinally Hammer the chicken out until it is around ¼-inch thick using a meat mallet.

2. Put out each chicken slice and arrange 3 onion pieces and 4 green pepper pieces on the end nearest to you Start to firmly roll the onions and peppers into the chicken Both with toothpicks or a few strips of butcher's twine protect the roll.

3. Drizzle the chicken with coconut oil Sprinkle with cumin, chili powder, and garlic powder on either side Put all the rolls in the bucket of your Air Fryer.

4. Set the temperature and adjust the clock to about 350°F for around 25 minutes.

5. Serve it hot.

Nutrition: Calories: 201 | Fat: 3 g | Fiber: 5 g | Carbohydrates: 14 g | Protein: 7 g

## 106. Lemon Pepper Drumsticks

Ready in: 27 minutes | Servings: 5 | Difficulty: Normal

**Ingredients**

- 1 tbsp. lemon pepper seasoning
- 4 tbsps. salted butter, melted
- 8 chicken drumsticks
- ½ tsp garlic powder
- 2 tsps. baking powder

**Directions**

1. Sprinkle some baking powder over the drumsticks along with some garlic powder and massage it into the chicken skin Add your drumsticks into the bucket of your Air Fryer.

2. Set the temperature and adjust the clock to about 375°F for around 25 minutes.

3. Turn your drumsticks midway through the cooking process using tongs.

4. Take out from the fryer when the skin is golden in color, and the inside temperature is at a minimum of 165°F.

5. Put lemon pepper seasoning and some butter in a big dish To the dish, add your fried drumsticks and turn until the chicken is coated Serve it hot.

Nutrition: Calories: 201 | Fat: 3 g | Fiber: 5 g | Carbohydrates: 14 g | Protein: 7 g

## 107. Cilantro Lime Chicken Thighs

Ready in: 32 minutes | Servings: 5 | Difficulty: Normal

**Ingredients**

- ¼ c chopped fresh cilantro
- 2 medium limes
- 1 tsp cumin
- 2 tsps. chili powder
- ½ tsp garlic powder
- 1 tsp baking powder
- 4 bone-in, skin-on chicken thighs

**Directions**

1. Toss some baking powder on your chicken thighs and rinse them.

2. Mix the chili powder, garlic powder, and cumin in a small bowl and sprinkle uniformly over the thighs, rubbing softly on and under the chicken's skin.

3. Halve 1 lime and squeeze the liquid across the thighs Place the chicken in the bucket of an Air Fryer.

4. Set the temperature and adjust the clock to about 380°F for around 22 minutes.

5. For serving, split the other lime into 4 slices and garnish the fried chicken with lemon wedges and some cilantro.

Nutrition: Calories: 199 | Fat: 3 g | Fiber: 6 g | Carbohydrates: 13 g | Protein: 8 g

## 108. Lemon Thyme Roasted Chicken

Ready in: 70 minutes | Servings: 6 | Difficulty: Hard

**Ingredients**

- 2 tbsps. salted butter, melted
- 1 medium lemon
- 1 tsp baking powder
- ½ tsp onion powder
- 2 tsps. dried parsley
- 1 tsp garlic powder
- 2 tsps. dried thyme
- 1 (4 lbs.) chicken

**Directions**

1. Rub the garlic powder, thyme, parsley, onion powder, and baking powder with the chicken.

2. Slice the lemon and put 4 slices using a toothpick on top of the chicken, chest side up, and secure Put the leftover slices inside your chicken.

3. Put the whole chicken in the bucket of your Air Fryer, chest side down.

4. Set the temperature and adjust the clock to about 350°F for around 60 minutes.

5. Switch the sides of your chicken after 30 minutes, so its breast side is up.

6. The internal temperature should be at about 165°F when finished, and the skin should be golden in color and crispy Pour the melted butter over the whole chicken before serving.

Nutrition: Calories: 199 | Fat: 3 g | Fiber: 6 g | Carbohydrates: 13 g | Protein: 8 g

## 109. Teriyaki Wings
Ready in: 1 hour and 40 minutes | Servings: 4 | Difficulty: Hard

**Ingredients**
- 2 tsps. baking powder
- ¼ tsp ground ginger
- 2 tsps. minced garlic
- ½ c sugar-free teriyaki sauce
- 2 lbs. chicken wings

**Directions**
1. Put all of your ingredients in a big bowl or bag, excluding the baking powder, and leave to marinate in the fridge for at least 1 hour.

2. Bring the wings into the bucket of your Air Fryer and dust with baking powder Rub the wings softly.

3. Set the temperature and adjust the clock to about 400°F for around 25 minutes.

4. When frying, rotate the bucket 2–3 times.

5. Wings, when finished, should be crunchy and cooked internally to a minimum of 165°F Instantly serve.

Nutrition: Calories: 200 | Fat: 4 g | Fiber: 3 g | Carbohydrates: 7 g | Protein: 8 g

## 110. Crispy Buffalo Chicken Tenders
Ready in: 32 minutes | Servings: 4 | Difficulty: Normal

**Ingredients**
- 1 tsp garlic powder
- 1 tsp chili powder
- 1 ½ oz. pork rinds, finely ground
- ¼ c hot sauce
- 1 lb. boneless, skinless chicken tenders

**Directions**
1. Put the chicken tenders in a big bowl and pour them over with hot sauce In the hot sauce, toss tender, rubbing uniformly.

2. Mix the ground pork rinds with chili powder and garlic powder in a separate, wide bowl.

3. Put each tender, fully coated, in the ground pork rinds With some water, wet your hands and push down the rinds of pork onto the chicken.

4. Put the tenders in a single layer into the basket of the Air Fryer

5. Set the temperature and adjust the clock to about 375°F for around 20 minutes.

6. Serve it hot.

Nutrition: Calories: 200 | Fat: 4 g | Fiber: 3 g | Carbohydrates: 7 g | Protein: 8 g

## 111. Mushroom and Bell Pepper Pizza
Ready in: 15 minutes | Servings: 9 | Difficulty: Easy

**Ingredients**
- Salt and pepper according to taste
- 2 tbsps. parsley
- 1 vegan pizza dough
- 1 shallot, chopped
- 1 c oyster mushrooms, chopped
- ¼ red bell pepper, chopped

**Directions**
1. Preheat your Air Fryer to about 400°F.

2. Cut the pizza dough into small squares Just set them aside.

3. Put your bell pepper, shallot, oyster mushroom, and parsley all together into a mixing dish.

4. According to taste, sprinkle with some pepper and salt.

5. On top of your pizza cubes, put your topping.

6. Put your pizza cubes into your Air Fryer and cook for about 10 minutes.

Nutrition: Calories: 237 | Fat: 5 g | Fiber: 4 g | Carbohydrates: 12 g | Protein: 9 g

## 112. Veggies Stuffed Eggplants
Ready in: 19 minutes | Servings: 6 | Difficulty: Easy

**Ingredients**
- 2 tbsps. tomato paste
- Salt and ground black pepper, as required
- ½ tsp garlic, chopped
- 1 tbsp. vegetable oil
- 1 tbsp. fresh lime juice
- ½ green bell pepper, seeded and chopped
- ¼ c Cottage cheese, chopped
- 1 tomato, chopped
- 1 onion, chopped
- 10 small eggplants, halved lengthwise

**Directions**
1. Preheat your Air Fryer to about 320°F and oil the container of your Air Fryer.

2. Cut a strip longitudinally from all sides of your eggplant and scrape out the pulp in a medium-sized bowl.

3. Add lime juice on top of your eggplants and place them in the container of your Air Fryer.

4. Cook for around a couple of minutes and extract from your Air Fryer.

5. Heat the vegetable oil on medium-high heat in a pan and add the onion and garlic.

6. Sauté for around 2 minutes and mix in the tomato, salt, eggplant flesh, and black pepper.

7. Sauté and add bell pepper, tomato paste, cheese, and cilantro for roughly 3 minutes.

8. Cook for around 1 minute and put this paste into your eggplants.

9. Shut each eggplant with its lids and adjust the Air Fryer to 360°F.

10. Organize and bake for around 5 minutes in your Air Fryer basket.

11. Dish out on a serving tray and eat hot.

Nutrition: Calories: 200 | Fat: 5 g | Fiber: 3 g | Carbohydrates: 9 g | Protein: 8 g

## 113. Air-Fried Falafel

Ready in: 35 minutes | Servings: 6 | Difficulty: Normal

**Ingredients**

- Salt and black pepper according to taste
- 1 tsp chili powder
- 2 tsps. ground cilantro
- 2 tsps. ground cumin
- 1 onion, chopped
- 4 garlic cloves, chopped
- Juice of 1 lemon
- 1 c fresh parsley, chopped
- ½ c chickpea flour

**Directions**

1. Add chickpeas flour, cilantro, lemon juice, parsley, onion, garlic, chili, cumin, salt, and pepper to a processor and mix until mixed, not too battery; several chunks should be present.
2. Morph the paste into spheres and hand-press them to ensure that they are still round.
3. Spray using some spray oil and place them in a paper-lined Air Fryer bucket; if necessary, perform in groups.
4. Cook for about 14 minutes at around 360°F, rotating once mid-way through the cooking process.
5. They must be light brown and crispy.

Nutrition: **Calories: 185 | Fat: 3 g | Fiber: 2 g | Carbohydrates: 6 g | Protein: 8 g**

## 114. Almond Flour Battered Wings

Ready in: 32 minutes | Servings: 4 | Difficulty: Normal

**Ingredients**

- Salt and pepper according to taste
- 4 tbsps. minced garlic
- 2 tbsps. Stevia powder
- 16 pieces of chicken wings
- ¾ c almond flour
- ¼ c butter, melted

**Directions**

1. Preheat your Air Fryer for about 5 minutes.
2. Mix the Stevia powder, almond flour, chicken wings, and garlic in a mixing dish According to taste, sprinkle with some black pepper and salt.
3. Please put it in the bucket of your Air Fryer and cook at about 400°F for around 25 minutes.
4. Ensure you give your fryer container a shake midway through the cooking process.
5. Put in a serving dish after cooking and add some melted butter on top Toss it to coat it completely.

Nutrition: **Calories: 180 | Fat: 10 g | Fiber: 6 g | Carbohydrates: 13 g | Protein: 8 g**

## 115. Spicy Tofu

Ready in: 15 minutes | Servings: 6 | Difficulty: Easy

**Ingredients**

- Salt and black pepper, according to taste
- 1 tsp garlic powder
- 1 tsp onion powder
- 1½ tsp paprika
- 1½ tbsp. avocado oil
- 3 tsps. cornstarch
- 1 (14 oz.) block extra-firm tofu, pressed and cut into ¾-inch cubes

**Directions**

1. Preheat your Air Fryer to about 390°F and oil the container of your Air Fryer with some spray oil.
2. In a medium-sized bowl, blend the cornstarch, oil, tofu, and spices and mix to cover properly.
3. In the Air Fryer basket, place the tofu bits and cook for around 1 minute, flipping twice between the cooking times.
4. On a serving dish, spread out the tofu and enjoy it warm.

Nutrition: **Calories: 170 | Fat: 5 g | Fiber: 7 g | Carbohydrates: 8 g | Protein: 10 g**

## 116. Sautéed Bacon with Spinach

Ready in: 15 minutes | Servings: 2 | Difficulty: Easy

**Ingredients**

- 1 garlic clove, minced
- 2 tbsps. olive oil
- 4 oz. fresh spinach
- 1 onion, chopped
- 3 meatless bacon slices, chopped

**Directions**

1. Preheat your Air Fryer at about 340°F and oil the Air Fryer's tray with some olive oil or cooking oil spray.
2. In the Air Fryer basket, put garlic and olive oil.
3. Cook and add in the onions and bacon for around 2 minutes.
4. Cook and mix in the spinach for approximately 3 minutes.
5. Cook for 4 more minutes and plate out in a bowl to eat.

Nutrition: **Calories: 130 | Fat: 1 g | Fiber: 2 g | Carbohydrates: 7 g | Protein: 6 g**

## 117. Garden Fresh Veggie Medley

Ready in: 20 minutes | Servings: 6 | Difficulty: Easy

**Ingredients**

- 1 tbsp. balsamic vinegar
- 1 tbsp. olive oil
- 2 tbsps. herbs de Provence
- 2 garlic cloves, minced
- 2 small onions, chopped
- 3 tomatoes, chopped
- 1 zucchini, chopped
- 1 eggplant, chopped
- 2 yellow bell peppers seeded and chopped
- Salt and black pepper, according to taste

**Directions**

1. Preheat your Air Fryer at about 355°F and oil up the Air Fryer basket.
2. In a medium-sized bowl, add all the ingredients and toss to cover completely.
3. Move to the basket of your Air Fryer and cook for around 15 minutes.
4. After completing the cooking time, let it sit in the Air Fryer for around 5 minutes and plate out to serve warm.

Nutrition: **Calories: 130 | Fat: 1 g | Fiber: 2 g | Carbohydrates: 7 g | Protein: 6 g**

## 118. Colorful Vegetable Croquettes

Ready in: 15 minutes | Servings: 4 | Difficulty: Easy

### Ingredients

- ½ c Parmesan cheese, grated
- 2 eggs
- ¼ c coconut flour
- ½ c almond flour
- 2 tbsps. olive oil
- 3 tbsps. scallions, minced
- 1 clove garlic, minced
- 1 bell pepper, chopped
- ½ c mushrooms, chopped
- ½ tsp cayenne pepper
- Salt and black pepper, according to taste
- 2 tbsps. butter
- 4 tbsps. milk
- ½ lb. broccoli

### Directions

1. Boil your broccoli in a medium-sized saucepan for up to around 20 minutes With butter, milk, black pepper, salt, and cayenne pepper, and then rinse the broccoli and mash it.

2. Add in the bell pepper, mushrooms, garlic, scallions, and olive oil and blend properly Form into patties with the blend.

3. Put the flour in a deep bowl; beat your eggs in a second bowl; then put the Parmesan cheese in another bowl.

4. Dip each patty into your flour, accompanied by the eggs and lastly the Parmesan cheese, push to hold the shape.

5. Cook for around 16 minutes, turning midway through the cooking period, in the preheated Air Fryer at about 370°F Bon appétit!

Nutrition: Calories: 70 | Fat: 2 g | Fiber: 2 g | Carbohydrates: 6 g | Protein: 4 g

## 119. Cheesy Mushrooms

Ready in: 11 minutes | Servings: 4 | Difficulty: Easy

### Ingredients

- 1 tsp dried dill
- 2 tbsps. Italian dried mixed herbs
- 2 tbsps. olive oil
- 2 tbsps. Cheddar cheese, grated
- 2 tbsps. Mozzarella cheese, grated
- Salt and freshly ground black pepper, according to taste
- 6 oz. button mushrooms stemmed

### Directions

1. Preheat the Air Fryer at around 355°F and oil your Air Fryer basket.

2. In a mixing bowl, combine the Italian dried mixed herbs, mushrooms, salt, oil, and black pepper and mix well to cover.

3. In the Air Fryer bucket, place the mushrooms and cover them with some Cheddar cheese and Mozzarella cheese.

4. To eat, cook for around 8 minutes and scatter with dried dill.

Nutrition: Calories: 70 | Fat: 2 g | Fiber: 2 g | Carbohydrates: 6 g | Protein: 4 g

## 120. Greek-Style Roasted Vegetables

Ready in: 32 minutes | Servings: 3 | Difficulty: Normal

### Ingredients

- ½ c Kalamata olives, pitted
- 1 (28 oz.) canned diced tomatoes with juice
- ½ tsp dried basil
- Sea salt and freshly cracked black pepper, according to taste
- 1 tsp dried rosemary
- 1 c dry white wine
- 2 tbsps. extra-virgin olive oil
- 2 bell peppers, cut into 1-inch chunks
- 1 red onion, sliced
- ½ lb. zucchini, cut into 1-inch chunks
- ½ lb. cauliflower, cut into 1-inch florets
- ½ lb. butternut squash, peeled and cut into 1-inch chunks

### Directions

1. Add some rosemary, wine, olive oil, black pepper, salt, and basil along with your vegetables toss until well-seasoned.

2. Onto a lightly oiled baking dish, add ½ of the canned chopped tomatoes; scatter to fill the base of your baking dish.

3. Add in the vegetables and add the leftover chopped tomatoes to the top On top of tomatoes, spread the Kalamata olives.

4. Bake for around 20 minutes at about 390°F in the preheated Air Fryer, turning the dish midway through your cooking cycle Serve it hot and enjoy it!

Nutrition: Calories: 120 | Fat: 2 g | Fiber: 1 g | Carbohydrates: 7 g | Protein: 1 g

## 121. Vegetable Kabobs with Simple Peanut Sauce

Ready in: 40 minutes | Servings: 4 | Difficulty: Hard

### Ingredients

- 1/3 tsp granulated garlic
- 1 tsp dried rosemary, crushed
- 1 tsp red pepper flakes, crushed
- Sea salt and ground black pepper, according to your taste
- 2 tbsps. extra-virgin olive oil
- 8 small button mushrooms, cleaned
- 8 pearl onions, halved
- 2 bell peppers, diced into 1-inch pieces
- 8 whole baby potatoes, diced into 1-inch pieces
- Wooden chopsticks

### For the peanut sauce:

- ½ tsp garlic salt
- 1 tbsp. soy sauce
- 1 tbsp. balsamic vinegar
- 2 tbsps. peanut butter

### Directions

1. For a few minutes, dunk the wooden chopsticks in water.

2. String the vegetables onto your chopsticks; drip some olive oil all over your chopsticks with the vegetables on it; dust with seasoning.

3. Cook for about 1 minute at 400°F in the preheated Air Fryer.

### For the peanut sauce:

4. In the meantime, mix the balsamic vinegar with some peanut butter, garlic salt, and some soy sauce in a tiny dish Offer the kabobs with a side of peanut sauce Eat warm!

Nutrition: Calories: 130 | Fat: 3 g | Fiber: 6 g | Carbohydrates: 10 g | Protein: 3 g

## 122. Hungarian Mushroom Pilaf

Ready in: 60 minutes | Servings: 4 | Difficulty: Hard

**Ingredients**

- 1 tsp sweet Hungarian paprika
- ½ tsp dried tarragon
- 1 tsp dried thyme
- ¼ c dry vermouth
- 1 onion, chopped

- 2 garlic cloves
- 2 tbsps. olive oil
- 1 lb. fresh porcini mushrooms, sliced
- 2 tbsps. olive oil
- 3 c vegetable broth
- 1 ½ c white rice

**Directions**

1. In a wide saucepan, put the broth and rice, add some water, and bring it to a boil.

2. Cover with a lid and turn the flame down to a low temperature and proceed to cook for the next 18 minutes or so After cooking, let it rest for 5–10 minutes, and then set aside.

3. Finally, in a lightly oiled baking dish, mix the heated, fully cooked rice with the rest of your ingredients.

4. Cook at about 200°F for around 20 minutes in the preheated Air Fryer, regularly monitoring to even cook.

5. In small bowls, serve Bon appétit!

Nutrition: **Calories: 140 | Fat: 2 g | Fiber: 2 g | Carbohydrates: 7 g | Protein: 7 g**

## 123. Chinese Cabbage Bake

Ready in: 50 minutes | Servings: 4 | Difficulty: Hard

**Ingredients**

- 1 c Monterey Jack cheese, shredded
- ½ tsp cayenne pepper
- 1 c cream cheese
- ½ c milk
- 4 tbsps. flaxseed meal
- ½ stick butter
- 2 garlic cloves, sliced

- 1 onion, thickly sliced
- 1 jalapeño pepper, seeded and sliced
- Sea salt and freshly ground black pepper, according to taste
- 2 bell peppers, seeded and sliced
- ½ lb. Chinese cabbage, roughly chopped

**Directions**

1. Heat the salted water in a pan and carry it to a boil For around 2–3 minutes, steam the Chinese cabbage To end the cooking process, switch the Chinese cabbage to cold water immediately.

2. Put your Chinese cabbage in a lightly oiled casserole dish Add in the garlic, onion, and peppers.

3. Next, over low fire, melt some butter in a skillet Add in your flaxseed meal steadily and cook for around 2 minutes to create a paste.

4. Add in the milk gently, constantly whisking until it creates a dense mixture Add in your cream cheese Sprinkle some cayenne pepper, salt, and black pepper To the casserole tray, transfer your mixture.

5. Cover with some Monterey Jack cheese and cook for about 2 minutes at around 390°F in your preheated Air Fryer Serve it warm.

Nutrition: **Calories: 120 | Fat: 2 g | Fiber: 2 g | Carbohydrates: 7 g | Protein: 2 g**

## 124. Brussels Sprouts with Balsamic Oil

Ready in: 15 minutes | Servings: 4 | Difficulty: Easy

**Ingredients**

- 2 tbsps. olive oil
- 2 c Brussels sprouts, halved
- 1 tbsp. balsamic vinegar
- ¼ tsp salt

**Directions**

1. For 5 minutes, preheat your Air Fryer.

2. In a mixing bowl, blend all of your ingredients and ensure the zucchini fries are very well coated Put the fries in the basket of an Air Fryer.

3. Close it and cook it at about 350°F for around 15 minutes.

Nutrition: **Calories: 120 | Fat: 3 g | Fiber: 3 g | Carbohydrates: 7 g | Protein: 5 g**

## 125. Aromatic Baked Potatoes with Chives

Ready in: 50 minutes | Servings: 2 | Difficulty: Hard

**Ingredients**

- 2 tbsps. chives, chopped
- 2 garlic cloves, minced
- 1 tbsp. sea salt
- ¼ tsp smoked paprika

- ¼ tsp red pepper flakes
- 2 tbsps. olive oil
- 4 medium baking potatoes, peeled

**Directions**

1. Toss the potatoes with your seasoning, olive oil, and garlic.

2. Put them in the basket of your Air Fryer Cook at about 400°F for around 40 minutes just until the potatoes are fork soft in your preheated Air Fryer.

3. Add in some fresh minced chives to garnish Bon appétit!

Nutrition: **Calories: 87 | Fat: 1 g | Fiber: 2 g | Carbohydrates: 4 g | Protein: 7 g**

## 126. Easy Vegan "Chicken"

Ready in: 32 minutes | Servings: 5 | Difficulty: Normal

**Ingredients**

- 1 tsp celery seeds
- ½ tsp mustard powder
- 1 tsp cayenne pepper
- ¼ c all-purpose flour

- ½ c cornmeal
- 8 oz. soy chunks
- Sea salt and ground black pepper, according to taste

**Directions**

1. In a skillet over medium-high flame, cook the soya chunks in plenty of water Turn off the flame and allow soaking for several minutes Drain the remaining water, wash, and strain it out.

2. In a mixing bowl, combine the rest of the components Roll your soy chunks over the breading paste, pressing lightly to stick

3. In the slightly oiled Air Fryer basket, place your soy chunks.

4. Cook at about 390°F for around 10 minutes in your preheated Air Fryer, rotating them over midway through the cooking process; operate in batches if required Bon appétit!

Nutrition: **Calories: 87 | Fat: 1 g | Fiber: 2 g | Carbohydrates: 4 g | Protein: 7 g**

## 127. Paprika Vegetable Kebab's

Ready in: 32 minutes | Servings: 5 | Difficulty: Normal

**Ingredients**

- ½ tsp ground black pepper
- 1 tsp sea salt flakes
- 1 tsp smoked paprika
- ¼ c sesame oil
- 2 tbsps. dry white wine
- 1 red onion, cut into wedges
- 2 cloves garlic, pressed
- 1 tsp whole grain mustard
- 1 fennel bulb, diced
- 1 parsnip, cut into thick slices
- 1 celery, cut into thick slices

**Directions**

1. Toss all of the above ingredients together in a mixing bowl to uniformly coat Thread the vegetables alternately onto the wooden skewers.

2. Cook for around 15 minutes at about 380°F on your Air Fryer grill plate.

3. Turn them over midway during the cooking process.

4. Taste, change the seasonings if needed, and serve steaming hot.

Nutrition: Calories: 120 | Fat: 4 g | Fiber: 2 g | Carbohydrates: 7 g | Protein: 12 g

## 128. Spiced Soy Curls

Ready in: 15 minutes | Servings: 6 | Difficulty: Easy

**Ingredients**

- 1 tsp poultry seasoning
- 2 tsps. Cajun seasoning
- ¼ c fine ground cornmeal
- ¼ c nutritional yeast
- 4 oz. soy curls
- 3 c boiling water
- Salt and ground white pepper, as needed

**Directions**

1. Dip the soy curls for around 1 minute or so in hot water in a heat-resistant bowl.

2. Drain your soy coils using a strainer and force the excess moisture out using a broad spoon.

3. Mix the cornmeal, nutritional yeast, salt, seasonings, and white pepper well in a mixing bowl.

4. Transfer your soy curls to the bowl and coat well with the blend Let the Air Fryer temperature to about 380°F Oil the basket of your Air Fryer.

5. Adjust soy curls in a uniform layer in the lined Air Fryer basket Cook for about 10 minutes in the Air Fryer, turning midway through the cycle.

6. Take out the soy curls from your Air Fryer and put them on a serving dish Serve them steaming hot.

Nutrition: Calories: 130 | Fat: 4 g | Fiber: 5 g | Carbohydrates: 8 g | Protein: 6 g

## 129. Cauliflower and Egg Rice Casserole

Ready in: 20 minutes | Servings: 6 | Difficulty: Easy

**Ingredients**

- 2 eggs, beaten
- 1 tbsp. soy sauce
- Salt and black pepper according to taste
- ½ c chopped onion
- 1 c okra, chopped
- 1 yellow bell pepper, chopped
- 2 tsps. olive oil
- Cauliflower

**Directions**

1. Preheat your Air Fryer to about 380°F Oil a baking tray with spray oil Pulse the cauliflower till it becomes like thin rice-like capsules in your food blender.

2. Now, add your cauliflower rice to a baking tray mix in the okra, bell pepper, salt, soy sauce, onion, and pepper, and combine well

3. Drizzle a little olive oil on top along with the beaten eggs Put the tray in your Air Fryer and cook for about 1 minute Serve it hot.

Nutrition: Calories: 120 | Fat: 3 g | Fiber: 2 g | Carbohydrates: 5 g | Protein: 9 g

## 130. Hollandaise Topped Grilled Asparagus

Ready in: 15 minutes | Servings: 6 | Difficulty: Easy

**Ingredients**

- 1 pinch of ground white pepper
- 1 pinch of mustard powder
- 3 lbs. asparagus spears, trimmed
- 3 egg yolks
- 2 tbsps. olive oil
- 1 tsp chopped tarragon leaves
- ½ tsp salt
- ½ lemon juice
- ½ c butter, melted
- ¼ tsp black pepper

**Directions**

1. Preheat your Air Fryer to about 330°F In your Air Fryer, put the grill pan attachment.

2. Mix the olive oil, salt, asparagus, and pepper into a Ziplock bag To mix all, give everything a quick shake Load onto the grill plate and cook for about 15 minutes.

3. In the meantime, beat the lemon juice, egg yolks, and salt in a double boiler over a moderate flame until velvety.

4. Add in the melted butter, mustard powder, and some white pepper Continue whisking till the mixture is creamy and thick Serve with tarragon leaves as a garnish.

5. Pour the sauce over the asparagus spears and toss to blend.

Nutrition: Calories: 110 | Fat: 2 g | Fiber: 2 g | Carbohydrates: 4 g | Protein: 7 g

## 131. Crispy Asparagus Dipped in Paprika-Garlic Spice

Ready in: 15 minutes | Servings: 6 | Difficulty: Easy

**Ingredients**

- ¼ c almond flour
- ½ tsp garlic powder
- ½ tsp smoked paprika
- 10 medium asparagus, trimmed
- 2 large eggs, beaten
- 2 tbsps. parsley, chopped
- Salt and pepper according to your taste

**Directions**

1. For about 5 minutes, preheat your Air Fryer.

2. Mix the almond flour, garlic powder, parsley, and smoked pa-

prika in a mixing dish Season with some salt and black pepper to taste.

3. Soak your asparagus in the beaten eggs, and then dredge it in a combination of almond flour.

4. Put in the bowl of your Air Fryer Close the lid Cook for a few minutes at about 350°F.

Nutrition: **Calories: 120 | Fat: 2 g | Fiber: 2 g | Carbohydrates: 3 g | Protein: 4 g**

## 132. Eggplant Gratin with Mozzarella Crust

Ready in: 40 minutes | Servings: 3 | Difficulty: Hard

### Ingredients

- 1 tbsp. breadcrumbs
- ¼ c grated Mozzarella cheese
- Cooking spray
- Salt and pepper according to your taste
- ¼ tsp dried marjoram
- ¼ tsp dried basil
- 1 tsp capers
- 1 tbsp. sliced pimiento-stuffed olives
- 1 clove garlic, minced
- 1/3 c chopped tomatoes
- ¼ c chopped onion
- ¼ c chopped green pepper
- ¼ c chopped red pepper
- Eggplant

### Directions

1. Put the green pepper, eggplant, onion, red pepper, olives, tomatoes, basil marjoram, garlic, s alt, capers, and pepper in a container and preheat your Air Fryer to about 300°F.

2. Lightly oil a baking tray with a spray of cooking olive oil.

3. Fill your baking with the eggplant combination and line it with the vessel.

4. Place some Mozzarella cheese on top of it and top with some breadcrumbs Put the dish in the frying pan and cook for a few minutes.

Nutrition: **Calories: 120 | Fat: 2 g | Fiber: 2 g | Carbohydrates: 3 g | Protein: 4 g**

## 133. Asian-Style Cauliflower

Ready in: 32 minutes | Servings: 5 | Difficulty: Normal

### Ingredients

- 2 tbsps. sesame seeds
- ¼ c lime juice
- 1 tbsp. fresh parsley, finely chopped
- 1 tbsp. ginger, freshly grated
- 2 cloves of garlic, peeled and pressed
- 1 tbsp. sake
- 1 tbsp. tamari sauce
- 1 tbsp. sesame oil
- 1 onion, peeled and finely chopped
- 2 c cauliflower, grated

### Directions

1. In a mixing bowl, mix your onion, cauliflower, tamari sauce, sesame oil, garlic, sake, and ginger; whisk until all is well integrated.

2. Air fry it for around a minute at about 400°F.

3. Pause your Air Fryer Add in some parsley and lemon juice.

4. Cook for an extra 10 minutes at about 300°F in the Air Fryer.

5. In the meantime, in a nonstick pan, toast your sesame seeds;

swirl them continuously over medium-low heat Serve hot on top of the cauliflower with a pinch of salt and pepper

Nutrition: **Calories: 120 | Fat: 2 g | Fiber: 2 g | Carbohydrates: 3 g | Protein: 4 g**

## 134. 2-Cheese Vegetable Frittata

Ready in: 40 minutes | Servings: 4 | Difficulty: Hard

### Ingredients

- 1/3 c crumbled Feta cheese
- 1/3 c grated Cheddar cheese
- Salt and pepper according to taste
- 1/3 c milk
- 4 eggs, cracked into a bowl
- 2 tsps. olive oil
- ¼ lb. asparagus, trimmed and sliced thinly
- ¼ c chopped chives
- 1 small red onion, sliced
- 1 large zucchini, sliced with a 1-inch thickness
- 1/3 c sliced mushrooms
- Baby spinach

### Directions

1. Preheat your Air Fryer to about 380°F Set aside your baking dish lined with some parchment paper Put salt, milk, and pepper into the egg bowl; whisk evenly.

2. Put a skillet on the stovetop over a moderate flame, and heat your olive oil Add in the zucchini, asparagus, baby spinach, onion, and mushrooms; stir-fry for around 5 minutes Transfer the vegetables into your baking tray, and finish with the beaten egg.

3. Put the tray into your Air Fryer and finish with Cheddar and Feta cheese.

4. For about 15 minutes, cook Take out your baking tray and add in some fresh chives to garnish.

Nutrition: **Calories: 100 | Fat: 2 g | Fiber: 2 g | Carbohydrates: 3 g | Protein: 6 g**

## 135. Rice and Beans Stuffed Bell Peppers

Ready in: 25 minutes | Servings: 5 | Difficulty: Normal

### Ingredients

- 1 tbsp. Parmesan cheese, grated
- ½ c Mozzarella cheese, shredded
- 5 large bell peppers, tops removed and seeded
- 1 ½ tsp Italian seasoning
- 1 c cooked rice
- 1 (15 oz.) can of red kidney beans, rinsed and drained
- 1 (15 oz.) can of diced tomatoes with juice
- ½ small bell pepper, seeded and chopped

### Directions

1. Combine the tomatoes with juice, small bell pepper, rice, beans, and Italian seasoning in a mixing dish Using the rice mixture, fill each large bell pepper uniformly.

2. Preheat the Air Fryer to 300°F Oil the basket of your Air Fryer with some spray oil Put the bell peppers in a uniform layer in your Air Fryer basket.

3. Cook for around 12 minutes in the Air Fryer In the meantime, combine the Parmesan and Mozzarella cheese in a mixing dish.

4. Remove the peppers from the Air Fryer basket and top each with some cheese mix Cook for another 3–4 minutes in the Air Fryer.

5. Take the bell peppers from the Air Fryer and put them on a serving dish Enable to cool slowly before serving Serve it hot.

Nutrition: **Calories: 100 | Fat: 2 g | Fiber: 2 g | Carbohydrates: 3 g | Protein: 6 g**

## 136. Parsley-Loaded Mushrooms
Ready in: 20 Minutes | Servings: 5 | Difficulty: Normal
**Ingredients**
• 2 tbsps. parsley, finely chopped
• 2 tsps. olive oil
• 1 garlic clove, crushed
• 2 slices white bread
• Salt and black pepper according to your taste
• Mushrooms

**Directions**
1. Preheat the Air Fryer to about 360°F Crush your bread into crumbs in a food blender Add the parsley, garlic, salt, and pepper; blend with the olive oil and mix.

2. Remove the stalks from the mushrooms and stuff the caps with breadcrumbs In your Air Fryer basket, position the mushroom heads Cook for a few minutes, just until golden brown and crispy.

Nutrition: **Calories: 100 | Fat: 1 g | Fiber: 1 g | Carbohydrates: 7 g | Protein: 6 g**

## 137. Cheesy Vegetable Quesadilla
Ready in: 15 minutes | Servings: 6 | Difficulty: Easy
**Ingredients**
• 1 tsp olive oil
• 1 tbsp. cilantro, chopped
• ½ green onion, sliced
• ¼ zucchini, sliced
• ¼ yellow bell pepper, sliced
• ¼ c shredded Gouda cheese
• Flour tortilla

**Directions**
1. Preheat your Air Fryer to about 390°F Oil a basket of Air Fryer with some cooking oil.

2. Put a flour tortilla in your Air Fryer basket and cover it with some bell pepper, Gouda cheese, cilantro, zucchini, and green onion Take the other tortilla to cover and spray with some olive oil.

3. Cook until slightly golden brown, for around 10 minutes Cut into 4 slices for serving when ready Enjoy!

Nutrition: **Calories: 100 | Fat: 1 g | Fiber: 1 g | Carbohydrates: 7 g | Protein: 6 g**

## 138. Creamy and Cheese Broccoli Bake
Ready in: 40 minutes | Servings: 2 | Difficulty: Hard
**Ingredients**
• 1 ½ tsps. butter, or to taste
• ½ c cubed sharp Cheddar cheese
• ½ (14 oz.) can evaporate milk, divided
• 2 tbsps. all-purpose flour
• 1 lb. fresh broccoli, coarsely diced

**Directions**
1. Lightly oil the Air Fryer baking pan with cooking oil Add half of the milk and flour into a pan and simmer at about 360°F for around 5 minutes.

2. Mix well midway through the cooking period Remove the broccoli and the extra milk Cook for the next 5 minutes after fully blending.

3. Mix in the cheese until it is fully melted Mix the butter and breadcrumbs well in a shallow bowl Sprinkle the broccoli on top

4. Cook for around 20 minutes at about 360°F until the tops are finely golden brown Enjoy and serve warm.

Nutrition: **Calories: 110 | Fat: 0 g | Fiber: 3 g | Carbohydrates: 6 g | Protein: 8 g**

## 139. Sweet and Spicy Parsnips
Ready in: 53 minutes | Servings: 4 | Difficulty: Hard
**Ingredients**
• ¼ tsp red pepper flakes, crushed
• 1 tbsp. dried parsley flakes, crushed
• 2 tbsps. honey
• 1 tbsp. butter, melted
• 2 lbs. a parsnip, peeled and cut into 1-inch chunks
• Salt and ground black pepper, according to your taste

**Directions**
1. Let the Air Fryer temperature to about 355°F Oil the basket of your Air Fryer Combine the butter and parsnips in a big dish.

2. Transfer the parsnip pieces into the lined Air Fryer basket arranges them in a uniform layer Cook for a few minutes in the fryer.

3. In the meantime, combine the leftover ingredients in a large mixing bowl.

4. Move the parsnips into the honey mixture bowl after around 40 minutes and toss them to coat properly.

5. Again, in a uniform layer, organize the parsnip chunks into your Air Fryer basket.

6. Air fry for another 3–4 minutes Take the parsnip pieces from the Air Fryer and pass them onto the serving dish Serve it warm.

Nutrition: **Calories: 100 | Fat: 1 g | Fiber: 3 g | Carbohydrates: 6 g | Protein: 7 g**

## 140. Zucchini with Mediterranean Dill Sauce
Ready in: 1 hour and 10 minutes | Servings: 4 | Difficulty: Hard
**Ingredients**
• ½ tsp freshly cracked black peppercorns
• 2 sprigs thyme, leaves only, crushed
• 1 sprig rosemary, leaves only, crushed
• 1 tsp sea salt flakes
• 2 tbsps. melted butter
• 1 lb. zucchini, peeled and cubed

**For the Mediterranean dipping:**
- 1 tbsp. olive oil
- 1 tbsp. fresh dill, chopped
- 1/3 c yogurt
- ½ c mascarpone cheese

**Directions**

1. To start, preheat your Air fryer to 350°F Now, add ice-cold water to the container with your zucchini cubes and let them sit in the bath for about 35 minutes.

2. Dry your potato cubes with a hand towel after that Whisk together the sea salt flakes, melted butter, thyme, rosemary, and freshly crushed peppercorns in a mixing container This butter/spice mixture can be rubbed onto the potato cubes.

3. In the cooking basket of your Air Fryer, air fry your potato cubes for around 18–20 minutes or until cooked completely; ensure you shake the potatoes at least once during cooking to cook them uniformly.

4. In the meantime, by mixing the rest of the ingredients, create the Mediterranean dipping sauce to dip and eat, serve warm potatoes with Mediterranean sauce!

Nutrition: **Calories: 120 | Fat: 2 g | Fiber: 1 g | Carbohydrates: 8 g | Protein: 2 g**

## 141. Zesty Broccoli

Ready in: 25 minutes | Servings: 4 | Difficulty: Normal

**Ingredients**
- 1 tbsp. butter
- 1 large crown broccoli, chopped into bite-sized pieces
- 1 tbsp. white sesame seeds
- 2 tbsps. vegetable stock
- ½ tsp red pepper flakes, crushed
- 3 garlic cloves, minced
- ½ tsp fresh lemon zest, grated finely
- 1 tbsp. pure lemon juice

**Directions**

1. Preheat the Air Fryer to about 355°F and oil an Air Fryer pan with cooking spray In the Air Fryer plate, combine the vegetable stock, butter, and lemon juice.

2. Move the mixture and cook for about 2 minutes into your Air Fryer Cook for a minute after incorporating the broccoli and garlic.

3. Cook for a minute with lemon zest, sesame seeds, and red pepper flakes Remove the dish from the oven and eat immediately.

Nutrition: **Calories: 120 | Fat: 2 g | Fiber: 1 g | Carbohydrates: 8 g | Protein: 2 g**

## 142. Chewy Glazed Parsnips

Ready in: 1 hour | Servings: 5 | Difficulty: Hard

**Ingredients**
- ¼ tsp red pepper flakes, crushed
- 1 tbsp. dried parsley flakes, crushed
- 2 tbsps. maple syrup
- 1 tbsp. butter, melted
- 2 lbs. parsnips, skinned and chopped into 1-inch chunks

**Directions**

1. Preheat the Air Fryer to about 355°F and oil your Air Fryer basket In a wide mixing bowl, combine the butter and parsnips and toss well to cover Cook for around 40 minutes with the parsnips in the Air Fryer basket.

2. In the meantime, combine in a wide bowl the rest of your ingredients Move this mix to your basket of the Air Fryer and cook for another 4 minutes or so Remove the dish from the oven and eat promptly.

Nutrition: **Calories: 170 | Fat: 4 g | Fiber: 8 g | Carbohydrates: 14 g | Protein: 11 g**

## 143. Hoisin-Glazed Bok Choy

Ready in: 15 minutes | Servings: 4 | Difficulty: Easy

**Ingredients**
- 1 tbsp. all-purpose flour
- 2 tbsps. sesame oil
- 2 tbsps. hoisin sauce
- ½ tsp sage
- 1 tsp onion powder
- 2 garlic cloves, minced
- 1 lb. baby bok choy, roots removed, leaves separated

**Directions**

1. In a lightly oiled Air Fryer basket, put the onion powder, garlic, bok choy, and sage Cook for around 3 minutes at about 350°F in a preheated Air Fryer.

2. Whisk together the sesame oil, hoisin sauce, and flour in a deep mixing dish Drizzle over the bok choy with the gravy Cook for an extra minute Bon appétit!

Nutrition: **Calories: 130 | Fat: 2 g | Fiber: 2 g | Carbohydrates: 6 g | Protein: 8 g**

## 144. Green Beans with Okra

Ready in: 32 minutes | Servings: 2 | Difficulty: Normal

**Ingredients**
- 3 tbsps. balsamic vinegar
- ¼ c nutritional yeast
- ½ (10 oz.) of bag chilled cut green beans
- ½ (10 oz.) of bag chilled cut okra
- Salt and black pepper, according to your taste

**Directions**

1. Preheat your Air Fryer to about 400°F and oil the Air Fryer basket.

2. In a wide mixing bowl, toss together the salt, green beans, okra, vinegar, nutritional yeast, and black pepper.

3. Cook for around 20 minutes with the okra mixture in your Air Fryer basket Dish out into a serving plate and eat warm.

Nutrition: **Calories: 120 | Fat: 1 g | Fiber: 3 g | Carbohydrates: 7 g | Protein: 8 g**

## 145. Celeriac with some Greek Yogurt Dip

Ready in: 35 minutes | Servings: 4 | Difficulty: Normal

**Ingredients**

- ½ tsp sea salt
- ½ tsp ground black pepper, to taste
- 1 tbsp. sesame oil
- 1 red onion, chopped into 1 ½-inch piece
- ½ lb. celeriac, chopped into 1 ½-inch piece

**For the spiced yogurt:**

- ½ tsp chili powder
- ½ tsp mustard seeds
- 2 tbsps. mayonnaise
- ¼ c Greek yogurt

**Directions**

1. In the slightly oiled cooking basket, put the veggies in one uniform layer Pour sesame oil over the veggies.

2. Season with a pinch of black pepper and a pinch of salt Cook for around 20 minutes at about 300°F, tossing the basket midway through your cooking cycle.

3. In the meantime, whisk all the leftover ingredients into the sauce Spoon the sauce over the veggies that have been cooked Bon appétit!

Nutrition: **Calories: 120 | Fat: 1 g | Fiber: 3 g | Carbohydrates: 7 g | Protein: 8 g**

## 146. Wine and Garlic Flavored Vegetables

Ready in: 32 minutes | Servings: 5 | Difficulty: Normal

**Ingredients**

- 4 cloves of garlic, minced
- 3 tbsps. red wine vinegar
- 1/3 c olive oil
- 1 red onion, diced
- 1 package frozen diced vegetables
- 1 c baby Portobello mushrooms, diced
- 1 tsp Dijon mustard
- 1 ½ tbsp. honey
- Salt and pepper according to your taste
- ¼ c chopped fresh basil

**Directions**

1. Preheat the Air Fryer to about 330°F Put the grill pan attachment in the Air Fryer.

2. Combine the veggies and season with pepper, salt, and garlic in a Ziplock container and shake to mix all Cook for around 15 minutes on the grill pan.

3. Additionally, add the remainder of the ingredients into a mixing bowl and season with some more salt and pepper Drizzle the sauce over your grilled vegetables.

Nutrition: **Calories: 140 | Fat: 1 g | Fiber: 10 g | Carbohydrates: 10 g | Protein: 7 g**

## 147. Spicy Braised Vegetables

Ready in: 32 minutes | Servings: 5 | Difficulty: Normal

**Ingredients**

- ½ c tomato puree
- ¼ tsp ground black pepper
- ½ tsp fine sea salt
- 1 tbsp. garlic powder
- ½ tsp fennel seeds
- ¼ tsp mustard powder
- ½ tsp porcini powder
- ¼ c olive oil
- 1 celery stalk, chopped into matchsticks
- 2 bell peppers, deveined and thinly diced
- 1 Serrano pepper, deveined and thinly diced
- 1 large-sized zucchini, diced

**Directions**

1. In your Air Fryer cooking basket, put your peppers, zucchini, bell pepper, and celery.

2. Drizzle with some olive oil and toss to cover completely; cook for around 15 minutes in a preheated Air Fryer at about 350°F.

3. Make the sauce as the vegetables are frying by quickly whisking the remaining ingredients (except the tomato ketchup) Slightly oil up a baking dish that fits your fryer.

4. Add the cooked vegetables to the baking dish, along with the sauce, and toss well to cover.

5. Turn the Air Fryer to about 390°F and cook for 2–4 more minutes with the vegetables Bon appétit!

Nutrition: **Calories: 90 | Fat: 1 g | Fiber: 3 g | Carbohydrates: 7 g | Protein: 2 g**

## 148. Tuna and Chimichurri Sauce

Ready in: 24 minutes | Servings: 5 | Difficulty: Normal

**Ingredients**

- 8 oz. baby arugula
- 3 avocados, pitted, peeled, and sliced
- 4 garlic cloves, minced
- 2 tsps. thyme, chopped
- 2 tsps. red pepper flakes
- Salt and black pepper according to your taste
- 2 lbs. sushi tuna steak
- 2 jalapeño pepper, chopped
- 3 tbsps. basil, chopped
- 3 tbsps. parsley, chopped
- 4 tbsps. balsamic vinegar
- 2 small red onion, chopped
- 2/3 C olive oil, plus 2 tbsps.
- 1 c cilantro, chopped

**Directions**

1. Mix 2/3 c vinegar, jalapeño, oil, cilantro, avocados, onion, garlic, basil, flakes of pepper, parsley, salt, thyme, and pepper in a small bowl, stir together well, and set aside for now.

2. Season the tuna with some salt and black pepper, fry with the remainder of the oil, put in the fryer, and sear on each side for about 3 minutes at around 360°F.

3. Mix the arugula with half of the chimichurri mixture that you made and cover it with a throw.

4. Split arugula on bowls, dice tuna, and divide between plates as well, top and serve with the remainder of the chimichurri and avocado Enjoy!

Nutrition: **Calories: 145 | Fat: 3 g | Fiber: 5 g | Carbohydrates: 5 g | Protein: 8 g**

## 149. Creamy Shrimp and Veggies

Ready in: 45 minutes | Servings: 4 | Difficulty: Hard

**Ingredients**

- 2 c heavy cream
- 4 garlic cloves, minced
- 2 c Parmesan cheese, grated
- ½ c butter, melted
- 2 tsps. red pepper flakes, crushed
- 2 yellow onion, chopped
- 3 tsps. Italian seasoning
- 3 tbsps. olive oil
- 2 spaghetti squash, cut into halves
- Salt and black pepper according to your taste

- 2 lbs. shrimp, peeled and deveined
- 2 asparagus bunch, cut into medium pieces
- 10 oz. mushrooms, chopped

## Directions

1. Put the squash halves in the basket of your Air Fryer, cook for about 17 minutes at around 390°F, move to a chopping board, scoop inside and move to a dish.
2. Put some water in a kettle, add some salt, bring it to a boil over medium heat, add some asparagus, steam for a few minutes, move to a bowl of cold water, drain and set aside.
3. Over medium fire, heat a pan that suits your Air Fryer with some oil, add onions and mushrooms, mix and cook for about 7 minutes.
4. Add the flakes of pepper, shrimp, salt, Italian seasoning, melted butter, squash, pepper, asparagus, Parmesan, heavy cream, and garlic, and steam for about 6 minutes in your Air Fryer around 360°F.
5. Split and serve all on dishes Enjoy!

Nutrition: Calories: 140 | Fat: 1 g | Fiber: 4 g | Carbohydrates: 6 g | Protein: 4 g

## 150. Italian Barramundi Fillets and Tomato Salsa

Ready in: 22 minutes | Servings: 5 | Difficulty: Normal

### Ingredients

- 2 barramundi fillets, boneless
- 3 tbsps. olive oil
- 4 tsps. Italian seasoning
- ½ c green olives, pitted and chopped
- ½ c cherry tomatoes, chopped
- ½ c black olives, chopped
- 2 tbsps. lemon zest
- 4 tbsps. lemon juice
- Salt and black pepper according to your taste
- 4 tbsps. parsley, chopped

### Directions

1. Stir in pepper, salt, Italian seasoning, and 2 tsps. olive oil, move to your Air Fryer, and cook for about 8 minutes at around 360°F, flipping halfway through.
2. Mix the black olives, tomatoes, salt, green olives, lemon zest, pepper, parsley, lemon juice, and 1 tbsp. olive oil in a bowl and toss thoroughly.
3. Divide the fish into bowls, stir in the tomato salsa, and eat Enjoy!

Nutrition: Calories: 140 | Fat: 1 g | Fiber: 4 g | Carbohydrates: 6 g | Protein: 4 g

## 151. Salmon and Avocado Salsa

Ready in: 1 hour and 10 minutes | Servings: 4 | Difficulty: Hard

### Ingredients

- 2 tsps. garlic powder
- 1 tsp chili powder
- 2 tsps. sweet paprika
- 2 tsps. cumin, ground
- Salt and black pepper according to your taste
- 2 tbsps. olive oil
- 6 salmon fillets

**For the salsa:**
- Salt and black pepper according to your taste
- Juice from 2 ½ limes
- 32 tbsps. cilantro, chopped
- 2 avocados, pitted, peeled, and chopped
- 2 small red onions, chopped

### Directions

1. Mix pepper, salt, garlic powder, chili powder, cumin, and paprika in a small bowl, swirl, brush the salmon with this mixture, drizzle with some oil, brush it again, move it to your Air Fryer and cook on both sides for about 5 minutes at around 350°F.
2. Meanwhile, combine the avocado with red onion, pepper, salt, cilantro, and lime juice in a bowl and mix well.
3. On bowls, split fillets, cover with avocado salsa, and eat Enjoy!

Nutrition: Calories: 2 | Protein: 0 g | Carbohydrates: 1 g | Fat: 0 g | Fiber: 0 g

## 152. Creamy Salmon

Ready in: 24 minutes | Servings: 5 | Difficulty: Normal

### Ingredients

- 1 c coconut cream
- 2 ½ tsp mustard
- 2/3 c Cheddar cheese, grated
- Salt and black pepper according to your taste
- 2 tbsps. olive oil
- 5 salmon fillets, boneless

### Directions

1. Add salt and pepper to the salmon, drizzle with the oil and rub properly.
2. Mix the mustard, Cheddar, salt, and black pepper with coconut cream in a small bowl and shake well.
3. Move the salmon to a pan that suits your Air Fryer Apply the coconut cream blend, place it in the Air Fryer, and cook for about 10 minutes at around 320°F.
4. Split and serve between dishes Enjoy!

Nutrition: Calories: 140 | Fat: 2 g | Fiber: 2 g | Carbohydrates: 4 g | Protein: 6 g

## 153. Trout and Butter Sauce

Ready in: 28 minutes | Servings: 5 | Difficulty: Normal

### Ingredients

- 4 tsps. lemon juice
- 4 tbsps. olive oil
- 8 tbsps. butter
- 6 tbsps. chives, chopped
- 6 tsps. lemon zest, grated
- Salt and black pepper according to your taste
- 6 trout fillets, boneless

### Directions

1. Add salt and pepper to the trout, drizzle with olive oil, brush, move to your Air Fryer and cook for about 10 minutes at around 360°F, tossing once.
2. Meanwhile, over medium-high flame, heat a skillet with butter, add pepper, salt, lemon juice, chives, and zest, whisk thoroughly, cook for about 1–2 minutes, and turn the heat off.
3. On bowls, split fish fillets, drizzle butter sauce all over and eat Enjoy!

Nutrition: Calories: 2 | Protein: 0 g | Carbohydrates: 1 g | Fat: 0 g | Fiber: 0 g

## 154. Thyme and Parsley Salmon

Ready in: 32 minutes | Servings: 5 | Difficulty: Normal

**Ingredients**

• Salt and black pepper according to your taste
• 4 tbsps. extra-virgin olive oil
• 5 parsley sprigs
• 5 thyme sprigs
• 5 tomatoes, sliced
• 2 yellow onion, chopped
• Juice from 2 lemon
• 8 salmon fillets, boneless

**Directions**

1. Add a layer of tomatoes, pepper, and salt drizzle 1 tbsp. oil, add fish, add some salt and black pepper, drizzle with remaining oil, add some onions, thyme, lemon juice, and parsley springs Put in the basket of your Air Fryer, and cook for around 360°F for about 12 minutes, shake once.
2. Split and serve all on plates straight away Enjoy!

Nutrition: **Calories: 140 | Fat: 2 g | Fiber: 2 g | Carbohydrates: 4 g | Protein: 6 g**

## 155. Cod Fillets and Peas

Ready in: 28 minutes | Servings: 5 | Difficulty: Normal

**Ingredients**

• Salt and pepper according to your taste
• 4 garlic cloves, minced
• 1 tsp sweet paprika
• 6 tbsps. wine
• 4 c peas
• 1 tsp oregano, dried
• 4 tbsps. parsley, chopped
• 6 cod fillets, boneless

**Directions**

1. Mix the parsley, garlic, pepper, salt, paprika, oregano, and wine in your food processor and blend properly.
2. Rub the fish with half of this paste, position it in your fryer and cook for about 10 minutes at around 360°F.
3. Meanwhile, place the peas in a kettle, cover with water, add salt, bring to a simmer over medium-high flame, simmer for about 10 minutes, drain, and split between the plates.
4. Divide fish among plates as well, sprinkle all over the remainder of the herb seasoning, and eat Enjoy!

Nutrition: **Calories: 231 | Fat: 12 g | Fiber: 6 g | Carbohydrates: 15 g | Protein: 14 g**

## 156. Trout Fillet and Orange Sauce

Ready in: 24 minutes | Servings: 5 | Difficulty: Normal

**Ingredients**

• Juice and zest from 1 orange
• Salt and black pepper according to your taste
• 2 tbsps. ginger, minced
• 2 tbsps. olive oil
• 6 spring onions, chopped
• 6 trout fillets, skinless and boneless

**Directions**

1. Add green onions, ginger, orange zest, and juice, mix well, put in your Air Fryer, and cook for about 10 minutes at around 360°F Season the trout fillets with some salt, black pepper, rub them with olive oil Put them in a pan that suits your Air Fryer.
2. Split the fish and sauce into bowls, and then eat immediately Enjoy!

Nutrition: **Calories: 200 | Fat: 12 g | Fiber: 4 g | Carbohydrates: 9 g | Protein: 7 g**

## 157. Seafood Casserole

Ready in: 1 hour and 4 minutes | Servings: 4 | Difficulty: Hard

**Ingredients**

• 2 tsps. sweet paprika
• 1 handful of parsley, chopped
• 4 tbsps. Cheddar cheese, grated
• 2/3 c breadcrumbs
• 2 tbsps. lemon juice
• 1 tsp mustard powder
• 6 oz. lobster meat, already cooked and cut into small pieces
• 6 sea scallops, sliced
• 1 c heavy cream
• 2 ½ c milk
• 1 c white wine
• 6 tbsps. flour
• 6 oz. haddock, skinless, boneless, and cut into small pieces
• Salt and black pepper according to your taste
• 2 small yellow onions, chopped
• 4 garlic cloves, minced
• 2 celery stalks, chopped
• Salt and black pepper according to your taste
• 2 small green bell pepper, chopped
• 3 oz. mushrooms, chopped
• 8 tbsps. butter

**Directions**

1. Heat a skillet over a medium-high flame with 4 tablespoons of butter, add mushrooms, bell pepper, onion, salt, pepper, garlic, celery, and white wine, mix, and simmer for about 10 minutes.
2. Add the cream, flour, and milk and mix well, and then simmer for about 6 minutes.
3. Add the salt, lemon juice, mustard powder, pepper, lobster meat, scallops, and haddock, mix well, take off the flame and move to the Air Fryer's plate.
4. Mix the leftover butter with the paprika, breadcrumbs, and cheese in a small bowl and brush with the seafood mixture.
5. Switch the pan to an Air Fryer and cook for about 16 minutes at around 360°F.
6. Split between plates and finish with the top sprinkled with parsley Enjoy!

Nutrition: **Calories: 200 | Fat: 12 g | Fiber: 4 g | Carbohydrates: 9 g | Protein: 7 g**

## 158. Shrimp and Crab Mix

Ready in: 45 minutes | Servings: 4 | Difficulty: Hard

**Ingredients**

- 1 c yellow onion, chopped
- 2 c green bell pepper, chopped
- 2 c celery, chopped
- 2 lbs. shrimp, peeled and deveined
- 2 c crab meat, flaked
- 2 c mayonnaise
- 2 tsps. Worcestershire sauce
- Salt and black pepper according to your taste
- 4 tbsps. breadcrumbs
- 2 tbsps. butter, melted
- 2 tsps. sweet paprika

**Directions**

1. Combine shrimp with bell pepper, crab meat, onion, mayonnaise, salt, pepper, celery, and Worcestershire sauce in a small bowl, mix well and move to an air-fryer-friendly plate.
2. Sprinkle with breadcrumbs and paprika, apply melted butter, put in the fryer, and steam for about 25 minutes at around 320°F, shaking halfway through.
3. Divide between plates and serve immediately Enjoy!

Nutrition: Calories: 234 | Fat: 12 g | Fiber: 5 g | Carbohydrates: 14 g | Protein: 7 g

## 159. Cod and Vinaigrette

Ready in: 35 minutes | Servings: 5 | Difficulty: Normal

**Ingredients**

- 2 bunch basil, chopped
- 4 tbsps. olive oil
- Salt and black pepper according to your taste
- 4 tbsps. lemon juice
- 10 black olives, pitted and roughly chopped
- 14 cherry tomatoes, halved
- 6 cod fillets, skinless and boneless

**Directions**

1. Season the cod with salt and pepper to taste, put it in the basket of your Air Fryer, and cook for about 10 minutes at around 360°F, flipping after every 5 minutes.
2. In the meantime, over medium-high flame, heat the pan with the oil, add the olives, tomatoes, and lemon juice, mix, bring to a boil, add the salt, basil, and pepper, mix well and remove from the flame.
3. Split the fish among plates and serve on top with the drizzled vinaigrette Enjoy!

Nutrition: Calories: 100 | Fat: 3 g | Fiber: 4 g | Carbohydrates: 8 g | Protein: 5 g

## 160. Asian Halibut

Ready in: 44 minutes | Servings: 4 | Difficulty: Hard

**Ingredients**

- 2 garlic cloves, minced
- ½ tsp ginger, grated
- ½ c orange juice
- ½ tsp red pepper flakes, crushed
- 1 c mirin
- 4 tbsps. lime juice
- ½ c sugar
- 1 c soy sauce
- 2 lbs. halibut steaks

**Directions**

1. Heat up over medium-high flame, add lime, sugar, mirin, and orange juice, ginger, pepper flakes, and garlic, mix well, bring it to a boil and turn off the flame Throw soy sauce in a small bowl.
2. Move half of the marinade to a dish, apply the halibut, coat, and leave for 30 minutes in the refrigerator.
3. Switch your halibut to your Air Fryer and cook for about 10 minutes at around 390°F, turning once.
4. Split the halibut steaks into bowls, drizzle all over the rest of the marinade, and serve warm Enjoy!

Nutrition: Calories: 149 | Fat: 4 g | Fiber: 2 g | Carbohydrates: 14 g | Protein: 5 g

## 161. Lemony Saba Fish

Ready in: 22 minutes | Servings: 2 | Difficulty: Normal

**Ingredients**

- 3 tbsps. garlic, minced
- 3 tbsps. olive oil
- 3 tbsps. lemon juice
- 4 red chili pepper, chopped
- Salt and black pepper according to your taste
- 8 Saba fish fillets, boneless

**Directions**

1. Place the fish fillets in a bowl and season them with salt and pepper.
2. To coat, apply lemon juice, oil, chili, and garlic, then toss, move the fish to the Air Fryer, and sear for about 8 minutes at around 360°F, flipping midway.
3. Split into dishes and serve with fries Enjoy!

Nutrition: Calories: 188 | Fat: 4 g | Fiber: 6 g | Carbohydrates: 8 g | Protein: 6 g

## 162. Salmon with Capers and Mash

Ready in: 40 minutes | Servings: 4 | Difficulty: Hard

**Ingredients**

- 2 tsps. olive oil
- Juice from 2 lemon
- Salt and black pepper according to your taste
- 2 tbsps. capers, drained
- 5 salmon fillets, skinless and boneless

**For the potato mash:**
- 1 c milk
- 2 lbs. potatoes, chopped
- 2 tbsps. dill, dried
- 2 tbsps. olive oil

**Directions**

1. Place the potatoes in a big pot Add some salt; bring it to a boil over medium-high flame Simmer for about 15 minutes, rinse, move to a big bowl, mash with a hand blender Add 2 tablespoons of oil, salt, dill, pepper, and milk Mix well, and set aside for now.
2. Season the salmon with some salt and black pepper, drizzle over 2 tablespoons of oil, brush Move to the basket of your Air Fryer, cover with capers, and cook at around 360°F for about 8 minutes.
3. Split the salmon and capers on the dishes, transfer the mashed potatoes on the side, drizzle all over with the lemon juice and eat
4. Enjoy!

Nutrition: Calories: 199 | Fat: 3 g | Fiber: 4 g | Carbohydrates: 12 g | Protein: 5 g

## 163. Flavored Air-Fried Salmon

Ready in: 1 hour and 20 minutes | Servings: 4 | Difficulty: Hard

### Ingredients

• 2 tbsps. olive oil
• 2/3 c brown sugar
• 4 scallions, chopped
• 2/3 c soy sauce
• 1 tsp garlic powder
• Salt and black pepper according to your taste
• 4 tbsps. lemon juice
• 4 salmon fillets

### Directions

1. Mix the sugar, garlic powder, soy sauce, pepper, oil, salt, and lemon juice in a pot, stir well, apply the salmon fillets, coat, and keep in the refrigerator for about 1 hour or so.
2. Move the salmon fillets to the basket and cook for about 8 minutes at around 360°F, turning them midway.
3. Split the salmon among the bowls, scatter on top with the scallions and serve immediately Enjoy!

Nutrition: Calories: 330 | Fat: 7 g | Sodium: 360 mg | Carbohydrates: 57 g | Fiber: 8 g | Protein: 14 g

## 164. Cod Steaks with Plum Sauce

Ready in: 40 minutes | Servings: 4 | Difficulty: Hard

### Ingredients

• Cooking spray
• 2 tbsps. plum sauce
• ½ tsp turmeric powder
• 1 tsp ginger powder
• 1 tsp garlic powder
• Salt and black pepper according to your taste
• 3 big cod steaks

### Directions

1. Add some salt and black pepper to the cod steaks, brush them with cooking oil, add turmeric powder, ginger powder, garlic powder, and rub thoroughly
2. In your Air Fryer, put the cod steaks and cook for about 15 minutes at around 360°F, tossing them after 7 minutes
3. Over medium heat, heat a skillet, add plum sauce, stir and simmer for 2 minutes
4. Split the cod steaks between bowls, drizzle all over with the plum sauce, and eat Enjoy!

Nutrition: Calories: 174 | Fat: 10 g | Sodium: 36 mg | Carbohydrates: 20 g | Protein: 4 g

## 165. Asian Salmon

Ready in: 1 hour and 40 minutes | Servings: 3 | Difficulty: Hard

### Ingredients

• 8 tbsps. honey
• 2 tsps. water
• 6 tsps. mirin
• 12 tbsps. light soy sauce
• 4 medium salmon fillets

### Directions

1. Mix some soy sauce with water, honey, and mirin in a small bowl, brush well Apply salmon, rub well, and allow resting for at least 1 hour in the fridge.
2. Move the salmon to your Air Fryer and cook for about 15 minutes at around 360°F, turning after about 7 minutes.
3. In the meantime, in a skillet, position the soy marinade, warm up over medium flame, stir well, cook for about 2 minutes, and turn off the flame.
4. Split the salmon between bowls, drizzle all over with the marinade, and eat Enjoy!

Nutrition: Calories: 122 | Fat: 5 g | Sodium: 157 mg | Carbohydrates: 30 g | Fiber: 78 g | Protein: 34 g

## 166. Buttered Shrimp Skewers

Ready in: 18 minutes | Servings: 6 | Difficulty: Easy

### Ingredients

• 2 tbsps. butter, melted
• 2 tbsps. rosemary, chopped
• 10 green bell pepper slices
• Salt and black pepper according to your taste
• 6 garlic cloves, minced
• 10 shrimps, peeled and deveined

### Directions

1. Mix the shrimp in a bowl with the slices of butter, garlic, pepper, rosemary, salt, and bell pepper, toss to cover, and let stand for about 10 minutes.
2. On a skewer, place 2 bell pepper slices and 2 shrimp and repeat for the remaining bits of seafood and bell pepper.
3. Put them all in the basket of your Air Fryer and cook for about 6 minutes at around 360°F.
4. Split between plates and serve immediately Enjoy!

Nutrition: Calories: 287 | Protein: 124 g | Carbohydrates: 504 g

## 167. Tabasco Shrimp

Ready in: 32 minutes | Servings: 5 | Difficulty: Normal

### Ingredients

• 1 tsp smoked paprika
• 1 tsp parsley, dried
• Salt and black pepper according to your taste
• 2 tsps. oregano, dried
• 2 tsps. Tabasco sauce
• 2 tbsps. olive oil
• 2 tsps. red pepper flakes
• 2 lbs. shrimp, peeled and deveined

### Directions

1. Mix the oil, pepper flakes, Tabasco sauce, parsley, oregano, salt, paprika, pepper, and shrimp in a bowl and toss to cover properly.
2. Move the shrimp to your preheated Air Fryer at around 370°F and cook for about 10 minutes, rotating the fryer.
3. Split the shrimp into dishes and eat with a side salad Enjoy!

Nutrition: Calories: 355 | Protein: 124 g | Carbohydrates: 504 g

## 168. Cod Fillets with Fennel and Grapes Salad

Ready in: 32 minutes | Servings: 4 | Difficulty: Normal

**Ingredients**

- 1 c pecans
- 2 c grapes, halved
- 2 fennel bulbs, thinly sliced
- Salt and black pepper according to your taste
- 2 tbsps. olive oil
- 4 black cod fillets, boneless

**Directions**

1. Sprinkle half of the oil over the fish fillets, season with salt and pepper, fry well, put the fillets in the basket of your Air Fryer, and cook at about 400°F for around 10 minutes and move to a tray.

2. Mix the pecans with the fennel, grapes, the rest of the oil, salt, and black pepper in a small bowl, toss to cover, transfer to the pan that fits your Air Fryer, and cook for about 5 minutes at around 400°F.

3. Split the cod between the bowls, apply the side blend of fennel and grapes, and eat Enjoy!

Nutrition: **Calories: 287 | Protein: 124 g |Carbohydrates: 504 g | Fat: 42 g | Fiber: 9 g | Cholesterol: 0 mg**

## 169. Delicious Catfish

Ready in: 40 minutes | Servings: 5 | Difficulty: Hard

**Ingredients**

- 2 tbsps. olive oil
- 2 tbsps. lemon juice
- 2 tbsps. parsley, chopped
- 1 pinch of sweet paprika
- Salt and black pepper according to your taste
- 5 catfish fillets

**Directions**

1. Season using pepper, salt, paprika, drizzle oil on the catfish fillets, brush well, put in the basket of your Air Fryer, and cook at around 400°F for about 20 minutes, turning the fish after every 10 minutes.

2. Split the fish into bowls, drizzle with the lemon juice, scatter with the parsley, and serve Enjoy!

Nutrition: **Calories: 287 | Protein: 124 g | Carbohydrates: 504 g | Fat: 42 g | Fiber: 9 g | Cholesterol: 0 mg**

## 170. Tasty Air-Fried Cod

Ready in: 40 minutes | Servings: 4 | Difficulty: Hard

**Ingredients**

- 4 tbsps. cilantro, chopped
- 6 spring onions, chopped
- 8 ginger slices
- 6 tbsps. olive oil
- 2 tbsps. sugar
- 8 tbsps. light soy sauce
- 2 tsps. dark soy sauce
- 2 c water
- Salt and black pepper according to your taste
- 1 drizzle of sesame oil
- 3 (7 oz. each) codfish

**Directions**

1. Season the fish with salt, pepper, sesame oil, and drizzle, rub properly, and let stand for 10 minutes.

2. Transfer the fish to your Air Fryer and steam for about 12 minutes at around 356°F.

3. In the meantime, over medium flame, heat a pot with the water, add light and dark soy sauce and sugar, mix, bring to boil, and take off the flame.

4. Over medium pressure, heat the pan with the olive oil, add the ginger and green onions Mix; simmer for a few minutes, and heat off.

5. Split the fish into bowls, cover with the ginger and green onions, drizzle with the combination of soy sauce, sprinkle with the cilantro Serve immediately Enjoy!

Nutrition: **Calories: 99 | Protein: 29 g | Carbohydrates: 113 g | Fat: 5 g | Fiber: 18 g**

## 171. Mini Cheesecake

Ready in: 25 minutes | Servings: 2 | Difficulty: Normal

**Ingredients**

- ⅛ c powdered Erythritol
- ½ tsp vanilla extract
- 1 large egg
- 4 oz. full-fat cream cheese, softened
- 2 tbsps. granular Erythritol
- 2 tbsps. salted butter
- ½ c walnuts

**Directions**

1. In a food mixer, put the butter, walnuts, and granular Erythritol Pulse until the items bind together to shape the dough.

2. Push the dough into a 4-inch spring-form pan and put the pan in the bucket of your Air Fryer.

3. Set the temperature and adjust the clock to about 400°F for around 5 minutes

4. Pick the crust when the timer dings, and let it cool

5. Mix your cream cheese with the vanilla extract, egg, and powdered Erythritol in a medium-sized bowl until creamy

Nutrition: **Calories: 94 | Protein: 54 g | Carbohydrates: 142 g | Fat: 36 g**

## 172. Pecan Brownies

Ready in: 32 minutes | Servings: 6 | Difficulty: Normal

**Ingredients**

- ¼ c low-carb, sugar-free chocolate chips
- ¼ c chopped pecans
- 1 large egg
- ¼ c unsalted butter, softened
- ½ tsp baking powder
- 2 tbsps. unsweetened cocoa powder
- ½ c powdered Erythritol
- ½ c blanched finely ground almond flour

**Directions**

1. Mix the almond flour, cocoa powder, Erythritol, and baking powder in a big bowl Stir in the egg and butter.

2. Fold in the chocolate chips and pecans Pour the mixture into a 6-inch circular baking tray Place the pan in the bucket of your Air Fryer.

3. Set the temperature and adjust the clock to about 300°F for around 20 minutes.

4. A toothpick placed in the middle will come out clean once completely fried Let it cool off entirely for about 20 minutes

Nutrition: **Calories: 59 | Protein: 11 g | Carbohydrates: 109 g | Fat: 17 g**

## 173. Cinnamon Sugar Pork Rinds

Ready in: 10 minutes | Servings: 2 | Difficulty: Easy

### Ingredients
- ¼ c powdered Erythritol
- ½ tsp ground cinnamon
- 2 tbsps. unsalted butter, melted
- 2 oz. pork rinds

### Directions
1. Toss the pork rinds and butter into a wide pan Sprinkle some Erythritol and cinnamon, and toss to cover uniformly.
2. Put the pork rinds into the bucket of your Air Fryer.
3. Set the temperature and adjust the clock to about 400°F for around 5 minutes.
4. Instantly serve.

Nutrition: Calories: 59 | Protein: 11 g | Carbohydrates: 109 g | Fat: 17 g

## 174. Almond Butter Cookie Balls

Ready in: 15 minutes | Servings: 10 | Difficulty: Easy

### Ingredients
- ½ tsp ground cinnamon
- ¼ c low-carb, sugar-free chocolate chips
- ¼ c shredded unsweetened coconut
- ¼ c powdered Erythritol
- ¼ c low-carb protein powder
- 1 tsp vanilla extract
- 1 large egg
- 1 c almond butter

### Directions
1. Mix the almond butter with the egg in a big pot Add protein powder, vanilla, and Erythritol to it.
2. Fold in the coconut, chocolate chips, and cinnamon Roll into 1-inch spheres Put the balls in a 6-inch circular baking tray and place them in the bucket of your Air Fryer.
3. Set the temperature and adjust the clock to about 10 minutes to around 320°F.
4. Please enable it to cool fully Up to 4 days in an airtight jar placed in the fridge.

Nutrition: Calories: 105 | Protein: 32 g | Carbohydrates: 88 g | Fat: 75 g | Fiber: 8 g

## 175. Almond-Apple Treat

Ready in: 15 minutes | Servings: 6 | Difficulty: Easy

### Ingredients
- 2 tbsps. sugar
- ¾ oz. raisins
- 1 ½ oz. almonds

### Directions
1. Preheat your Air Fryer to around 360°F.
2. Mix the almonds, sugar, and raisins in a dish Blend using a hand mixer.
3. Load the apples with a combination of the almond mixture Please put them in the Air Fryer basket and cook for a few minutes Enjoy!

Nutrition: Calories: 108 | Protein: 5 g | Carbohydrates: 89 g | Fat: 73 g | Fiber: 48 g

## 176. Pepper-Pineapple with Butter-Sugar Glaze

Ready in: 15 minutes | Servings: 6 | Difficulty: Easy

### Ingredients
- Salt according to taste
- 2 tsps. melted butter
- 1 tsp brown sugar
- 1 red bell pepper, seeded and julienned
- 1 medium-sized pineapple, peeled and sliced

### Directions
1. Preheat your Air Fryer to about 390°F Put the grill pan attachment in your Air Fryer.
2. Combine all ingredients and shake well in a Ziplock bag.
3. Put and cook on the grill pan for around 10 minutes to ensure you turn the pineapples over every 5 minutes during cooking.

Nutrition: Calories: 108 | Protein: 5 g | Carbohydrates: 89 g | Fat: 73 g | Fiber: 48 g

## 177. True Churros with Yummy Hot Chocolate

Ready in: 35 minutes | Servings: 6 | Difficulty: Normal

### Ingredients
- 1 tsp ground cinnamon
- 1/3 c sugar
- 1 tbsp. cornstarch
- 1 c milk
- 2 oz. dark chocolate
- 1 c all-purpose flour
- 1 tbsp. canola oil
- 1 tsp lemon zest
- ¼ tsp sea salt
- 2 tbsps. granulated sugar
- ½ c water

### Directions
1. To create the churro dough, boil the water in a pan over a medium-high flame; then, add the salt, granulated sugar, and lemon zest and fry, stirring continuously, until fully dissolved.
2. Take the pan off the heat and add in some canola oil Stir the flour in steadily, constantly stirring until the solution turns to a ball.
3. With a broad star tip, pipe the paste into a piping bag In the oiled Air Fryer basket, squeeze 4-inch slices of dough Cook for around 6 minutes at a temperature of 300°F.
4. Make the hot cocoa for dipping in the meantime In a shallow saucepan, melt some chocolate and ½ c milk over low flame.
5. In the leftover ½ c milk, mix the cornstarch and blend it into the hot chocolate mixture Cook for around 5 minutes on low flame
6. Mix the sugar and cinnamon; roll your churros in this combination Serve with a side of hot cocoa Enjoy!

Nutrition: Calories: 105 | Protein: 19 g | Carbohydrates: 10 g | Fat: 73 g | Fiber: 35 g

# CHAPTER 4

## DINNER RECIPES

## 178. Chinese Duck

Ready in: 40 minutes | Servings: 6 | Difficulty: Hard

**Ingredients**

- 1 tsp Chinese 5-spice powder
- 1 tsp Szechuan peppercorns
- 3 tbsps. Shaoxing rice wine
- 2 lbs. duck breast, boneless
- 2 green onions, chopped
- 1 tbsp. light soy sauce
- ½ tsp ground black pepper
- 1 tsp coarse salt

**For the glaze:**

- 3 tbsps. orange juice
- 1 tbsp. soy sauce
- ¼ c molasses

**Directions**

1. Put the duck breasts, green onions, light soy sauce, 5-spice Chinese powder, Szechuan peppercorns, and Shaoxing rice wine in a ceramic cup Enable it to marinate in your fridge for 1 hour.

2. For 5 minutes, preheat your Air Fryer to 400°F.

3. Just remove the marinade and season with salt and pepper on the duck breasts The duck breasts should be cooked for 12–15 minutes or until golden brown.

4. Meanwhile, apply to the saucepan the reserved marinade, heated up over moderate flame Remove molasses, orange juice, and add 1 tbsp. soy sauce.

5. Get it to a boil, and whisk it continuously until it becomes syrupy Scrub the surface with a glaze on the duck breasts, so they are covered.

6. Put the duck breasts back in the basket of the Air Fryer; cook an appropriate 5 minutes Enjoy!

Nutrition: **Calories: 105 | Protein: 19 g | Carbohydrates: 10 g | Fat: 73 g | Fiber: 35 g**

## 179. Special Maple-Glazed Chicken

Ready in: 35 minutes | Servings: 5 | Difficulty: Normal

**Ingredients**

- 1 tsp fresh lemon juice
- Seasoned salt and freshly ground pepper to taste
- 2 boneless, skinless chicken breasts
- 1 tsp minced fresh ginger
- 1 tsp garlic puree
- 2 ½ tbsp. maple syrup
- 1 tbsp. tamari soy sauce
- 1 tbsp. oyster sauce

**Directions**

1. Combine the maple syrup, tamari sauce, lemon juice, oyster sauce, fresh ginger, and garlic puree in a dish It's your marinade here.

2. Drizzle salt and pepper over the chicken breasts.

3. With the marinade, cover the chicken breasts Put some foil over the bowl and, if necessary, chill in the fridge for hours or overnight.

4. Remove the chicken from the marinade Place them in the Air Fryer, then fry at 365°F for 15 minutes, rotating each once or twice.

5. Meanwhile, over a moderate flame, apply the leftover marinade to a pan Enable the marinade to boil for 3 minutes until the mixture has reduced to a half.

6. Pour the fried chicken over, and then eat.

Nutrition: **Calories: 259 | Protein: 54 g | Carbohydrates: 143 g | Fat: 223 g | Fiber: 64 g**

## 180. Chicken Cheese Wings

Ready in: 35 minutes | Servings: 2 | Difficulty: Normal

**Ingredients**

- 2 tbsps. Parmesan cheese, grated
- ⅛ tsp paprika
- ½ tsp oregano
- ¼ tsp salt
- ½ tsp rosemary
- 1 lb. chicken wings
- 1 garlic clove, minced
- 2 tbsps. butter

**Directions**

1. Preheat the fryer to 390°F

2. In the Air Fryer basket, put the chicken wings and continue cooking When you roast, rotate the basket 2–3 times.

3. In the meantime, warm the butter in a skillet over medium heat for a sauce Stir in the garlic and sauté for a few seconds.

4. Put the herbs and spices together and apply them to the pan.

5. Simply throw the chicken wings with the pan sauce and the cheese topping.

6. Enjoy and serve.

Nutrition: **Calories: 31 | Protein: 14 g | Carbohydrates: 53 g | Fat: 11 g**

## 181. Turkey and Coconut Broccoli

Ready in: 30 minutes | Servings: 4 | Difficulty: Normal

**Ingredients**

- 2 broccoli heads, florets separated and then halved
- 1 pinch of salt and black pepper
- 1 tsp chili paste
- 2 garlic cloves, minced
- 1 tsp ginger, grated
- 1 lb. turkey meat, ground
- 2 tsps. coconut aminos
- 3 tbsps. olive oil

**Directions**

1. Burn up a pan with the oil over the moderate flame that suits the Air Fryer, add the meat, and brown for 5 minutes.

2. Apply the remainder products, turn, place the bowl in the fryer and cook for 20 minutes at 380°F.

3. Split and serve everything between plates.

Nutrition: **Calories: 63 | Protein: 24 g | Carbohydrates: 69 g | Fat: 39 g**

## 182. Mixed Vegetable Breakfast Frittata

Ready in: 55 minutes | Servings: 6 | Difficulty: Hard

**Ingredients**

- ½ c milk or cream
- ½ tsp black pepper
- 6 eggs
- ½ lb. breakfast sausage
- 1 c Cheddar cheese shredded
- 1 tsp kosher salt

- 8 oz. frozen mixed vegetables (bell peppers, broccoli, etc.), thawed

**Directions**

1. Lightly oil the Air Fryer casserole dish with cooking oil Cook the breakfast sausage for 4 minutes at 360°F and crunch it Crumble some more sausage midway into the cooking process till it feels like ground beef If the cooking is finished, discard the extra fat.

2. Mix in thawed mixed vegetables and simmer, turning halfway through cooking time, for 10 minutes or until cooked through.

3. In the meantime, whisk the eggs, milk, salt, and pepper well in a mug.

4. Take the basket out, spread the vegetable mixture uniformly, and add in the egg mixture—Pan with foil cover.

5. Cook for another 2 minutes, cut the foil, and cook for another 5–10 minutes until the eggs' optimal doneness is reached.

6. Enjoy and serve with cheese.

**Nutrition: Calories: 149 | Protein: 62 g | Carbohydrates: 321 g | Fat: 21 g**

## 183. Parmesan and Dill Chicken

Ready in: 30 minutes | Servings: 6 | Difficulty: Normal

**Ingredients**

- 3 eggs, beaten
- 1 tsp chili flakes
- 1 tsp ground paprika
- 2 tbsps. avocado oil
- 1 tsp cayenne pepper
- 1 chili pepper, minced
- ½ tsp dried dill
- 1 tsp Erythritol
- ¼ tsp onion powder
- 18 oz. chicken breast, skinless, boneless
- 5 oz. pork rinds
- 3 oz. Parmesan, grated

**Directions**

1. Comb the chili flakes, ground paprika, and Erythritol in a small dish Onion powder and pepper of cayenne Apply the dried dill and gently stir the mixture After which, in the spice mixture, massage the chicken breast.

2. Then brush with minced chili pepper on the chicken Dip the pounded eggs with the chicken breast Cover it in the Parmesan cheese after this and drop in the eggs again.

3. Then coat the pork rinds with the chicken and spray them with avocado oil Preheat the fryer to 380°F for air In an Air Fryer, place the chicken breast and cook for a few minutes.

4. Then turn another side of the chicken breast and roast it for another 4 minutes.

**Nutrition: Calories: 149 | Protein: 62 g | Carbohydrates: 321 g | Fat: 21 g**

## 184. Broccoli-Rice and Cheese Casserole

Ready in: 30-40 minutes | Servings: 4 | Difficulty: Hard

**Ingredients**

- ½ lb. processed cheese food
- 2 tbsps. butter
- 1 c uncooked instant rice
- 1 c water
- 8 oz. frozen chopped broccoli
- 1 (10 oz.) can chunk chicken, drained
- ½ (1075 oz.) can condense cream of tomato soup
- ½ (1075 oz.) can condense cream of mushroom sauce
- ½ c milk
- ½ small white onion, chopped

**Directions**

1. Lightly oil the Air Fryer casserole dish with cooking spray Add water and get it to a 390°F boil Add rice to the mixture and simmer for 3 minutes.

2. Add the refined cheese, onion, broccoli, milk, butter, mushroom sauce, tomato soup, and chicken Mix thoroughly.

3. Cook for 15 minutes, mix with the fluff and cook for another 10 minutes before the tops are browned.

4. Enjoy and serve.

**Nutrition: Calories: 115 | Protein: 15 g | Carbohydrates: 122 g | Fat: 72 g**

## 185. Chicken Pot Pie with Coconut Milk

Ready in: 40 minutes | Servings: 8 | Difficulty: Hard

**Ingredients**

- 1 c chicken broth
- 1/3 c coconut flour
- 1 lb. ground chicken
- 2 cloves of garlic, minced
- 4 ½ tbsps. butter, melted
- 4 eggs
- Salt and pepper to taste
- 2 tbsps. butter
- ¼ small onion, chopped
- ½ c broccoli, chopped
- ¾ c coconut milk

**Directions**

1. Preheat the Air Fryer for 5 minutes.

2. In a casserole tray that suits your Air Fryer, put 2 tablespoons of butter, broccoli, onion, garlic, coconut milk, chicken broth, and ground chicken Season with salt and pepper to taste.

3. Combine the remaining butter, coconut flour, and eggs in a mixing dish.

4. Using the coconut flour dough to spread the surface of the chicken and broccoli mixture uniformly.

5. Put the bowl in the Air Fryer.

6. Cook at 350°F for 30 minutes.

**Nutrition: Calories: 115 | Protein: 15 g | Carbohydrates: 122 g | Fat: 72 g**

## 186. Sweet Curried Chicken Cutlets

Ready in: 50 minutes | Servings: 3 | Difficulty: Hard

**Ingredients**

- 1 tbsp. sugar
- 1 tbsp. soy sauce
- 1 tbsp. mayonnaise
- 2 eggs
- 1 tbsp. chili pepper
- 1 tbsp. curry powder
- Chicken

**Directions**

1. Place the chicken cutlets on a clean, flat surface and slice them diagonally using a knife Add soy sauce, sugar, curry powder, and chili pepper and put them in a cup.

2. Shake well and chill in the fridge for 1 hour; preheat to 350°F for the Air Fryer Drop the chicken and break in the eggs.

3. Mix and add the mayonnaise To extract as much liquid as possible, eliminate each chicken piece and turn well Put them in the bucket of a fryer and cook for 10 minutes.

4. Switch and finish cooking for 6 minutes Remove and finish cooking with the leftover chicken on a serving platter Just serve.

Nutrition: **Calories: 103 | Protein: 39 g | Carbohydrates: 193 g | Fat: 25 g**

## 187. Malaysian Chicken Satay with Peanut Sauce

Ready in: 2 hours 25 minutes | Servings: 4 | Difficulty: Normal

### Ingredients

- 1 tbsp. yellow curry powder
- 1 tsp fish sauce
- 1 tsp white sugar
- 1 lb. skinless, boneless chicken breasts, cut into strips
- ½ c unsweetened coconut milk

**For the peanut sauce:**

- ½ c chicken broth
- 2 tsps. yellow curry powder
- ¾ c unsweetened coconut milk
- ¼ c creamy peanut butter
- 1 tbsp. fish sauce
- 1 tbsp. lime juice
- 1 tbsp. white sugar

### Directions

1. Combine the garlic, 1 tsp fish sauce, 1 tsp sugar, and 2 tablespoons of powdered curry, and ½ c coconut milk in the re-sealable container To cover, add chicken and toss well Flush the bag with waste air and seal For 2 hours, caramelize.
2. Hook the chicken into the skewer and set it on the skewer shelf.
3. Cook for 10 minutes Turn skewers over midway across the cooking process.
4. In the meantime, render the peanut sauce in a medium saucepan by taking the remaining coconut milk to a simmer Mix in the curry powder and cook for a few minutes or more Add 1 tbsp. fish sauce, lime juice, 1 tbsp. sugar, chicken broth, and peanut butter Comb well and cook once thoroughly heated Move it to a tiny bowl.
5. Serve and enjoy with the peanut sauce.

Nutrition: **Calories: 128 | Protein: 37 g | Carbohydrates: 164 g | Fat: 69 g**

## 188. Chicken Burgers

Ready in: 30 minutes | Servings: 4 | Difficulty: Normal

### Ingredients

- Sea salt and ground black pepper, to taste
- ½ tsp paprika
- ½ tsp ground cumin
- 1 lb. chicken breast, ground
- 2 tsps. Dijon mustard
- 4 tbsps. green onions, chopped
- 4 pickles, sliced
- 4 soft rolls
- 4 tbsps. ketchup
- 4 tbsps. mayonnaise
- 1 tbsp. olive oil
- 1 onion, peeled and finely chopped
- 2 garlic cloves, minced

### Directions

1. Heat olive oil over a high flame in a cooker Next, sauté the onion for about 4 minutes until it becomes golden and translucent.
2. Add garlic and cook for 30 more seconds, or until the garlic is aromatic Add salt, pepper, paprika, and cumin to season; reserve.

3. Add the chicken and roast, mixing and cracking with a fork, for 2 minutes To blend properly, introduce the onion mixture and mix.
4. Form the mixture and pass it to the cooking basket into patties Heat at 360°F For 5 minutes, in the hot oven Air Fryer Switch them over and cook for an extra 5 minutes.
5. Using ketchup, mayo, and mustard to smear the base of the roll Place the chicken, green onions, and pickles on top Enjoy!

Nutrition: **Calories: 128 | Protein: 37 g | Carbohydrates: 164 g | Fat: 69 g**

## 189. Turkey Meatballs with Manchego Cheese

Ready in: 30 minutes | Servings: 4 | Difficulty: Normal

### Ingredients

- 1 tsp dried basil
- 1 tsp dried rosemary
- ¼ c Manchego cheese, grated
- 2 tbsps. yellow onions, finely chopped
- 1 tsp fresh garlic, finely chopped
- Sea salt and ground black pepper, to taste
- 1 lb. ground turkey
- ½ lb. ground pork
- 1 egg, well beaten

### Directions

1. Combine all the ingredients in a mixing bowl and mix properly
2. Form into 1-inch balls with the combination.
3. Heat the meatballs for 10 minutes in the hot Air Fryer oven Shake over the cooking time halfway Do this in batches.
4. Serve with your favorite pasta Bon appétit!

Nutrition: **Calories: 260 | Protein: 54 g | Carbohydrates: 393 g | Fat: 98 g**

## 190. Asian Chicken Fillets with Cheese

Ready in: 59 minutes | Servings: 4 | Difficulty: Hard

### Ingredients

- 1 tsp garlic, minced
- 1 (2-inch) piece ginger, peeled and minced
- 1 tsp black mustard seeds
- 1/3 c tortilla chips, crushed
- 4 rashers smoked bacon
- 1 tsp mild curry powder
- ½ c coconut milk
- 2 chicken fillets
- ½ tsp coarse sea salt
- ¼ tsp black pepper, preferably freshly ground
- ½ c Pecorino Romano cheese, freshly grated

### Directions

1. Begin by heating up to 400°F on your Air Fryer Cook the smoked bacon for 5–7 minutes in the hot oven Air Fryer.
2. Place your chicken fillets, salt, black pepper, garlic, ginger, mustard seeds, curry powder, and milk in a mixing dish Let everything marinate for about 30 minutes in your refrigerator.
3. Mix the smashed chips and grated Pecorino Romano cheese in another dish.

4. Drag the chicken fillets through the mixture of chips and move them to the cooking basket Lower the temperature to 380°F and cook for 6 minutes with the chicken.

5. Switch them over and simmer for 6 minutes longer Until you have run out of supplies, repeat the procedure.

6. With reserved bacon, serve Enjoy!

Nutrition: Calories: 124 | Protein: 103 g | Carbohydrates: 6 g | Fat: 66 g

## 191. Zaatar Chicken

Ready in: 45 minutes | Servings: 4 | Difficulty: Hard

**Ingredients**

- ¼ c olive oil
- ¼ tsp pepper
- 1 tsp salt
- 4 chicken thighs
- 2 ½ tbsp. avatar
- 2 sprigs thyme
- 1 onion, cut into chunks
- ½ tsp cinnamon
- 2 garlic cloves, smashed
- 1 lemon juice
- 1 lemon zest

**Directions**

1. In a big Ziplock container, add the oil, lemon juice, lemon zest, cinnamon, garlic, pepper, 2 tbsps. za'atar, and salt and shake well.

2. Fill the bag with chicken, thyme, and onion and shake well to coat Place them overnight in the refrigerator.

3. Preheat the vortex Air Fryer.

4. In an Air Fryer basket, add the sautéed chicken and cook for 15 minutes at 380°F.

5. Switch the chicken over and sprinkle with the remaining za'atar spice and cook for 8 more minutes at 380°F.

Nutrition: Calories: 124 | Protein: 58 g | Carbohydrates: 99 g | Fat: 73 g

## 192. Pesto Chicken

Ready in: 32 minutes | Servings: 2 | Difficulty: Normal

**Ingredients**

- 1 tbsp. ginger, sliced
- ½ c cilantro
- 1 tsp salt
- 4 chicken drumsticks
- 6 garlic cloves
- ½ jalapeño pepper
- 2 tbsps. lemon juice
- 2 tbsps. olive oil

**Directions**

1. Mix all the ingredients except chicken and combine them in the mixer.

2. Put in the mixed mixture in a large bowl.

3. Add the chicken and mix well Place it in the fridge for 2 hours

4. Spray the Air Fryer basket with cooking oil.

5. Place the sautéed chicken in the basket of the Air Fryer and cook at 390°F for 20 minutes Switch around halfway through.

6. Enjoy and serve.

Nutrition: Calories: 48 | Protein: 22 g | Carbohydrates: 45 g | Fat: 28 g | Fiber: 16 g

## 193. Garlic Chicken

Ready in: 55 minutes | Servings: 4 | Difficulty: Hard

**Ingredients**

- 2 tbsps. parsley, chopped
- 2 tbsps. olive oil
- Pepper
- 2 lbs. chicken drumsticks
- 1 fresh lemon juice
- 9 garlic cloves, sliced
- 4 tbsps. butter, melted
- Salt

**Directions**

1. Preheat the 400°F Air Fryer.

2. In a broad mixing cup, add all the ingredients and toss properly.

3. Shift the chicken wings to the basket of the Air Fryer and cook for several minutes Toss through midway.

4. Enjoy and serve.

Nutrition: Calories: 63 | Protein: 5 g | Carbohydrates: 128 g | Fat: 04 g | Fiber: 57 g

## 194. Old-Fashioned Chicken Drumettes

Ready in: 42 minutes | Servings: 3 | Difficulty: Hard

**Ingredients**

- 1 tsp garlic paste
- 1 tsp rosemary
- 6 chicken drumettes
- 1 whole egg + 1 egg white
- 1 heaping tbsp. fresh chives, chopped
- 1/3 c all-purpose flour
- ½ tsp ground white pepper
- 1 tsp seasoning salt

**Directions**

1. Begin by heating up to 390°F on your Air Fryer.

2. Comb the white pepper, salt, garlic paste, and rosemary with the flour Tiny-sized bowl.

3. Beat the eggs in another container until foamy.

4. Soak the chicken into the combination of flour, then into the beaten eggs; cover with the mixture of flour one more time.

5. Cook for 22 minutes with the chicken drumettes Offer warm, coated with chives.

Nutrition: Calories: 80 | Protein: 39 g | Carbohydrates: 105 g | Fat: 39 g | Fiber: 43 g

## 195. Spicy Chicken Legs

Ready in: 35 minutes | Servings: 3 | Difficulty: Normal

**Ingredients**

- 1 tsp garlic powder
- 1 tsp onion powder
- Salt and ground black pepper, as required
- 1 tsp ground cumin
- 1 tsp paprika
- 1 tbsp. olive oil
- 3 (8 oz.) chicken legs
- 1 c buttermilk
- 2 c white flour

**Directions**

1. Preheat the 360°F Air Fryer and oil the basket with an Air Fryer.

2. In a bowl, mix the chicken legs and buttermilk and chill in the fridge for about a few hours.

3. In a separate dish, combine the flour and spices and soak the chicken legs into this mixture.

4. Then, dunk the chicken in the buttermilk and cover the flour mixture with it again.

5. Organize the chicken legs and sleet with the oil in the Air Fryer basket.

6. Heat for about 25 minutes and serve on a serving platter.

Nutrition: Calories: 169 | Protein: 4 g | Carbohydrates: 359 g | Fat: 15 g | Fiber: 54 g

## 196. Mediterranean Chicken Breasts with Roasted Tomatoes

Ready in: 1 hour and 10 minutes | Servings: 4 | Difficulty: Hard

### Ingredients

- 1 tsp cayenne pepper
- 2 tbsps. fresh parsley, minced
- 1 tsp fresh basil, minced
- 4 medium-sized Roma tomatoes, halved
- 1 tsp fresh rosemary, minced
- 2 tsps. olive oil, melted
- 3 lbs. chicken breasts, bone-in
- ½ tsp black pepper, freshly ground
- ½ tsp salt

### Directions

1. Begin by heating up to 370°F with your Air Fryer Rub 1 tsp olive oil over the baking basket.

2. Spray all the ingredients mentioned above with the chicken breasts.

3. Cook for 25 minutes just until chicken breasts are finely browned.

4. Place the tomatoes and clean them with the leftover tsp olive oil in the baking basket Sprinkle with salt from the sea.

5. Cook the tomatoes for 10 minutes at 3°F, shaking halfway through the process Add to the chicken breasts Bon appétit!

Nutrition: Calories: 158 | Protein: 64 g | Carbohydrates: 252 g | Fat: 38 g | Fiber: 47 g

## 197. Chicken Enchiladas II

Ready in: 1 hour and 15 minutes | Servings: 6 | Difficulty: Hard

### Ingredients

- 12 flour tortillas
- 2 cans of enchilada sauce
- 2 c cheese, grated
- ½ c salsa
- 1 can green chilies, chopped
- Chicken, minced

### Directions

1. Preheat the fryer to 400°F.

2. Mix the salsa and enchilada sauce in a bowl Simply throw to cover with the minced chicken.

3. Put the chicken and roll it on the tortillas; cover it with cheese In the Air Fryer cooking basket, put the ready tortillas and cook for 60 minutes.

4. Offer with green chilies and serve.

Nutrition: Calories: 158 | Protein: 64 g | Carbohydrates: 252 g | Fat: 38 g | Fiber: 47 g

## 198. Chicken and Black Olives Sauce Recipe

Ready in: 25 minutes | Servings: 2 | Difficulty: Easy

### Ingredients

- 1 c black olives, pitted
- 2 tbsps. olive oil
- 1 tbsp. lemon juice
- Salt and black pepper to the taste
- ¼ c parsley, chopped
- 1 chicken breast cut into 4 pieces
- 3 garlic cloves, minced

### Directions

1. Combine the olives with salt, pepper in your mixing bowl Blend well with olive oil, lemon juice, and parsley, and switch to à bowl.

2. Season the chicken with salt and pepper, brush with the garlic and oil Put it in the preheated fryer, and cook for 8 minutes at 370°F Segregate the chicken into bowls, cover with the sauce and serve with the olives.

Nutrition: Calories: 105 | Protein: 27 g | Carbohydrates: 178 g | Fat: 28 g | Fiber: 3 g

## 199. Eggs Benedict on English Muffins

Ready in: 55 minutes | Servings: 5 | Difficulty: Hard

### Ingredients

- ½ tsp salt
- 3 English muffins, cut into ½-inch dice
- 4 large eggs
- ¼ tsp paprika
- 2 tbsps. margarine
- 6 oz. Canadian bacon, cut into ½-inch dice
- ½ tsp onion powder
- 1 ½ c milk
- 1 stalk green onions, chopped
- ½ (9 oz.) package hollandaise sauce mix

### Directions

1. Lightly oil the Air Fryer casserole dish with cooking oil.

2. Placed half of the bacon on the bottom of the plate, English muffins died on top uniformly spaced Spread the leftover bacon uniformly on top.

3. Combine the eggs, 1 c milk, green onions, onion powder, and salt in a big dish Pour the English muffin mixture on top Sprinkle with paprika on top Cover and refrigerate overnight with foil.

4. Preheat the Air Fryer at 390°F.

5. Cook for 2 minutes in an Air Fryer wrapped in Parchment paper Remove the paper and cook for an additional 15 minutes just until set.

6. In the meantime, render the hollandaise sauce in a saucepan by heating the margarine In a shallow cup, combine the remaining milk and the Hollandaise sauce and whisk in the melted margarine Simmer until it thickens when stirring constantly.

7. Serve with sauce and enjoy.

Nutrition: Calories: 155 | Protein: 122 g | Carbohydrates: 207 g | Fat: 84 g | Fiber: 29 g

## 200. Paprika Liver Spread

Ready in: 15 minutes | Servings: 6 | Difficulty: Easy

### Ingredients

- 1 tsp smoked paprika
- ¼ c hot water
- 1 lb. chicken liver
- 2 tbsps. ghee
- 1 tsp salt

**Directions**

1. Preheat the Air Fryer to 400°F Clean the chicken liver and trim and place it in the basket of the Air Fryer for 5 minutes.

2. After that: Turn them to the other side and cook them for another 3 minutes.

3. Move it into the blender when the chicken liver is fried.

4. Add salt, ghee, and smoked paprika.

5. Hot water is added, and the mixture is mixed until smooth Then move the cooked chicken pâté into the bowl and prepare it for up to 3 days in the fridge.

Nutrition: **Calories: 83 | Protein: 7 g | Carbohydrates: 17 g | Fat: 62 g | Fiber: 08**

## 201. Buttery Turkey and Mushroom Sauce

Ready in: 35 minutes | Servings: 4 | Difficulty: Normal

**Ingredients**

- 1 lb. mushrooms, sliced
- 2 spring onions, chopped
- 1 pinch of salt and black pepper
- 1 tbsp. parsley, chopped
- 6 c leftover turkey meat, skinless, boneless, and shredded
- 1 c chicken stock
- 3 tbsps. butter, melted

**Directions**

1. Heat a pan that suits the Air Fryer over a moderate flame with the butter; add the mushrooms and sauté for 5 minutes.

2. Apply the remainder of the ingredients, toss, place the pan in the machine and cook for 20 minutes at 370°F.

3. Split and serve everything between dishes.

Nutrition: **Calories: 2 | Protein: 0 g | Carbohydrates: 1 g | Fat: 0 g | Fiber: 0 g**

## 202. Air-Fried Cheese Chicken

Ready in: 25 minutes | Servings: 6 | Difficulty: Normal

**Ingredients**

- ½ c Mozzarella cheese, shredded
- 1 tbsp. marinara sauce
- Cooking spray as needed
- 6 tbsps. seasoned breadcrumbs
- 2 tbsps. Parmesan cheese, grated
- 1 tbsp. melted butter
- Chicken bits

**Directions**

1. Preheat your 390°F Air Fryer with cooking oil, oil the cooking basket Stir the breadcrumbs with the Parmesan cheese in a small cup With butter, wash the chicken bits and dredge them into the breadcrumbs.

2. To the cooking basket, add the chicken and simmer for 5 minutes Switch over and finish with sliced Mozzarella or marinara sauce; cook for 3 more minutes.

Nutrition: **Calories: 70 | Protein: 26 g | Carbohydrates: 69 g | Fat: 41 g | Fiber: 15 g**

## 203. Chicken, Pineapple and Veggie Kabobs

Ready in: 25 minutes | Servings: 5 | Difficulty: Normal

**Ingredients**

- Salt and ground black pepper, as required
- 1 (20 oz.) pineapple chunks, drained
- 1 tbsp. jerk sauce, cut into cubes
- 8 (4 oz.) boneless, skinless chicken thigh fillets, trimmed
- 1 tbsp. jerk seasoning
- 2 large zucchinis, sliced
- 8 oz. white mushrooms, stems removed

**Directions**

1. Place the chicken cubes and jerk spice together in a dish.

2. Cover and chill the bowl afterward.

3. Add salt and black pepper to the zucchini slices and mushrooms.

4. Thread onto oiled metal skewers with the chicken, vegetables, and pineapple.

5. Preheat the Air Fryer to a level of 370°F Oil the basket of an Air Fryer.

6. Arrange 2 batches of skewers into the packed Air Fryer basket

7. Air Fry for about 8–9 minutes, tossing and brushing until halfway through with jerk sauce.

8. Pull the chicken skewers from the Air Fryer and pass them to a serving platter

9. Serve it warm.

Nutrition: **Calories: 70 | Protein: 26 g | Carbohydrates: 69 g | Fat: 41 g | Fiber: 15 g**

## 204. Chicken Drumsticks

Ready in: 55 minutes | Servings: 4 | Difficulty: Hard

**Ingredients**

- 1/3 c cauliflower
- 1/3 c oats
- Pepper and salt to taste
- 8 chicken drumsticks
- 2 tbsps. mustard powder
- 2 tbsps. oregano
- 1 tsp cayenne pepper
- 2 tbsps. thyme
- 3 tbsps. coconut milk
- 1 large egg, lightly beaten

**Directions**

1. Preheat the Air Fryer to 350°F.

2. Over the chicken drumsticks, scatter salt and pepper and rub the coconut milk into them.

3. To produce a breadcrumb-like paste, throw all the items except for the egg into the food processor.

4. Switch to a bowl.

5. Place the beaten egg in a different dish; until dredging it into the egg, coat each chicken drumstick in the breadcrumb blend Roll it again into the breadcrumbs.

Nutrition: **Calories: 180 | Protein: 36 g | Carbohydrates: 243 g | Fat: 88 g | Fiber: 71 g**

## 205. Pizza Spaghetti Casserole

Ready in: 40 minutes | Servings: 4 | Difficulty: Hard

**Ingredients**

- 1 tbsp. Italian seasoning mix
- 3 tbsps. Romano cheese, grated
- 1 tbsp. fresh basil leaves, chiffonier
- 8 oz. spaghetti
- 1 lb. smoked chicken sausage, sliced
- 2 tomatoes, pureed
- ½ c Asiago cheese, shredded

**Directions**

1. Put a big pot of mildly salted water to simmer For 5 minutes or until al dente, cook your spaghetti; drain and reserve, holding warm.

2. Add the chicken sausage, tomato puree, Asiago cheese, and a combination of Italian seasoning.

3. Sprinkle the baking tray with the cooking spray; apply the mixture of spaghetti to the pan Cook at 5°F in a hot oven Air Fryer for 11 minutes.

4. Cover with the Romano grated cheese Turn the temperature to 390°F and cook for an extra 5 minutes or until it is all cooked thoroughly and the cheese gets melted.

5..Caramelize with new basil leaves Bon appetite!

Nutrition: **Calories: 180** | **Protein: 36 g** | **Carbohydrates: 243 g** | **Fat: 88 g** | **Fiber: 71 g**

## 206. Spicy Chicken and Tomato Sauce

Ready in: 20 minutes | Servings: 8 | Difficulty: Easy

**Ingredients**

- ¼ tsp jalapeño pepper, minced
- ½ tsp ground cumin
- 1 tsp keto tomato sauce
- 1 tbsp. almond oil
- 1 tsp dried thyme
- ½ tsp salt
- 8 chicken drumsticks
- ½ tsp cayenne pepper
- ½ tsp chili powder

**Directions**

1. Combine the tomato sauce and almond oil together in a mixing dish Then apply the minced jalapeño pepper and stir until homogeneous with the mixture Using chili powder, cayenne pepper, cumin, dried thyme, and sprinkle with salt to rub the chicken drumsticks Spray the tomato sauce mixture with the chicken and leave to marinate at least 8 hours or overnight.

2. Preheat the Air Fryer to 375°F In the Air Fryer, put the marinated chicken drumsticks and cook them for a few minutes.

Nutrition: **Calories: 24** | **Protein: 12 g** | **Carbohydrates: 29 g** | **Fat: 13 g** | **Fiber: 09 g**

## 207. Air-Fried Crispy Chicken Tenders

Ready in: 40 minutes | Servings: 4 | Difficulty: Hard

**Ingredients**

- 2 (6 oz.) boneless, skinless chicken breasts, pounded into ½-inch thick and cut into tenders
- ¼ c Parmesan cheese, finely grated
- 2 large eggs
- 1 ½ tsps. Worcestershire sauce, divided
- ½ c all-purpose flour
- 1 ½ c panko breadcrumbs
- Buttermilk
- Paprika, salt, and pepper to taste

**Directions**

1. Preheat the Air Fryer to 400°F and oil the basket with the Air Fryer.

2. In a cup, mix the buttermilk, ¾ tsps. Worcestershire sauce, tablespoons of paprika, salt, and black pepper.

3. In another dish, combine the flour, remaining paprika, salt, and black pepper.

4. In a third mug, whisk the eggs and leftover Worcestershire sauce.

5. In the fourth cup, combine the panko breadcrumbs and Parmesan cheese.

6. Bring the chicken tenders in and chill in the fridge in the buttermilk mixture.

7. Drop the chicken tenders in the flour mixture from the buttermilk mixture.

8. Soak the breadcrumb mixture into the egg and coat it.

9. In the Air Fryer basket, place half the chicken tenders and cook for about 15 minutes, rotating once in between.

10. To serve sweet, repeat with the remaining combination and dish out.

Nutrition: **Calories: 187** | **Protein: 42 g** | **Carbohydrates: 16 g** | **Fat: 12 g** | **Fiber: 37 g**

## 208. Cajun Chicken Tenders

Ready in: 35 minutes | Servings: 5 | Difficulty: Normal

**Ingredients**

- ½ tbsp. garlic powder, plus ½ tbsp.
- 1 tbsp. salt
- 3 tbsps. Cajun seasoning, divided
- ¼ c milk
- 3 eggs
- 2 c flour, plus ¼ c
- 1 tbsp. olive oil
- Pepper to taste
- Chicken

**Directions**

1. With salt, pepper, ½ tbsps. Garlic powder and tablespoons of Cajun seasoning, season the chicken In a dish, combine 2 c flour, the majority of the Cajun seasoning, and the garlic powder's remainder Put the eggs, milk, olive oil, and ¼ c flour in another dish Preheat the fryer to 370°F for air.

2. Line the parchment paper with a baking sheet Soak the chicken into the mixture of eggs and then into the mixture of flour Arrange the sheet over it Work in 2 batches if there is not enough space Fry for about 1 minute.

Nutrition: **Calories: 187** | **Protein: 42 g** | **Carbohydrates: 16 g** | **Fat: 12 g** | **Fiber: 37 g**

## 209. Chicken with Carrots

Ready in: 35 minutes | Servings: 2 | Difficulty: Normal

**Ingredients**

- 1 tbsp. fresh rosemary, chopped
- Salt and black pepper, as required
- 2 tbsps. fresh lemon juice
- 1 carrot, peeled and thinly sliced
- 2 tbsps. butter
- 2 (4 oz.) chicken breast halves

**Directions**

1. Preheat the Air Fryer to 375°F, and grease the Air Fryer basket.
2. On a flat surface, place square-shaped parchment paper and arrange carrot slices equally in the middle of each parchment paper.
3. Drizzle ½ tbsp. butter and season with salt and black pepper over the carrot slices.
4. Layer the chicken breasts with rosemary, lemon juice, and the remaining butter on top.
5. On both ends, fold the parchment paper and pass it into the Air Fryer.
6. Prep and dish out in a casserole plate for about 25 minutes to serve.

Nutrition: **Calories: 231 | Protein: 113 g | Carbohydrates: 339 g | Fat: 66 g | Fiber: 96 g**

## 210. Easy Chicken Sliders

Ready in: 40 minutes | Servings: 3 | Difficulty: Hard

**Ingredients**

• 1 egg
• 2 chicken breasts, cut in thirds
• 6 small-sized dinner rolls
• ½ tsp black pepper, preferably freshly ground
• 1 tsp celery seeds
• ½ c all-purpose flour
• 1 tsp garlic salt
• ½ tsp mustard seeds
• ½ tsp dried basil

**Directions**

1. Sift the flour and the spices well in a mixing bowl.
2. Shake the egg in a different shallow bowl until foamy.
3. Put the chicken into the egg through the flour mixture, and then roll it over the flour mixture again.
4. Spray the chicken bits on both sides with the cooking water Move them to the basket for frying.
5. Cook at 380°F for 1 minute in a hot oven Air Fryer; switch over and cook for a further 12–15 minutes.
6. Check doneness and change the seasonings Offer on dinner rolls instantly.

Nutrition: **Calories: 113 | Protein: 61 g | Carbohydrates: 194 g | Fat: 14 g | Fiber: 41 g**

## 211. Almond Flour Coco-Milk Battered Chicken

Ready in: 40 minutes | Servings: 4 | Difficulty: Hard

**Ingredients**

• 1 egg, beaten
• 4 small chicken thighs
• Salt and pepper to taste
• ¼ c coconut milk
• ½ c almond flour
• 1 ½ tbsp. old bay Cajun seasoning

**Directions**

1. Preheat the Air Fryer for 5 minutes.
2. Combine the egg with coconut milk in a cup.
3. Moisten the chicken thighs in the pounded egg mixture.
4. Integrate the almond flour, Cajun seasoning, salt, and pepper in a mixing dish.
5. Put the chicken thighs in the almond flour mixture.

6. Put it in the basket of an Air Fryer.
7. Cook at 350°F for 30 minutes.

Nutrition: **Calories: 235 | Protein: 105 g | Carbohydrates: 354 g | Fat: 67 g | Fiber: 10 g**

## 212. Crispy Chicken Wings

Ready in: 35 minutes | Servings: 2 | Difficulty: Normal

**Ingredients**

• Salt and ground white pepper, as required
• 1 lb. chicken wings, rinsed and trimmed
• ½ c cornstarch
• 2 lemongrass stalks (white portion), minced
• 1 onion, finely chopped
• 1 tbsp soy sauce
• 1 ½ tbsps. honey

**Directions**

1. Combine the lemongrass, onion, soy sauce, honey, salt, and white pepper together in a dish.
2. Add the wings, and coat with the marinade generously.
3. Cover and chill overnight to caramelize.
4. Set the Air Fryer to a temperature of 355°F Oil the Air Fryer basket.
5. Strip the chicken wings from the casserole and apply the cornstarch to the coat.
6. Organize the chicken wings in a thin layer in the ready Air Fryer basket.
7. Air fry for 25 minutes or so, tossing halfway around once.
8. Take the chicken wings from the Air Fryer and pass them to a serving platter.
9. Offer it warm.

Nutrition: **Calories: 235 | Protein: 105 g | Carbohydrates: 354 g | Fat: 67 g | Fiber: 10 g**

## 213. Delicious Whole Chicken

Ready in: 40 minutes | Servings: 4 | Difficulty: Hard

**Ingredients**

• 3 lbs. whole chicken, remove giblets and pat dry chicken
• ¼ tsp pepper
• 1 ½ tsp salt
• 1 tsp Italian seasoning
• ½ tsp garlic powder
• ½ tsp onion powder
• ¼ tsp paprika

**Directions**

1. Put the Italian seasoning, garlic powder, onion powder, paprika, pepper, and salt together in a shallow dish.
2. Drag the combination of spices in and out of the chicken.
3. Add the chicken breast side down in the basket of the Air Fryer.
4. At 360°F, roast chicken for 30 minutes.
5. Switch the chicken and roast for 20 minutes, or the chicken's core temperature hits 160°F.
6. Cherish and serve.

Nutrition: **Calories: 235 | Protein: 105 g | Carbohydrates: 354 g | Fat: 67 g | Fiber: 10 g**

## 214. Paprika Turkey and Shallot Sauce

Ready in: 40 minutes | Servings: 4 | Difficulty: Hard

**Ingredients**

• Salt and black pepper to the taste
• 1 c chicken stock
• 3 tbsps. butter, melted
• 4 shallots, chopped
• 1 big turkey breast, skinless, boneless, and cubed
• 1 tbsp. olive oil
• ¼ tsp sweet paprika

**Directions**

1. Warm the Air Fryer tray with the olive oil and butter over a moderate flame, introduce the turkey cubes, and brown per side for 3 minutes Insert shallots, mix and sauté for an additional 5 minutes.
2. Apply the paprika, stock, salt, and pepper, toss, place the pan in the fryer, and bake for 20 minutes at 370°F.
3. Slice and serve.

Nutrition: Calories: 378 | Protein: 183 g | Carbohydrates: 454 g | Fat: 151 g | Fiber: 215 g

## 215. Buffalo Chicken

Ready in: 35 minutes | Servings: 4 | Difficulty: Normal

**Ingredients**

• 2 beaten eggs
• 1 tbsp. sweet paprika
• 1 tbsp. garlic powder
• ½ c yogurt
• 1 lb. chicken breasts cut into strips
• 1 tbsp. ground cayenne pepper
• 1 tbsp. hot sauce
• Breadcrumbs

**Directions**

1. Preheat a 390°F Air Fryer Beat the eggs along with the yogurt and hot sauce Combine the breadcrumbs, paprika, pepper in a shallow dish, and garlic powder—line a parchment paper baking bowl.
2. First, dunk the chicken in the egg/yogurt mixture, and then cover it with breadcrumbs Arrange it on a tray and bake for 10 minutes in an Air Fryer Flip over the chicken and roast for an extra 10 minutes Just serve.

Nutrition: Calories: 211 | Protein: 23 g | Carbohydrates: 132 g | Fat: 25 g | Fiber: 212 g

## 216. Middle Eastern Chicken BBQ with Tzatziki Sauce

Ready in: 35 minutes | Servings: 5 | Difficulty: Normal

**Ingredients**

• 2 tsps. white vinegar
• Salt to taste
• ½ cucumber, peeled, seeded, and grated
• 1 ½ lbs. skinless, boneless chicken breast halves, cut into bite-sized pieces
• ¼ c olive oil
• 2 cloves garlic, minced
• 2 tbsps. lemon juice
• 1 tsp dried oregano

**For the tzatziki dip:**

• 1 (6 oz.) container plain Greek-style yogurt
• 1 tbsp. olive oil

**Directions**

1. Combine all the tzatziki dip ingredients together in a moderate dish To encourage the flavor to mix, put it in the fridge for at least 2 hours.
2. Mix the cucumber, oregano, garlic, lemon juice, and olive oil well in the re-sealable container Include chicken, salt, vinegar, and marinate excess air for a couple of hours.
3. Thread the chicken into skewers and put it on the skewer shelf Cook them in batches.
4. Heat at 360°F for 12 minutes Midway into the cooking process, turn skewers and re-sealable bag marinade baste
5. Serve and enjoy with tzatziki sauce.

Nutrition: Calories: 109 | Protein: 54 g | Carbohydrates: 168 g | Fat: 25 g | Fiber: 32 g

## 217. Vortex Fryer Meatballs

Ready in: 15 minutes | Servings: 4 | Difficulty: Easy

**Ingredients**

• 1 tsp pepper
• 1 egg
• 1 clove garlic
• ¼ c Parmesan cheese
• 1 tsp salt
• ¼ c breadcrumbs
• 1 tbsp. Worcestershire sauce
• 1 lb. ground beef or pork or turkey

**Directions**

1. Preheat your Air Fryer to 400°F.
2. In a mixing cup, combine all of the ingredients.
3. Make 1 ½ inch meatballs with a tiny volume of the mixture.
4. Place them on a sheet and placed them in the heated fryer.
5. When finished, flip every few minutes

Nutrition: Calories: 109 | Protein: 54 g | Carbohydrates: 168 g | Fat: 25 g | Fiber: 32 g

## 218. Leftover Turkey Pot Pie

Ready in: 18 minutes | Servings: 6 | Difficulty: Easy

**Ingredients**

• 2 c shredded cooked turkey
• 1/3 c chopped onion
• 1 c chicken broth
• ½ tsp pepper
• 1 tsp salt
• 1 can of crescent rolls
• ½ c milk or cream (depends on how creamy you like it!)
• 1/3 c all-purpose flour
• 1 small bag of frozen mixed vegetables
• 3 tbsps. butter or margarine

**Directions**

1. Preheat the Air Fryer to 350°F Melt butter in a saucepan over

medium heat Add onion and cook, constantly stirring, for 2 minutes, or it's soft.

2. Mix in the flour, salt, and pepper, so it is well together Cook, often stirring, until the broth and milk have thickened and become bubbly Combine the turkey and mixed vegetables in a mixing bowl.

3. Remove the pan from the flame in a pan that will work in your Air Fryer, position half of the crescents.

4. Preheat oven to 350°F and bake for 6 minutes, or until golden brown.

5. It must be completed in its entirety Otherwise, it would be too late.

6. Check for firmness before removing Remove the turkey filling and replace it Add the other half of the crescent rolls on top.

7. You may also be a little more creative and make a template or a lattice.

8. Bake for 8 minutes, or until golden brown on top Take the pan from the oven and set it aside for 5 minutes before eating.

Nutrition: **Calories: 303 | Protein: 105 g | Carbohydrates: 494 g | Fat: 64 g | Fiber: 37 g**

## 219. Cracker Chicken Strips

Ready in: 20 minutes | Servings: 4 | Difficulty: Easy

**Ingredients**
- ½ tsp pepper
- 2 eggs
- ½ tsp garlic powder
- 1 c crushed butter crackers Ritz
- ¼ c milk
- ½ c butter cut into pieces
- 1 ½ lbs. boneless skinless chicken breast cut into strips

**Directions**

1. Preheat the Air Fryer to 375°F and lightly oil a baking dish with nonstick frying oil Make sure your rack is in the center of the place.

2. Whisk the eggs and milk together in a small dish Add the crushed crackers to a different bowl Garlic powder and pepper to taste.

3. Each chicken strip should be dipped in the egg mixture before being dipped in the cracker mixture To protect the flesh, press the cracker crumbs into it.

4. Place each coated chicken strip in the baking dish that has been packed.

5. Place a slice of butter on top of each chicken strip

6. Bake for 30–40 minutes in the Air Fryer, or until chicken is cooked through and golden brown.

Nutrition: **Calories: 303 | Protein: 105 g | Carbohydrates: 494 g | Fat: 64 g | Fiber: 37 g**

## 220. Whole Chicken in Basket

Ready in: 1 hour and 5 minutes | Servings: 4 | Difficulty: Hard

**Ingredients**
- 2 tbsps. olive oil
- 1 tbsp. salt and pepper
- 1 tbsp. paprika
- 1 whole chicken

**Directions**

1. Don't rinse the chicken; pat it off.

2. Season and coat with olive oil.

3. Place the chicken in the basket after tying it up.

4. Preheat the Air Fryer to 350°F; you can air fry or bake .

5. Preheat the oven before adding the chicken You don't want to get burned!.

6. Cook for 60 minutes or until the internal temperature reaches 165°F.

Nutrition: **Calories: 522 | Protein: 601 g | Carbohydrates: 311 g | Fat: 182 g | Fiber: 22 g**

## 221. Hot Dog

Ready in: 30 minutes | Servings: 4 | Difficulty: Normal

**Ingredients**
- 2 tbsps. butter
- Mustard
- Mayo
- 1 sweet pepper or red bell pepper
- 4 strips bacon
- ½ onion
- Ketchup
- ½ bell pepper
- 4 buns
- 4 hot dogs (Hebrew National is our preferred brand)

**Directions**

1. Preheat the Air Fryer to 400°F Set up your rack in the center of the room.

2. Place the peppers and onions in a pan and slice them Place the pan on the bottom of the oven and the bacon on the rack above it

3. The bacon should be put on the center shelf Cook for another 4 minutes before tossing Cook for a further 4 minutes.

4. Cook the hotdogs for 4 minutes on a rack, tossing once Leave the peppers and onions in so these can cook if they aren't cooked yet.

5. Then, butter your buns and place them on the Air Fryer's middle shelf for a few minutes.

6. Serve with mayo, ketchup, and mustard Enjoy!

Nutrition: **Calories: 109 | Protein: 53 g | Carbohydrates: 77 g | Fat: 73 g | Fiber: 19 g**

## 222. Butternut Squash and Kielbasa Sausage

Ready in: 25 minutes | Servings: 2 | Difficulty: Normal

**Ingredients**
- ½ c diced pre-cooked kielbasa
- ¼ tsp garlic salt
- ½ tbsp. olive oil
- ¼ diced medium red or white onion
- 1 c diced butternut squash

**Directions**

1. Preheat the Air Fryer to 370°F in the air fry environment.

2. Butternut squash can be cut into 1-inch squares In a mixing dish, combine the butternut squash, onion, oil, and seasoning.

3. Coat, to be precise.

4. Arrange the butternut squash in a single layer on a rack Both of them should be willing to be laid flat.

5. Squash should be cooked for 10 minutes.

6. Remove the rack, introduce the kielbasa, and cook for another. 5 minutes, or until it is crispy and done.

7. The size of the sausage and squash will determine how long it takes to cook The total time could be about 20 minutes.

Nutrition: **Calories: 109 | Protein: 53 g |
Carbohydrates: 77 g | Fat: 73 g | Fiber: 19 g**

## 223. Rotisserie Basket Meatballs

Ready in: 15 minutes | Servings: 4 | Difficulty: Easy

**Ingredients**

- 1 tsp pepper
- ½ c breadcrumbs
- 1 tsp salt
- 1 clove garlic
- ¼ c Parmesan cheese
- 1 tbsp. Worcestershire sauce
- 1 lb. ground beef or pork or turkey

**Directions**

1. The Air Fryer cannot be preheated.

2. In a mixing cup, combine all of the ingredients Ensure they're a bit drier and well-knit If required, add more breadcrumbs.

3. Make 1 ½-inch meatballs with a tiny volume of the mixture.

4. Cover the Rotisserie Basket after placing them in it.

5. Place the basket in the machine and set the rotation speed to 380°F.

6. Cook for 10 minutes before serving.

Nutrition: **Calories: 154 | Protein: 148 g |
Carbohydrates: 83 g | Fat: 82 g | Fiber: 02 g**

## 224. Sausage Stuffed Portobello Mushroom With Balsamic

Ready in: 25 minutes | Servings: 4 | Difficulty: Easy

**Ingredients**

- 2 tbsps. balsamic vinegar
- 1 tbsp. olive oil
- 2 cloves garlic minced
- 1 red bell pepper finely diced
- 1 c minced onion, about half of 1 large
- 1 c spinach
- 1 lb. smoked sausage (we use Bradley's)
- 4–6 slices Swiss cheese
- 4–6 Portobello mushroom caps

**Directions**

1. Preheat the Vortex Air Fryer to 350°F For this recipe, the rack should be adjusted to the middle level Sausage, garlic, bell pepper, and onions must all be chopped.

2. Place on a baking sheet and roast in the Air Fryer for 4 minutes or until the onions are wilted.

3. When the sausage is in the oven, clean the mushrooms lightly Scrape the gills from the interior of the mushrooms with a spoon and discard Set aside the washed mushrooms.

4. Remove the sausage mixture from the pan and place it in a mixing bowl Add the spinach and stir to combine The heat from the sausage can cause it to wilt.

5. Carefully place the caps on the trays; they can be sticky Evenly spread the filling among the mushroom caps.

6. For 10 minutes, air fry the caps Keep an eye on them to make sure they don't smoke.

7. Cook for a further 1–2 minutes after adding a slice of cheese to the top of each.

8. Enjoy with a drizzle of Balsamic!

Nutrition: **Calories: 132 | Protein: 78 g |
Carbohydrates: 25 g | Fat: 107 g | Fiber: 1 g**

## 225. Apple Cheddar Stuffed Chicken Breast

Ready in: 40 minutes | Servings: 2 | Difficulty: Hard

**Ingredients**

- ½ c chicken broth
- ½ c apple peeled and diced
- 1 tbsp. butter
- 1 tbsp. fine breadcrumbs
- ¼ c shredded Cheddar cheese
- Chopped fresh parsley for serving
- 2 chicken breasts flattened to ¼-inch
- Salt and pepper to taste
- 1 egg

**Directions**

1. Preheat your Air Fryer to 350°F with the "Bake" mode Set the rack to the lowest spot.

2. Set aside the chicken after seasoning it with salt and pepper Combine the fruit, egg, and breadcrumbs in a little dish Mix well.

3. In the middle of the chicken breast, spread half of the apple mixture and roll it up Toothpicks are used to keep everything together.

4. Place the chicken in a pan and cook it Pour the chicken broth into the bowl Only enough to reach the bottom of the container Using tin foil, cover the plate.

5. The cooking time is 20 minutes Check the temperature Cook uncovered before the internal temperature reaches 165°F Cook for another 10 minutes if necessary The length of time depends on the thickness of the material.

6. Remove from the oven and set aside for 5 minutes Put butter on top Serve garnished with cheese and sliced new parsley.

Nutrition: **Calories: 123 | Protein: 32 g |
Carbohydrates: 81 g | Fat: 101 g | Fiber: 26 g**

## 226. Roast Beef

Ready in: 25 minutes | Servings: 6 | Difficulty: Normal

**Ingredients**

- 1 tsp salt and pepper
- 1 medium onion optional
- 1 tbsp. olive oil
- 2 tsps. rosemary and thyme fresh or dried
- 2 lbs. beef roast

**Directions**

1. Preheat the vortex Air Fryer to 390°F Using paper towels, pat the beef roast dry Rub the roast with olive oil and seasonings to coat it thoroughly.

2. Place the roast on a rack in the Air Fryer and cook it The rack should be set to the lowest position At 15 minutes in the oven, check the temperature If the temperature isn't quite right, return it for a few minutes.

3. When the roast beef has achieved the target temperature, remove it from the Air Fryer Until eating, cover with aluminum foil and set aside for at least 10 minutes This helps the meat to finish cooking and consume the juices.

4. Carve the roast beef against the grain into thin slices and serve with vegetables.

Nutrition: Calories: 289 | Protein: 44 g | | Carbohydrates: 416 g | Fat: 134 g | Fiber: 56 g

## 227. Keto Philly Cheesesteak Stuffed Tomatoes

Ready in: 15 minutes | Servings: 3 | Difficulty: Easy

**Ingredients**
- ¼ c Mozzarella cheese
- 4 slices of frozen Philly cheesesteak meat of your choosing
- ½ medium bell pepper sliced
- ¼ large onion thinly sliced
- 1 c shredded lettuce
- ½ tbsp. olive oil
- Salt and pepper to taste
- 2 medium tomatoes

**Directions**

1. Using a tiny quantity of olive oil, coat the peppers and onions in strips.

2. Preheat the Air Fryer to 360°F Cook for 3 minutes on the center rack with the onions and peppers.

3. Remove your basket from the Air Fryer Place the frozen cheesesteak meat in the Air Fryer for 5 minutes at the same temperature Season with salt and pepper to taste.

4. Return the vegetables to the rack after shredding Toss all around Cook for 2 more minutes before removing it from the oven.

5. Place the tomatoes on a flat surface, stem side down with a sharp knife, gently sliced 6 wedges out of the tomato, being cautious not to cut into the tomato's bottom.

6. To separate the tomato wedges, gently peel back the skin Half of the shredded lettuce should be placed in the bottom of each cut tomato.

7. Half of the meat and vegetable mixture should be filled into each tomato Serve with some melted Mozzarella cheese on top of each stuffed tomato.

8. If you want the cheese to melt, return them to the Air Fryer for 1 minute.

Nutrition: Calories: 289 | Protein: 44 g | Carbohydrates: 416 g | Fat: 134 g | Fiber: 56 g

## 228. Garlic Pizza

Ready in: 20 minutes | Servings: 4 | Difficulty: Easy

**Ingredients**
- 1 bowl of garlic butter or use the recipe below
- 1 jar of your favorite pizza sauce
- 1 package of shredded Mozzarella cheese
- 1 package of pepperoni
- 1 package of Italian bread (can be found in the bakery section of your local grocery store)

**Directions**

1. Preheat your Air Fryer to 360°F and make sure your rack is in the center spot.

2. Spread butter on all sides of the bread and place it on a cookie sheet.

3. Carefully put 3 pieces of bread in the Air Fryer's basket.

4. 1 tbsp. pizza sauce, pepperoni, and cheese on each slice of bread.

5. Cook for 5 minutes at 360°F (If you prefer lighter toast, cook for 4 minutes instead).

6. Enable to cool for a couple of minutes before serving.

Nutrition: Calories: 82 | Protein: 44 g | Carbohydrates: 97 g | Fat: 34 g | Fiber: 24 g

## 229. Garlic Butter

Ready in: 10 minutes | Servings: 1 | Difficulty: Easy

**Ingredients**
- 1 pinch of salt and pepper to taste
- 1 tbs parsley
- 2 cloves of minced garlic or 2 tbs garlic powder
- 1 stick of butter softened best if left out at room temperature about ½ hour before making

**Directions**
- Mix all of the components.
- Refrigerate leftovers for up to 1 week or freeze for up to 3 months in an airtight bag.

Nutrition: Calories: 416 | Protein: 152 g | Carbohydrates: 438 g | Fat: 218 g | Fiber: 181 g

## 230. Low-Carb Spaghetti Squash Bowls

Ready in: 55 minutes | Servings: 4 | Difficulty: Hard

**Ingredients**
- 2 medium spaghetti squash
- 1 small onion diced
- 1 c shredded Mozzarella cheese + extra for topping
- 24 oz. low-carb marinara sauce
- ½ c shredded Parmesan cheese
- 2 tsps. minced garlic
- Salt and pepper
- 1 lb. ground beef

**Directions**

1. Every spaghetti squash should be split in half, with the seeds scooped out and discarded Pour 1-inch of water in an 8x8-inch or 9x9-inch baking dish.

2. Put 2 spaghetti squash halves in the baking bowl, rounded side down Microwave on high for 18 minutes Go on for the second spaghetti squash in the same manner.

3. When the squash is finished, scrape the insides into a wide mixing bowl and put them aside.

4. Preheat your Vortex Air Fryer to 350°F on the "Bake" level During cooking, the rack will be placed in the lowest location.

5. Drain the fat after browning the ground beef, diced onion, and minced garlic.

6. Set aside the 24 oz. low-carb marinara sauce and the baked ground beef.

7. Combine the fried spaghetti squash with both slices of cheese Season with salt and pepper.

8. Cover each squash shell halfway with the cheese-squash mixture Serve with the meat/marinara combination on top.

9. Extra melted cheese can be spread on top Bake for 10 minutes with the squash boats on a shelf You can need to do them separately, depending on the distance.

10. Remove from the Air Fryer and set aside to cool for a few minutes before serving.

Nutrition: **Calories: 50 | Protein: 12 g | Carbohydrates: 41 g | Fat: 38 g | Fiber: 18 g**

## 231. Grouper Tacos with Corn Salsa
Ready in: 20 minutes | Servings: 6 | Difficulty: Normal
### Ingredients
- Lime juice
- ½ c corn
- ¼ c Roma tomatoes diced
- ¼ c red onion diced
- Salt and Pepper
- ½ lb. grouper

### Directions
1. Preheat the Air Fryer to 350°F on bake.
2. Set the rack to the middle position.
3. Toss the vegetables together and season with lime juice, salt, and pepper.
4. If you like more fire, add red pepper.
5. Refrigerate for at least 10 minutes before serving.
6. Season the grouper with salt and pepper.
7. In your Air Fryer, bake the grouper for 5 minutes (possibly more depending on thickness).
8. Flake the grouper and bring the tacos together.

Nutrition: **Calories: 171 | Protein: 135 g | Carbohydrates: 73 g | Fat: 112 g | Fiber: 01 g**

## 232. Rotisserie Chicken Nuggets
Ready in: 18 minutes | Servings: 6 | Difficulty: Easy
### Ingredients
- 2 tbsps. grated Parmesan optional
- 1 c Panko breadcrumbs
- ⅛ tsp black pepper
- ¼ tsp salt
- ¼ c milk
- 1 egg
- 1 boneless skinless chicken breast cut into ½-inch chunks

### Directions
1. In a single dish, mix the egg and the milk.
2. Place Panko crumbs in another bowl, making sure it can hold a skewer.
3. It fits well with a paper plate.
4. Season the chicken pieces with salt and pepper before placing them in the egg mixture.
5. Remove the bits from the pan and skewer them.
6. Then, when both of them are finished, dunk them in the Panko mixture.
7. Preheat the Air Fryer to 390°F.
8. Add the rotisserie tray and cook for 7 minutes until it has heated up.
9. Check the temperature.

10. The temperature should be about 165°F.
11. If not, proceed to cook for a few more minutes before golden brown.
12. Top with cheese and serve.

Nutrition: **Calories: 171 | Protein: 135 g | Carbohydrates: 73 g | Fat: 112 g | Fiber: 01 g**

## 233. Mini Bourbon Gouda Stuffed Meat Loaves
Ready in: 20 minutes | Servings: 4 | Difficulty: Easy
### Ingredients
- 1 tsp crushed red pepper flakes
- 2 tbsps. Bourbon, plus 1 tbsp.
- ¼ c brown sugar
- ¼ c ketchup
- 1 tbsp. Worcestershire sauce
- 1 tbsp. Chili Sauce
- 6 oz. Gouda cheese, either sliced or cut into strips
- 1 egg lightly beaten
- 2 cloves garlic minced
- ¼ medium red onion grated
- ¼ c panko breadcrumbs
- 1 lb. ground beef

### Directions
1. Preheat the Air Fryer to bake at 400°F The rack will be adjusted to the lowest setting.
2. Combine the whiskey and breadcrumbs in a big mixing dish Allow the whiskey to soak into the breadcrumbs for a few minutes Combine the ground beef, chili sauce, red onion, garlic, eggs, and Worcestershire sauce in a large mixing bowl.
3. Gently mix with your hands, so it is well mixed Don't overwork the meat; otherwise, your meatloaf would be rough and chewy.
4. In the cup, split the meat into 4 pieces Create a patty with half of one beef Place the cheese in the center of the meatloaf, leaving an inch of meatloaf on both sides.
5. Cover with the leftover meatloaf mixture and press the sides tightly to properly close the sandwich Any opened holes would enable the cheese to leak out during the cooking process.
6. Rep before you've completed all 4 and put them on a shelf Add them to the Air Fryer on the lowest setting until it has heated up Cook for 10 minutes, or until well browned on the outside.
7. In a shallow bowl, add all of the ingredients Combine the sauce ingredients and spill over the meatloaf's top, causing it to drip down the sides a little.
8. Take the plate from the oven and fill it with the sauce Return to the oven for another 1–2 minutes, just until the mixture is bubbly.
9. At this stage, keep an eye on them as they will burn quickly.
10. When the mixture starts to bubble, remove it.
11. Serve with mashed potatoes or vegetables as a side dish!

Nutrition: **Calories: 105 | Protein: 106 g | Carbohydrates: 62 g | Fat: 51 g | Fiber: 2 g**

## 234. Turkey Pot Pie with Puff Pastry
Ready in: 32 minutes | Servings: 4 | Difficulty: Normal
### Ingredients
- 1 large egg beaten
- 1 sheet frozen puff pastry thawed but still cold
- 15 c shredded leftover turkey

- Kosher salt and ground black pepper to taste
- 1 tbsp. heavy cream
- 1 c chicken stock
- 3 tbsps. all-purpose flour
- 1 clove garlic minced
- ½ bag mixed veggies 6 oz. or 1 c chopped veggies (green beans, carrots, peas, and corn)
- 1 tsp chopped fresh rosemary
- 1 tsp chopped fresh thyme
- ½ small yellow onion chopped
- 3 tbsps. unsalted butter

**Directions**

1. Preheat the Air fryer to 375°F The rack would be set to its lowest position.

2. Melt the butter in a big skillet over medium-high flame Add the yellow onion, fresh thyme, and fresh rosemary until the butter has melted.

3. Cook, sometimes stirring, until the onion is smooth and golden in color.

4. Add the garlic and simmer for 30 seconds, or until fragrant Combine the turkey, vegetables, and stock in a large mixing bowl.

5. Cook for 5 minutes, or until it is well mixed Remove the pan from the heat and apply the cream Enable 5–10 minutes for the mixture to sit It has to be thickened If not, leave it to rest for a few minutes longer or apply a little more flour (1 tbsp. flour and 1 tbsp. water mixed).

6. Divide the mixture into 2–4 oven-safe bowls Don't overfill; there should be at least 1 ½-inch of space at the end Puff pastry can be cut to match and covered Cook, occasionally stirring, for 8 minutes or until golden brown.

7. If you want your toppings extra crispy, this is the way to go Until putting it in the dishes, bake it for 2 minutes Then, with the crispy side down, clip it over.

Nutrition: **Calories: 105 | Protein: 106 g | Carbohydrates: 62 g | Fat: 51 g | Fiber: 2 g**

## 235. Cuban Mojo Pork Loin
Ready in: 32 minutes | Servings: 4 | Difficulty: Normal
**Ingredients**
- Salt to taste
- ¼ tsp ground cumin
- 1 tbsp. fresh oregano chopped
- ¼ c olive oil
- 2 tbsps. lime juice
- ½ c orange juice
- 1 tsp salt
- 3 cloves garlic diced
- 2 lbs. pork tenderloin

**Directions**

1. Trim the excess fat from the pork loin or roast, but leave a ½-inch thick coating on top.

2. In a mixing cup, combine both of the other components You should use either a pocket or a lidded mug Seal the pork with the marinade Refrigerate for at least 1 hour or up to 24 hours in the refrigerator.

3. Preheat your Vortex to 350°F using the "Bake" mode Remove from the fridge and set aside for 20 minutes to get to room temperature Any of the marinades can be injected into the loin If you want to give more flair, cut the top of the pork loin diagonally.

4. Wrap the pork loin securely in tin foil Place the rack on the lowest level until the Air Fryer has reached the temperature Cook for 10 minutes before removing and unwrapping the loin.

5. Return to the oven and cook for another 15–20 minutes, or until the internal temperature reaches 145°F Enable to rest for 5 minutes before slicing and serving.

Nutrition: **Calories: 102 | Protein: 37 g | Carbohydrates: 11 g | Fat: 49 g | Fiber: 25 g**
Note: Cooking times differ considerably based on the size and form of the loin It is strongly recommended that you begin monitoring temperatures at the 10 minutes mark and check every 5–10 minutes after that

## 236. Low-Carb Chicken Enchiladas
Ready in: 20 minutes | Servings: 4 | Difficulty: Easy
**Ingredients**
- 3 c shredded skinless, boneless rotisserie chicken breast
- 1 c salsa can use tomato sauce
- ¼ tsp salt
- ½ tsp crushed red pepper
- ¾ tsp garlic powder
- 2 tsps. ground cumin
- 1 ½ tbsps. chili powder
- 1 c chicken stock
- 1 c prechopped onion
- 6 tbsps. sour cream
- ¼ c chopped fresh cilantro
- 1 c chopped tomato
- 1 c 4-cheese Mexican blend cheese, shredded
- 12 (6-inch) carb-conscious tortillas
- 1 (15 oz.) can of black beans, rinsed and drained

**Directions**

1. Preheat the Vortex Air Fryer to 350°F.

2. In a medium saucepan, combine the first 9 ingredients Cook for 2 minutes on medium heat or until the sauce has thickened 1 ½ c sauce mixture can be set back Cook for 2 minutes, or until the chicken is fully cooked, in the pan with the beans.

3. Stack tortillas, roll in wet paper towels, and then microwave for 25 seconds on high Serve with the remaining sauce and cheese on top.

4. Fill each tortilla with around 1/3 c chicken mixture and roll it up Place tortillas in the bottom of a 13 x 9-inch glass or ceramic baking dish coated with cooking spray, seam sides down 3 minutes under the broiler, or before the cheese is finely browned and the sauce is bubbling Toss with tomato and cilantro before serving Serve with sour cream on the side.

Nutrition: **Calories: 80 | Protein: 59 g | Carbohydrates: 79 g | Fat: 34 g | Fiber: 21 g**

## 237. Beef Burger
Ready in: 15 minutes | Servings: 1 | Difficulty: Easy
**Ingredients**
- Pepper to taste
- Salt to taste
- 1 envelope French onion dip
- 1 tsp garlic powder
- 1 tbsp. Worcestershire sauce
- ½ onion finely chopped
- 1 package kaiser rolls
- 1 lb. ground beef or pork or turkey

**Directions**

1. Preheat the Vortex Air Fryer to 400°F Place the rack in the center of the space.

2. In a mixing cup, combine all of the ingredients.

3. Create patties with the combination.

4. Place in the Air Fryer and flip after 4 minutes, it will take 8–15 minutes to cook depending on how finished you like them.

5. Add the cheese and toast for another minute.

6. Butter the buns and toast them for 2–3 minutes.

7. Create your burgers!

Nutrition: **Calories: 109 | Protein: 61 g | Carbohydrates: 63 g | Fat: 66 g | Fiber: 37 g**

## 238. Sausage, Peppers, and Onions

Ready in: 15 minutes | Servings: 4 | Difficulty: Easy

**Ingredients**

- 2 tbsps. olive oil
- 1 lb. sausage of your choice
- 1 bell pepper
- 1 onion

**Directions**

1. Preheat the Air Fryer to 400°F on the air fry setting Place your rack in the center of the space.

2. Pepper and onion can be finely cut Pour 2 tablespoons of olive oil over the peppers and onions.

3. Arrange the products on the tray in a pleasing manner Cook for 10 minutes until the Air Fryer is ready And sure to turn the side halfway through.

4. To check whether the sausage is finished, cut it Halfway into the cooking period, you should break them in half.

5. Serve with buns or your favorite side dish!

Nutrition: **Calories: 41 | Protein: 16 g | Carbohydrates: 81 g | Fat: 06 g | Fiber: 16 g**

## 239. Ginger Cod

Ready in: 15 minutes | Servings: 2 | Difficulty: Easy

**Ingredients**

- ½ tsp ground black pepper
- ½ tsp ground ginger
- 1 tbsp. sunflower oil
- ½ tsp salt
- ½ tsp dried rosemary
- ½ tsp ground paprika
- 10 oz. cod fillet
- ½ tsp cayenne pepper
- ¼ tsp ground cilantro

**Directions**

1. Combine the cayenne pepper, ground cilantro, ginger, ground black pepper, salt, dried rosemary, and dried paprika in a small dish.

2. After that, with the spice combination, brush the cod fillet.

3. Sprinkle it with sunflower oil after this.

4. Preheat the fryer to 390°F for air.

5. In an Air Fryer, put the cod fillet and cook this for 4 minutes.

6. Then flip the fish gently on the other side and simmer for 4 more minutes.

Nutrition: **Calories: 30 | Protein: 07 g | Carbohydrates: 65 g | Fat: 04 g | Fiber: 05 g**

## 240. Buttery Chives Trout

Ready in: 17 minutes | Servings: 2 | Difficulty: Easy

**Ingredients**

- Juice of 1 lime
- 1 tbsp. chives, chopped
- 4 trout fillets, boneless
- 1 tbsp. parsley, chopped
- 4 tbsps. butter, melted
- Salt and black pepper to the taste

**Directions**

1. Combine the melted butter, salt, and pepper with the fillets, brush softly, and place the fish in the bucket of your Air Fryer Then cook for 6 minutes on each side at 390°F.

2. Divide plates and serve at the end with lime juice slathered on top and with scattered parsley and chives.

Nutrition: **Calories: 30 | Protein: 07 g | Carbohydrates: 65 g | Fat: 04 g | Fiber: 05 g**

## 241. Buttered Scallops

Ready in: 9 minutes | Servings: 2 | Difficulty: Easy

**Ingredients**

- ½ tbsp. fresh thyme, minced
- Salt and black pepper, as required
- ¾ lb. sea scallops, cleaned and patted very dry
- 1 tbsp. butter, melted

**Directions**

1. Preheat the Air Fryer to 390°F and oil the basket with the Air Fryer.

2. In a mug, whisk together the scallops, butter, thyme, salt, and black pepper.

3. Organize the prawns in the Air Fryer's basket and fry them for about 4 minutes.

4. Dish out a platter of scallops and serve sweet.

Nutrition: **Calories: 351 | Protein: 171 g | Carbohydrates: 416 g | Fat: 131 g | Fiber: 233 g**

## 242. Shrimp and Celery Salad

Ready in: 10 minutes | Servings: 4 | Difficulty: Easy

**Ingredients**

- ½ tsp salt
- ½ tsp chili flakes
- 4 oz. celery stalk, chopped
- 3 oz. chevre
- 1 tsp avocado oil
- ½ tsp dried oregano
- 8 oz. shrimps, peeled
- 1 tsp butter, melted

**Directions**

1. Spray the dried oregano and melted butter on the shrimps and put them in the Air Fryer For 5 minutes, fry the seafood at 400°F.

2. In the meantime, let the chevre break Place a stalk of sliced celery in a salad bowl Insert collapsed chevre, chili flakes, avocado oil, and then salt.

3. Mix the salad well and cover with the shrimps fried in it.

Nutrition: **Calories: 351 | Protein: 171 g | Carbohydrates: 416 g | Fat: 131 g | Fiber: 233 g**

## 243. Cajun Cod Fillets with Avocado Sauce

Ready in: 30 minutes | Servings: 2 | Difficulty: Normal

### Ingredients

- ½ avocado, peeled, pitted, and mashed
- 1 tbsp. mayonnaise
- 3 tbsps. sour cream
- ½ tsp yellow mustard
- 1 tsp lemon juice
- ¼ tsps. salt
- ¼ tsps. hot pepper sauce
- 2 cod fish fillets
- 1 garlic clove, minced
- ¼ tsps. black pepper
- 1 egg
- Sea salt, to taste
- ½ c tortilla chips, crushed
- 2 tsps. olive oil

### Directions

1. Begin by heating up to 360°F for your Air Fryer Spray the basket of the Air Fryer with cooking oil.
2. Pat a dish towel to dry the fish fillets.
3. Combine the salt, crushed tortilla chips, and olive oil thoroughly in a separate dish.
4. Soak the fish into the mixture of crumbs, making sure to thoroughly cover it—Cook for about 12 minutes in the preheated Air Fryer.
5. In the meantime, by combining the rest of the ingredients in a cup, make your avocado sauce Place it in your fridge until it is ready for serving.
6. On the side, eat the fish fillets with chilled avocado sauce Bon appétit!

Nutrition: Calories: 168 | Protein: 67 g | Carbohydrates: 239 g | Fat: 63 g | Fiber: 6 g

## 244. Jumbo Shrimp

Ready in: 25 minutes | Servings: 2 | Difficulty: Normal

### Ingredients

- ½ tsp garlic salt
- 12 jumbo shrimps
- ¼ tsp freshly cracked mixed peppercorns

**For the sauce:**

- 1 tsp chipotle powder
- ½ tsp cumin powder
- 1 tsp Dijon mustard
- 4 tbsps. Mayonnaise
- 1 tsp lemon zest

### Directions

1. Spray the garlic salt with the crushed peppercorns over the shrimp and coat.
2. In the frying basket, fried the shrimp for 5 minutes at 395°F.
3. Switch the shrimp over and allow for an additional 2 minutes to cook.
4. Meanwhile, blend all the sauce items with a whisk.
5. Pour over the shrimp and serve.

Nutrition: Calories: 168 | Protein: 67 g | Carbohydrates: 239 g | Fat: 63 g | Fiber: 6 g

## 245. Halibut Steaks

Ready in: 20 minutes | Servings: 2 | Difficulty: Easy

### Ingredients

- 2 tbsps. honey
- ¼ c vegetable oil
- 2 ½ tbsp. Worcester sauce
- 2 tbsps. vermouth
- 1 tbsp. fresh parsley leaves, coarsely chopped
- 1 tbsp. freshly squeezed lemon juice
- 1 lb. halibut steaks
- Salt and pepper to taste
- 1 tsp dried basil

### Directions

1. In a big bowl, placed all of the supplies With the seasoning, mix and cover the fish fully.
2. Move to your Air Fryer and bake for 5 minutes, at 390°F.
3. Switch the fish over and enable it for an additional 5 minutes to cook.
4. Ensure the fish is fried through, leaving it, if possible, in the fryer for a few more minutes.
5. Offer a potato salad on the side.

Nutrition: Calories: 168 | Protein: 67 g | Carbohydrates: 239 g | Fat: 63 g | Fiber: 6 g

## 246. Spiced Coco-Lime Skewered Shrimp

Ready in: 17 minutes | Servings: 2 | Difficulty: Easy

### Ingredients

- 1 lb. uncooked medium shrimp, peeled and deveined
- 2 garlic cloves
- 2 jalapeño peppers, seeded
- 1 lime, zested and juiced
- 1/3 c shredded coconut
- 1/3 c chopped fresh cilantro
- ¼ c olive oil
- ¼ c soy sauce

### Directions

1. Heat the soy sauce, olive oil, coconut, cilantro, garlic, lime juice, lime zest, and jalapeño in the food processor until smooth.
2. Mix the shrimp and dried marinade well into a shallow bowl Toss well for 3 hours to coat and sauté in ref.
3. Shrimps on the thread in skewers Put it in an Air Fryer on a skewer stand.
4. Cook at 360°F for 6 minutes Cook in batches if needed.
5. Enjoy and serve.

Nutrition: Calories: 118 | Protein: 85 g | Carbohydrates: 31 g | Fat: 86 g | Fiber: 11 g

## 247. Pecan Crusted Tilapia

Ready in: 35 minutes | Servings: 5 | Difficulty: Normal

### Ingredients

- 1 tsp garlic paste
- 2 tbsps. extra-virgin olive oil
- ½ c pecans, ground
- 5 tilapia fillets, slice into halves
- 2 tbsps. ground flaxseeds
- 1 tsp paprika
- Sea salt and white pepper, to taste

### Directions

1. In a Ziplock bag, blend the ground flaxseeds, paprika, salt, white pepper, garlic paste, olive oil, and ground pecans To cover properly, apply the fish fillets and shake.
2. Spray the basket of the Air Fryer with cooking oil Cook for 10 minutes in the hot oven Air Fryer at 400°F; turn over and bake for another 5 minutes In lots, work.
3. If needed, offer lemon wedges Enjoy!

Nutrition: Calories: 187 | Protein: 45 g | Carbohydrates: 316 g | Fat: 56 g | Fiber: 61 g

## 248. Crab Cakes

Ready in: 1 hour and 5 minutes | Servings: 4 |
Difficulty: Hard

### Ingredients

- ¼ c breadcrumbs
- 2 tbsps. chopped parsley
- Old bay seasoning, as desired
- Cooking spray
- ¼ c chopped red onion
- ¼ c chopped red pepper
- 3 tbsps. mayonnaise
- 1 tbsp. chopped basil
- ¼ c chopped celery
- Zest of ½ lemon

### Directions

1. Preheat the fryer to 390°F for air.
2. In a wide bowl, place all the ingredients and blend well.
3. Create 4 big mixed crab cakes and put them on a lined sheet of paper For 30 minutes, refrigerate.
4. Spay the air basket with cooking spray and organize it inside of the crab cakes.
5. Fry on each side for 10 minutes, when crispy.

Nutrition: Calories: 67 | Protein: 24 g | Carbohydrates: 9 g | Fat: 31 g | Fiber: 19 g

## 249. Sole Fish and Cauliflower Fritters

Ready in: 40 minutes | Servings: 2 | Difficulty: Hard

### Ingredients

- 1 tbsp. coconut aminos
- ½ tsp paprika
- Salt and white pepper, to taste
- ½ lb. sole fillets
- 2 tbsps. fresh parsley, chopped
- 1 bell pepper, finely chopped
- ½ tsp scotch bonnet pepper, minced
- ½ lb. mashed cauliflower
- 1 egg, well beaten
- ½ c red onion, chopped
- 2 garlic cloves, minced
- 1 tbsp. olive oil

### Directions

1. Begin by heating up to 395°F for your Air Fryer With cooking spray, spray the bottom and sides of the frying basket.
2. Fry the sole fillets for 10 minutes in the hot oven Air Fryer, turning them midway through the cooking process.
3. Then, mash the sole fillets into flakes in a mixing bowl Mix the rest of the ingredients in Form the mixture of the fish into patties.
4. Bake for 1 minute at 390°F in the hot oven Air Fryer, rotating them halfway through the cooking process Bon appétit!

Nutrition: Calories: 157 | Protein: 29 g | Carbohydrates: 153 g | Fat: 96 g | Fiber: 23 g

## 250. Louisiana-Style Shrimp

Ready in: 28 minutes | Servings: 4 | Difficulty: Normal

### Ingredients

- 2 tbsps. Cajun seasoning
- Salt and black pepper to taste
- 1 lemon, cut into wedges
- 1 egg, beaten
- ¼ c flour
- ¼ c white breadcrumbs
- Shrimps

### Directions

1. Preheat to 390°F for your Air Fryer Sprinkle the basket of the Air Fryer with cooking spray.

2. In a cup, beat the egg and season with some salt and black pepper Comb the white breadcrumbs with the Cajun seasoning in a different dish Drop the flour into the third bowl.
3. Soak the shrimp into the flour, then into the eggs, then into the mixture of breadcrumbs Spray and put it in the cooking basket with cooking spray Cook for 6 minutes, move the basket out of the fryer and turn; cook for a further 6 minutes Serve with slices of lemon.

Nutrition: Calories: 211 | Fat: 4 g | Fiber: 5 g | Carbohydrates: 14 g | Protein: 11 g

## 251. Grilled Salmon with Butter and Wine

Ready in: 55 minutes | Servings: 4 | Difficulty: Hard

### Ingredients

- 1 tbsp. lime juice
- ¼ c dry white wine
- 4 salmon steaks
- 2 cloves garlic, minced
- Sea salt and ground black pepper to taste
- 1 tsp smoked paprika
- 4 tbsps. butter, melted
- ½ tsp onion powder

### Directions

1. In a large ceramic bowl, put all of the items Wrap it and let it soak in the fridge for 30 minutes.
2. Organize the grilled pan with the salmon steaks Bake for 5 minutes, at 390°F, just until the salmon steaks are quickly fork-flaked.
3. Switch the steaks fish; baste them with the allocated marinade and simmer for another 5 minutes Bon appétit!

Nutrition: Calories: 231 | Fat: 4 g | Fiber: 7 g | Carbohydrates: 14 g | Protein: 15 g

## 252. Lemony-Parsley Linguine with Grilled Tuna

Ready in: 30 minutes | Servings: 2 | Difficulty: Normal

### Ingredients

- 2 c parsley leaves, chopped
- Juice from 1 lemon
- Salt and pepper to taste
- 1 tbsp. capers, chopped
- 1 tbsp. olive oil
- 12 oz. linguine, cooked according to package directions
- 1 lb. fresh tuna fillets

### Directions

1. Preheat the Air Fryer to 390°F.
2. Place the attachment for the grill pan in the Air Fryer.
3. Including salt and pepper, season the tuna with an oil-based brush.
4. Barbecue for 20 minutes.
5. Tear with forks until the tuna is fried and put on top of the fried linguine Insert the capers and parsley Season with pepper and salt and combine lemon juice.

Nutrition: Calories: 235 | Fat: 5 g | Fiber: 6 g | Carbohydrates: 14 g | Protein: 15 g

## 253. Tilapia with Cheesy Caper Sauce

Ready in: 20 minutes | Servings: 4 | Difficulty: Easy

**Ingredients**
- Celery salt, to taste
- Freshly cracked pink peppercorns, to taste
- 4 tilapia fillets
- 1 tbsp. extra-virgin olive oil

For the creamy caper sauce:
- ½ c Crème Fraiche
- 1 tbsp. capers, finely chopped
- 2 tbsps. mayonnaise
- ¼ c Cottage cheese, at room temperature

**Directions**

1. Sprinkle the olive oil, celery salt, and crushed peppercorns with the tilapia fillets until they are well seasoned.

2. At the Air Fryer frying basket base, put the fillets into a single plate Air fry for approximately 1 minute at 360°F; switch over once while baking.

3. In the meantime, by combining the remaining products, prepare the sauce.

4. Finally, garnish the sauce with the air-fried tilapia fillets and serve immediately!

Nutrition: **Calories: 235 | Fat: 5 g | Fiber: 6 g | Carbohydrates: 14 g | Protein: 15 g**

## 254. Crusty Pesto Salmon

Ready in: 20 minutes | Servings: 2 | Difficulty: Easy

**Ingredients**
- 2 (4 oz.) salmon fillets
- 2 tbsps. unsalted butter, melted
- ¼ c S roughly chopped
- ¼ c pesto

**Directions**

1. Bring together the S and the pesto.

2. Put the salmon fillets, about 6-inch in diameter, in a circular baking dish.

3. Brush the butter on the fillets, followed by the pesto paste, making sure the top and bottom are brushed Then placed them in the interior of the baking dish.

4. Simmer for 12 minutes at 390°F.

5. When it flakes quickly nudged with a fork, the salmon is primed Serve it hot.

Nutrition: **Calories: 235 | Fat: 5 g | Fiber: 6 g | Carbohydrates: 14 g | Protein: 15 g**

## 255. Shrimp Skewers

Ready in: 10 minutes | Servings: 5 | Difficulty: Easy

**Ingredients**
- 1 tsp ground cilantro
- 1 tbsp. avocado oil
- Cooking spray
- 4 lbs. shrimps, peeled
- 2 tbsps. fresh cilantro, chopped
- 2 tbsps. apple cider vinegar

**Directions**

1. Match the avocado oil, dried cilantro, apple cider vinegar, and new cilantro in a shallow dish After that, put the shrimp in a large bowl and spray it with a combination of avocado oil.

2. Mix them well and leave to marinate for a few minutes.

3. Preheat the Air Fryer to 400°F.

4. In an Air Fryer, place the shrimp skewers and cook them for 5 minutes.

Nutrition: **Calories: 254 | Fat: 12 g | Fiber: 6 g | Carbohydrates: 15 g | Protein: 20 g**

## 256. Herbed Trout Mix

Ready in: 30 minutes | Servings: 6 | Difficulty: Normal

**Ingredients**
- 4 trout fillets, boneless and skinless
- 1 tbsp. lemon juice
- 2 tbsps. olive oil
- 1 pinch of salt and black pepper
- 1 bunch asparagus, trimmed
- 2 tbsps. ghee, melted
- ¼ c mixed chives and tarragon

**Directions**

1. Mash half the oil, salt, and pepper with the asparagus, place it in the basket of your Air Fryer, cook for 5 minutes, at 380°F, and break between dishes.

2. Mix the trout with salt, pepper, lemon juice, the rest of the oil, and the herbs in a bowl and shake.

3. Place the fillets in the Air Fryer's basket and cook on either side at 380°F for 7 minutes.

4. Split the fish.

Nutrition: **Calories: 254 | Fat: 12 g | Fiber: 6 g | Carbohydrates: 15 g | Protein: 20 g**

## 257. Thyme Catfish

Ready in: 15 minutes | Servings: 4 | Difficulty: Easy

**Ingredients**
- 1 tsp apple cider vinegar
- 1 tsp avocado oil
- ¼ tsp cayenne pepper
- 1/3 c coconut flour
- 20 oz. (4 oz. each) catfish fillet
- 2 eggs, beaten
- 1 tsp dried thyme
- ½ tsp salt

**Directions**

1. Spray with dried thyme, salt, apple cider vinegar, eggs, cayenne pepper, and coconut flour over the catfish fillets.

2. Then brush avocado oil on the fish fillets.

3. Preheat the fryer to 385F for air.

4. In the Air Fryer basket, put the catfish fillets and cook them for 8 minutes After that, flip the fish to the other side and simmer for an additional 4 minutes.

Nutrition: **Calories: 254 | Fat: 12 g | Fiber: 6 g | Carbohydrates: 15 g | Protein: 20 g**

## 258. Lemony Grilled Halibut and Tomatoes

Ready in: 20 minutes | Servings: 4 | Difficulty: Easy

### Ingredients

- 4 halibut fillets
- Juice from 1 lemon
- Salt and pepper to taste
- ½ c hearts of palm, rinse and drained
- 1 c cherry tomatoes
- 2 tbsps. oil

### Directions

1. Preheat the Air Fryer to 390°F.
2. Put the attachment for the grill pan in the Air Fryer.
3. Mix lemon juice, salt, and pepper; season the halibut fillets—oil-based brush.
4. Put the fish in a barbecue pan.
5. On the side, place the palm hearts and cherry tomatoes and scatter with far more salt and pepper.
6. Cook for 15 minutes.

Nutrition: Calories: 241 | Fat: 4 g | Fiber: 8 g | Carbohydrates: 15 g | Protein: 16 g

## 259. Cajun Shrimps

Ready in: 11 minutes | Servings: 4 | Difficulty: Easy

### Ingredients

- 8 oz. shrimps, peeled
- 1 tsp Cajun seasonings
- 1 tsp cream cheese
- 1 egg, beaten
- ½ tsp salt
- 1 tsp avocado oil

### Directions

1. Spray Cajun seasoning and salt over the shrimps.
2. Combine cream cheese and egg in the mixing bowl and dip each shrimp in the egg mixture.
3. Preheat the Air Fryer to 400°F In an Air Fryer, arrange the shrimps and sprinkle them with avocado oil Cook the popcorn shrimps for 5 minutes Upon 3 minutes of frying, shake them good.

Nutrition: Calories: 241 | Fat: 4 g | Fiber: 8 g | Carbohydrates: 15 g | Protein: 16 g

## 260. Pollock with Kalamata Olives and Capers

Ready in: 30 minutes | Servings: 3 | Difficulty: Normal

### Ingredients

- 2 tbsps. capers
- 1 tsp oregano
- 1 tsp rosemary
- Sea salt, to taste
- ½ c white wine
- 2 cloves garlic, chopped
- 1 Florina pepper, deveined and minced
- 3 Pollock fillets, skinless
- 2 tbsps. olive oil
- 1 red onion, sliced
- 2 ripe tomatoes, diced
- 12 Kalamata olives, pitted and chopped

### Directions

1. Begin by heating up to 360°F for your Air Fryer In a baking pan, heat the oil When it is light, sauté the onion, garlic, and pepper for 2–3 minutes or until aromatic.
2. To the baking pan, apply the fish fillets Place the tomatoes, olives, and capers on top Spray with oregano, salt, and rosemary

Pour in the white wine and pass it to the basket for preparation.
3. Switch the heat down to 5°F and simmer for 10 minutes Season to taste and serve on individual dishes, if desired, garnished with some extra Mediterranean herbs Enjoy!

Nutrition: Calories: 241 | Fat: 4 g | Fiber: 7 g | Carbohydrates: 15 g | Protein: 15 g

## 261. Chinese Garlic Shrimp

Ready in: 20 minutes | Servings: 5 | Difficulty: Easy

### Ingredients

- ¼ tsp Chinese powder
- Chopped chili to taste
- Salt and black pepper to taste
- 4 garlic cloves
- Juice of 1 lemon
- 1 tsp sugar
- 3 tbsps. peanut oil
- 2 tbsps. cornstarch
- 2 scallions, chopped
- Shrimp

### Directions

1. Preheat the Air Fryer to 370°F Combine the lemon juice, sugar, spice, half the oil, the cornstarch, the pepper, the Chinese powder, and the salt in a Ziplock container To cover uniformly, put it in the shrimp and massage Let them wait for a few minutes.
2. In a pan, add remaining peanut oil, garlic, scallions, and chili, and fry over moderate flame for 5 minutes Put the brined shrimp in the basket of your Air Fryer and cover the sauce with it Cook until soft and crispy for 10 minutes Just serve.

Nutrition: Calories: 241 | Fat: 4 g | Fiber: 7 g | Carbohydrates: 15 g | Protein: 15 g

## 262. Savory Backload Tapas Recipe from Portugal

Ready in: 25 minutes | Servings: 4 | Difficulty: Normal

### Ingredients

- 1 lb. codfish fillet, chopped
- 2 hard-cooked eggs, chopped
- 2 tbsps. butter
- 2 Yukon Gold potatoes, peeled and diced
- ¾ tsp red pepper flakes
- 5 pitted black olives
- 5 pitted green olives
- freshly ground pepper to taste
- 1 clove garlic, chopped, divided
- 1 yellow onion, thinly sliced
- ¼ c chopped fresh parsley, divided
- ¼ c olive oil

### Directions

1. Lightly oil the Air Fryer baking pan with cooking oil At 360°F, melt the butter Mix in the onion and roast, until caramelized, for 5 minutes.
2. Mix the black pepper, the red pepper, half the parsley, the garlic, the olive oil, the sliced potatoes, and the sliced fish—Cook at 360°F for 10 minutes Mix well to blend midway across the cooking process.
3. Cook for 10 minutes until the tops are finely browned.
4. Garnish with the leftover parsley, black and green olives, and eggs.

Nutrition: Calories: 233 | Fat: 4 g | Fiber: 6 g | Carbohydrates: 15 g | Protein: 20 g

## 263. Fish and Chips II

Ready in: 35 minutes | Servings: 4 | Difficulty: Normal

### Ingredients

- 2 tbsps. flour
- 1 egg, beaten
- 1 c breadcrumbs
- Cooking spray
- Salt and black pepper to taste
- 4 white fish fillets

### Directions

1. Use olive oil to brush the slices and season with salt and black pepper.
2. Put them in an Air Fryer and cook at 400°F for 20 minutes.
3. Pour the flour and cover the fish on a tray.
4. Season with salt and black pepper and drop in the egg, then into the crumbs Bring the fish to the fryer at the 15 minutes mark and cook with the chips Heat until they're crispy.
5. Offer with mayo, ketchup, and lemon slices.

Nutrition: Calories: 233 | Fat: 4 g | Fiber: 6 g | Carbohydrates: 15 g | Protein: 20 g

## 264. Trout and Almond Butter Sauce

Ready in: 35 minutes | Servings: 5 | Difficulty: Normal

### Ingredients

- 4 trout fillets, boneless
- Cooking spray
- Salt and black pepper to taste

**For the sauce:**

- 1 c almond butter
- 4 tsps. soy sauce
- ¼ c lemon juice
- 1 tsp almond oil
- ¼ c water

### Directions

1. In your Air Fryer, place the fish fillets, season with salt and pepper, and oil with the frying spray.
2. Cook on each side for 5 minutes, at 380°F, and split between plates.
3. Cook the almond butter in a saucepan over medium heat, and combine the soy sauce, lemon juice, almond oil, and water.
4. Mix well the sauce and simmer for 2–3 minutes.
5. Sprinkle the sauce with almond butter over the fish and eat.

Nutrition: Calories: 310 | Fat: 6 g | Fiber: 4 g | Carbohydrates: 14 g | Protein: 20 g

## 265. Crab Cake Burgers

Ready in: 2 hours and 15 minutes | Servings: 3 | Difficulty: Hard

### Ingredients

- 1 c tortilla chips, crushed
- ½ tsp cayenne pepper
- ½ tsp ground black pepper
- Sea salt, to taste
- ¾ c fresh breadcrumbs
- 2 eggs, beaten
- 1 shallot, chopped
- 2 garlic cloves, crushed
- 1 tbsp. olive oil
- 1 tsp yellow mustard
- ü1 tsp fresh cilantro, chopped
- 10 oz. crab meat

### Directions

1. Mash the eggs, shallot, garlic, olive oil, mustard, cilantro, crab meat, tortilla chips, cayenne pepper, and black pepper with salt thoroughly in a mixing dish Mix once mixed properly.

2. Form 6 patties into the combination Soak the crab patties, covering well on both sides, into the fresh breadcrumbs Place it for 2 hours in your refrigerator.
3. Spritz the crab patties on both sides with cooking oil—Cook for 15 minutes in the preheated Air Fryer Offer if needed on dinner rolls Bon appétit!.

Nutrition: Calories: 287 | Fat: 10 g | Fiber: 2 g | Carbohydrates: 14 g | Protein: 19 g

## 266. Chili Loin Medallions

Ready in: 25 minutes | Servings: 4 | Difficulty: Normal

### Ingredients

- 1 tsp coconut oil, melted
- ½ tsp salt
- ½ tsp chili flakes
- 1 lb. pork loin
- 4 oz. bacon, sliced
- 1 tsp ground cumin

### Directions

1. Cut the beef medallions with the pork loin and dust with ground cumin, salt, and chili flakes.
2. Then wrap the sliced bacon with each meat medallion and spray it with coconut oil.
3. Put the wrapped medallions in one layer in the Air Fryer basket and cook at 375°F for a few minutes.
4. Then rotate the meat medallions gently on the other side and cook them for 5 more minutes.

Nutrition: Calories: 311 | Fat: 5 g | Fiber: 4 g | Carbohydrates: 13 g | Protein: 4 g

## 267. Air-Fried Grilled Steak

Ready in: 1 hour and 5 minutes | Servings: 2 | Difficulty: Hard

### Ingredients

- 3 tbsps. olive oil
- Salt and pepper to taste
- 2 top sirloin steaks
- 3 tbsps. butter, melted

### Directions

1. Preheat the Air Fryer for 5 minutes.
2. Including olive oil, salt, and pepper, season the sirloin steaks.
3. Put the beef in the basket of an Air Fryer.
4. Cook at 350°F for several minutes.
5. Offer with butter when baked.

Nutrition: Calories: 311 | Fat: 5 g | Fiber: 4 g | Carbohydrates: 13 g | Protein: 4 g

## 268. Fried Pork with Sweet and Sour Glaze

Ready in: 38 minutes | Servings: 4 | Difficulty: Normal

### Ingredients

- 2 lbs. pork chops cut into chunks
- 2 tbsps. cornstarch + 3 tbsps. water
- 5 tbsps. brown sugar
- Salt and pepper to taste
- ¼ c rice wine vinegar
- ¼ tsp Chinese 5-spice powder
- 1 c potato starch
- 1 green onion, chopped
- 2 large eggs, beaten

## Directions

1. Preheat the Air Fryer to 390°F.

2. Season the pork chops with salt and pepper to taste.

3. Soak the pork chops into the egg Only put aside.

4. Combine the potato starch and Chinese spice powder in a dish

5. Put the pork chops in the dry mixture.

6. Place and cook for 30 minutes in the double-layer rack.

7. In the meantime, in a saucepan, put the vinegar and the brown sugar To taste, season with salt and pepper Mix in the slurry of cornstarch and enable it to boil until thick.

8. Offer the sauce over the pork chops and garnish with green onions.

Nutrition: **Calories: 311 | Fat: 5 g | Fiber: 4 g | Carbohydrates: 13 g | Protein: 4 g**

## 269. Dill Beef and Artichokes

Ready in: 40 minutes | Servings: 4 | Difficulty: Hard

**Ingredients**

• 2 shallots, chopped
• 1 c beef stock
• 2 garlic cloves, minced
• ½ tsp dill, chopped

• 12 oz. artichoke hearts,drained and chopped
• 1 ½ lbs. beef stew meat, cubed
• 1 pinch of salt and black pepper
• 2 tbsps. olive oil

**Directions**

1. Over moderate high pressure, heat a pan that matches the Air Fryer with oil.

2. Insert the meat and brown for 5 minutes.

3. Except for the dill, introduce the remaining ingredients, move the pan to your Air Fryer and cook for 25 minutes at 380°F, shaking the Air Fryer in half.

4. Serve with the dill scattered on top.

Nutrition: **Calories: 254 | Fat: 6 g | Fiber: 4 g | Carbohydrates: 16 g | Protein: 22 g**

## 270. Rich Meatball and Mushroom Cassoulet

Ready in: 48 minutes | Servings: 4 | Difficulty: Hard

**Ingredients**

• ½ c heavy cream
• ½ c Monterey Jack cheese, preferably freshly grated
• ½ c celery, peeled and grated
• 1 ½ c mushrooms, sliced

**For the meatballs:**

• ½ tsp dried dill weed
• 2 small-sized egg
• ½ tsp cumin
• ½ tsp fine sea salt
• Freshly ground black pepper, to taste

• 2 tbsps. pork rinds
• 12 oz. lean ground pork
• 1 tsp saffron
• 2 tsps. Fennel seeds
• 1 medium-sized lee, finely chopped

**Directions**

1. Start by preheating to 400°F the Air Fryer.

2. Mix all the ingredients for the meatballs in a bowl Form into mini meatballs with the combination.

3. Simply throw the celery and mushrooms with the cream in an Air Fryer baking dish; cook in the hot oven Air Fryer for 2 minutes.

4. Stop the unit and put the allocated meatballs on top of the celery-mushroom mixture in a thin line.

5. Place the grated Monterey Jack cheese on top; cook for 9 extra minutes Serve it hot.

Nutrition: **Calories: 210 | Fat: 3 g | Fiber: 4 g | Carbohydrates: 12 g | Protein: 9 g**

## 271. Sirach-Hoisin Glazed Grilled Beef

Ready in: 3 hours 10 minutes | Servings: 5 | Difficulty: Normal

**Ingredients**

• ½ tsp sesame oil (optional)
• ½ tsp chili-garlic sauce
• 1 ½ tsps. toasted sesame seeds
• ¼ c hoisin sauce
• ¼ tsp crushed red pepper flakes
• ⅛ tsp ground black pepper
• 1 chopped green onion

• 1 ½ tsps. honey
• ½ clove garlic, minced
• 1 lb. flank steak, sliced at an angle 1x¼-inch thick
• 1 tbsp. lime juice
• ½ tsp kosher salt
• ½ tsp peeled and grated fresh ginger root

**Directions**

1. Combine pepper, red pepper flakes, chili sauce, sesame oil, ginger, salt, honey, garlic, lime juice, and hoisin sauce well in a shallow bowl To coat, add steak and toss well Caramelize for 3 hours with the ref.

2. Steak thread in skewers Put it in an Air Fryer on a skewer stand

3. Cook for 10 minutes Cook in groups if required.

4. Accompany with a downpour of green onions and sesame seeds and eat.

Nutrition: **Calories: 209 | Fat: 5 g | Fiber: 5 g | Carbohydrates: 13 g | Protein: 9 g**

## 272. Creamy Burger and Potato Bake

Ready in: 1 hour and 5 minutes | Servings: 3 | Difficulty: Hard

**Ingredients**

• 1 ½ c peeled and thinly sliced potatoes
• ½ c shredded Cheddar cheese
• ¼ c chopped onion
• ¼ c milk, plus 2 tbsps.
• Salt to taste
• Freshly ground pepper, to taste
• ½ (1075 oz.) can condense cream of mushroom soup
• ½ lb. lean ground beef

**Directions**

1. Lightly oil the Air Fryer baking pan with cooking spray Add ground beef Cook at 360°F for several minutes At cooking time, mix and break midway.

2. In the meantime, whisk the herb, salt, milk, onion, and mushroom soup into a cup Mix thoroughly.

3. Drain the fat from the ground beef and place the beef on a pan

4. Layer ½ of the potatoes on the bottom, then ½ of the soup mixture, and then ½ of the beef in the same Air Fryer baking tray Repeat.

5. Cover the pan with foil.

6. For 30 minutes, cook Remove the foil and simmer till the potatoes are moist, or for another 15 minutes.

7. Top with cheese Enjoy and serve.

Nutrition: **Calories: 209 | Fat: 5 g | Fiber: 5 g | Carbohydrates: 13 g | Protein: 9 g**

## 273. Grilled Beef Ribs

Ready in: 1 hour and 5 minutes | Servings: 4 | Difficulty: Hard

### Ingredients

- 1 chipotle powder
- 1 tsp fennel seeds
- 1 tsp hot paprika
- Kosher salt and black pepper, to taste
- ½ c vegetable oil
- 1 lb. meaty beef ribs
- 3 tbsps. apple cider vinegar
- 1 c cilantro, finely chopped
- 1 heaped tbsp. fresh basil leaves, chopped
- 2 garlic cloves, finely chopped

### Directions

1. Wash the ribs and dry them.

2. With the remaining supplies, cover the ribs and refrigerate for 3 hours.

3. Split the marinade from the ribs and position them on an Air Fryer grill tray.

4. Cook for 10 minutes at 360°F, or longer as desired.

5. Until serving right away, spill the leftover marinade over the ribs.

Nutrition: **Calories: 202 | Fat: 6 g | Fiber: 4 g | Carbohydrates: 8 g | Protein: 12 g**

## 274. Greek Souvlaki with Eggplant

Ready in: 1 hour and 50 minutes | Servings: 4 | Difficulty: Hard

### Ingredients

- 1 tbsp. yellow mustard
- 1 tbsp. Worcestershire sauce
- 1 c pearl onions
- 1 small-sized eggplant, 1 ½-inch cube
- Sea salt and ground black pepper, to taste
- 1 ½ lb. beef stew meat cubes
- ¼ c mayonnaise
- ¼ c sour cream

### Directions

1. Simply throw all ingredients in a mixing bowl until everything is well covered.

2. Put it in your fridge, seal it, and allow it to soak for 1 hour.

3. For 15 minutes, soak the wooden skewers in water.

4. Thread onto skewers with the beef balls, pearl onions, and eggplant Cook for 12 minutes in the preheated Air Fryer at 395°F, rotating halfway through the cooking process Serve it hot.

Nutrition: **Calories: 291 | Fat: 5 g | Fiber: 8 g | Carbohydrates: 10 g | Protein: 12 g**

## 275. Glazed Ham

Ready in: 55 minutes | Servings: 4 | Difficulty: Hard

### Ingredients

- 2 tbsps. French mustard
- 2 tbsps. honey
- 1 lb. (10 ½ oz.) ham joint
- ¾ c whiskey

### Directions

1. Preheat the 320°F Air Fryer and oil the pan with an Air Fryer.

2. Mix the ingredients, excluding ham, in a bowl.

3. Hold the ham joint at ambient temperature for around a few minutes and put it in the pan of the Air fryer.

4. Top, then switch to the Air Fryer with half of the whisky mixture.

5. Cook and flip the side for roughly 1 minute.

6. Use the leftover whisky mixture to coat and simmer for about 25 minutes.

7. Dish it out in a dish and serve it hot.

Nutrition: **Calories: 291 | Fat: 5 g | Fiber: 8 g | Carbohydrates: 10 g | Protein: 12 g**

## 276. Beef, Pearl Onions, and Cauliflower

Ready in: 1 hour and 50 minutes | Servings: 4 | Difficulty: Hard

### Ingredients

- 1 ½ lb. beef strip, cut into strips
- 1 (1 lb.) head cauliflower, broken into florets
- 1 c pearl onion, sliced

**For the marinade:**
- 1 tbsp. olive oil
- 2 cloves garlic, minced
- 1 tsp ground ginger
- ¼ c tomato paste
- ½ c red wine

### Directions

1. Combine with all of the marinade components Apply the marinade to the beef and let it rest for 1 hour in your fridge.

2. Preheat to 400°F for your Air Fryer Shift the meat to the basket with the Air Fryer Add the onions and Cauliflower.

3. Sprinkle all over the meat and vegetables with a few tbsp., of marinade Cook for 8 minutes, nearly halfway through the cooking process, rotating the basket Serve it warm.

Nutrition: **Calories: 291 | Fat: 5 g | Fiber: 8 g | Carbohydrates: 10 g | Protein: 12 g**

## 277. Beef Tips with Onion

Ready in: 15 minutes | Servings: 2 | Difficulty: Easy

### Ingredients

- 1 tsp onion powder
- 1 tsp garlic powder
- Salt and black pepper, to taste
- 1 lb. top round beef, cut into 1½-inch cubes
- ½ yellow onion, chopped
- 2 tbsps. Worcestershire sauce
- 1 tbsp. avocado oil

### Directions

1. Preheat the 360°F Air Fryer and oil the basket with an Air Fryer.

2. Combine the beef tips, onion, Worcestershire sauce, oil, and spices in a cup.

3. In the Air Fryer basket, place the beef mixture and cook for about 10 minutes.

4. Dish the steak combination onto serving plates and split to serve into slices of the required size.

Nutrition: **Calories: 199 | Fat: 3 g | Fiber: 5 g | Carbohydrates: 6 g | Protein: 11 g**

## 278. Pork Sausage with Mashed Cauliflower
Ready in: 30–35 minutes | Servings: 6 | Difficulty: Hard
**Ingredients**
- 1 tsp cumin powder
- ½ tsp sea salt
- 3 beaten eggs
- 6 pork sausages, chopped
- 1 lb. cauliflower, chopped
- ½ tsp tarragon
- 1/3 c Colby cheese
- ½ tsp ground black pepper
- ½ onion, peeled and sliced

**Directions**
1. Once tender, boil the Cauliflower After this, in your mixer, purée the Cauliflower Move it with the other products to a mixing bowl.

2. Divide 6 thinly oiled ramekins into the prepared mixture; now, put the ramekins in your Air Fryer.

3. Bake for 27 minutes in the preheated Air Fryer Serve warm.

Nutrition: **Calories: 223 | Fat: 2 g | Fiber: 4 g | Carbohydrates: 11 g | Protein: 8 g**

## 279. Pork Belly with Sweet–Sour Sauce
Ready in: 1 hour and 15 minutes | Servings: 4 | Difficulty: Hard
**Ingredients**
- 2 tbsps. hoisin sauce
- 3 tbsps. brown sugar
- 3-star anise
- Salt and pepper to taste
- ¼ c lemon juice
- ½ c soy sauce
- 1 bay leaf
- 2 lbs. pork belly

**Directions**
1. Put all the ingredients in a Ziplock bag and wait for at least 2 hours to marinate in the refrigerator.

2. Preheat the Air Fryer to 390°F.

3. Insert the attachment for the grill pan in the Air Fryer.

4. Grill the pork for at least 20 minutes per batch.

5. Please ensure to flip the pork every 10 minutes.

6. To serve, chop the pork and garnish it with green onions.

Nutrition: **Calories: 223 | Fat: 2 g | Fiber: 4 g | Carbohydrates: 11 g | Protein: 8 g**

## 280. Cheesy Beef Meatballs
Ready in: 44 minutes | Servings: 8 | Difficulty: Hard
**Ingredients**
- ¼ c fresh parsley, chopped
- 1 small garlic clove, chopped
- 1 tsp dried oregano, crushed
- Salt and black pepper to taste
- 2 lbs. ground beef
- 1 ¼ c breadcrumbs

- ¼ c Parmigiano-Reggiano cheese, grated
- 2 large eggs

**Directions**
1. Preheat the Air Fryer to 350°F, and oil it.

2. In a bowl, mix all of the ingredients until integrated.

3. Form the mixture gently into 2-inch balls and arrange half the meatballs in the Air Fryer basket.

4. Fry and turn the side for about 10 minutes.

5. Fry and dish out for about a few minutes to serve warm.

Nutrition: **Calories: 269 | Fat: 5 g | Fiber: 6 g | Carbohydrates: 13 g | Protein: 12 g**

## 281. Creamy Cheesy Bacon Dip
Ready in: 17 minutes | Servings: 6 | Difficulty: Easy
**Ingredients**
- 1 tbsp. chives, chopped
- 1 tsp avocado oil
- ½ tsp salt
- 6 oz. bacon, chopped
- 6 tsps. cream cheese
- ½ c heavy cream
- 1 tsp dried sage
- 1 c Monterey Jack cheese, shredded
- ½ tsp chili flakes

**Directions**
1. Preheat the fryer to 400°F for air.

2. In an Air Fryer, place the chopped bacon in it and cook for 6 minutes.

3. After 3 minutes in the oven, mix.

4. Place the cooked bacon in the baking pan after that.

5. Add the cream cheese, the heavy cream, the Monterey Jack cheese, the flakes of chili, the chives, the avocado oil, the sage, and the salt Mix the mixture up.

6. Clean the basket of the Air Fryer and insert the casserole dish inside with bacon dip.

7. Cook it for 5 minutes at 385°F.

Nutrition: **Calories: 205 | Fat: 8 g | Fiber: 3 g | Carbohydrates: 12 g | Protein: 6 g**

## 282. Spicy Bacon–Pork Pops
Ready in: 40 minutes | Servings: 6 | Difficulty: Hard
**Ingredients**
- 1 tsp curry powder
- 2 lbs. pork tenderloin, cut into bite-sized cubes
- 4 oz. bacon, cut into pieces
- 12 bamboo skewers, soaked in water
- 1 c cream of celery soup
- 1 (13 ½ oz.) coconut milk, unsweetened
- 2 tbsps. tamari sauce
- 1 tsp yellow mustard
- Salt and freshly ground white pepper, to taste
- ½ tsp cayenne pepper
- ½ tsp chili powder

**Directions**
1. Put the celery soup cream, coconut milk, tamari sauce, mus-

tard, salt, white pepper, cayenne pepper, chili powder, and curry powder to a boil in a large saucepan.

2. Then raise the heat to simmer; cook for about 13 minutes till the liquid is cooked through.

3. Include the bacon, whisk softly, and put for 2 hours in your refrigerator.

4. Thread the pork into the skewers, replacing the beef cubes with the bacon bits.

5. Preheat to 370°F with your Air Fryer Cook for 1 minute, backing down a few times Bon appétit!

Nutrition: Calories: 245 | Fat: 2 g | Fiber: 3 g | Carbohydrates: 5 g | Protein: 6 g

## 283. Beef Recipe Texas-Rodeo Style
Ready in: 1 hour and 32 minutes | Servings: 6 | Difficulty: Hard

**Ingredients**
- 2 onions, chopped
- 3 lbs. beef steak sliced
- Salt and pepper to taste
- ½ c honey
- ½ c ketchup
- ½ tsp dry mustard
- 1 clove of garlic, minced
- 1 tbsp. chili powder

**Directions**
1. Place all the ingredients in a Ziplock bag and wait for at least 2 hours to marinate in the fridge.
2. Preheat the Air Fryer to 390°F.
3. Put the attachment for the grill pan in the Air Fryer.
4. Grill the beef for 15 minutes per batch to guarantee that you flip it for grilling every 8 minutes.
5. In the meantime, pour the marinade over a saucepan and allow boiling until the sauce thickens over moderate flame.
6. Until cooking, baste the beef with sauce.

Nutrition: Calories: 245 | Fat: 2 g | Fiber: 3 g | Carbohydrates: 5 g | Protein: 6 g

## 284. Cheesy Meatball and Mushroom Casserole
Ready in: 55 minutes | Servings: 4 | Difficulty: Hard

**Ingredients**
- 1 ½ c mushrooms, sliced
- 3 carrots, peeled and shredded
- 1/3 c cream
- 1/3 c Monterey Jack cheese, preferably freshly grated
For the meatballs:
- 2 medium-sized leeks, finely chopped
- ½ tsp dried dill weed
- 2 small-sized egg
- ½ tsp cumin
- 10 oz. lean ground pork
- 1 tsp saffron
- 2 tsps. fennel seeds
- ½ tsp fine sea salt

- Freshly ground black pepper, to taste
- 2 tbsps. Italian breadcrumbs

**Directions**
1. Start by warming the Air Fryer to 400°F for preheating.
2. Mix the ingredients for the meatballs in a dish Shape into mini meatballs with the combination.
3. Simply throw the carrots and mushrooms with the cream in an Air Fryer baking dish; cook in the preheated Air Fryer for 2 minutes.
4. Stop the unit and put the allocated meatballs on the upper edge of the carrot/mushroom mixture in a single layer.
5. Place the grated Monterey Jack cheese on top; bake for 9 extra minutes Serve it hot.

Nutrition: Calories: 210 | Fat: 12 g | Fiber: 3 g | Carbohydrates: 10 g | Protein: 23 g

## 285. Skirt Steak with Veggies
Ready in: 15 minutes | Servings: 4 | Difficulty: Easy

**Ingredients**
- ½ lb. fresh mushrooms, quartered
- 6 oz. snow peas
- 1 onion, cut into half rings
- Salt and ground black pepper, as required
- ¼ c olive oil, divided
- 2 tbsps. soy sauce
- 2 tbsps. honey
- 1 (12 oz.) skirt steak, cut into thin strips

**Directions**
1. Mix tablespoons of the oil, soy sauce, and honey in a cup.
2. Insert the strips of steak and cover them appropriately with the oil mixture.
3. Add the onion, leftover oil, salt, and black pepper to another dish To coat properly, turn.
4. Let the Air Fryer temperature to 390°F Oil the Air Fryer basket, place steak strips and vegetables.
5. Air fry for around 5 minutes or before frying is needed.
6. Remove from the Air Fryer and put the steak before slicing on a cutting board for about 10 minutes.
7. Cut every steak into slices of the desired size and pass them to serving plates.
8. Serve alongside the veggies instantly.

Nutrition: Calories: 210 | Fat: 12 g | Fiber: 3 g | Carbohydrates: 10 g | Protein: 23 g

## 286. Comforting Sausage Casserole
Ready in: 40 minutes | Servings: 4 | Difficulty: Hard

**Ingredients**
- 8 small sausages
- 1 tbsp. olive oil

- 1 garlic clove, minced
- Salt and black pepper, to taste
- 6 oz. flour
- 2 eggs
- 1 red onion, sliced thinly
- ¾ c milk
- 2 c water
- Rosemary to taste

**Directions**

1. Preheat the 320°F Air Fryer and oil a casserole platter.
2. In a cup, sift the flour and whisk the eggs in.
3. Add the onion, garlic, cream, cold water, salt, and black pepper, and mix well.
4. Pierce each sausage with rosemary sprig and pass it to the casserole dish.
5. Cover uniformly with the mixture of flour and simmer for 30 minutes or so.
6. Dish out, serve hot.

Nutrition: **Calories: 210 | Fat: 12 g | Fiber: 3 g | Carbohydrates: 10 g | Protein: 23 g**

## 287. Tangy Pork Chops with Vermouth
Ready in: 25-35 minutes | Servings: 5 | Difficulty: Hard

**Ingredients**

- ½ lemon, cut into wedges
- 1 tsp freshly cracked black pepper
- 3 tbsps. lemon juice
- 3 cloves garlic, minced
- 2 tbsps. canola oil
- 5 pork chops
- 1/3 c vermouth
- ½ tsp paprika
- 2 sprigs thyme, only leaves, crushed
- ½ tsp dried oregano
- Fresh parsley, to serve
- 1 tsp garlic salt

**Directions**

1. First, melt the canola oil over low heat in a saucepan Sweat the garlic now until it's all fragrant.
2. Take the pan from the fire and add in the vermouth and lemon juice Then, put your seasonings in there Load the sauce into the mixture of a baking bowl, along with the chops of pork.
3. Tuck the lemon wedges between the pork chops and air fry for 27 minutes Serve garnish with parsley Bon appétit!.

Nutrition: **Calories: 190 | Fat: 3 g | Fiber: 4 g | Carbohydrates: 7 g | Protein: 10 g**

## 288. Traditional Walliser Schnitzel
Ready in: 25 minutes | Servings: 2 | Difficulty: Normal

**Ingredients**

- ½ c pork rinds
- 2 eggs, beaten

- ½ tsp fennel seed
- 2 pork schnitzel, halved
- 1/3 tbsp. cider vinegar
- 1/3 tsp ground black pepper
- 1 tsp garlic salt
- ½ tsp mustard
- ½ heaping tbsp. fresh parsley

**Directions**

1. Blitz your food processor with vinegar, black pepper, garlic salt, mustard, fennel seeds, fresh parsley, and pork rinds until standardized and smooth.
2. In a small bowl, pour the mixed mixture into it In another small bowl, add the beaten eggs.
3. Use the beaten egg to cover the pork schnitzel, and then dredge them in the herb mixture.
4. Cook for around 1 minute at 355°F in the preheated Air Fryer Bon appétit!

Nutrition: **Calories: 250 | Fat: 5 g | Fiber: 3 g | Carbohydrates: 7 g | Protein: 12 g**

# CHAPTER 5

## SLIDE DISH RECIPES

## 289. Creamy Endives

Ready in: 35 minutes | Servings: 8 | Difficulty: Normal

**Ingredients**

- 5 tbsps. lemon juice
- Salt and black pepper according to your taste
- 1 tsp curry powder
- 1 c Greek yogurt
- 2 tsps. garlic powder
- 8 endives, trimmed and halved

**Directions**

1. Mix the endives with the garlic powder, curry powder, yogurt, pepper, salt, and lemon juice in a pot, mix well, leave for about 10 minutes and move to the 350°F preheated Air Fryer.

2. For about 10 minutes, roast the endives, split them into dishes, and use them as a side dish Enjoy!

Nutrition: **Calories: 250 | Fat: 5 g | Fiber: 3 g | Carbohydrates: 7 g | Protein: 12 g**

## 290. Pita-Style Chips

Ready in: 15 minutes | Servings: 4 | Difficulty: Easy

**Ingredients**

- 1 large egg
- ¼ c blanched finely ground almond flour
- ½ oz. pork rinds, finely ground
- 1 c shredded Mozzarella cheese

**Directions**

1. Put Mozzarella in a wide oven-safe dish and microwave for about 30 seconds or until melted Add the rest of the ingredients and mix until largely smooth dough shapes into a ball quickly; if your dough is too hard, microwave for an additional 15 seconds.

2. Roll the dough into a wide rectangle among 2 parchment paper sheets and then use a sharp knife to make the triangle-shaped chips Put the prepared chips in the bucket of your Air Fryer.

3. Set the temperature and adjust the clock to about 350°F for around 5 minutes.

4. Chips, when finished, would be golden in color and crunchy When they cool down, they will become even crispier.

Nutrition: **Calories: 230 | Fat: 5 g | Fiber: 5 g | Carbohydrates: 12 g | Protein: 9 g**

## 291. Avocado Fries

Ready in: 20 minutes | Servings: 4 | Difficulty: Easy

**Ingredients**

- 1 oz. pork rinds, finely ground
- 2 medium avocados

**Directions**

1. Split each avocado in half Now have the pit removed Peel the outer gently and then split the flesh into ¼-inch-thick strips.

2. Put the pork rinds in a medium-sized pot and drop each slice of avocado onto your pork rinds to cover it fully Put the pieces of avocado in the bucket of your Air Fryer.

3. Set the temperature and adjust the clock to about 350°F for around 5 minutes.

4. Instantly serve.

Nutrition: **Calories: 214 | Fat: 3 g | Fiber: 3 g | Carbohydrates: 14 g | Protein: 15 g**

## 292. Flatbread

Ready in: 20 minutes | Servings: 4 | Difficulty: Easy

**Ingredients**

- 1 oz. full-fat cream cheese softened
- ¼ c blanched finely ground almond flour
- 1 c shredded Mozzarella cheese

**Directions**

1. Melt some Mozzarella in your microwave for about 30 seconds in a wide oven-safe container Mix in some almond flour to make it smooth, and add some cream cheese to the mix Proceed to blend until dough shapes, slowly kneading using wet hands if needed.

2. Split the dough into 2 parts and roll between 2 pieces of parchment paper to a thickness of about ¼-inch Cut an extra piece of parchment paper to fit in the container of your Air Fryer.

3. Put a small piece of flatbread; try working in 2 batches if necessary, on your parchment paper and into the Air Fryer.

4. Set the temperature and adjust the clock to about 320°F for around 7 minutes.

5. Rotate the flatbread midway through the cooking process Serve it hot.

Nutrition : **Calories: 214 | Fat: 3 g | Fiber: 3 g | Carbohydrates: 14 g | Protein: 15 g**

## 293. Radish Chips

Ready in: 15 minutes | Servings: 4 | Difficulty: Easy

**Ingredients**

- 2 tbsps. coconut oil, melted
- ½ tsp garlic powder
- ¼ tsp paprika
- ¼ tsp onion powder
- 1 lb. radishes
- 2 c water

**Directions**

1. Put the water in a medium-sized saucepan and bring the water to a boil.

2. Cut the upper part and bottom of each radish, then cut each radish thinly and evenly using a mandolin For this stage, you can use the cutting blade in your food processor.

3. For about 5 minutes or until transparent, put the radish pieces in hot water To trap extra humidity, extract them from the boiling water and put them on a dry paper towel.

4. In a wide pot, combine the radish pieces and the rest of the ingredients until thoroughly covered in oil and seasoned Put the radish chips in the basket of an Air Fryer.

5. Set the temperature and adjust the clock to about 320°F for around 5 minutes.

6. During the cooking process, rotate the basket at least 2–3 times Serve it hot.

Nutrition: **Calories: 220 | Fat: 4 g | Fiber: 2 g | Carbohydrates: 12 g | Protein: 10 g**

## 294. Coconut Flour Cheesy Garlic Biscuits

Ready in: 22 minutes | Servings: 4 | Difficulty: Easy

**Ingredients**

- 1 scallion, sliced
- ½ c shredded sharp Cheddar cheese
- ¼ c unsalted butter, melted and divided
- 1 large egg
- ½ tsp garlic powder
- ½ tsp baking powder
- 1/3 c coconut flour

**Directions**

1. Combine the baking powder, coconut flour, and garlic powder in a wide dish.

2. Add half the melted butter, some Cheddar cheese, egg, and scallions, and mix well Pour the mixture into a rectangular 6-inch baking tray Put it in the basket of your Air Fryer.

3. Set the temperature and adjust the clock to about 320°F for around a 12 minutes timer.

4. Take out from the pan to enable it to cool thoroughly Slice into 4 parts and add leftover melted butter on top of each piece.

Nutrition: **Calories: 260 | Fat: 5 g | Fiber: 11 g | Carbohydrates: 30 g | Protein: 24 g**

## 295. Dinner Rolls

Ready in: 22 minutes | Servings: 6 | Difficulty: Easy

**Ingredients**

- 1 large egg
- ½ tsp baking powder
- ¼ c ground flaxseed
- 1 c blanched finely ground almond flour
- 1 oz. full-fat cream cheese
- 1 c shredded Mozzarella cheese

**Directions**

1. In a big oven-safe dish, put the cream cheese, Mozzarella, and almond flour Microwave for about 1 minute Blend until smooth.

2. When thoroughly mixed and soft, add baking powder, flaxseed, and egg Suppose the dough is too hard, microwave for an extra 15 seconds.

3. Split your dough into 6 portions and shape it into small balls Put the balls into the bucket of your Air Fryer.

4. Set the temperature and adjust the clock to about 320°F for around a 12 minutes timer.

5. Let the rolls cool fully before serving.

Nutrition: **Calories: 260 | Fat: 5 g | Fiber: 11 g | Carbohydrates: 30 g | Protein: 24 g**

## 296. Cilantro Lime Roasted Cauliflower

Ready in: 17 minutes | Servings: 4 | Difficulty: Easy

**Ingredients**

- 2 tbsps. chopped cilantro
- 1 medium lime
- ½ tsp garlic powder
- 2 tsps. chili powder
- 2 tbsps. coconut oil, melted
- 2 c chopped cauliflower florets

**Directions**

1. Toss your cauliflower with coconut oil in a big dish Dust some garlic powder and chili powder Put the prepared cauliflower in the bucket of your Air Fryer.

2. Set the temperature and adjust the clock to about 350°F for around 7 minutes.

3. At the sides, the cauliflower would be soft and starting to become golden Put in the serving dish.

4. Slice the lime and squeeze the juice over your cauliflower Garnish using cilantro.

Nutrition: **Calories: 330 | Fat: 7 g | Sodium: 360 mg | Carbohydrates: 57 g | Fiber: 8 g | Protein: 14 g**

## 297. Green Bean Casserole

Ready in: 25 minutes | Servings: 4 | Difficulty: Easy

**Ingredients**

- ½ oz. pork rinds, finely ground
- 1 lb. fresh green beans, edges trimmed
- ¼ tsp xanthan gum
- ½ c chicken broth
- 1 oz. full-fat cream cheese
- ½ c heavy whipping cream
- ½ c chopped white mushrooms
- ¼ c diced yellow onion
- 4 tbsps. unsalted butter

**Directions**

1. Melt some butter in a medium-sized skillet over medium flame Sauté the mushrooms and onion for around 3–5 minutes before they become tender and fragrant.

2. Transfer the cream cheese, heavy whipped cream, and broth Mix until thick Bring it to a boil and decrease the flame to let it simmer Sprinkle your xanthan into the pan and turn off the flame.

3. Cut the green beans into 2-inch pieces and put them in a circular 4-cup baking tray Pour the combination of sauce over them and swirl until they are covered Cover the dish with the rinds of ground pork Place it in the bucket of your Air Fryer.

4. Set the temperature and adjust the clock to about 320°F for around 15 minutes.

5. When completely baked, the top will be golden brown, and green beans would be fork tender Serve it hot.

Nutrition: **Calories: 174 | Fat: 10 g | Sodium: 36 mg | Carbohydrates: 20 g | Protein: 4 g**

## 298. Buffalo Cauliflower

Ready in: 10 minutes | Servings: 4 | Difficulty: Easy

**Ingredients**

- ¼ c buffalo sauce
- ½ (1 oz.) dry ranch seasoning packet
- 2 tbsps. salted butter, melted
- 4 c cauliflower florets

**Directions**

1. Toss the cauliflower with the butter and dry ranch in a wide pot Place it in the bucket of your Air Fryer.

2. Set the temperature and adjust the clock to about 400°F for around 5 minutes.

3. During frying, rotate the basket at least 2–3 times Take out the cauliflower from the fryer basket when soft, and then toss in the buffalo sauce Serve it hot.

Nutrition: **Calories: 174 | Fat: 10 g | Sodium: 36 mg | Carbohydrates: 20 g | Protein: 4 g**

## 299. Kale Chips

Ready in: 10 minutes | Servings: 4 | Difficulty: Easy

**Ingredients**

- ½ tsp salt
- 2 tsps. avocado oil
- 4 c stemmed kale

**Directions**

1. Toss the kale in some avocado oil in a wide bowl and dust it with some salt Put it in the bucket of your Air Fryer.

2. Set the temperature and adjust the clock to about 400°F for around 5 minutes.

3. Kale, when cooked completely, would be crisp Instantly serve.

Nutrition: **Calories: 174 | Fat: 10 g | Sodium: 36 mg | Carbohydrates: 20 g | Protein: 4 g**

## 300. Roasted Garlic

Ready in: 32 minutes | Servings: 2 | Difficulty: Normal

**Ingredients**

- 2 tsps. avocado oil
- 1 medium head garlic

**Directions**

1. Remove the garlic from any remaining excess peel However, keep the cloves protected Slice ¼ of the garlic head off, showing the tops of the cloves.

2. Add your avocado oil to it In a small layer of aluminum foil, put the garlic head, tightly enclosing it Put it in the bucket of your Air Fryer.

3. Set the temperature and adjust the clock to about 400°F for around 20 minutes Monitor it after about 15 minutes if the garlic head is a little shorter.

4. Garlic should be nicely browned when finished and very tender.

5. Cloves can pop out to eat and be scattered or sliced quickly Up to 2–5 in an airtight jar store in the fridge You can even freeze individual cloves on a baking tray and then put them together in a fridge-safe storage bag when frozen completely.

Nutrition: **Calories: 122 | Fat: 5 g | Sodium: 157 mg | Carbohydrates: 30 g | Fiber: 78 g | Protein: 34 g**

## 301. Zucchini Parmesan Chips

Ready in: 20 minutes | Servings: 4 | Difficulty: Easy

**Ingredients**

- ½ c grated Parmesan cheese
- 1 large egg
- 1 oz. pork rinds
- 2 medium zucchinis

**Directions**

1. Cut zucchini into thick slices of about ¼-inch To extract excess water, put on 1 dry kitchen towel or 2 paper towels for around 30 minutes.

2. Put pork rinds and process until finely ground in the food processor Put into a medium-sized bowl and blend with Parmesan

3. In a shallow bowl, beat your egg.

4. Add the egg into pork rind mixture; soak zucchini pieces in it, covering as thoroughly as possible Put each piece gently in a thin layer in the Air Fryer bucket, working as required in groups or individually.

5. Set the temperature and adjust the clock to about 320°F for around 10 minutes.

6. Midway through the cooking process, turn your chips Serve hot.

Nutrition: **Calories: 287 | Protein: 124 g | Carbohydrates: 504 g**

## 302. Crispy Brussels Sprouts

Ready in: 15 minutes | Servings: 4 | Difficulty: Easy

**Ingredients**

- 1 tbsp. unsalted butter, melted
- 1 tbsp. coconut oil
- 1 lb. Brussels sprouts

**Directions**

1. Remove all of the loose leaves from the Brussels sprouts and break them in half.

2. Sprinkle the sprouts with some coconut oil and placed them in the bowl of your Air Fryer.

3. Set the temperature and adjust the clock to about 400°F for around 10 minutes Based on how they tend to cook, you might want to softly mix midway through the cooking period.

4. They should be soft with deeper caramelized spots when fully baked Take out from the bucket of fryers and drizzle some melted butter Serve instantly.

Nutrition: **Calories: 287 | Protein: 124 g | Carbohydrates: 504 g | Fat: 42 g | Fiber: 9 g | Cholesterol: 0 mg**

## 303. Cheesy Cauliflower Tots

Ready in: 25 minutes | Servings: 4 | Difficulty: Easy

**Ingredients**

- ⅛ tsp onion powder
- ¼ tsp dried parsley
- ¼ tsp garlic powder
- 1 large egg
- ½ c grated Parmesan cheese
- 1 c shredded Mozzarella cheese
- 1 large head cauliflower
- 2 c water

**Directions**

1. Fill a big pot with 2 c water on the cooktop and put a steamer in the pot Bring the water to a boil Chop the cauliflower into florets and put it on a steamer bowl Close the pot with a lid.

2. Enable cauliflower to steam for around 7 minutes before they are tender fork Take out your cauliflower from the steamer basket and put it in a cheesecloth or dry kitchen towel, and leave it

to cool down Squeeze over the sink and extract as much extra moisture as necessary If all the moisture is not extracted, the mixture would be too fragile to shape into tots Crush to a smooth consistency using a fork.

3. Add in some Parmesan, Mozzarella, parsley, garlic powder, egg, and onion powder, and place the cauliflower in a big mixing dish Stir when thoroughly mixed The paste should be sticky but hard to shape.

4. Roll into tot form by taking 2 tablespoons of the mix Repeat for the remaining mixture Put in the bucket of your Air Fryer

5. Set the temperature and adjust the clock to about 320°F for around 12 minutes.

6. Switch tots midway through the cooking period When fully baked, cauliflower tots should be crispy Serve hot.

Nutrition: Calories: 99 | Protein: 29 g | Carbohydrates: 113 g | Fat: 5 g | Fiber: 18 g

## 304. Sausage-Stuffed Mushroom Caps

Ready in: 18 minutes | Servings: 2 | Difficulty: Easy

**Ingredients**
• 1 tsp minced fresh garlic
• ¼ c grated Parmesan cheese
• 2 tbsps. blanched finely ground almond flour
• ¼ c chopped onion
• ½ lb. Italian sausage
• 6 large Portobello mushroom caps

**Directions**

1. Using a spoon, voiding scrapings, to hollow out each mushroom shell.

2. Brown the sausage for approximately 10 minutes or until thoroughly baked, and no red exists in a small-sized skillet over medium flame Drain and then add some reserved mushroom scrapings, Parmesan, almond flour, onion, and garlic Fold ingredients softly together and proceed to cook for an extra minute, and then remove from flame.

3. Pour the mixture uniformly into mushroom caps and put the caps in a circular 6-inch pot Put the pan in the bucket of your Air Fryer.

4. Set the temperature and adjust the clock to about 375°F for around 8 minutes.

5. The tops would be browned and fizzing when it is cooked completely Serve it hot.

Nutrition: Calories: 94 | Protein: 54 g | Carbohydrates: 142 g | Fat: 36 g

## 305. Garlic Herb Butter Roasted Radishes

Ready in: 20 minutes | Servings: 4 | Difficulty: Easy

**Ingredients**
• ¼ tsp ground black pepper
• ¼ tsp dried oregano
• ½ tsp dried parsley
• ½ tsp garlic powder
• 2 tbsps. unsalted butter, melted
• 1 lb. radishes

**Directions**

1. Remove the radish roots and split them into quarters.

2. Put seasonings and butter in a shallow dish In the herb butter, turn the radishes and put them in your Air Fryer basket.

3. Set the temperature and adjust the clock to about 350°F for around 10 minutes.

4. Simply throw the radishes in the Air Fryer basket midway through the cooking time Keep cooking until the edges start to turn dark brown.

5. Serve it hot.

Nutrition: Calories: 59 | Protein: 11 g | Carbohydrates: 109 g | Fat: 17 g

## 306. Loaded Roasted Broccoli

Ready in: 20 minutes | Servings: 4 | Difficulty: Easy

**Ingredients**
• 1 scallion, sliced on the bias
• 4 slices sugar-free bacon, cooked and crumbled
• ¼ c full-fat sour cream
• ½ c shredded sharp Cheddar cheese
• 1 tbsp. coconut oil
• 3 c fresh broccoli florets

**Directions**

1. In the Air Fryer basket, put the broccoli and drizzle with some coconut oil.

2. Set the temperature and adjust the clock to about 350°F for around 10 minutes.

3. During frying, turn the basket at least 2–3 times to prevent burning.

4. Remove from the fryer as the broccoli continues to crisp at the ends Garnish with some scallion slices and finish with sour cream, shredded cheese, and crumbled bacon.

Nutrition: Calories: 59 | Protein: 11 g | Carbohydrates: 109 g | Fat: 17 g

## 307. Roasted Peppers

Ready in: 25 minutes | Servings: 4 | Difficulty: Easy

**Ingredients**
• 2 yellow onions, chopped
• 6 yellow bell peppers, cut into medium strips
• 6 green bell peppers, cut into medium strips
• 6 red bell peppers, cut into medium strips
• 2 tbsps. olive oil
• 2 tbsps. sweet paprika
• Salt and black pepper according to your taste

**Directions**

1. Mix the red bell peppers with the green and yellow ones in your Air Fryer.

2. Add some oil, paprika, salt, onion, and black pepper, mix, and bake for about 20 minutes at around 350°F.

3. Split as a side dish between plates and eat Enjoy!

Nutrition: Calories: 105 | Protein: 32 g | Carbohydrates: 88 g | Fat: 75 g | Fiber: 8 g

## 308. Herbed Tomatoes

Ready in: 35 minutes | Servings: 5 | Difficulty: Normal

**Ingredients**

• 1 tsp thyme, chopped
• 3 garlic cloves, minced
• 2 tbsps. olive oil
• Salt and black pepper according to your taste
• 5 big tomatoes, halved and insides scooped out

**Directions**

1. Mix the tomatoes and pepper, salt, garlic, oil, and thyme in your Air Fryer, combine and cook at around 390°F for about 15 minutes.
2. Split into dishes and enjoy as a side dish with your favorite food.

Nutrition: **Calories: 105 | Protein: 32 g | Carbohydrates: 88 g | Fat: 75 g | Fiber: 8 g**

## 309. Zucchini Fries

Ready in: 35 minutes | Servings: 5 | Difficulty: Normal

**Ingredients**

• 1 c flour
• 2 c breadcrumbs
• 3 eggs, whisked
• Salt and black pepper according to your taste
• 1 drizzle of olive oil
• 2 zucchinis, cut into medium sticks

**Directions**

1. Put the flour in a container and add salt and pepper to the mixture and shake it to mix well.
2. Put some breadcrumbs in a separate bowl.
3. Mix the eggs along with a touch of salt and pepper in a third bowl.
4. Add flour, dredge zucchini fries, then add eggs, and at last, breadcrumbs.
5. Oil your Air Fryer with some olive oil, warm it up to around 400°F, add the zucchini fries, and cook for about 12 minutes.
6. Offer as a side dish for everyone Enjoy!

Nutrition: **Calories: 108 | Protein: 5 g | Carbohydrates: 89 g | Fat: 73 g | Fiber: 48 g**

## 310. Cheddar Biscuits

Ready in: 40 minutes | Servings: 10 | Difficulty: Hard

**Ingredients**

• 2 c flour
• 2 1/3 c buttermilk
• 1 c Cheddar cheese, grated
• 3 tbsps. sugar
• 1 c butter + 1 tbsp. melted
• 3 1/3 c self-rising flour

**Directions**

1. Mix 1 c butter, Cheddar cheese, sugar, and buttermilk in a bowl of self-rising flour and mix until you have a dough.
2. On a working surface, place 1 c flour, shape the dough, flatten it, slice 10 circles with a cookie cutter and cover them with flour.
3. Cover the basket of your Air Fryer with aluminum foil, add the

cookies, spray them with some melted butter and fry them for about 20 minutes at around 380°F.
4. Split between plates and serve them as a side dish Enjoy!

Nutrition: **Calories: 105 | Protein: 19 g | Carbohydrates: 10 g | Fat: 73 g | Fiber: 35 g**

## 311. Creamy Brussels Sprouts II

Ready in: 45 minutes | Servings: 10 | Difficulty: Hard

**Ingredients**

• 4 lbs. Brussels sprouts, halved
• 1 drizzle of olive oil
• 2 lbs. bacon, chopped
• Salt and black pepper according to your taste
• 5 tbsps. butter
• 4 shallots, chopped
• 2 c milk
• 3 c heavy cream
• ½ tsp nutmeg, ground
• 4 tbsps. prepared horseradish

**Directions**

1. Preheat the Air Fryer to around 370°F; add some oil, salt, bacon, and pepper, and sprouts of Brussels and mix
2. Add in the shallots, butter, milk, cream, horseradish, and nutmeg, toss again and simmer for around 25 minutes
3. Split as a side dish between plates and eat Enjoy!

Nutrition: **Calories: 259 | Protein: 54 g | Carbohydrates: 143 g | Fat: 223 g | Fiber: 64 g**

## 312. Cauliflower Cakes

Ready in: 30 minutes | Servings: 8 | Difficulty: Normal

**Ingredients**

• Cooking spray
• Salt and black pepper according to your taste
• 1 c Parmesan, grated
• ½ c white flour
• 3 eggs
• 4 ½ c cauliflower rice

**Directions**

1. Combine the cauliflower rice with some salt and black pepper in a pot, mix and squeeze out the excess water.
2. Move the cauliflower rice to a big bowl, add in the salt, eggs, flour, pepper, and Parmesan, mix well and form the cakes.
3. Oil your Air Fryer with some cooking spray, heat it up to around 400°F, add your cauliflower cakes and steam them for about 10 minutes, rotating halfway.
4. On bowls, divide the cakes and offer them as a side dish with your choice of food Enjoy!

Nutrition: **Calories: 31 | Protein: 14 g | Carbohydrates: 53 g | Fat: 11 g**

## 313. Fried Tomatoes

Ready in: 25 minutes | Servings: 5 | Difficulty: Easy

**Ingredients**

• Cooking spray
• 1 tbsp. Creole seasoning
• 2 c panko breadcrumbs
• 2 c buttermilk
• 1 c flour

- Salt and black pepper according to your taste
- 3 green tomatoes, sliced

**Directions**

1. With some salt and black pepper, spice the tomato slices.
2. Put some flour in a bowl, buttermilk in a different bowl, and panko crumbs Add Creole seasoning in the final bowl.
3. Dig the tomato slices in flour then placed them in your buttermilk and the panko breadcrumbs Put them in the oiled Air Fryer basket with some cooking spray, and fry them for about 5 minutes at around 400°F.
4. Split as a side dish between dishes and eat Enjoy!

Nutrition: **Calories: 63 | Protein: 24 g | Carbohydrates: 69 g | Fat: 39 g**

## 314. Eggplant Fries

Ready in: 25 minutes | Servings: 5 | Difficulty: Easy

**Ingredients**

- 1 pinch of salt and black pepper to the taste
- 1 c Italian cheese, shredded
- 3 c panko breadcrumbs
- 2 eggs, whisked
- 3 tbsps. milk
- 2 eggplant, peeled and cut into medium fries
- Cooking spray

**Directions**

1. Mix the eggs with the salt, milk, and pepper in a pot, then stir well.
2. Add the panko with some cheese in another bowl and mix well.
3. Dip the eggplant fries in your egg mix, then cover them in the panko mix, put them in your Air Fryer sprayed with some cooking spray, then cook for about 5 minutes at around 400°F.
4. Split as a side dish between dishes and serve Enjoy!

Nutrition: **Calories: 149 | Protein: 62 g | Carbohydrates: 321 g | Fat: 21 g**

## 315. Mushrooms and Sour Cream

Ready in: 30 minutes | Servings: 8 | Difficulty: Normal

**Ingredients**

- Salt and black pepper according to your taste
- 1 ½ c Cheddar cheese, grated
- 1 ½ c sour cream
- 2 carrot, grated
- 28 mushrooms, stems removed
- 2 green bell pepper, chopped
- 2 yellow onion, chopped
- 4 bacon strips, chopped

**Directions**

1. Heat a skillet over medium-high heat; add onion, bacon, carrot, and bell pepper Mix and cook for about 1 minute.
2. Add some salt, black pepper, and some sour cream, cook for an extra minute Remove from flame and cool off.
3. Stuff the mushrooms with this combination; sprinkle the cheese on top, and simmer for about 8 minutes at around 360°F.
4. Split as a side dish between plates and serve Enjoy!

Nutrition: **Calories: 149 | Protein: 62 g | Carbohydrates: 321 g | Fat: 21 g**

## 316. Eggplant Side Dish

Ready in: 30 minutes | Servings: 5 | Difficulty: Normal

**Ingredients**

- 2 tomato chopped
- 2 yellow onion, chopped
- 2 tbsps. olive oil
- 1 tsp garlic powder
- 2 bunch cilantros, chopped
- 2 tbsps. tomato paste
- 2 green bell pepper, chopped
- 1 pinch of oregano, dried
- Salt and black pepper according to your taste
- 10 baby eggplants, scooped in the center and pulp reserved

**Directions**

1. Over medium-high heat, warm a pan with some oil, add the onion, mix and cook for about 1 minute.
2. Add some salt, the pulp of eggplant, black pepper, green bell pepper, oregano, tomato paste, cilantro, powdered garlic, and tomato, mix, cook for about 1–2 more minutes, take off the flame and cool down.
3. Pack the eggplants with this blend, put them in the basket of your Air Fryer, and cook for about 8 minutes at around 360°F.
4. On bowls, split the eggplants and offer them as a side dish with your choice of food Enjoy!

Nutrition: **Calories: 115 | Protein: 15 g | Carbohydrates: 122 g | Fat: 72 g**

## 317. Garlic Potatoes

Ready in: 37 minutes | Servings: 8 | Difficulty: Normal

**Ingredients**

- 1/3 c Parmesan, grated
- 3 tbsps. butter
- Salt and black pepper according to your taste
- 3 tbsps. olive oil
- 2 tsps. thyme, dried
- 5 lbs. red potatoes, halved
- 1 tsp oregano, dried
- 1 tsp basil, dried
- 6 garlic cloves, minced
- 3 tbsps. parsley, chopped

**Directions**

1. Mix the potato halves with garlic, parsley, oregano, basil, thyme, pepper, salt, oil, and butter in a bowl, mix very well and move to the basket of your Air Fryer.
2. Cover and cook for about 20 minutes at around 400°F, switching them over once.
3. Toss on top some Parmesan, split the potatoes on the dishes, and serve them as a side dish Enjoy!

Nutrition: **Calories: 103 | Protein: 39 g | Carbohydrates: 193 g | Fat: 25 g**

## 318. Parmesan Mushrooms

Ready in: 45 minutes | Servings: 5 | Difficulty: Hard

**Ingredients**

- 2 tbsps. butter, melted
- 1 pinch of salt and black pepper
- 2 tsps. Italian seasoning
- 3 tbsps. Parmesan, grated
- 2 egg white

- 6 cream cracker slices, crumbled
- 10 button mushroom caps

**Directions**

1. Put the egg white with crackers, Italian seasoning, Parmesan, salt, butter, and pepper in a bowl, whisk well, and transfer the mushrooms to the mixture.
2. Organize the mushrooms in the basket of your Air Fryer and cook them for about 15 minutes at around 360°F.
3. Split as a side dish between dishes and serve Enjoy!

Nutrition: **Calories: 103 | Protein: 39 g | Carbohydrates: 193 g | Fat: 25 g**

## 319. Roasted Pumpkin

Ready in: 30 minutes | Servings: 5 | Difficulty: Normal

**Ingredients**

- 1 pinch of cinnamon powder
- 1 pinch of nutmeg, ground
- 1 pinch of brown sugar
- 1 pinch of sea salt
- 2 tbsps. olive oil
- 4 garlic cloves, minced
- 2 ½ lb. pumpkin, deseeded, sliced, and roughly chopped

**Directions**

1. Combine the pumpkin with oil, garlic, brown sugar, salt, nutmeg, and cinnamon in the Air Fryer's basket, mix good, cover and cook for about 12 minutes at around 370°F.
2. Split as a side dish between dishes and serve Enjoy!

Nutrition: **Calories: 128 | Protein: 37 g | Carbohydrates: 164 g | Fat: 69 g**

## 320. Green Beans Side Dish

Ready in: 45 minutes | Servings: 5 | Difficulty: Hard

**Ingredients**

- 3 tbsps. olive oil
- ½ c almonds, toasted
- 1 lb. shallots, chopped
- Salt and black pepper according to your taste
- 2 ½ lbs. green beans, trimmed and steamed for 2 minutes

**Directions**

1. Mix the green beans with pepper, salt, almonds, shallots, and oil in the basket of your Air Fryer Mix gently, and steam for about 25 minutes at around 400°F.
2. Split as a side dish between dishes and eat Enjoy!

Nutrition: **Calories: 260 | Protein: 54 g | Carbohydrates: 393 g | Fat: 98 g**

## 321. Creamy Air-Fried Potato Side Dish

Ready in: 1 hour and 45 minutes | Servings: 5 | Difficulty: Hard

**Ingredients**

- 3 tbsps. heavy cream
- 2 tbsps. butter
- Salt and black pepper according to your taste
- 2 tbsps. green onions, chopped
- 2/3 c Cheddar cheese, shredded
- 2 tsps. olive oil
- 4 bacon strips, cooked and chopped
- 2 big potato
- Eggs

**Directions**

1. Rub the potatoes with oil, season with some salt and black pepper Put them in a preheated Air Fryer, and steam for about 30 minutes at around 400°F.
2. Flip the potato, cook an extra 30 minutes, move to a chopping board, cool it off, cut lengthwise in the quarter, and scoop the pulp in a bowl.
3. Use this blend to include eggs, bacon, heavy cream, butter, salt, green onions, and black pepper mix gently and stuff the potato skin.
4. Put the potatoes back in your fryer and fry them for about 20 minutes at around 400°F.
5. Split as a side dish between dishes and eat garnish with cheese Enjoy!

Nutrition: **Calories: 260 | Protein: 54 g | Carbohydrates: 393 g | Fat: 98 g**

## 322. Brussels Sprouts Side Dish

Ready in: 35 minutes | Servings: 5 | Difficulty: Normal

**Ingredients**

- 3 tbsps. roasted garlic, crushed
- 1 c mayonnaise
- 1 tsp thyme, chopped
- 8 tsps. olive oil
- Salt and black pepper according to your taste
- 2 lbs. Brussels sprouts, trimmed and halved

**Directions**

1. Combine the Brussels sprouts with pepper, salt, and oil in your Air Fryer, mix properly, and sear for about 15 minutes at around 390°F.
2. In the meantime, blend thyme with garlic and mayo in a bowl and blend well.
3. Brussels sprouts are placed on bowls; garlic sauce is drizzled all over and eaten as a side dish Enjoy!

Nutrition: **Calories: 260 | Protein: 54 g | Carbohydrates: 393 g | Fat: 98 g**

## 323. Hassel Back Potatoes

Ready in: 40 minutes | Servings: 4 | Difficulty: Hard

**Ingredients**

- 1 tsp sweet paprika
- 1 tsp basil, dried
- 1 tsp oregano, dried
- Salt and black pepper according to your taste
- 2 tsps. garlic, minced
- 4 tbsps. olive oil
- 4 potatoes, peeled and thinly sliced almost all the way horizontally

**Directions**

1. Combine the oil, salt, garlic, oregano, basil, pepper, and paprika in a bowl and mix well.
2. Brush the potatoes with this blend, put them in the basket of your Air Fryer, and cook them for about 20 minutes at around 360°F.
3. Split them and serve them as a side dish on bowls Enjoy!

Nutrition: **Calories: 260 | Protein: 54 g | Carbohydrates: 393 g | Fat: 98 g**

## 324. Corn With Lime and Cheese

Ready in: 35 minutes | Servings: 4 | Difficulty: Normal

**Ingredients**

• Juice from 3 limes
• 4 tsps. sweet paprika
• 1 c Feta cheese, grated
• 1 drizzle of olive oil
• 4 corns on the cob, husks removed

**Directions**

1. Rub the corn with the oil and some paprika, bring it in your Air Fryer, and steam for about 15 minutes at around 400°F, turning once.
2. Split the corn into bowls, cover with the cheese, drizzle with the lime juice and serve as a side dish with your choice of food Enjoy!

Nutrition: **Calories: 260 | Protein: 54 g | Carbohydrates: 393 g | Fat: 98 g**

## 325. Sweet Potato Fries

Ready in: 40 minutes | Servings: 5 | Difficulty: Hard

**Ingredients**

• 1 pinch of cinnamon powder
• 1 pinch of ginger powder
• 1 tsp cumin, ground
• 4 tbsps. mayonnaise
• ½ c ketchup
• ½ tsp cilantro, ground
• 1 tsp curry powder
• 4 tbsps. olive oil
• Salt and black pepper according to your taste
• 4 sweet potatoes, peeled and cut into medium fries

**Directions**

1. Mix the sweet potato fries with pepper, salt, curry powder, cilantro, and oil in your Air Fryer's basket, mix well and steam for about 20 minutes at around 370°F, turning once.
2. Meanwhile, blend the ginger, cumin, mayo, and cinnamon with some ketchup in a container and stir well.
3. On bowls, split fries, drizzle ketchup blend over them and eat as a side dish Enjoy!

Nutrition: **Calories: 260 | Protein: 54 g | Carbohydrates: 393 g | Fat: 98 g**

## 326. Mushroom Side Dish

Ready in: 25 minutes | Servings: 5 | Difficulty: Easy

**Ingredients**

• 2 tbsps. dill, chopped
• 4 tbsps. Mozzarella, grated
• 2 tbsps. olive oil
• 4 tbsps. Cheddar cheese, grated
• Salt and black pepper
• according to your taste
• 2 tbsps. Italian seasoning
• 12 button mushrooms, stems removed

**Directions**

1. Mix the Italian seasoning, mushrooms, oil, pepper, salt, and dill in a bowl and massage well.
2. Organize the mushrooms in the basket of your Air Fryer, brush each one with Mozzarella and Cheddar and bake for about 8 minutes at around 360°F.
3. Split them and offer as a side dish on bowls Enjoy!

Nutrition: **Calories: 260 | Protein: 54 g | Carbohydrates: 393 g | Fat: 98 g**

## 327. Potato Wedges

Ready in: 45 minutes | Servings: 5 | Difficulty: Hard

**Ingredients**

• 3 tbsps. sweet chili sauce
• 4 tbsps. sour cream
• Salt and black pepper according to your taste
• 2 tbsps. olive oil
• 3 potatoes, cut into wedges

**Directions**

1. Combine the potato wedges with the salt, oil, and pepper in a pot, mix well, transfer to the Air Fryer's basket, and steam for about 25 minutes at around 360°F, rotating once.
2. Split your potato wedges into bowls, spoon all over with sour cream and chili sauce, and offer as a side dish Enjoy!

Nutrition: **Calories: 260 | Protein: 54 g | Carbohydrates: 393 g | Fat: 98 g**

## 328. Crispy and Tasty Spring Rolls

Ready in: 20 minutes | Servings: 4 | Difficulty: Easy

**Ingredients**

• 8 spring roll wrappers
• 1 tsp nutritional yeast
• 1 tsp corn starch + 2 tbsps. water
• 1 tsp coconut sugar
• 1 tbsp. soy sauce
• 1 medium carrot, shredded
• 1 c shiitake mushroom, sliced thinly
• 1 celery stalk, chopped
• ½ tsp ginger, finely chopped

**Directions**

1. Mix your carrot, celery stalk, soy sauce, coconut sugar, ginger, mushrooms, and nutritional yeast with each other in a mixing dish.
2. Have 1 tbsp. your vegetable mix and put it in the middle of your spring roll wrappers.
3. Roll up and secure the sides of your wraps with some cornstarch.
4. Cook for about 15 minutes or till your spring roll wraps is crisp in a preheated Air Fryer at 200°F.

Nutrition: **Calories: 124 | Protein: 103 g | Carbohydrates: 6 g | Fat: 66 g**

## 329. Spinach and Feta Crescent Triangles

Ready in: 35 minutes | Servings: 4 | Difficulty: Normal

**Ingredients**

- ¼ tsp salt
- 1 tsp chopped oregano
- ¼ tsp garlic powder
- 1 c crumbled Feta cheese
- 1 c steamed spinach

**Directions**

1. Preheat your Air Fryer to about 350°F, and then roll up the dough over a level surface that is gently floured.
2. In a medium-sized bowl, mix the spinach, Feta, salt, oregano, and ground garlic cloves Split your dough into 4 equal chunks.
3. Split the mix of Feta/spinach among the 4 chunks of dough Fold and seal your dough using a fork.
4. Please put it on a baking tray covered with parchment paper, and then put it in your Air Fryer.
5. Cook until nicely golden, for around 1 minute.

Nutrition: **Calories: 124 | Protein: 103 g | Carbohydrates: 6 g | Fat: 66 g**

## 330. Healthy Avocado Fries

Ready in: 25 minutes | Servings: 2 | Difficulty: Easy

**Ingredients**

- ¼ c Aquafina
- 1 avocado, cubed
- Salt as required
- Bread crumbs

**Directions**

1. Mix the Aquafina, crumbs, and salt in a mixing bowl.
2. Preheat your Air Fryer to about 390°F and cover the avocado pieces uniformly in the crumbs blend.
3. Put the ready pieces in the cooking bucket of your Air Fryer and cook for several minutes.

Nutrition: **Calories: 124 | Protein: 58 g | Carbohydrates: 99 g | Fat: 73 g**

## 331. Twice-Fried Cauliflower Tater Tots

Ready in: 20 minutes | Servings: 12 | Difficulty: Easy

**Ingredients**

- 3 tbsps. oats flaxseed meal + 3 tbsps. water
- 1 lb. cauliflower, steamed and chopped
- 1 tsp parsley, chopped
- 1 tsp oregano, chopped
- 1 tsp garlic, minced
- 1 tsp chives, chopped
- 1 onion, chopped
- 1 flax egg
- 3 tbsps. desiccated coconuts
- ½ c nutritional yeast
- Salt and pepper according to taste
- ½ c breadcrumbs

**Directions**

1. Preheat your Air Fryer to about 390°F.
2. To extract extra moisture, place the steamed cauliflower onto a ring and a paper towel.
3. Put and mix the remainder of your ingredients, excluding your breadcrumbs, in a small mixing container.
4. Use your palms, blend it until well mixed, and shapes into a small ball.

5. Roll your tater tots over your breadcrumbs and put them in the bucket of your Air Fryer.
6. For a minute, bake Raise the cooking level to about 400°F and cook for the next 10 minutes.

Nutrition: **Calories: 124 | Protein: 58 g | Carbohydrates: 99 g | Fat: 73 g**

## 332. Cheesy Mushroom and Cauliflower Balls

Ready in: 1 hour | Servings: 4 | Difficulty: Hard

**Ingredients**

- Salt and pepper according to taste
- 2 sprigs chopped fresh thyme
- ¼ c coconut oil
- 1 c Grana Padano cheese
- 1 c breadcrumbs
- 2 tbsps. chicken stock
- 3 c cauliflower, chopped
- 3 cloves garlic, minced
- 1 small red onion, chopped
- 3 tbsps. olive oil
- Mushrooms

**Directions**

1. Over moderate flame, put a pan Add some olive oil When the oil is heated, stir-fry your onion and garlic till they become transparent.
2. Add in the mushrooms and cauliflower and stir-fry for about 5 minutes Add in your stock, add thyme and cook till your cauliflower has consumed the stock Add pepper, Grana Padano cheese, and salt.
3. Let the mix cool down and form bite-size spheres of your paste To harden, put it in the fridge for about 30 minutes.
4. Preheat your Air Fryer to about 350°F.
5. Add your coconut oil and breadcrumbs into a small bowl and blend properly.
6. Take out your mushroom balls from the fridge, swirl the breadcrumb paste once more, and drop the balls into your breadcrumb paste.
7. Avoid overcrowding, put your balls into your Air Fryer's container and cook for about 15 minutes, flipping after every 5 minutes to ensure even cooking.
8. Serve with some tomato sauce and brown sugar.

Nutrition: **Calories: 48 | Protein: 22 g | Carbohydrates: 45 g | Fat: 28 g | Fiber: 16 g**

## 333. Italian Seasoned Easy Pasta Chips

Ready in: 15 minutes | Servings: 2 | Difficulty: Easy

**Ingredients**

- 2 c whole wheat bowtie pasta
- 1 tbsp. olive oil
- 1 tbsp. nutritional yeast
- 1 ½ tsp Italian seasoning blend
- ½ tsp salt

**Directions**

1. Put the accessory for the baking tray into your Air Fryer.
2. Mix all the ingredients in a medium-sized bowl, offer it a gentle stir.

3. Add the mixture to your Air Fryer basket.

4. Close your Air Fryer and cook at around 400°degrees F for about 10 minutes.

Nutrition: **Calories: 48 | Protein: 22 g | Carbohydrates: 45 g | Fat: 28 g | Fiber: 16 g**

## 334. Thai Sweet Potato Balls

Ready in: 1 hour | Servings: 4 | Difficulty: Hard

**Ingredients**

- 1 c coconut flakes
- 1 tsp baking powder
- ½ c almond meal
- ¼ tsp ground cloves
- ½ tsp ground cinnamon
- 2 tsps. orange zest
- 1 tbsp. orange juice
- 1 c brown sugar
- 1 lb. sweet potatoes

**Directions**

1. Bake your sweet potatoes for around 25–30 minutes at about 380°F till they become soft; peel and mash them in a medium-sized bowl.

2. Add orange zest, orange juice, brown sugar, ground cinnamon, almond meal, cloves, and baking powder Now blend completely.

3. Roll the balls around in some coconut flakes.

4. Bake for around 15 minutes or until fully fried and crunchy in the preheated Air Fryer at about 360°F.

5. For the rest of the ingredients, redo the same procedure Bon appétit!

Nutrition: **Calories: 48 | Protein: 22 g | Carbohydrates: 45 g | Fat: 28 g | Fiber: 16 g**

## 335. Barbecue Roasted Almonds

Ready in: 25 minutes | Servings: 6 | Difficulty: Easy

**Ingredients**

- 1 tbsp. olive oil
- ¼ tsp smoked paprika
- ½ tsp cumin powder
- ¼ tsp mustard powder
- ¼ tsp garlic powder
- Sea salt and ground black pepper, according to taste
- 1 ½ c raw almonds

**Directions**

1. In a mixing pot, mix all your ingredients.

2. Line the container of your Air Fryer with some baking parchment paper Arrange the covered almonds out in the basket of your Air Fryer in a uniform layer.

3. Roast for around 8–9 minutes at about 340°F, tossing the bucket once or twice If required, work in groups.

4. Enjoy!

Nutrition: **Calories: 48 | Protein: 22 g | Carbohydrates: 45 g | Fat: 28 g | Fiber: 16 g**

## 336. Croissant Rolls

Ready in: 10 minutes | Servings: 8 | Difficulty: Easy

**Ingredients**

- 4 tbsps. butter, melted
- 1 (8 oz.) can croissant rolls

**Directions**

1. Adjust the Air Fryer temperature to about 320°F Oil the basket of your Air Fryer.

2. Into your Air Fryer basket, place your prepared croissant rolls

3. Airs fry them for around 4 minutes or so.

4. Flip to the opposite side and cook for another 2–3 minutes.

5. Take out from your Air Fryer and move to a tray.

6. Glaze with some melted butter and eat warm.

Nutrition: **Calories: 80 | Protein: 39 g | Carbohydrates: 105 g | Fat: 39 g | Fiber: 43 g**

## 337. Curry and Cilantro Spiced Bread Rolls

Ready in: 20 minutes | Servings: 5 | Difficulty: Easy

**Ingredients**

- Salt and pepper according to taste
- 5 large potatoes, boiled
- 2 sprigs, curry leaves
- 2 small onions, chopped
- 2 green chilies, seeded and chopped
- 1 tbsp. olive oil
- 1 bunch of cilantro, chopped
- ½ tsp turmeric powder
- 8 slices of vegan wheat bread, brown sides discarded
- ½ tsp mustard seeds

**Directions**

1. Mash your potatoes in a bowl and sprinkle some black pepper and salt according to taste Now set aside.

2. In a pan, warm up the olive oil over medium-low heat and add some mustard seeds Mix until the seeds start to sputter.

3. Now add in the onions and cook till they become transparent Mix in the curry leaves and turmeric powder.

4. Keep on cooking till it becomes fragrant for a couple of minutes Take it off the flame and add the mixture to the potatoes.

5. Mix in the green chilies and some cilantro This is meant to be the filling.

6. Wet your bread and drain excess moisture In the center of the loaf, put one tablespoon of the potato filling and gently roll the bread so that the potato filling is fully enclosed within the bread.

7. Brush with some oil and put them inside your Air Fryer basket.

8. Cook for around 15 minutes in a preheated Air Fryer at about 400°F.

9. Ensure that the Air Fryer basket is shaken softly midway through the cooking period for an even cooking cycle.

Nutrition: **Calories: 169 | Protein: 4 g | Carbohydrates: 359 g | Fat: 15 g | Fiber: 54 g**

## 338. Scrumptiously Healthy Chips

Ready in: 15 minutes | Servings: 2 | Difficulty: Easy

**Ingredients**

- 2 tbsps. olive oil
- 2 tbsps. almond flour
- 1 tsp garlic powder
- 1 bunch kale
- Salt and pepper according to taste

**Directions**

1. Preheat your Air Fryer for around 5 minutes.

2. In a mixing bowl, add all your ingredients, add the kale leaves at the end and toss to completely cover them.

3. Put in the basket of your fryer and cook until crispy for around 10 minutes.

Nutrition: Calories: 169 | Protein: 4 g | Carbohydrates: 359 g | Fat: 15 g | Fiber: 54 g

## 339. Kid-Friendly Vegetable Fritters

Ready in: 25 minutes | Servings: 4 | Difficulty: Easy

**Ingredients**

- 2 tbsps. olive oil
- ½ c cornmeal
- ½ c all-purpose flour
- ½ tsp ground cumin
- 1 tsp turmeric powder
- 2 garlic cloves, pressed
- 1 carrot, grated
- 1 sweet pepper, seeded and chopped
- 1 yellow onion, finely chopped
- 1 tbsp. ground flaxseeds
- Salt and ground black pepper, according to taste
- 1 lb. broccoli florets

**Directions**

1. In salted boiling water, blanch your broccoli until al dente, for around 3–5 minutes Drain the excess water and move to a mixing bowl; add in the rest of your ingredients to mash the broccoli florets.

2. Shape the paste into patties and position them in the slightly oiled Air Fryer basket.

3. Cook for around 6 minutes at about 400°F, flipping them over midway through the cooking process; if needed, operate in batches.

4. Serve hot with some Vegenaise of your choice Enjoy it!

Nutrition: Calories: 158 | Protein: 64 g | Carbohydrates: 252 g | Fat: 38 g | Fiber: 47 g

## 340. Avocado Fries with Parmesan and Sauce

Ready in: 1 hour | Servings: 4 | Difficulty: Hard

**Ingredients**

- 2 avocados, cut into wedges
- ½ c Parmesan cheese, grated
- 2 eggs
- Sea salt and ground black pepper, according to taste
- ½ c almond meal
- ½ head garlic (6–7 cloves)

**For the sauce:**
- 1 tsp mustard
- 1 tsp lemon juice
- ½ c mayonnaise

**Directions**

1. On a piece of aluminum foil, put your garlic cloves and spray some cooking spray on it Wrap your garlic cloves in the foil.

2. Cook for around 1–2 minutes at about 400°F in your preheated Air Fryer Inspect the garlic, open the foil's top end, and keep cooking for an additional 10–12 minutes.

3. Once done, let them cool for around 10–15 minutes; take out the cloves by pressing them out of their skin; mash your garlic and put them aside.

4. Mix the salt, almond meal, and black pepper in a small dish.

5. Beat the eggs until foamy in a separate bowl.

6. Put some Parmesan cheese in the final shallow dish.

7. In your almond meal blend, dip the avocado wedges, dusting off any excess.

8. In the beaten egg, dunk your wedges; eventually, dip in some Parmesan cheese.

9. Spray your avocado wedges on both sides with some cooking oil spray.

10. Cook for around 8 minutes in the preheated Air Fryer at about 395°F, flipping them over midway thru the cooking process.

11. In the meantime, mix the ingredients of your sauce with your cooked crushed garlic.

12. Split the avocado wedges between plates and cover with the sauce before serving Enjoy!

Nutrition: Calories: 158 | Protein: 64 g | Carbohydrates: 252 g | Fat: 38 g | Fiber: 47 g

## 341. Crispy Wings with Lemony Old Bay Spice

Ready in: 35 minutes | Servings: 4 | Difficulty: Normal

**Ingredients**

- Salt and pepper according to taste
- 3 lbs. chicken wings
- 1 tsp lemon juice, freshly squeezed
- 1 tbsp. old bay spices
- ¾ c of almond flour
- ½ c butter

**Directions**

1. Preheat your Air Fryer for about 5 minutes Mix all your ingredients in a mixing dish, excluding the butter Put in the bowl of an Air Fryer.

2. Preheat the oven to about 350°F and bake for around 25 minutes Rock the fryer container midway thru the cooking process, also for cooking.

3. Drizzle with some melted butter when it's done frying Enjoy!

Nutrition: Calories: 105 | Protein: 27 g | Carbohydrates: 178 g | Fat: 28 g | Fiber: 3 g

## 342. Cold Salad with Veggies and Pasta

Ready in: 2 hours and 2 minutes | Servings: 5 | Difficulty: Hard

**Ingredients**

- ½ c fat-free Italian dressing
- 2 tbsps. olive oil, divided
- ½ c Parmesan cheese, grated
- 8 c cooked pasta
- 4 medium tomatoes, cut in eighths
- 3 small eggplants, sliced into ½-inch thick rounds
- 3 medium zucchinis, sliced into ½-inch thick rounds
- Salt, according to your taste

**Directions**

1. Preheat your Air fryer to about 355°F and oil the inside of your Air Fryer basket In a dish, mix 1 tbsp. olive oil and zucchini and swirl to cover properly.

2. Cook for around 25 minutes your zucchini pieces in your Air fryer basket In another dish, mix your eggplants with a tbsp. olive oil and toss to coat properly.

3. Cook for around 40 minutes your eggplant slices in your Air fryer basket Reset the Air Fryer temperature to about 320°F and put the tomatoes next in the ready basket.

4. Cook and mix all your air-fried vegetables for around 30 minutes To serve, mix in the rest of the ingredients and chill for at least 2 hours, covered.

Nutrition: Calories: 155 | Protein: 122 g | Carbohydrates: 207 g | Fat: 84 g | Fiber: 29 g

## 343. Zucchini and Minty Eggplant Bites

Ready in: 55 minutes | Servings: 8 | Difficulty: Hard

**Ingredients**
• 3 tbsps. olive oil
• 1 lb. zucchini, peeled and cubed
• 1 lb. eggplant, peeled and cubed
• 2 tbsps. melted butter
• 1 ½ tsp red pepper chili flakes
• 2 tsps. fresh mint leaves, minced

**Directions**
1. In a large mixing container, add all of the ingredients mentioned above.

2. Roast the zucchini bites and eggplant in your Air Fryer for around 30 minutes at about 300°F, flipping once or twice during the cooking cycle Serve with some homemade dipping sauce.

Nutrition: Calories: 83 | Protein: 7 g | Carbohydrates: 17 g | Fat: 62 g | Fiber: 08 g

## 344. Stuffed Potatoes

Ready in: 55 minutes | Servings: 4 | Difficulty: Hard

**Ingredients**
• 3 tbsps. canola oil
• ½ c Parmesan cheese, grated
• 2 tbsps. chives, chopped
• ½ of brown onion, chopped
• 1 tbsp. butter
• 4 potatoes, peeled

**Directions**
1. Preheat the Air fryer to about 390°F and oil the Air Fryer basket Coat the canola oil on the potatoes and place them in your Air Fryer Basket.

2. Cook for around 20 minutes before serving on a platter Halve each potato and scrape out the middle from each half of it.

3. In a frying pan, melt some butter over medium heat and add the onions Sauté in a bowl for around 5 minutes and dish out.

4. Combine the onions with the middle of the potato, chives, and half of the cheese Stir well and uniformly cram the onion potato mixture into the potato halves.

5. Top and layer the potato halves in your Air Fryer basket with the leftover cheese Cook for around 6 minutes before serving hot.

Nutrition: Calories: 83 | Protein: 7 g | Carbohydrates: 17 g | Fat: 62 g | Fiber: 08 g

## 345. Paneer Cutlet

Ready in: 20 minutes | Servings: 1 | Difficulty: Easy

**Ingredients**
• ½ tsp salt
• ½ tsp oregano
• 1 small onion, finely chopped
• ½ tsp garlic powder
• 1 tsp butter
• ½ tsp chai masala
• 1 c grated cheese

**Directions**
1. Preheat the Air Fryer to about 350°F and lightly oil a baking dish In a mixing bowl, add all ingredients and stir well Split the mixture into cutlets and put them in an oiled baking dish.

2. Put the baking dish in your Air Fryer and cook your cutlets until crispy, around a minute or so.

Nutrition: Calories: 70 | Protein: 26 g | Carbohydrates: 69 g | Fat: 41 g | Fiber: 15 g

## 346. Spicy Roasted Cashew Nuts

Ready in: 30 minutes | Servings: 4 | Difficulty: Normal

**Ingredients**
• ½ tsp ancho chili powder
• ½ tsp smoked paprika
• Salt and ground black pepper, according to taste
• 1 tsp olive oil
• 1 c whole cashews

**Directions**
1. In a mixing big bowl, toss all your ingredients.

2. Line parchment paper to cover the Air Fryer container Space out the spiced cashews in your basket in a uniform layer.

3. Roast for about 6–8 minutes at 300°F, tossing the basket once or twice during the cooking process Work in batches if needed Enjoy!

Nutrition: Calories: 180 | Protein: 36 g | Carbohydrates: 243 g | Fat: 88 g | Fiber: 71 g

## 347. Lemongrass Rice Mix

Ready in: 15 minutes | Servings: 4 | Difficulty: Easy

**Ingredients**
• ½ c broccoli, shredded
• ¼ c beef broth
• 1 tsp butter
• ½ tsp salt
• 3 oz. Cheddar cheese, shredded
• ½ c cauliflower, shredded
• ¼ tsp lemongrass
• 1 tsp ground turmeric
• Keto rice

**Directions**
1. Blend the shredded broccoli and cauliflower in a baking dish.

2. Combine lemongrass, salt, and turmeric.

3. Then pour the mixture into the baking pan of the Air Fryer and insert the beef broth .

4. Add the butter and top with Cheddar cheese on top of the keto rice.

5. Heat the Air Fryer to 365°F Put the Air Fryer in the oven with "Rice" and fry it for 8 minutes.

Nutrition: Calories: 24 | Protein: 12 g | Carbohydrates: 29 g | Fat: 13 g | Fiber: 09 g

## 348. Family Vegetable Gratin

Ready in: 45 minutes | Servings: 4 | Difficulty: Hard

**Ingredients**
- Sea salt and freshly ground black pepper, to taste
- ½ tsp cayenne pepper
- 1 c Monterey Jack cheese, shredded
- 1 lb. Chinese cabbage, roughly chopped
- 2 garlic cloves, sliced
- ½ stick butter
- 4 tbsps. all-purpose flour
- 2 bell peppers, seeded and sliced
- 1 jalapeño pepper, seeded and sliced
- 1 onion, thickly sliced
- 1 c milk
- 1 c cream cheese

**Directions**

1. Warm salted water in a pan and get it to a boil For 3 minutes, boil the Chinese cabbage Switch the cabbage from hot to cold water to make the frying cycle end.

2. Put a thinly oiled casserole dish with the Chinese cabbage Add the onion, garlic, and peppers.

3. Then, over low heat, melt the butter in a saucepan Add the flour steadily and cook for 2 minutes to form a paste.

4. Slowly pour the milk in; frequently stirring till it creates a creamy paste Apply the cream cheese to the milk Sprinkle with salt, black pepper, and cayenne pepper Transfer the mixture to the casserole bowl.

5. Cover with sliced Monterey Jack cheese and bake for 2 minutes at 390°F in the hot oven Air Fryer Serve hot.

Nutrition: **Calories: 24 | Protein: 12 g | Carbohydrates: 29 g | Fat: 13 g | Fiber: 09 g**

## 349. Spicy Ricotta Stuffed Mushrooms

Ready in: 45 minutes | Servings: 4 | Difficulty: Hard

**Ingredients**
- 4 tbsps. all-purpose flour
- 1 egg
- ½ c fresh breadcrumbs
- Sea salt and ground black pepper, to taste
- ½ lb. small white mushrooms
- 2 tbsps. Ricotta cheese
- ½ tsp ancho chili powder
- 1 tsp paprika

**Directions**

1. Strip and peel the stems from the mushroom caps; add the sliced steamed mushrooms with salt, black pepper, cheese, chili powder, and paprika.

2. Fill the mushroom caps for the cheese filling.

3. In a baking dish, put the flour and smash the egg in another bowl Place a third shallow bowl with the breadcrumbs.

4. In the flour, brush the mushrooms, after which dip in the egg mixture; ultimately, add in the breadcrumbs and press to stay together Spritz cooking oil on the stuffed mushrooms.

5. Cook at 360°F for 18 minutes in the hot oven Air Fryer Bon appétit!

Nutrition: **Calories: 187 | Protein: 42 g | Carbohydrates: 16 g | Fat: 12 g | Fiber: 37 g**

## 350. Breaded Mushrooms

Ready in: 1 hour and 5 minutes | Servings: 4 | Difficulty: Hard

**Ingredients**
- Salt and pepper to taste
- 2 c Parmigiano-Reggiano cheese, grated
- 2 c breadcrumbs
- 2 eggs, beaten
- Mushrooms

**Directions**

1. Preheat to 360°F the Air Fryer.

2. In a cup, pour the breadcrumbs, add salt and pepper and blend properly.

3. In a separate cup, pour in the cheese.

4. Dip each of the mushrooms into the eggs, then the crumbs, therefore the cheese.

5. Float the basket out of the fryer and add 6 mushrooms for 20 minutes.

6. Offer a dip in the cheese.

Nutrition: **Calories: 187 | Protein: 42 g | Carbohydrates: 16 g | Fat: 12 g | Fiber: 37 g**

## 351. Easy Sweet Potato Bake

Ready in: 40 minutes | Servings: 3 | Difficulty: Hard

**Ingredients**
- 1/3 c coconut milk
- ¼ c flour
- ½ c fresh breadcrumbs
- 1 stick butter, melted
- 1 lb. sweet potatoes, mashed
- 2 tbsps. honey
- 2 eggs, beaten

**Directions**

1. Begin by heating up to 325°F for your Air Fryer.

2. Spritz a saucepan with the cooking oil.

3. Mix all the ingredients, except the breadcrumbs and about 1 tbsp. butter, in a mixing dish In the prepared casserole bowl, spoon the mixture into it.

4. Cover with the breadcrumbs and add the remaining 1 tbsp. butter to brush the top—Bake for 30 minutes in the hot oven Air Fryer.

5. Bon appétit!

Nutrition: **Calories: 187 | Protein: 42 g | Carbohydrates: 16 g | Fat: 12 g | Fiber: 37 g**

## 352. Simple Tomatoes and Bell Pepper Sauce

Ready in: 30 minutes | Servings: 4 | Difficulty: Normal

**Ingredients**
- 1 tsp rosemary, dried
- 3 bay leaves
- Salt and black pepper to the taste
- 2 red bell peppers, chopped
- 2 garlic cloves, minced
- 2 tbsps. olive oil
- 1 tbsp. balsamic vinegar
- 1 lb. cherry tomatoes, halved

**Directions**

1. Comb tomatoes with garlic, salt, black pepper, rosemary, bay leaves, a quarter of the oil, and half the vinegar in a cup, toss to cover, place in the Air Fryer and bake at 320°F for a few minutes.

2. In the meantime, mix the bell peppers with a touch of sea salt,

black pepper, the remainder of the oil, and the remaining vinegar in your food processor And mix very well.

3. Split the roasted tomatoes between bowls, drizzle over them with the bell pepper sauce and eat.

Nutrition: **Calories: 113 | Protein: 61 g | Carbohydrates: 194 g | Fat: 14 g | Fiber: 41 g**

## 353. Jalapeño Clouds

Ready in: 8 minutes | Servings: 4 | Difficulty: Easy

### Ingredients

• 1 tsp almond flour
• 1 oz. Jarlsberg cheese, grated
• 2 egg whites
• 1 jalapeño pepper

### Directions

1. Whisk the egg whites till you have the high peaks.
2. Afterward, combine the egg white tops, almond flour, and Jarlsberg cheese carefully.
3. Cut 4 slices of Jalapeño pepper.
4. Preheat the Air Fryer to 385°F.
5. Line the basket of an Air Fryer with baking parchment.
6. Create white clouds on the baking paper with the aid of the spoon.
7. Cover the clouds with a jalapeño slice.
8. Fry them just until the clouds are light brown for about 4 minutes.

Nutrition: **Calories: 113 | Protein: 61 g | Carbohydrates: 194 g | Fat: 14 g | Fiber: 41 g**

## 354. Parmesan Artichoke Hearts

Ready in: 20 minutes | Servings: 4 | Difficulty: Easy

### Ingredients

• 1 tsp garlic powder
• Salt and black pepper to taste
• 1 egg
• ¼ c flour
• ¼ Parmesan cheese, grated
• 1/3 c panko breadcrumbs
• Artichokes

### Directions

1. Preheat the Air Fryer to 390°F Oil a basket of the Air Fryer with cooking spray.
2. Pat dry the artichokes with paper towels and cut them into wedges Mix the egg with salt in a mug.
3. Now, in another bowl, mix Parmesan, breadcrumbs, and ground garlic.
4. Blend the flour with pepper and salt.
5. Dip the artichokes on the flour mix, then dip in the egg mix, and cover with the breadcrumb mixture Place the cooker in your Air Fryer's basket and cook for 10 minutes, turning once Before serving, let it cool.

Nutrition: **Calories: 235 | Protein: 105 g | Carbohydrates: 354 g | Fat: 67 g | Fiber: 10 g**

## 355. Easy Veggie Fried Balls

Ready in: 20 minutes | Servings: 3 | Difficulty: Hard

### Ingredients

• ½ c Romano cheese, grated
• ½ c dried bread flakes
• 1 tbsp. olive oil
• ½ lb. sweet potatoes, grated
• 1 shallot, chopped
• Sea salt and ground black pepper, to taste
• 1 c carrots
• 1 c corn
• 2 garlic cloves, minced
• 2 tbsps. fresh parsley, chopped
• 1 egg, well beaten
• ½ c purpose flour

### Directions

1. When all is well blended, mix the veggies, spices, egg, flour, and Romano cheese.
2. Take about 1 tbsp. the mixture of vegetables and roll them into a ball Into the dry bread flakes, roll the cubes On both ends, spray the veggie balls with olive oil.
3. Heat for 20 minutes or until fully fried and crisp in the hot oven Air Fryer.
4. Unless you run out of supplies, repeat the procedure Bon appétit!

Nutrition: **Calories: 378 | Protein: 183 g | Carbohydrates: 454 g | Fat: 151 g | Fiber: 215 g**

## 356. Cheesy Sticks with Sweet Thai Sauce

Ready in: 30 minutes | Servings: 4 | Difficulty: Normal

### Ingredients

• 1 c sweet Thai sauce
• 4 tbsps. skimmed milk
• 2 c breadcrumbs
• 3 eggs
• Cheese, cut into sticks

### Directions

1. In a bowl, pour in the crumbs Add the eggs with milk in another cup Dip sticks one after the other in the beaten egg, in the crumbs, and again in the egg mixture, then again in the crumbs Hourly freeze.
2. Preheat the Air Fryer to 380°F Organize the sticks in the fryer Cook for 5 minutes, tossing them to brown equally halfway through cooking Fry in batches Offer them along with Thai sweet sauce.

Nutrition: **Calories: 378 | Protein: 183 g | Carbohydrates: 454 g | Fat: 151 g | Fiber: 215 g**

## 357. Broccoli Cheese Stuff Pepper

Ready in: 25 minutes | Servings: 4 | Difficulty: Normal

### Ingredients

• 4 eggs
• 2 medium bell peppers, cut in half, and de-seeded
• 1 tsp dried sage
• 2 ½ oz. Cheddar cheese, grated
• 7 oz. almond milk
• ¼ c baby broccoli florets
• ¼ c cherry tomatoes
• Pepper
• Salt

## Directions

1. Preheat the Air Fryer to 370°F.
2. Toss the eggs, milk, broccoli, cherry tomatoes, sage, pepper, and salt together in a dish.
3. Mist the Air Fryer's basket with cooking spray.
4. Put the bell pepper halves in the basket of the Air Fryer.
5. Load the beaten eggs into the halves of the bell pepper.
6. Spray on top of the bell pepper with the cheese and roast for 20 minutes.
7. Enjoy and serve.

Nutrition: Calories: 211 | Protein: 23 g | Carbohydrates: 132 g | Fat: 25 g | Fiber: 212 g

## 358. Coconut Celery and Sprouts

Ready in: 17 minutes | Servings: 4 | Difficulty: Easy

**Ingredients**

- 1 tbsp. parsley, chopped
- 1 tbsp. coconut oil, melted
- ½ lb. Brussels sprouts, halved
- 1 celery stalks, roughly chopped
- 1 c coconut cream
- Salt and black pepper to the taste

**Directions**

1. Over moderate heat, prepare a pan that matches the Air Fryer with the oil, insert the sprouts and celery, stir, and cook for 2 minutes.
2. Insert the cream and remaining items, toss, place the pan in the Air Fryer and cook for a few minutes at 380°F.
3. Transfer and serve in pots.

Nutrition: Calories: 211 | Protein: 23 g | Carbohydrates: 132 g | Fat: 25 g | Fiber: 212 g

## 359. Cheesy Spinach

Ready in: 10-15 minutes | Servings: 4 | Difficulty: Easy

**Ingredients**

- 3 oz. Cottage cheese
- Salt and black pepper to taste
- 1 yellow onion, chopped
- 14 oz.' spinach
- 1 tbsp. olive oil
- 2 eggs, whisked
- 2 tbsps. milk

**Directions**

1. Heat the oil over medium heat in a saucepan that suits your Air Fryer; add the onions, stir, and sauté for 2 minutes.
2. Add and toss the other ingredients.
3. Place the pan in an Air Fryer and cook for 8 minutes.
4. Divide the spinach and serve as a side dish between dishes.

Nutrition: Calories: 109 | Protein: 54 g | Carbohydrates: 168 g | Fat: 25 g | Fiber: 32 g

## 360. Parmesan Squash

Ready in: 35 minutes | Servings: 4 | Difficulty: Normal

**Ingredients**

- ½ tsp dried cilantro
- ½ tsp ground nutmeg
- 2 tsps. butter
- 1 medium spaghetti squash
- 2 oz. Mozzarella, shredded
- 1 oz. Parmesan, shredded
- 1 tsp avocado oil
- ½ tsp dried oregano

**Directions**

1. Slice the spaghetti squash and separate the seeds into halves.
2. Then apply avocado oil, dried oregano, dried cilantro, the dried nutmeg.
3. In each half of the spaghetti squash, put ½ tbsp. butter and move the vegetables to the Air Fryer.
4. Cook them at 365°F for 15 minutes.
5. Cover the squash with Mozzarella and Parmesan after this, and simmer at the same temperature for 10 more minutes.

Nutrition: Calories: 303 | Protein: 105 g | Carbohydrates: 494 g | Fat: 64 g | Fiber: 37 g

## 361. Indian Malai Kofta

Ready in: 55 minutes | Servings: 4 | Difficulty: Hard

**Ingredients**

**For the veggie balls:**

- 1 tbsp. Garam masala
- 1 c chickpea flour
- Himalayan pink salt and ground black pepper, to taste
- 1 lb. potatoes, peeled and diced
- ½ lb. cauliflower, broken into small florets
- 2 tbsps. olive oil
- 2 cloves garlic, minced

**For the sauce:**

- 1 Kashmiri chili pepper, seeded and minced
- 1 (1-inch) piece ginger, chopped
- 1 tsp paprika
- 1 tsp turmeric powder
- 1 tbsp. sesame oil
- ¼ full fat coconut milk
  2 ripe tomatoes, pureed
- ½ tsp cumin seeds
- 2 cloves garlic, roughly chopped
- 1 onion, chopped
- ½ c vegetable broth

**Directions**

1. Begin by heating up to 400°F on your Air Fryer In a lightly oiled cooking basket, put the potato and cauliflower in it.
2. Cook for 15 minutes, halfway through the cooking time, rotating the basket In a mixing bowl, mash the cauliflower and potatoes.
3. For the veggie balls, add the remaining ingredients and mix to combine properly Form small balls of the vegetable combination and place them in the cooking basket.
4. Cook for 15 minutes or until completely fried and crispy in the preheated Air Fryer at 360°F Repeat the procedure before you are running out of ingredients.
5. In a saucepan over moderate pressure, warm the sesame oil and add the cumin seeds Add the garlic, onions, chili pepper, and ginger until the cumin seeds turn orange Sauté for between 2–3 minutes.
6. Add paprika, turmeric powder, tomatoes, and broth; let boil, covered, stirring periodically, for 4–5 minutes.
7. Add the milk from the coconut Heat off; to mix, add the vegan balls and gently stir Bon appétit!

Nutrition: Calories: 303 | Protein: 105 g | Carbohydrates: 494 g | Fat: 64 g | Fiber: 37 g

## 362. Kid-Friendly Veggie Tots

Ready in: 30 minutes | Servings: 4 | Difficulty: Normal

**Ingredients**

- 2 eggs, whisked
- ½ c tortilla chips, crushed
- ¼ c pork rinds
- Sea salt and ground black pepper, to taste
- 1 zucchini, grated
- 1 onion, chopped
- 1 parsnip, grated
- 1 carrot, grated
- 1 garlic clove, minced
- 2 tbsps. ground flax seeds

**Directions**

1. Begin by heating up to 400°F on your Air Fryer.
2. Then, add all ingredients properly in a mixing bowl until all is well mixed Shape the mixture into tot forms and put it in the cooking basket, which is lightly oiled.
3. Bake for 9–12 minutes until crispy golden around the outside, rotating midway through Bon appétit!

Nutrition: Calories: 522 | Protein: 601 g | Carbohydrates: 311 g | Fat: 182 g | Fiber: 22 g

## 363. Greek-Style Vegetable Bake

Ready in: 30 minutes | Servings: 4 | Difficulty: Hard

**Ingredients**

- 1 tsp smoked paprika
- Salt and ground black pepper, to taste
- 1 tomato, sliced
- 6 oz. halloumi cheese, sliced lengthways
- 1 eggplant, peeled and sliced
- 1 red onion, sliced
- 1 tsp fresh garlic, minced
- 4 tbsps. olive oil
- 2 bell peppers, seeded and sliced
- 1 tsp mustard
- 1 tsp dried oregano

**Directions**

1. Begin by heating up to 370°F for your Air Fryer Spritz out a nonstick cooking spray with a baking pan.
2. On the bottom of the baking pan, put the eggplant, peppers, onion, and garlic Olive oil, mustard, and spices are added Place them in the cooking basket and cook for 15 minutes.
3. Cover with the tomatoes and cheese; lift the temperature and simmer until bubbling, for 5 more minutes For 10 minutes before serving, let it rest on a cooling rack.
4. Bon appétit!

Nutrition: Calories: 109 | Protein: 53 g | Carbohydrates: 77 g | Fat: 73 g | Fiber: 19 g

## 364. Mushroom Cakes

Ready in: 15 minutes | Servings: 4 | Difficulty: Easy

**Ingredients**

- ½ tsp ground black pepper
- 1 tsp sesame oil
- 1 oz. spring onion, chopped
- ¼ c coconut flour
- 9 oz. mushrooms, finely chopped
- 1 tsp salt
- 1 egg, beaten
- 3 oz. Cheddar cheese, shredded
- 1 tsp dried parsley

**Directions**

1. Combine the diced mushrooms, coconut flour, salt, egg, dried parsley, ground black pepper, and grated onion in a mixing dish.
2. Mix once smooth and apply the Cheddar cheese to the mixture.
3. With the aid of the fork, stir it and preheat the Air Fryer to 385°F.
4. Cover the pan with baking paper for the Air Fryer.
5. Create medium-sized patties with the aid of the spoon and place them in the bowl.
6. Spray the sesame oil with the patties and roast for 4 minutes on either side.

Nutrition: Calories: 154 | Protein: 148 g | Carbohydrates: 83 g | Fat: 82 g | Fiber: 02 g

## 365. Sweet Corn Fritters

Ready in: 11-15 minutes | Servings: 4 | Difficulty: Normal

**Ingredients**

- 1 tbsp. fresh cilantro, chopped
- 1 medium-sized egg, whisked
- 2 tbsps. plain milk
- 1 c Parmesan cheese, grated
- ¼ c flour
- 1/3 tsp baking powder
- 1/3 tsp sugar
- 1 medium-sized carrot, grated
- 1 yellow onion, finely chopped
- 4 oz. canned sweet corn kernels, drained
- 1 tsp sea salt flakes

**Directions**

1. In a saucepan, put the sliced carrot and press it down to push any excess moisture out With a clean cloth, rinse it.
2. Combine the rest of the ingredients with the carrot.
3. Shape a ball of 1 tbsp. the mixture and press it down to flatten it with your hand or a pipe Repeat until you've used up the majority of the mixture.
4. Spritz the cooking spray balls.
5. Organize the Air Fryer in the basket; take care not to cross any balls Cook for 8–11 minutes or until solid.
6. Serve hot.

Nutrition: Calories: 154 | Protein: 148 g | Carbohydrates: 83 g | Fat: 82 g | Fiber: 02 g

## 366. Roasted Vegetables

Ready in: 35 minutes | Servings: 6 | Difficulty: Normal

**Ingredients**

- 1 tbsp. fresh thyme needles
- 1 tbsp. olive oil
- Salt and pepper to taste
- 1 1/3 c small parsnips
- 1 1/3 c celery (3–4 stalks)
- 2 red onions
- 1 1/3 c small butternut squash

**Directions**

1. Preheat the Air Fryer to 390°F.

2. Shave the onions and parsnips and cut them into 1-inch chunks Cut the celery together into wedges.

3. Do not remove the squash with the butternut Halve it, deseed it, and slice it.

4. Integrate the thyme, olive oil, salt, and pepper with the chopped vegetables.

5. In the bowl, position the vegetables and move the basket to the Air Fryer.

6. Cook for 20 minutes till the vegetables are well golden brown and cooked completely, moving once in the cooking time.

Nutrition: **Calories: 132 | Protein: 78 g | Carbohydrates: 25 g | Fat: 107 g | Fiber: 1 g**

## 367. Crumbed Beans

Ready in: 15 minutes | Servings: 4 | Difficulty: Easy

**Ingredients**

- 2 eggs, beaten
- ½ c crushed saltines
- 10 oz. wax beans
- ½ c flour
- 1 tsp Smoky chipotle powder
- ½ tsp ground black pepper
- 1 tsp sea salt flakes

**Directions**

1. In a dish, combine the flour, chipotle powder, black pepper, and salt In a second cup, placed the eggs In a third bowl, put the crushed saltine.

2. In cold water, wash the beans and discard any tough strings.

3. Until inserting them into the beaten egg, cover the beans with the flour mix Finally, coat them with crushed saltine.

4. Using a cooking spray to spritz the beans.

5. Air fry for 4 minutes at 360°F Give a strong shake to the cooking basket and finish cooking for 3 minutes Serve warm.

Nutrition: **Calories: 132 | Protein: 78 g | Carbohydrates: 25 g | Fat: 107 g | Fiber: 1 g**

# CHAPTER 6

## SNACK AND APPETIZER RECIPES

## 368. Thai Spring Rolls

Ready in: 35 minutes | Servings: 5 | Difficulty: Normal

**Ingredients**

- 4 oz. dry thin rice noodles
- 1 tbsp. vegetable oil
- 1 c carrot
- 2 c shiitake mushrooms
- 1 tbsp. scallions
- 2 clove garlic
- 1 tbsp. ginger
- 1 tsp sesame oil
- 3 tbsps. soy sauce
- 2 tbsps. cilantro
- 8 rice paper spring roll wrappers

**For the soy dipping sauce:**

- 1 tsp chili paste
- ¼ c soy sauce
- 3 scallions, minced

**Directions**

1. Make rice noodles as directed on the box Heat some oil and carrots in a pan over high temperatures Cook, frequently mixing until the carrots are softened (for around 3 minutes).

2. Add shiitake mushrooms to the mix Cook for another 3 minutes Combine the garlic, scallions, and ginger in a mixing bowl Cook for approximately 1 minute.

3. Remove the pan from the flame Add the vegetable blend with the rice noodles that have been cooked before.

4. Add the sesame oil, soy sauce, and cilantro in a mixing bowl Allow cooling before serving.

5. Wet spring roll wrappers in tepid water, one piece at a time, till pliable.

6. Place the wrappers on a wet, smooth surface Fill each wrapper with around a ¼ c the rice noodle blend.

7. Roll from the lower end up, folding the corners around the filling To avoid sticking to your counter, place on top of a wet cloth Redo with the rest of the wrappers.

8. Preheat your Air Fryer for around 2 minutes at about 400°F Put 3 spring rolls in your Fry Container, hem side down Cook for 10 minutes at 400°F.

9. Halfway into the cooking period, flip the rolls Continue before all of the spring rolls have been fried.

10. To make the soy dipping sauce, combine the chili paste, soy sauce, and minced scallions in a mixing bowl.

11. Serve your hot spring rolls with a soy dipping sauce.

Nutrition: **Calories: 132 | Protein: 78 g | Carbohydrates: 25 g | Fat: 107 g | Fiber: 1 g**

## 369. Bread Sticks

Ready in: 30 minutes | Servings: 4 | Difficulty: Normal

**Ingredients**

- 1 pinch of nutmeg
- ½ c brown sugar
- 2 tbsps. honey
- 2 tsps. cinnamon powder
- ½ c milk
- 3 eggs
- 6 bread slices, each cut into 6 sticks

**Directions**

1. Add the eggs with brown sugar, milk, nutmeg, cinnamon, and honey in a bowl and mix together well.

2. Dunk your sticks of bread in this blend, put them in the basket of your Air Fryer, and cook for about 10 minutes at around 360°F.

3. Split the sticks of bread into dishes to use as snacks Enjoy!

Nutrition: **Calories: 123 | Protein: 32 g | Carbohydrates: 81 g | Fat: 101 g | Fiber: 26 g**

## 370. Apple Chips

Ready in: 30 minutes | Servings: 4 | Difficulty: Normal

**Ingredients**

- 2 tbsps. white sugar
- 1 tsp cinnamon powder
- 1 pinch of salt
- 2 apples, cored and sliced

**Directions**

1. Mix salt, apple slices, sugar, and cinnamon in a pot, mix well, move to the basket of your Air Fryer, cook for about 10 minutes at around 390°F and turn once.

2. Split the bowls of apple chips to use as a party snack Enjoy!

Nutrition: **Calories: 123 | Protein: 32 g | Carbohydrates: 81 g | Fat: 101 g | Fiber: 26 g**

## 371. Sweet Popcorn

Ready in: 25 minutes | Servings: 4 | Difficulty: Easy

**Ingredients**

- 3 oz. brown sugar
- 3 ½ tbsps. butter
- 4 tbsps. corn kernels

**Directions**

1. Place the corn kernels in the pan of your Air Fryer, cook for about 6 minutes at around 400°F, move them to a dish, scatter and set aside for now.

2. On a low flame, heat up a plate, add butter, warm it up, add some sugar, and mix until it is completely dissolved.

3. Add corn kernel, flip to cover fully, remove from the flame Then scatter again on the plate.

4. Refrigerate, split into bowls and serve as a snack or lunch Enjoy!

Nutrition: **Calories: 123 | Protein: 32 g | Carbohydrates: 81 g | Fat: 101 g | Fiber: 26 g**

## 372. Chicken Dip

Ready in: 45 minutes | Servings: 12 | Difficulty: Hard

**Ingredients**

- 1 c chutney
- Salt and black pepper according to your taste
- 1 c almonds, sliced
- ½ c cilantro, chopped
- 2/3 c raisins
- 8 oz. Monterey Jack cheese, grated

- 6 scallions, chopped
- 4 tsps. curry powder
- 3 c chicken meat, cooked and shredded
- 14 oz. cream cheese
- 2 c yogurt
- 4 tbsps. butter, melted

**Directions**

1. Mix the cream cheese and yogurt in a bowl and blend with your mixer.
2. Stir in the scallions, curry powder, raisins, cheese, chicken meat, salt, cilantro, and pepper.
3. Put this into an Air Fryer's baking dish, scatter almonds on top, put in your Air Fryer, bake for about 25 minutes at around 300°F, split into dishes, top with some chutney and melted butter, and use as an appetizer Enjoy!

Nutrition: **Calories: 123 | Protein: 32 g | Carbohydrates: 81 g | Fat: 101 g | Fiber: 26 g**

## 373. Sausage Balls

Ready in: 35 minutes | Servings: 10 | Difficulty: Normal

**Ingredients**

- 4 tbsps. breadcrumbs
- 2 small onion, chopped
- 1 tsp garlic, minced
- 2 tsps. sage
- Salt and black pepper according to your taste
- 6 oz. sausage meat, ground

**Directions**

1. Mix the sausage with pepper, salt, onion, sage, garlic, and breadcrumbs in a pot, blend well and form the mixture into tiny balls.
2. Put them into the basket of your Air Fryer, cook for about 15 minutes at around 360°F, split into batches and use them as a snack Enjoy!

Nutrition: **Calories: 289 | Protein: 44 g | Carbohydrates: 416 g | Fat: 134 g | Fiber: 56 g**

## 374. Chickpeas Snack

Ready in: 24 minutes | Servings: 6 | Difficulty: Easy

**Ingredients**

- Salt and black pepper according to your taste
- 2 tsps. smoked paprika
- 2 tbsps. olive oil
- 1 tsp cumin, ground
- 17 oz. canned chickpeas, drained

**Directions**

1. Combine the chickpeas with the cumin, oil, salt, paprika, and pepper in a pan, toss to cover, put them in the basket of your fryer and cook for about 10 minutes at around 390°F.
2. Split and use as a snack in tiny bowls Enjoy!

Nutrition: **Calories: 82 | Protein: 44 g | Carbohydrates: 97 g | Fat: 34 g | Fiber: 24 g**

## 375. Air-Fried Dill Pickles

Ready in: 25 minutes | Servings: 6 | Difficulty: Easy

**Ingredients**

- ½ c ranch sauce
- Cooking spray
- 1 tsp sweet paprika
- 1 tsp garlic powder
- Salt
- ½ c milk

- 2 egg
- 1 c white flour
- 18 oz. jarred dill pickles, cut into wedges and pat dry

**Directions**

1. Mix the milk with the egg in a bowl and whisk well.
2. Mix the flour with the garlic powder, salt, and paprika in a separate bowl and whisk as well.
3. Soak the pickles in the flour, then in the mixture of the eggs and then in the flour once more Finally, put them in your Air Fryer.
4. Oil them with cooking oil, cook pickle wedges for about 5 minutes at around 400°F Move to a bowl and offer on the side with some ranch sauce Enjoy!

Nutrition: **Calories: 82 | Protein: 44 g | Carbohydrates: 97 g | Fat: 34 g | Fiber: 24 g**

## 376. Crab Sticks

Ready in: 30 minutes | Servings: 5 | Difficulty: Normal

**Ingredients**

- 4 tsps. Cajun seasoning
- 4 tsps. sesame oil
- 12 crabsticks, halved

**Directions**

1. Place the crabsticks in a pot; add some sesame oil and the Cajun seasoning, mix Move them to the basket of your Air Fryer, and cook for about 12 minutes at around 350°F.
2. Arrange to use as an appetizer on a platter Enjoy!

Nutrition: **Calories: 82 | Protein: 44 g | Carbohydrates: 97 g | Fat: 34 g | Fiber: 24 g**

## 377. Crispy Radish Chips

Ready in: 30 minutes | Servings: 5 | Difficulty: Normal

**Ingredients**

- 2 tbsps. chives, chopped
- Salt and black pepper according to your taste
- 18 radishes, sliced
- Cooking spray

**Directions**

1. Arrange slices of radish in the basket of your Air Fryer; brush them with some cooking oil.
2. Sprinkle with some salt and some black pepper to taste.
3. Cook for about 10 minutes at around 350°F.
4. Turn them halfway, move to bowls, and offer with scattered chives on top.
5. Enjoy!

Nutrition: **Calories: 82 | Protein: 44 g | Carbohydrates: 97 g | Fat: 34 g | Fiber: 24 g**

## 378. Spring Rolls

Ready in: 45 minutes | Servings: 10 | Difficulty: Hard

**Ingredients**

- 4 tbsps. water
- 4 tbsps. corn flour
- 12 spring roll sheets
- 4 tbsps. olive oil
- 2 tsps. soy sauce

- Salt and black pepper according to your taste
- 2 tsps. sugar
- 4 garlic cloves, minced
- 2 tbsps. ginger, grated
- 1 chili pepper, minced
- 2 carrot, grated
- 4 yellow onions, chopped
- 4 c green cabbage, shredded

## Directions

1. Over medium-high heat, heat a skillet with some oil, add the cabbage, carrots, onions, ginger, chili pepper, sugar, garlic, pepper, salt, and soy sauce, mix well, cook for about 2–3 minutes, remove from flame and cool off.

2. Split spring roll sheets into circles, cut each one with a cabbage mix, and turn them.

3. Mix the corn flour and water in a pot, blend well and seal the spring rolls with this paste.

4. Place the spring rolls in the basket of your Air Fryer and cook them for about 10 minutes at around 360°F.

5. Turn the roll and cook it for another 10 minutes.

6. Arrange and offer them as an appetizer on a platter Enjoy!

Nutrition: Calories: 416 | Protein: 152 g | Carbohydrates: 438 g | Fat: 218 g | Fiber: 181 g

## 379. Banana Chips

Ready in: 35 minutes | Servings: 5 | Difficulty: Hard

### Ingredients

- 2 tsps. olive oil
- 1 tsp chaat masala
- 1 tsp turmeric powder
- 1 pinch of salt
- 6 bananas, peeled and sliced

### Directions

1. Combine banana slices with turmeric, salt, chaat masala, and oil in a small bowl, mix and leave for about 10 minutes to put aside.

2. Switch banana slices at around 360°F to your preheated Air Fryer and cook for about 15 minutes, rotating them once.

3. Offer as a small snack Enjoy!

Nutrition: Calories: 50 | Protein: 12 g | Carbohydrates: 41 g | Fat: 38 g | Fiber: 18 g

## 380. Salmon Party Patties

Ready in: 45 minutes | Servings: 6 | Difficulty: Hard

### Ingredients

- Cooking spray
- 4 tbsps. breadcrumbs
- 2 egg
- Salt and black pepper according to your taste
- 4 tbsps. dill, chopped
- 4 tbsps. parsley, chopped
- 2 big salmon fillet, skinless, boneless
- 6 big potatoes, boiled, drained, and mashed

### Directions

1. Place your salmon in the basket of your Air Fryer and cook at around 360°F for about 10 minutes.

2. Move the salmon to a chopping board, cool it off, place it in a pot, and flake it.

3. Using this combination to combine salt, mashed potatoes, dill,

pepper, egg, parsley, and breadcrumbs Blend well and create 8 or more patties.

4. Put the salmon patties in the basket of your Air Fryer; spray them with some cooking oil Cook for about 12 minutes at around 360°F, turn them halfway, move them to a dish, and offer as an appetizer Enjoy!

Nutrition: Calories: 50 | Protein: 12 g | Carbohydrates: 41 g | Fat: 38 g | Fiber: 18 g

## 381. Honey Party Wings

Ready in: 1 hour and 45 minutes | Servings: 8 | Difficulty: Hard

### Ingredients

- 4 tbsps. lime juice
- Salt and black pepper according to your taste
- 4 tbsps. honey
- 4 tbsps. soy sauce
- 20 chicken wings, halved

### Directions

1. Add the chicken wings with the honey, soy sauce, pepper, salt, and lime juice in a small bowl Mix thoroughly and refrigerate for about 1 hour.

2. Move the chicken wings to your Air Fryer and cook them for about 12 minutes at around 360°F, rotating them halfway through.

3. Arrange them to offer as an appetizer on a platter Enjoy!

Nutrition: Calories: 50 | Protein: 12 g | Carbohydrates: 41 g | Fat: 38 g | Fiber: 18 g

## 382. Beef Jerky Snack

Ready in: 4 hours and 25 minutes | Servings: 4 | Difficulty: Hard

### Ingredients

- 4 lbs. beef round, sliced
- 4 tbsps. black pepper
- 4 tbsps. black peppercorns
- 1 c Worcestershire sauce
- 4 c soy sauce

### Directions

1. Mix black pepper, black peppercorns, and Worcestershire sauce with soy sauce in a small bowl and whisk thoroughly.

2. Add slices of beef, mix to coat, and then set aside for about 6 hours in the refrigerator.

3. Place the beef rounds in your fryer and cook them for about 1 hour and 30 minutes at around 370°F.

4. Move and eat cold in a container Enjoy!

Nutrition: Calories: 171 | Protein: 135 g | Carbohydrates: 73 g | Fat: 112 g | Fiber: 01 g

## 383. Zucchini Chips

Ready in: 1 hour and 35 minutes | Servings: 8 | Difficulty: Hard

### Ingredients

- 4 tbsps. balsamic vinegar
- 4 tbsps. olive oil
- Salt and black pepper according to your taste
- 6 zucchinis, thinly sliced

**Directions**

1. Mix the salt, vinegar, oil, and pepper in a small bowl and stir well.
2. Add the slices of zucchini, coat well, place them in your Air Fryer and cook for about 1 hour at around 200°F.
3. As a snack, eat cold zucchini chips Enjoy!

Nutrition: **Calories: 171 | Protein: 135 g | Carbohydrates: 73 g | Fat: 112 g | Fiber: 01 g**

## 384. Pumpkin Muffins

Ready in: 35 minutes | Servings: 20 | Difficulty: Normal

**Ingredients**

- 1 tsp baking powder
- 2 egg
- 1 tsp baking soda
- 2 tsps. cinnamon powder
- 1 tsp nutmeg, ground
- 1 c sugar
- ½ c flour
- 4 tbsps. flaxseed meal
- 1 c pumpkin puree
- ½ c butter

**Directions**

1. Mix the butter with the pumpkin puree and egg in a small bowl and mix properly.
2. Stir well and add flour, flaxseed meal, nutmeg, baking soda, sugar, baking powder, and cinnamon.
3. Place this in the fryer at around 350°F and bake for about 15 minutes in a muffin pan that suits your fryer.
4. Offer the muffins cold as a snack Enjoy!

Nutrition: **Calories: 105 | Protein: 106 g | Carbohydrates: 62 g | Fat: 51 g | Fiber: 2 g**

## 385. Pesto Crackers

Ready in: 35 minutes | Servings: 8 | Difficulty: Normal

**Ingredients**

- 4 tbsps. butter
- 4 tbsps. basil pesto
- 2 garlic cloves, minced
- ½ tsp basil, dried
- 1 ½ c flour
- Salt and black pepper according to your taste
- 1 tsp baking powder
- Cayenne pepper to taste

**Directions**

1. Combine the black pepper, salt, flour, baking powder, cayenne, garlic, pesto, basil, and butter in a bowl and mix until the dough is set.
2. Put this dough on a lined baking sheet that matches your Air Fryer Put in the fryer and bake at 325°F for about 17 minutes.
3. Put aside to cool off, break and eat crackers as a snack or lunch Enjoy!

Nutrition: **Calories: 102 | Protein: 37 g | Carbohydrates: 11 g | Fat: 49 g | Fiber: 25 g**

## 386. Cauliflower Bars

Ready in: 45 minutes | Servings: 15 | Difficulty: Hard

**Ingredients**

- Salt and black pepper according to your taste

- 2 tsps. Italian seasoning
- ½ c egg whites
- 1 c Mozzarella, shredded
- 2 big cauliflower head, florets separated

**Directions**

1. Place cauliflowers florets in your food mixer and process well, scatter on a lined baking sheet that suits your Air Fryer Put in the fryer and cook for about 10 minutes at around 360°F.
2. Move cauliflower to a small bowl and add pepper, salt, egg whites, cheese, and Italian seasoning, stir very well, and scatter this into a rectangular pan that suits your Air Fryer, pressing well, place in the fryer, and cook for about 15 minutes more at around 360°F.
3. Split into 12–15 bars, put them on a dish, and serve as a snack Enjoy!

Nutrition: **Calories: 102 | Protein: 37 g | Carbohydrates: 11 g | Fat: 49 g | Fiber: 25 g**

## 387. Zucchini Cakes

Ready in: 30 minutes | Servings: 15 | Difficulty: Normal

**Ingredients**

- 4 zucchinis, grated
- 4 garlic cloves, minced
- 2 yellow onion, chopped
- Salt and black pepper according to your taste
- 1 c whole wheat flour
- 2 egg
- 1 c dill, chopped
- Cooking spray

**Directions**

1. Combine zucchinis with onion, garlic, salt, flour, egg, pepper, and dill in a small bowl Stir well, form small patties from this mixture Spray with cooking spray; put them in the tray of your Air Fryer, and cook on each side at around 370°F for about 6 minutes.
2. Offer them right away as a snack Enjoy!

Nutrition: **Calories: 80 | Protein: 59 g | Carbohydrates: 79 g | Fat: 34 g | Fiber: 21 g**

## 388. Shrimp Muffins

Ready in: 45 minutes | Servings: 8 | Difficulty: Hard

**Ingredients**

- Cooking spray
- Salt and black pepper according to the taste
- 2 garlic cloves, minced
- 2 tsps. parsley flakes
- 2 ½ c panko
- 10 oz. shrimp, peeled, cooked, and chopped
- 2 c Mozzarella, shredded
- 4 tbsps. mayonnaise
- 2 spaghetti squash, peeled and halved

**Directions**

1. Put the squash halves in your Air Fryer, cook for about 16 minutes at around 350°F, leave to cool off, and grate the flesh into a small bowl.
2. Stir well and add pepper, salt, panko, parsley flakes, garlic, mayo, shrimp, and Mozzarella.

3. Spray some cooking spray on a muffin tray that matches your Air Fryer and split squash and shrimp mix in each cup.

4. Put them in the fryer and cook for about 10 minutes at around 360°F.

5. Arrange the muffins and offer them as lunch on a platter Enjoy!

Nutrition: **Calories: 80 | Protein: 59 g | Carbohydrates: 79 g | Fat: 34 g | Fiber: 21 g**

## 389. Mexican Apple Snack

Ready in: 25 minutes | Servings: 5 | Difficulty: Normal

**Ingredients**

- 1 c clean caramel sauce
- 1 c dark chocolate chips
- ½ c pecans, chopped
- 4 tsps. lemon juice
- 6 big apples, cored, peeled, and cubed

**Directions**

1. Mix the apples with the lemon juice in a small bowl, stir and move to a pan that's perfect for your Air Fryer.

2. Add pecans, chocolate chips, drizzle with caramel sauce, mix, place in the fryer, and steam for about 5 minutes at around 320°F.

3. Gently flip, split into little bowls, and offer as a snack straight away Enjoy!

Nutrition: **Calories: 109 | Protein: 61 g | Carbohydrates: 63 g | Fat: 66 g | Fiber: 37 g**

## 390. Potato Spread

Ready in: 35 minutes | Servings: 5 | Difficulty: Normal

**Ingredients**

- 1 pinch of salt and white pepper
- 4 tbsps. water
- 1 tsp cumin, ground
- 6 garlic cloves, minced
- 3 tbsps. olive oil
- 4 tbsps. lemon juice
- ½ c tahini
- 2 c sweet potatoes, peeled and chopped
- 20 oz. canned garbanzo beans, drained

**Directions**

1. Place the potatoes in the basket of your Air Fryer, cook them for about 15 minutes at around 360°F, cool them down, peel, position them in your food mixer, and pulse well.

2. Apply the tahini, the garlic, the beans, the lemon juice, the cumin, the water, and the oil.

3. Add some salt and white pepper, pump again Split, and serve in small bowls Enjoy!

Nutrition: **Calories: 41 | Protein: 16 g | Carbohydrates: 81 g | Fat: 06 g | Fiber: 16 g**

## 391. Banana Snack

Ready in: 25 minutes | Servings: 10 | Difficulty: Normal

**Ingredients**

- 2 tbsps. coconut oil
- 2 bananas, peeled and sliced into 16 pieces each
- 1 c chocolate chips
- ½ c peanut butter

**Directions**

1. In a small container, place the chocolate chips, heat them up over medium heat, mix until the chocolate melts, and take off the flame.

2. Mix the peanut butter and coconut oil in a cup and mix well.

3. Place 1 tablespoon of chocolate mix in a bowl, add 1 slice of banana, and finish with 1 tablespoon of butter mix.

4. Continue with the remaining cups; put them all in a dish that suits your Air Fryer Cook for about 5 minutes at around 320°F; move to a refrigerator, and keep until you offer them as a snack Enjoy!

Nutrition: **Calories: 41 | Protein: 16 g | Carbohydrates: 81 g | Fat: 06 g | Fiber: 16 g**

## 392. Buffalo Cauliflower Snacks

Ready in: 35 minutes | Servings: 5 | Difficulty: Normal

**Ingredients**

- ½ c buffalo sauce
- ½ c butter, melted
- 2 c panko breadcrumbs
- 6 c cauliflower florets
- Mayonnaise for serving

**Directions**

1. Combine the buffalo sauce and butter in a small bowl and whisk well.

2. In this combination, dip the cauliflower florets and brush them in panko breadcrumbs.

3. Put them within the basket of your Air Fryer and cook for about 15 minutes at around 350°F.

4. Organize them on a platter and serve on the side with mayo Enjoy!

Nutrition: **Calories: 30 | Protein: 07 g | Carbohydrates: 65 g | Fat: 04 g | Fiber: 05 g**

## 393. Coconut Chicken Bites

Ready in: 30 minutes | Servings: 5 | Difficulty: Normal

**Ingredients**

- 10 chicken tenders
- Cooking spray
- 1 c coconut, shredded
- 1 c panko breadcrumbs
- Salt and black pepper according to the taste
- 3 eggs
- 4 tsps. garlic powder

**Directions**

1. Combine the eggs, pepper, salt, and garlic powder in a small bowl and whisk gently.

2. Mix the coconut with the panko in a separate bowl and stir well.

3. Dip the chicken wings in a blend of eggs and then cover one well in coconut.

4. Spray the chicken bites with some cooking spray, put them in the basket of your Air Fryer, and cook for about 10 minutes at around 350°F.

5. Organize them to eat like an appetizer on a platter Enjoy!

Nutrition: **Calories: 30 | Protein: 07 g | Carbohydrates: 65 g | Fat: 04 g | Fiber: 05 g**

## 394. Bacon-Wrapped Brie
Ready in: 15 minutes | Servings: 8 | Difficulty: Easy

**Ingredients**
- 1 (8 oz.) round Brie
- 4 slices sugar-free bacon

**Directions**

1. Position 2 bacon strips to shape an X Put a 3rd bacon strip over the middle of the X sideways Position vertically over the X a fourth slice of bacon On top of your X, it could appear like an addition sign (+) Position the Brie in the middle of the bacon.

2. Tie the bacon from around Brie, using several toothpicks to hold it To suit your Air Fryer container, take a piece of parchment paper and put your bacon-wrapped Brie on it Put it in the container of your Air Fryer.

3. Set the temperature and set the clock to about 400°F for around 10 minutes.

4. At around 3 minutes left on the clock, rotate Brie gently.

5. The bacon will be crispy when grilled, and the cheese will be smooth and melted Cut into 8 pieces to serve.

Nutrition: **Calories: 351 | Protein: 171 g | Carbohydrates: 416 g | Fat: 131 g | Fiber: 233 g**

## 395. Crustless Meat Pizza
Ready in: 10 minutes | Servings: 1 | Difficulty: Easy

**Ingredients**
- 2 tbsps. low-carb, sugar-free pizza sauce for dipping
- 1 tbsp. grated Parmesan cheese
- 2 slices sugar-free bacon, cooked and crumbled
- ¼ c cooked ground sausage
- 7 slices pepperoni
- ½ c shredded Mozzarella cheese

**Directions**

1. Line the bottom of a Mozzarella 6-inch cake tray Put on top of your cheese some sausage, pepperoni, and bacon and cover with Parmesan Put the pan in the bowl of your Air Fryer.

2. Set the temperature and set the clock to about 400°F for around 5 minutes.

3. Remove from the flame once the cheese is fizzing and lightly golden Serve hot with some pizza sauce as dipping.

Nutrition: **Calories: 168 | Protein: 67 g | Carbohydrates: 239 g | Fat: 63 g | Fiber: 6 g**

## 396. Garlic Cheese Bread
Ready in: 20 minutes | Servings: 2 | Difficulty: Easy

**Ingredients**
- ½ tsp garlic powder
- 1 large egg1 large egg
- ¼ c grated Parmesan cheese
- 1 c shredded Mozzarella cheese

**Directions**

1. In a big bowl, combine all the ingredients To fit your Air Fryer bowl cut a piece of parchment paper Add the blend onto the parchment paper to form a circle and put it in the Air Fryer basket.

2. Set the temperature and adjust the timer to about 350°F for around 10 minutes.

3. Serve it hot.

Nutrition: **Calories: 168 | Protein: 67 g | Carbohydrates: 239 g | Fat: 63 g | Fiber: 6 g**

## 397. Mozzarella Pizza Crust
Ready in: 15 minutes | Servings: 1 | Difficulty: Easy

**Ingredients**
- 1 large egg white
- 1 tbsp. full-fat cream cheese
- 2 tbsps. blanched finely ground almond flour
- ½ c shredded whole-milk Mozzarella cheese

**Directions**

1. In a small oven-safe bowl, put almond flour, Mozzarella, and cream cheese Microwave for about 30 seconds Mix until the mixture becomes a softball Add egg white and mix until fluffy, circular dough forms.

2. Shape into 6 round crust pizza.

3. To suit your Air Fryer container, take a piece of parchment paper and put each crust on the parchment paper Place it in the basket of your Air Fryer.

4. Set the temperature and adjust the clock to about 350°F for around 10 minutes.

5. Switch sides after 5 minutes and put any preferred toppings on your crust at this stage like Mozzarella cheese Keep cooking until lightly golden Immediately serve.

Nutrition: **Calories: 118 | Protein: 85 g | Carbohydrates: 31 g | Fat: 86 g | Fiber: 11 g**

## 398. Spicy Spinach Artichoke Dip
Ready in: 20 minutes | Servings: 6 | Difficulty: Easy

**Ingredients**
- 1 c shredded Pepper Jack cheese
- ¼ c grated Parmesan cheese
- ½ tsp garlic powder
- ¼ c full-fat sour cream
- ¼ c full-fat mayonnaise
- 8 oz. full-fat cream cheese, softened
- ¼ c chopped pickled jalapeños
- 1 (14 oz.) can artichoke hearts, drained and chopped
- 10 oz. frozen spinach, drained and thawed

**Directions**

1. In a 4-cup baking dish, combine all your ingredients Put it in the basket of your Air Fryer.

2. Set the temperature and adjust the timer for around 10 minutes to about 320°F.

3. When dark brown and sizzling, remove from flame Serve it hot.

Nutrition: **Calories: 187 | Protein: 45 g | Carbohydrates: 316 g | Fat: 56 g | Fiber: 61 g**

## 399. Mini Sweet Pepper Poppers

Ready in: 25 minutes | Servings: 4 | Difficulty: Easy

**Ingredients**
- ¼ c shredded Pepper Jack cheese
- 4 slices sugar-free bacon, cooked and crumbled
- 4 oz. full-fat cream cheese, softened
- 8 mini sweet peppers

**Directions**

1. Cut the tops of your peppers and lengthwise cut each one in the quarter Remove the seeds and cut the membranes with a tiny knife.

2. Toss the bacon, cream cheese, and Pepper Jack in a tiny bowl

3. Put each sweet pepper with 3 tablespoons of the mixture and push down smoothly Put it in the Air Fryer basket.

4. Set the temperature and adjust the clock to about 400°F for around 8 minutes.

5. Serve it hot.

Nutrition: Calories: 67 | Protein: 24 g | Carbohydrates, 9 g | Fat: 31 g | Fiber: 19 g

## 400. Bacon-Wrapped Onion Rings

Ready in: 15 minutes | Servings: 4 | Difficulty: Easy

**Ingredients**
- 8 slices sugar-free bacon
- 1 tbsp. sriracha
- 1 large onion, peeled

**Directions**

1. Cut your onion into large ¼-inch pieces Sprinkle the sriracha on the pieces of your onion Take 2 pieces of onion and cover the circles with bacon Redo with the rest of the onion and bacon Put in the container of your Air Fryer.

2. Set the temperature and adjust the clock to about 350°F for around 10 minutes.

3. To rotate the onion rings midway through the frying period, use tongs The bacon would be crispy once completely fried Serve hot.

Nutrition: Calories: 67 | Protein: 24 g | Carbohydrates: 9 g | Fat: 31 g | Fiber: 19 g

## 401. Mozzarella Sticks

Ready in: 1 hour and 5 minutes | Servings: 4 | Difficulty: Hard

**Ingredients**
- 2 large eggs
- 1 tsp dried parsley
- ½ oz. pork rinds, finely ground
- ½ c grated Parmesan cheese
- 6 (1 oz.) Mozzarella string cheese sticks

**Directions**

1. Put Mozzarella sticks on a chopping board and slice in half Freeze for about 45 minutes or until solid Remove your frozen sticks after 1 hour if freezing overnight, then put them in a sealed zip-top plastic bag and put them back for potential usage in the freezer.

2. Mix the ground pork rinds, Parmesan, and parsley in a wide dish.

3. Whisk the eggs together in a medium dish separately.

4. Soak a stick of frozen Mozzarella into whisked eggs and then cover it in the Parmesan mixture Repeat for the leftover sticks Put the sticks of Mozzarella in the basket of your Air Fryer.

5. Set the temperature to about 400°F and adjust the clock for around 10 minutes or until it is golden.

6. Serve it hot.

Nutrition: Calories: 157 | Protein: 29 g | Carbohydrates: 153 g | Fat: 96 g | Fiber: 23 g

## 402. Pork Rind Tortillas

Ready in: 15 minutes | Servings: 4 | Difficulty: Easy

**Ingredients**
- 1 large egg
- 2 tbsps. full-fat cream cheese
- ¾ c shredded Mozzarella cheese
- 1 oz. pork rinds

**Directions**

1. Put pork rinds and pulses into the food processor pulse till finely ground.

2. Put Mozzarella in a big oven-safe bowl Cut the cream cheese into tiny bits and transfer them to the bowl Microwave for about 30 seconds or so; all cheeses are molten and can be combined into a ball quickly To the cheese mixture, add some ground pork rinds and eggs.

3. Keep mixing until the combination forms a ball If it cools too fast and the cheese hardens, microwave for another 10 seconds.

4. Divide the dough into 4 tiny balls Put each dough ball among 2 pieces of parchment paper and roll into a ¼-inch flat layer.

5. Put the tortilla chips in a thin layer in your Air Fryer basket, operating in groups if required.

6. Set the temperature and adjust the clock to about 400°F for around 5 minutes.

7. Tortillas, when thoroughly baked, would be crispy and solid.

8. Instantly serve.

Nutrition: Calories: 211 | Fat: 4 g | Fiber: 5 g | Carbohydrates: 14 g | Protein: 11 g

## 403. Bacon Cheeseburger Dip

Ready in: 30 minutes | Servings: 6 | Difficulty: Normal

**Ingredients**
- 2 large pickle spears, chopped
- 6 slices sugar-free bacon, cooked and crumbled
- ½ lb. cooked 80/20 ground beef
- 1 ¼ c shredded medium Cheddar cheese, divided
- 1 tbsp. Worcestershire sauce
- 1 tsp garlic powder
- ¼ c chopped onion
- ¼ c full-fat sour cream
- ¼ c full-fat mayonnaise
- 8 oz. full-fat cream cheese

**Directions**

1. Put the cream cheese in a big, oven-safe dish and microwave for about 45 seconds Add the Worcestershire sauce, sour cream, mayonnaise, garlic powder, onion, and 1 c Cheddar and mix well Add fried ground beef and your bacon to it Sprinkle the leftover Cheddar on top of the mixture.

2. Put in a 6-inch bowl and put into the basket of your Air Fryer.

3. Set the temperature and adjust the clock to about 400°F for around 10 minutes.

4. When the surface is golden brown and bubbling, dipping is cooked Scatter pickles over the dish Serve hot.

Nutrition : Calories: 231 | Fat: 4 g | Fiber: 7 g | Carbohydrates: 14 g | Protein: 15 g

## 404. Pizza Rolls

Ready in: 25 minutes | Servings: 8 | Difficulty: Easy

**Ingredients**

• 2 tbsps. grated Parmesan cheese
• ½ tsp dried parsley
• ¼ tsp garlic powder
• 2 tbsps. unsalted butter, melted
• 8 (1 oz.) Mozzarella string cheese sticks, cut into 3 pieces each
• 72 slices pepperoni
• 2 large eggs
• ½ c almond flour
• 2 c shredded Mozzarella cheese

**Directions**

1. Put almond flour and Mozzarella in a big oven-safe bowl Microwave for a minute Withdraw the bowl and blend until a ball of dough forms If required, microwave for an extra 30 seconds.

2. Crack the eggs into your bowl and blend until the ball becomes soft dough Wet your hands with some water and gently knead your dough.

3. Rip off 2 wide pieces of parchment paper and brush with nonstick cooking spray on each side Put your dough ball between the 2 pieces, facing dough with coated sides Use a rolling pin to roll dough to a thickness of ¼-inch.

4. Use a cutter to cut into 24 rectangles Put 3 pepperoni pieces and 1 strip of stringed cheese on each one of your rectangles.

5. Fold the rectangle in 2, lining the filling with cheese and pepperoni Ends closed by squeeze or roll To suit your Air Fryer bowl, take a piece of parchment paper and put it in the basket On the parchment paper, place the rolls.

6. Set the temperature and adjust the clock to about 350°F for around 10 minutes.

7. Open your fryer after 5 minutes and rotate the rolls of pizza Resume the fryer and proceed to cook until the rolls of pizza are golden brown

8. Put the garlic powder, butter, and parsley in a tiny bowl Brush the mix over the rolls of fried pizza and scatter the pizza with Parmesan Serve it hot.

Nutrition: Calories: 231 | Fat: 4 g | Fiber: 7 g | Carbohydrates: 14 g | Protein: 15 g

## 405. Bacon Jalapeño Cheese Bread

Ready in: 25 minutes | Servings: 4 | Difficulty: Easy

**Ingredients**

• 4 slices sugar-free bacon, cooked and chopped
• 2 large eggs
• ¼ c chopped pickled jalapeños
• ¼ c grated Parmesan cheese
• 2 c shredded Mozzarella cheese

**Directions**

1. In a wide bowl, combine all your ingredients Cut a slice of parchment to match the basket of your Air Fryer.

2. With a touch of water, dampen both of your hands and spread the mix out into a disk Depending on the fryer's scale, you would need to split this into 2 small cheese bread.

3. Put the parchment paper and your cheese bread into the basket of the Air Fryer.

4. Set the temperature and adjust the clock to about 320°F for around 15 minutes.

5. Turn the bread gently once you have 5 minutes remaining.

6. The top would be golden brown when completely baked Serve it hot.

Nutrition: Calories: 235 | Fat: 5 g | Fiber: 6 g | Carbohydrates: 1 g | Protein: 15 g

## 406. Spicy Buffalo Chicken Dip

Ready in: 20 minutes | Servings: 4 | Difficulty: Easy

**Ingredients**

• 2 scallions, sliced on the bias
• 1 ½ c shredded medium Cheddar cheese, divided
• 1/3 c chopped pickled jalapeños
• 1/3 c full-fat ranch dressing
• ½ c buffalo sauce
• 8 oz. full-fat cream cheese, softened
• 1 c cooked, diced chicken breast

**Directions**

1. Put the chicken in a spacious bowl Add some ranch dressing, cream cheese, and buffalo sauce Mix until the sauces are fully blended and completely soft Fold the jalapeños along with 1 cup of Cheddar in it.

2. Transfer the mixture into a circular 4-cup baking dish and put the leftover Cheddar on top Put the dish in your Air Fryer basket

3. Set the temperature and adjust the clock to about 350°F for around 10 minutes.

4. When cooked, it'll be brown at the top, and the dip will bubble Serve it hot with some cut-up scallions on top.

Nutrition: Calories: 235 | Fat: 5 g | Fiber: 6 g | Carbohydrates: 14 g | Protein: 15 g

## 407. Garlic Parmesan Chicken Wings

Ready in: 29 minutes | Servings: 4 | Difficulty: Easy

**Ingredients**

• ¼ tsp dried parsley
• 1/3 c grated Parmesan cheese
• 4 tbsps. unsalted butter, melted

- 1 tbsp. baking powder
- ½ tsp garlic powder
- 1 tsp pink Himalayan salt
- 2 lbs. raw chicken wings

**Directions**

1. Put the chicken wings, ½ tsp garlic powder, salt, and baking powder in a wide bowl, then toss Put the wings in the basket of your Air Fryer.

2. Set the temperature and adjust the clock to about 400°F for around 25 minutes.

3. During the cooking period, rotate the bowl 2–3 times to ensure even cooking.

4. Mix the Parmesan, butter, and parsley in a shallow dish.

5. Please take out your wings from the fryer and put them in a big, clean dish Over your wings, pour the butter mixture and toss until covered completely Serve it hot.

Nutrition: **Calories: 254 | Fat: 12 g | Fiber: 6 g | Carbohydrates: 15 g | Protein: 20 g**

## 408. Bacon-Wrapped Jalapeño Poppers

Ready in: 20 minutes | Servings: 6 | Difficulty: Easy

**Ingredients**

- 12 slices sugar-free bacon
- ¼ tsp garlic powder
- 1/3 c shredded medium Cheddar cheese
- 3 oz. full-fat cream cheese
- 6 jalapeños (about 4-inch long each)

**Directions**

1. Slice off the tops of the jalapeños and cut lengthwise down the middle into 2 sections Using a knife to gently detach the white membrane and seeds from the peppers.

2. Put the Cheddar, cream cheese, and garlic powder in a big, oven-proof dish Stir in the microwave for about 30 seconds Spoon the blend of cheese into your hollow jalapeño.

3. Place a bacon slice over each half of the jalapeño, totally covering the pepper Place it in the basket of an Air Fryer.

4. Set the temperature and adjust the clock to about 400°F for around 12 minutes.

5. Flip the peppers halfway into the cooking period Serve it hot.

Nutrition: **Calories: 241 | Fat: 4 g | Fiber: 8 g | Carbohydrates: 15 g | Protein: 16 g**

## 409. Prosciutto-Wrapped Parmesan Asparagus

Ready in: 20 minutes | Servings: 4 | Difficulty: Easy

**Ingredients**

- 2 tbsps. salted butter, melted
- 1/3 c grated Parmesan cheese
- ⅛ tsp red pepper flakes
- 2 tsps. lemon juice
- 1 tbsp. coconut oil, melted
- 12 (½ oz.) slices prosciutto
- 1 lb. asparagus

**Directions**

1. Put an asparagus spear on top of a slice of prosciutto on a clean cutting board.

2. Drizzle with coconut oil and lemon juice Sprinkle the asparagus with Parmesan and red pepper flakes Roll prosciutto across a spear of asparagus Put it in the basket of your Air Fryer.

3. Set the temperature and adjust the clock to about 375°F for around 10 minutes or so.

4. Dribble the asparagus roll with some butter before serving.

Nutrition: **Calories: 241 | Fat: 4 g | Fiber: 8 g | Carbohydrates: 15 g | Protein: 16 g**

## 410. Mozzarella Sticks II

Ready in: 40 minutes | Servings: 4 | Difficulty: Hard

**Ingredients**

- 1 c panko breadcrumbs
- ½ tsp salt
- 1 tsp Italian seasoning
- 4 Mozzarella cheese sticks cut in half
- 2 tbsps. milk
- 1 egg beaten

**Directions**

1. Break the Mozzarella sticks in half and put them in the freezer for at least 30 minutes.

2. In one bowl, whisk together the egg and milk; in another, combine everything else.

3. Preheat the Air Fryer to 400°F on "Air Fry" mode, with the rack in the center spot.

4. Dip the stick in the egg mixture first, then the panko crumbs, and then back in the egg and crumbs until fully covered.

5. Place the dish on the shelf.

6. Continue before all of the other sticks have been completed.

7. Return for another 8 minutes, flipping halfway around.

8. When they turn brownish, hold an eye on them and remove them.

9. Toss with marinara sauce and serve.

Nutrition: **Calories: 241 | Fat: 4 g | Fiber: 7 g | Carbohydrates: 15 g | Protein: 15 g**

## 411. Potato Wedges II

Ready in: 13 minutes | Servings: 2 | Difficulty: Easy

**Ingredients**

- ⅛ tsp ground black pepper
- ½ tsp sea salt
- ½ tsp paprika
- 1 ½ tbsps. olive oil
- 2 medium potatoes cut into wedges

**Directions**

1. Preheat the Air Fryer to 400°F.

2. Get wedges out of the potatoes Every potato should be quartered and then split into 8 sections.

3. In a wide mixing bowl, position the potato wedges Season with salt, pepper, and paprika and stir well to blend.

4. Stir olive oil Cook the wedges for 8 minutes, rotating once, on a rack in the center of the Air Fryer.

Nutrition: **Calories: 241 | Fat: 4 g | Fiber: 7 g | Carbohydrates: 15 g | Protein: 15 g**

## 412. Ham, Egg, and Cheese Hot Pockets

Ready in: 18 minutes | Servings: 8 | Difficulty: Easy

**Ingredients**
- 2 eggs scrambled
- 4 slices of cheese (shredded will work, too) (any flavor)
- 4 slice deli ham or bacon, sausage, etc.
- 1 roll biscuits 8 total (with butter inside works best)

**Directions**
1. Preheat the Vortex Air Fryer to 350°F using the "Bake" mode Place the rack in the center of the bed.
2. Cook the egg in the microwave after scrambling it Using a rolling pin, roll out the biscuits Stack the remaining ingredients within.
3. Cover and squeeze to shut Check to see if they're covered Cook 4 at a time on the center rack Flip after 4 minutes.

Nutrition: **Calories: 2 | Protein: 0 g | Carbohydrates: 1 g | Fat: 0 g | Fiber: 0 g**

## 413. Mini Egg, Ham, and Cheese Quiche

Ready in: 31 minutes | Servings: 6 | Difficulty: Normal

**Ingredients**
- ½ tsp salt and pepper
- ½ c cheese plus extra for topping Any cheese will go!
- 1 piece bread
- ½ c diced ham bacon, sausage, etc.
- 2 tbsps. milk
- 4 eggs

**Directions**
1. Preheat the Vortex Air Fryer to 350°F Bread, ham, and cheese can both be sliced.
2. In a mixing cup, combine all of the ingredients and stir until well mixed Place the cups on a rack and fill them ¾, complete with the mixture.
3. Making sure the treats are scooped into the cups, so you have ham and cheese instead of just the egg.
4. Cover and bake for 20 minutes Then cover and simmer for another 5 minutes Cook for a couple more minutes after adding the additional cheese.

Nutrition: **Calories: 233 | Fat: 4 g | Fiber: 6 g | Carbohydrates: 15 g | Protein: 20 g**

## 414. Oil-Free Fries

Ready in: 20 minutes | Servings: 1 | Difficulty: Easy

**Ingredients**
- 2 tsps. salt
- 3 potatoes baking (sliced into fries)

**Directions**
1. Preheat the Air Fryer to 400°F Slice the fries and arrange them on a rack on a single sheet.
2. At the moment, you should do 2 shelves Cook for 4 minutes, stirring occasionally.

3. You may also switch one rack up and one rack down if you have 2 racks Cooking would be more even as a result of this.
4. Before golden brown, check every 4 minutes You may have to shift the racks around and rotate them again before they're done sufficiently for your friends! Add salt to your taste.

Nutrition: **Calories: 310 | Fat: 6 g | Fiber: 4 g | Carbohydrates: 14 g | Protein: 20 g**

## 415. Garlic Parmesan Chicken Wings II

Ready in: 20 minutes | Servings: 6 | Difficulty: Easy

**Ingredients**
- Salt and pepper to taste
- 1 tsp dried basil
- 1 tsp dried oregano
- 1 tsp apple cider vinegar
- 1 tsp lemon juice
- 3 tbsps. grated Parmesan cheese
- 1 tbsp. honey
- ½ c mayonnaise
- 2 tbsps. olive oil
- 2 large cloves of garlic minced or pressed
- 2 lbs. bone-in chicken wings

**Directions**
1. Preheat the Air Fryer to 390°F on the air fry level, with the rack in the center place if you aren't using the rotisserie.
2. In a big mixing cup, whisk together all of the ingredients except the chicken wings Toss the wings in the bowl with the mixture and dust uniformly.
3. Put the wings on the central racks for cooking Cook for around 5 minutes before rotating racks or tossing the grill.
4. Cook for another 5 minutes and then switch back Preheat the oven to 165°F.
5. Place the wings in the basket and place the basket in the Air Fryer for rotisserie frying.
6. Cook at 390°F in an Air Fryer Check the temperature after 10 minutes by putting the thermometer into the basket Remove until the temperature reaches 160°F Serve directly with dipping sauce.

Nutrition: **Calories: 287 | Fat: 10 g | Fiber: 2 g | Carbohydrates: 14 g | Protein: 19 g**

## 416. Coconut Shrimp

Ready in: 15 minutes | Servings: 2 | Difficulty: Easy

**Ingredients**
- Oil for spraying
- ¼ tsp black pepper
- 1 tsp salt
- 1 tsp Cajun seasoning
- ¼ c panko breadcrumbs
- ½ c unsweetened shredded coconut
- ½ c all-purpose flour
- 1 egg beaten
- ½ lb. shrimp, about 2-dozen medium

**Directions**
1. Preheat the Air Fryer to 390°F using the "Air Fry" mode The rack should be set to the center location.
2. Keep the tails on the shrimp and peel them if necessary.
3. Three bowls are needed In one dish, combine the flour with all of the seasonings; in another, combine the egg; and in the final, combine the coconut and breadcrumbs.

4. Every shrimp should be dipped in flour, then egg, and finally coconut mixture, ensuring that all shrimp sides are coated.

5. Arrange the shrimp on the rack in a single layer Each rack will hold 1-dozen cookies Place the rack at the bottom of the stack.

6. Cook for 3 minutes after lightly spraying the shrimp with gasoline Cook for another minute or 2 after flipping the shrimp after 3 minutes.

7. Cook until the mixture is solid The amount of time would be calculated by the shrimp's scale Remove the shrimp from the pan and eat with the sauce.

Nutrition: **Calories: 287 | Fat: 10 g | Fiber: 2 g | Carbohydrates: 14 g | Protein: 19 g**

## 417. Pigs in a Blanket
Ready in: 15 minutes | Servings: 1 | Difficulty: Easy
**Ingredients**
• 1 package Little Smokies
• 1 can Crescent Rolls

**Directions**
1. Preheat the oven to 400°F for the Vortex Air Fryer Place your rack in the center of the space.

2. Roll out the Crescent Rolls after opening the bags Make triangles out of them.

3. Cover the Crescent Rolls with the Little Smokies Preheat oven to 350°F and bake for 5 minutes, turning halfway through.

Nutrition: **Calories: 311 | Fat: 5 g | Fiber: 4 g | Carbohydrates: 13 g | Protein: 4 g**

## 418. Chicken Legs in a Basket
Ready in: 15 minutes | Servings: 6 | Difficulty: Easy
**Ingredients**
• 2 tbsps. BBQ sauce
• 1 tsp onion powder
• 1 tsp paprika
• 1 tsp garlic powder
• 1 tsp pepper
• 1 tsp salt
• 1 tbsp. olive oil
• 2 lbs. chicken legs 6–8 drumsticks

**Directions**
1. Drizzle olive oil and seasoning over drumsticks in a big mixing bowl Toss to uniformly coat.

2. Place the basket in the Air Fryer with the chicken legs Since filling the fryer when it's hot is challenging, I placed these in before it heats up.

3. Preheat the Vortex Air Fryer to 375°F.

4. Cook for 5–10 minutes before checking the temperature As the temperature exceeds 165°F, switching off the Air Fryer Enable the basket to cool for a few minutes.

5. Remove the basket from the space It'll still be sticky, so be careful!

6. Brush with a small amount of BBQ sauce before serving as an option.

Nutrition: **Calories: 254 | Fat: 6 g | Fiber: 4 g | Carbohydrates: 16 g | Protein: 22 g**

## 419. Stromboli Rolls
Ready in: 20 minutes | Servings: 6 | Difficulty: Easy
**Ingredients**
• 1 c Mozzarella cheese
• ¼ c olive oil or butter
• ½ c sausage
• ½ c pepperoni slices
• 1 c marinara or spaghetti sauce
• 1 favorite pizza dough(see recipe below)

**Directions**
1. Preheat the Air Fryer to 400°F Place your rack in the center of the space Roll out the pizza dough until it is almost smooth.

2. Add sauce and layer the meats on top of the dough Place a slice of cheese on top.

3. It can be rolled up Cook for 10 minutes, often checking to ensure that it does not smoke.

Nutrition: **Calories: 210 | Fat: 3 g | Fiber: 4 g | Carbohydrates: 12 g | Protein: 9 g**

## 420. Favorite Pizza Dough
Ready in: 1 hour and 15 minutes | Servings: 1 | Difficulty: Hard
**Ingredients**
• 1 tbsp. salt
• 1 tbsp. honey
• 2 c warm water
• 1 tbsp. yeast
• 5 c flour

**Directions**
1. In a stand mixer equipped with the dough hook, combine all of the ingredients Alternatively, you should add anything in a bowl before it forms a ball.

2. Knead for a few minutes, and then set aside to grow in an olive oil-covered dish Allow cool down for at least 1 hour after covering Prepare a floured surface and cut out the dough.

Nutrition: **Calories: 209 | Fat: 5 g | Fiber: 5 g | Carbohydrates: 13 g | Protein: 9 g**

## 421. Sweet Bacon-wrapped Pork Tenderloin
Ready in: 15 minutes | Servings: 2 | Difficulty: Easy
**Ingredients**
• ¼ tsp black pepper
• ½ tsp salt
• ¼ c brown sugar
• 3 tbsps. Dijon honey mustard
• 1 pork tenderloin about 1 lb.
• 5 bacon slices approximately 10 oz.

**Directions**
1. Preheat the Air Fryer to 400°F on "Air Fry" mode, with the lowest shelf.

2. Cook the bacon in long strips for a few minutes or until they are halfway through.

3. Preheat the Air Fryer to 300°F on bake Using paper towels, pat the pork off.

4. Combine mustard, brown sugar, salt, and pepper in a shallow cup Stir in the sugar until it is fully dissolved in the mustard.

5. Arrange the pork loin on a tray Using a couple of tablespoons of the sauce, drizzle it over the bacon Do not touch the pork with your spoon.

6. Roll the bacon around your pork tenderloin On the lowest shelf, bake for 10 minutes Check the temperature and apply for a couple of minutes if it isn't 145°F.

7. Shift the bacon to the top rack for a minute or 2 if it isn't crispy enough.

Nutrition: Calories: 202 | Fat: 6 g | Fiber: 4 g | Carbohydrates: 8 g | Protein: 12 g

## 422. Stuffed Twice "Baked" Potatoes
Ready in: 17 minutes | Servings: 1 | Difficulty: Easy
**Ingredients**
- Salt and pepper to taste
- 1 tbsp. chives chopped
- 4 tbsps. bacon crispy and chopped
- ¼ tsp onion powder
- 1 tsp garlic powder
- 1 tbsp. lime juice
- 1/3 c sour cream
- 1 avocado
- 2 tsps. olive oil
- 2 potatoes washed and scrubbed

**Directions**
1. Preheat the Air Fryer to 350°F and cook on "Bake" mode The rack should be set to the lowest position.
2. Poke potatoes a couple of times with a fork Drizzle with olive oil and season with salt Cook for 30 minutes, or until the potatoes are tender.
3. Prepare the filling in the meantime Mash the avocado in a small cup, add the lime juice, garlic powder, onion powder, sour cream, salt, and pepper to taste.
4. Mix, so all of the ingredients are well combined.
5. Remove the potatoes from the Air Fryer and split them in half Stuff the tortillas with guacamole, pork, and chives.

Nutrition: Calories: 202 | Fat: 6 g | Fiber: 4 g | Carbohydrates: 8 g | Protein: 12 g

## 423. Chicken Bacon Ranch Poppers
Ready in: 20 minutes | Servings: 1 | Difficulty: Easy
**Ingredients**
- ¼ c ranch for dipping
- 1 tsp salt and pepper
- 1 tsp dill
- 1 tsp onion powder
- 1 tsp garlic, minced or ground
- 1 egg beaten
- ¼ c ground pork rinds
- ¼ c Mexican cheese
- 6 slices bacon
- 1 lb. ground chicken

**Directions**
1. Preheat the Vortex Air Fryer to 400°F Chop the bacon and beat the egg.
2. In a big mixing cup, combine all ingredients and vigorously blend with your fingertips.
3. Balls, such as meatballs, may be possible If required, add a couple more pork rinds Cook for 15 minutes in the oven at 165°F.
4. If not, cook for a couple more minutes until finished Don't overcook your dinner!

Nutrition: Calories: 291 | Fat: 5 g | Fiber: 8 g | Carbohydrates: 10 g | Protein: 12 g

## 424. Vortex Air Fryer Burgers
Ready in: 15 minutes | Servings: 1 | Difficulty: Easy
**Ingredients**
- Pepper to taste
- Salt to taste
- 1 envelope French onion dip
- 1 tsp garlic powder
- 1 tbsp. Worcestershire sauce
- ½ onion finely chopped
- 1 package kaiser rolls
- 1 lb. ground beef or pork or turkey

**Directions**
1. Preheat the Vortex Air Fryer to 400°F Place the rack in the center of the space.
2. In a mixing cup, combine all of the ingredients Create patties with the combination.
3. Place in the Air Fryer and flip after 4 minutes, it will take 8–15 minutes to cook depending on how finished you like them.
4. Add the cheese and toast for another minute Butter the buns and toast them for 2–3 minutes Build your burgers!

Nutrition: Calories: 199 | Fat: 3 g | Fiber: 5 g | Carbohydrates: 6 g | Protein: 11 g

## 425. Low-Carb Mexican Lasagna
Ready in: 35 minutes | Servings: 1 | Difficulty: Normal
**Ingredients**
- ¼ c corn (if not doing keto)
- ¼ c sour cream
- 1 avocado 6–8 oz.
- 8 oz. Mexican-blend shredded cheese
- 4 low-carb tortillas
- 1 can enchilada sauce
- 1 packet taco seasoning or make your own
- 1 lb. lean ground beef
- 2 tomatoes or 1 can drain
- Cooking spray

**Directions**
1. Preheat the Air Fryer to 400°F Spray a 9-inch cheesecake tray with cooking spray Preheat the Air Fryer to Sautee mode.
2. Place meat in the pan and cook for 5–7 minutes, occasionally stirring to crumble the meat to ensure no pink remains.
3. Drain the fat One cup of tomatoes and corn, with taco seasoning, are mixed into the beef Take the meat mixture out of the jar.
4. Cover bottom of the baking dish with ½ cup of enchilada sauce, 1 tortilla, ¼ cup of cheese, and 1 ½ cup of the beef mixture, spacing meat out equally.
5. Cover with a second tortilla, ¼ cup of cheese, and vegetables.
6. Layers can be repeated ¾ cup of enchilada salsa, ½ cup of onions, and 1 cup of cheese goes on top of the remaining tortilla.
7. Cover and bake for another 10 minutes, or until bubbly Allow 10 minutes for cooling Serve with sour cream and avocado on top.

Nutrition: Calories: 223 | Fat: 2 g | Fiber: 4 g | Carbohydrates: 11 g | Protein: 8 g

## 426. Aromatic Kale Chips

Ready in: 15 minutes | Servings: 4 | Difficulty: Easy

**Ingredients**

- 2 tbsps. lemon juice
- 1 ½ tsps. seasoned salt
- 2 ½ tbsps. olive oil
- 1 ½ tsp garlic powder
- 1 bunch of kale, torn into small pieces

**Directions**

1. Start throwing the other ingredients alongside your kale.
2. Heat for 5 minutes at 195°F, rotating the kale halfway through.
3. End up serving with your favorite sauce for dipping.

Nutrition: **Calories: 223 | Fat: 2 g | Fiber: 4 g | Carbohydrates: 11 g | Protein: 8 g**

## 427. Cocktail Sausage and Veggies on a Stick

Ready in: 35 minutes | Servings: 4 | Difficulty: Normal

**Ingredients**

- Salt and cracked black pepper, to taste
- ½ c tomato chili sauce
- 16 pearl onions
- 1 red bell pepper, cut into 1 ½-inch piece
- 16 cocktail sausages, halved
- 1 green bell pepper, cut into 1 ½-inch piece

**Directions**

1. Thread onto skewers simultaneously with the cocktail sausages, pearl onions, including peppers Spray with black pepper and salt.
2. Fry for 15 minutes in the hot oven Air Fryer at 380°F, flipping the skewers over once, maybe twice to guarantee the frying is even.
3. Serve on the hand with the tomato chili sauce Enjoy!

Nutrition: **Calories: 223 | Fat: 2 g | Fiber: 4 g | Carbohydrates: 11 g | Protein: 8 g**

## 428. Scallops and Bacon Kabobs

Ready in: 50 minutes | Servings: 6 | Difficulty: Hard

**Ingredients**

- Sea salt and ground black pepper, to taste
- ½ lb. bacon, diced
- 1 tsp garlic powder
- 1 tsp paprika
- 1 shallot, diced
- 1 lb. sea scallops
- ½ c coconut milk
- 1 tbsp. vermouth

**Directions**

1. Put the sea scallops, coconut milk, vermouth, salt, and black pepper in a glass bowl; let it soak for 30 minutes.
2. Prepare the skewers switching the scallops, bacon, and shallots Spray all over the skewers with garlic and paprika.
3. Cook in a hot oven fryer for 5 minutes, at 400°F Serve it hot and enjoy it!

Nutrition: **Calories: 269 | Fat: 5 g | Fiber: 6 g | Carbohydrates: 13 g | Protein: 12 g**

## 429. Tomato Smokies

Ready in: 20 minutes | Servings: 10 | Difficulty: Easy

**Ingredients**

- 1 tsp Erythritol
- ½ tsp cayenne pepper
- 1 tsp avocado oil
- 12 oz. pork and beef smokies
- 3 oz. bacon, sliced
- 1 tsp keto tomato sauce

**Directions**

1. Sprinkle cayenne pepper and tomato sauce over the smokies.
2. Next, spray with the Erythritol and olive oil.
3. Stuff every smokie in the bacon afterward, and seal it with the toothpick—preheat the Fryer to 400°F.
4. Put the bacon smokies in an Air Fryer and then cook them for 8 minutes.
5. Move them lightly throughout baking to avoid burning.
6. Serve with tomato sauce.

Nutrition: **Calories: 269 | Fat: 5 g | Fiber: 6 g | Carbohydrates: 13 g | Protein: 12 g**

## 430. Pickled Bacon Bowls

Ready in: 25 minutes | Servings: 4 | Difficulty: Easy

**Ingredients**

- 1 c avocado mayonnaise
- 4 dill pickle spears, sliced in half and quartered
- 8 bacon slices, halved

**Directions**

1. Cover each pickle spear in a slice of bacon, place it in the basket of your Air Fryer, and cook for 20 minutes at 400°F.
2. Split them into containers and serve the mayonnaise as a snack.

Nutrition: **Calories: 205 | Fat: 8 g | Fiber: 3 g | Carbohydrates: 12 g | Protein: 6 g**

## 431. Granny's Green Beans

Ready in: 15 minutes | Servings: 4 | Difficulty: Easy

**Ingredients**

- 1 c toasted pine nuts
- 1 c butter
- 1 lb. green beans, trimmed
- 2 cloves garlic, minced

**Directions**

1. Heat a water pot.
2. Insert the green beans and simmer for 5 minutes, till they are tender.
3. Warm the butter over a strong large skillet Add the garlic and pine nuts and sauté for 2 minutes until its finely golden brown with the pine nuts.
4. Switch to the skillet with the green beans and turn once brushed.
5. Just serve!

Nutrition: **Calories: 205 | Fat: 8 g | Fiber: 3 g | Carbohydrates: 12 g | Protein: 6 g**

## 432. Crispy Prawns

Ready in: 13 minutes | Servings: 4 | Difficulty: Easy

**Ingredients**

• 18 prawns, peeled and deveined
• 1 egg
• ½ lb. nacho chips, crushed

**Directions**

1. Put the eggs and mix them well in a shallow bowl.
2. In some other bowl, bring the smashed nacho chips in.
3. Now, drop the prawns in the egg mixture and brush the chips with the nacho.
4. Heat the Air Fryer to a level of 355°F.
5. Put the prawns in a thin layer in an Air Fryer basket.
6. Air fry for 10 minutes approximately.
7. End up serving it hot.

Nutrition: Calories: 245 | Fat: 2 g | Fiber: 3 g | Carbohydrates: 5 g | Protein: 6 g

## 433. Saucy Chicken Wings with Sage

Ready in: 1 hour and 11 minutes | Servings: 4 | Difficulty: Hard

**Ingredients**

• 1 tbsp. tamari sauce
• 1/3 tsp fresh sage
• 1 tsp mustard seeds
• ½ tsp garlic paste
• ½ tsp freshly ground mixed peppercorns
• ½ tsp seasoned salt
• 2 tsps. fresh basil
• 1/3 c almond flour
• 1/3 c buttermilk
• 1 ½ lb. chicken wings

**Directions**

1. In a large bowl, put the seasonings together with the garlic paste, chicken wings, buttermilk, including tamari sauce Just let soak for about 55 minutes; let the wings drain.
2. Put the wings in the almond flour and move them to the cooking basket for the Air Fryer.
3. Air fry for 16 minutes Offer with a dressing on the side on a good serving platter Bon appétit!

Nutrition: Calories: 210 | Fat: 12 g | Fiber: 3 g | Carbohydrates: 10 g | Protein: 23 g

## 434. Cheese Cookies

Ready in: 25 minutes | Servings: 10 | Difficulty: Normal

**Ingredients**

**For the dough:**

• 530 oz. flour, sifted
• ½ tsp baking powder
• 530 oz. margarine
• 635 oz. Gruyere cheese, grated
• 338 fl oz. cream
• 1 tsp paprika

• Salt, as required

**For the topping:**

• 2 tbsps. poppy seeds
• 1 tbsp. milk
• 2 egg yolks, beaten

**Directions**

1. Mix the cream, margarine, cheese, paprika, and then salt together in a dish.

2. Put the flour on a flat surface, along with the baking powder Only match them well.
3. Create a well in the middle of the flour by using your fingertips.
4. Attach the combination of cheese and knead it until a smooth dough forms.
5. Roll the dough up to 1–1 ½-inch thick.
6. And use a cookie cutter, cut the cookies.
7. Comb the milk and egg yolks together in the same dish.
8. Cover the milk mixture with the biscuits, and then scatter them with poppy seeds.
9. Level the Air Fryer to a maximum of 340°F.
10. Put the cookies in a baking tray on the Air Fryer grill pan and cook for 12 minutes.
11. Just serve.

Nutrition: Calories: 190 | Fat: 3 g | Fiber: 4 g | Carbohydrates: 7 g | Protein: 10 g

## 435. Crispy Shrimps

Ready in: 13 minutes | Servings: 6 | Difficulty: Easy

**Ingredients**

• 1 tbsp. olive oil
• Salt and black pepper, to taste
• 1 egg
• ¼ lb. nacho chips, crushed
• 10 shrimps, peeled and deveined

**Directions**

1. Preheat the Air Fryer to 365°F and oil the basket of the Air Fryer.
2. Break 1 egg and lb. it well in a shallow bowl.
3. In some other shallow dish, put the nacho chips.
4. Add salt and black pepper to the shrimps, brush them in 1 egg and then roll them into the nacho chips.
5. In the Air Fryer basket, place the seasoned shrimps and fry for about 10 minutes.
6. Food out, serve warm.

Nutrition: Calories: 190 | Fat: 3 g | Fiber: 4 g | Carbohydrates: 7 g | Protein: 10 g

## 436. Cauliflower Dip

Ready in: 50 minutes | Servings: 10 | Difficulty: Hard

**Ingredients**

• ¾ c mayonnaise
• 8 oz. cream cheese, softened
• 2 tbsps. olive oil
• 1 ½ c Parmesan cheese, shredded
• 1 cauliflower head, cut into florets
• 2 tbsps. green onions, chopped
• 2 garlic cloves
• 1 tsp Worcestershire sauce
• ½ c sour cream

**Directions**

1. Lob the olive oil with the cauliflower florets.
2. In the Air Fryer basket, put the cauliflower florets and steam for 25 minutes at 390°F Turn the basket quarter.

3. In the mixing bowl, add the cooked cauliflower, 1 c Parmesan, green onion, garlic, Worcestershire sauce, sour cream, mayonnaise, and then cream cheese process until smooth.

4. Move the cauliflower mixture to the 7-inch dish and cover with the remainder of the Parmesan cheese.

5. Put the dish in an Air Fryer basket and simmer for 10 minutes at 360°F.

6. Cherish and serve.

**Nutrition: Calories: 250 | Fat: 5 g | Fiber: 3 g | Carbohydrates: 7 g | Protein: 12 g**

## 437. Garlic Potatoes II

Ready in: 50 minutes | Servings: 4 | Difficulty: Hard

**Ingredients**

• ¼ tsp black pepper
• 1 tbsp. garlic powder
• 1–2 tbsps. olive oil
• 1 lb. russet baking potatoes
• 1 tbsp. freshly chopped parsley
• ½ tsp salt

**Directions**

1. Steam the potatoes and, with tidy paper towels, wipe them dry.

2. With a fork, penetrate each potato multiple times.

3. In a wide pot, put the potatoes, and then sprinkle with garlic powder, salt, and pepper.

4. Place the olive oil over and blend well.

5. Preheat to 360°F using the Air Fryer.

6. Put the potatoes in the Fryer and fry for about 30 minutes over the cooking process, rotating the basket a few times.

7. Marinade the sliced parsley with the potatoes and serve, if needed, with butter, sour cream, or some other dipping sauce.

**Nutrition: Calories: 250 | Fat: 5 g | Fiber: 3 g | Carbohydrates: 7 g | Protein: 12 g**

## 438. Mexican Cheesy Zucchini Bites

Ready in: 35 minutes | Servings: 4 | Difficulty: Normal

**Ingredients**

• ½ c Queso Añejo, grated
• Salt and cracked pepper, to taste
• ½ c flour
• 1 large-sized zucchini, thinly sliced
• ¼ c yellow cornmeal
• 1 egg, whisked
• ½ c tortilla chips, crushed

**Directions**

1. Use a kitchen towel to dry the zucchini pieces.

2. In a small bowl, combine the rest of the ingredients; blend until everything is well mixed In the ready batter, drop each zucchini slice.

3. Heat at 400°F for 10 minutes in the hot oven Air Fryer, tossing the basket midway through the cooking process.

4. Act in batches unless there are crispy and golden brown slices of zucchini Enjoy!

**Nutrition: Calories: 230 | Fat: 5 g | Fiber: 5 g | Carbohydrates: 12 g | Protein: 9 g**

## 439. Teriyaki Chicken Drumettes

Ready in: 55 minutes | Servings: 6 | Difficulty: Hard

**Ingredients**

• 2 tbsps. fresh chives, roughly chopped

**For the teriyaki sauce:**

• 1 ½ lbs. chicken drumettes
• ¼ c soy sauce
• Sea salt and cracked black pepper, to taste
• 1 tbsp. sesame oil
• ½ tsp fresh ginger, grated
• 2 cloves garlic, crushed
• 1 tbsp. corn starch dissolved in 3 tbsps. water
• ¼ c sugar
• ½ tsp 5-spice powder
• 2 tbsps. rice wine vinegar
• Butter

**Directions**

1. Begin by heating up to 380°F the Air Fryer and using salt and crushed black pepper to rub the chicken drumettes.

2. Heat for about 15 minutes in the preheated Air Fryer Switch them over and cook for 7 more minutes.

3. Integrate the sesame oil, soy sauce, sugar, butter, 5-Spice powder, vinegar, ginger, and garlic in a pan over medium heat, whereas the chicken drumettes are frying Cook for 5 minutes, frequently swirling.

4. Apply the slurry of cornstarch, turn the heat down and let it boil until it thickens with the glaze.

5. Rub the glaze all around the chicken drumettes afterward Air fry for 6 more minutes until it's crispy on the surface Serve finished and coated with fresh chives with the leftover glaze Bon Appetite!

**Nutrition: Calories: 230 | Fat: 5 g | Fiber: 5 g | Carbohydrates: 12 g | Protein: 9 g**

## 440. Thyme Fat Bombs

Ready in: 12 minutes | Servings: 4 | Difficulty: Easy

**Ingredients**

• 1 bacon slice, chopped
• ½ tsp avocado oil
• ½ tsp dried thyme
• 1 tsp bagel seasonings
• 2 tbsps. cream cheese
• 1 c Cheddar cheese, shredded

**Directions**

1. Preheat to 400°F the Air Fryer and place the bacon within Spray the avocado oil with it Bake it for 4 minutes.

2. Then shake it very well and let it simmer for 4 further minutes.

3. Move the bacon into the bowl afterward and chill it to ambient temperature.

4. Insert the cream cheese, dried thyme, Cheddar cheese, and bagel seasonings.

5. Once homogeneous, swirl it Create 4 fat bombs with the scooper's support Place them for up to 2 days in the refrigerator.

**Nutrition: Calories: 214 | Fat: 3 g | Fiber: 3 g | Carbohydrates: 14 g | Protein: 15 g**

## 441. Sweet Corn and Bell Pepper Sandwich with BBQ Sauce

Ready in: 35 minutes | Servings: 2 | Difficulty: Normal

**Ingredients**

• 1 roasted green bell pepper, chopped
• 4 bread slices, trimmed and cut horizontally
• 2 tbsps. butter, softened
• 1 c sweet corn kernels
• ¼ c BBQ sauce

**Directions**

1. Preheat the 355°F Air Fryer and oil an Air Fryer basket.
2. Warm the butter in a medium-hot skillet and add the kernels.
3. Sauté it in a bowl for about 2 minutes and dishes it out.
4. To the maize, apply bell pepper and barbecue sauce.
5. Lay the corn paste over 2 bread slices on one side and cover with the remaining slices.
6. Dish out, serve sweet.

Nutrition: **Calories: 220 | Fat: 4 g | Fiber: 2 g | Carbohydrates: 12 g | Protein: 10 g**

## 442. Bacon-Wrapped Onion Rings With Spicy Ketchup

Ready in: 35 minutes | Servings: 2 | Difficulty: Normal

**Ingredients**

• 8 strips bacon
• ¼ c spicy ketchup
• 1 tsp curry powder
• 1 onion, cut into ½-inch slices
• 1 tsp cayenne pepper
• Salt and ground black pepper, to your liking

**Directions**

1. Put the onion rings with ice water in the bowl; leave them to soak for about 20 minutes; remove the onion rings and use a dish towel to pat them dry.
2. Spray the onion rings with curry powder, cayenne pepper, salt, and black pepper.
3. Cover one layer of bacon around the onion and trim any surplus Using toothpicks protect the rings.
4. Lightly spray the Air Fryer basket with cooking spray; stack the Air Fryer basket with the breaded onion rings.
5. Cook for 1 minute in the hot oven Air Fryer at 360°F, flipping it over midway through the cooking process, and use hot ketchup to serve Bon appétit!

Nutrition: **Calories: 260 | Fat: 5 g | Fiber: 11 g | Carbohydrates: 30 g | Protein: 24 g**

## 443. Tomatoes and Herbs

Ready in: 20 minutes | Servings: 2 | Difficulty: Hard

**Ingredients**

• Cooking spray
• Pepper to taste
• Parsley, minced (optional)
• Parmesan, grated (optional)
• 2 large tomatoes, washed and cut into halves
• Herbs, such as oregano, basil, thyme, rosemary, sage to taste

**Directions**

1. Spray half of each tomato on both sides with a minor bit of cooking oil.
2. With a light coating of pepper and the herb of your choosing, cover the tomatoes.
3. Position the tomatoes, sawed, in the basket Cook for 20 minutes, or longer if desired.
4. Offer as a soothing summer snack, heated, at ambient temperature, or chilled Alternatively, before eating, you should garnish them with grated Parmesan and chopped parsley.

Nutrition: **Calories: 260 | Fat: 5 g | Fiber: 11 g | Carbohydrates: 30 g | Protein: 24 g**

## 444. Tomato and Avocado Egg Rolls

Ready in: 25 minutes | Servings: 5 | Difficulty: Normal

**Ingredients**

• 1 tomato, diced
• Salt and pepper, to taste
• 10 egg roll wrappers
• 3 avocados, peeled and pitted

**Directions**

1. Preheat to 350°F with your Air Fryer.
2. Place the avocados and tomatoes in a bowl Spray with some salt and pepper, then mash with a spoon once you reach a nice texture.
3. Into the wrappers, spoon equivalent proportions of the combination Roll the wrappers over the filling, completely enveloping them.
4. To a lined mixing bowl, switch the rolls and cook for 5 minutes.

Nutrition: **Calories: 2 | Protein: 0 g | Carbohydrates: 1 g | Fat: 0 g | Fiber: 0 g**

## 445. Healthy Broccoli Tots

Ready in: 15-20 minutes | Servings: 4 | Difficulty: Normal

**Ingredients**

• ½ tsp garlic powder
• 1 tsp salt
• ½ c almond flour
• 1 lb. broccoli, chopped
• ¼ c ground flaxseed

**Directions**

1. In a microwave-safe dish, insert the broccoli and microwave for 3 minutes.
2. Move and refine steamed broccoli into the mixing bowl till it appears like rice.
3. Move the broccoli to a large bowl with the mixture.
4. In the bowl, add the remaining ingredients and mix just until balanced.
5. Mist the Air Fryer basket with cooking spray.
6. Create little tots from the broccoli concentrate and put them in the basket of the Air Fryer.
7. Cook tots of broccoli for 10 minutes.
8. Enjoy and serve.

Nutrition: **Calories: 260 | Fat: 5 g | Fiber: 11 g | Carbohydrates: 30 g | Protein: 24 g**

## 446. Lava Rice Bites

Ready in: 30 minutes | Servings: 4 | Difficulty: Normal

**Ingredients**

- ¾ c  breadcrumbs
- 1 tbsp. olive oil
- 3 c cooked risotto
- 1/3 c Parmesan cheese, grated
- 1 egg, beaten
- 3 oz. Mozzarella cheese, cubed

**Directions**

1. Preheat the Air Fryer to 390°F and oil the basket with the Air Fryer.

2. In a bowl, mix the risotto, olive oil, Parmesan cheese, and egg together until mixed.

3. Create little balls of the same size out of the mixture and place a cube of Mozzarella in the middle of each ball.

4. To coat the cheese, brush the risotto mixture with your finger.

5. In a shallow bowl, put the breadcrumbs and cover the balls thinly with breadcrumbs.

6. Move the balls to the basket of an Air Fryer and cook for 10 minutes or so.

7. Dish out, serve hot.

Nutrition: Calories: 254 | Fat: 3 g | Fiber: 3 g | Carbohydrates: 7 g | Protein: 17 g

## 447. Southern Cheese Straws

Ready in: 45 minutes | Servings: 6 | Difficulty: Hard

**Ingredients**

- ½ tsp celery seeds
- 1 c all-purpose flour
- Sea salt and ground black pepper, to taste
- ¼ tsp smoked paprika
- 4 oz. mature Cheddar, cold, freshly grated
- 1 sticks butter

**Directions**

1. Begin by heating up the air Fryer to 330°F Line with parchment paper in the Air Fryer basket.

2. Comb the flour, salt, black pepper, paprika, and celery seeds well in a mixing dish.

3. And after that, in the bowl of a stand mixer, mix the cheese and butter Whisk in the flour mixture gently and blend to combine properly.

4. After that, pack the dough into a star disk-fitted cookie press Pipe through the parchment paper with the long ribbons of dough Split into 6-inch lengths, then.

5. Bake for 1 minute in the hot oven Air Fryer.

6. Repeat with the leftover dough On a shelf, just let cheese straws cold In an airtight jar, you can stack them between sheets of parchment Bon appétit!

Nutrition: Calories: 254 | Fat: 3 g | Fiber: 3 g | Carbohydrates: 7 g | Protein: 17 g

## 448. Turmeric Cauliflower Popcorn

Ready in: 18 minutes | Servings: 4 | Difficulty: Easy

**Ingredients**

- 2 tbsps. almond flour
- Cooking spray
- 1 c cauliflower florets
- 1 tsp ground turmeric
- 1 tsp salt
- 2 eggs, beaten

**Directions**

1. Break tiny chunks of the cauliflower florets and brush with ground turmeric and salt, after which dip the eggs into the vegetables and coat them with almond flour.

2. Preheat the Air Fryer to 400°F.

3. In the Air Fryer, put the cauliflower popcorn in one layer and cook for 5 minutes.

4. Give the veggies a gentle squeeze and cook them for an additional 4 minutes.

Nutrition: Calories: 304 | Fat: 11 g | Fiber: 4 g | Carbohydrates: 12 g | Protein: 17 g

## 449. Nutty Cauliflower Poppers

Ready in: 22 minutes | Servings: 4 | Difficulty: Easy

**Ingredients**

- 1 head of cauliflower, cut into small florets
- ½ c olive oil, plus 1 tsp divided
- 1 tbsp. curry powder
- ¼ tsp salt
- ¼ c golden raisins
- 1 c boiling water
- ¼ c toasted pine nuts

**Directions**

1. Preheat the Air Fryer to 390°F and oil the basket of the Air Fryer.

2. In a bowl, place the raisins in hot water and hold them aside.

3. Sprinkle the pine nuts with 1 tsp olive oil in another dish.

4. In an Air Fryer basket, put the pine nuts and cook for about 2 minutes.

5. Drop and hold aside the pine nuts from the Air Fryer.

6. In a wide bowl, combine the cauliflower, salt, curry powder, and the remaining olive oil together.

7. Switch this combination to the basket of an Air Fryer and cook for about 12 minutes.

8. In a serving cup, dish out the cauliflower and whisk in the pine nuts.

9. Drain the raisins and return them to the bowl for serving.

Nutrition: Calories: 304 | Fat: 11 g | Fiber: 4 g | Carbohydrates: 12 g | Protein: 17 g

## 450. Crispy Eggplant Slices

Ready in: 19 minutes | Servings: 4 | Difficulty: Easy

**Ingredients**

- 2 eggs, beaten
- 1 c Italian-style breadcrumbs
- ¼ c olive oil
- 1 medium eggplant, peeled and cut into ½-inch round slices
- Salt, as required
- ½ c all-purpose flour

**Directions**

1. Put the eggplant slices into a colander and sprinkle with salt.

2. Put down for roughly 45 minutes and tap the slices of eggplant dry.

3. Use a shallow dish to add the flour.

4. In the next dish, crack the eggs and lb. them well.

5. Stir the oil and breadcrumbs into a third bowl.

6. Cover each slice of eggplant with flour, after which dip in the beaten eggs and blend well Lastly, cover the combination of breadcrumbs equally.

7. Preheat the Air Fryer to a temperature of 390°F.

8. Organize the slices of eggplant in a basket of the Air Fryer in a single 2-batch layer.

9. Air Fry for 8 minutes approximately.

10. Just serve.

Nutrition: Calories: 225 | Fat: 12 g | Fiber: 5 g | Carbohydrates: 12 g | Protein: 27 g

## 451. Lemon Tofu
Ready in: 20 minutes | Servings: 4 | Difficulty: Easy

**Ingredients**
- 1 tbsp. arrowroot powder
- 1 lb. tofu, drained and pressed
- 1 tbsp. tamari

**For the sauce:**
- ½ c water
- 1/3 c lemon juice
- 1 tsp lemon zest
- 2 tsps. arrowroot powder
- 2 tbsps. Erythritol

**Directions**

1. Make tofu sliced into cubes In the Ziplock bag, insert tofu and tamari and mix well.

2. Apply 1 tbsp. arrowroot to the bag to cover the tofu and mix well Put down for 15 minutes.

3. In the meantime, combine all the sauce components together in a bowl and put them aside.

4. Spray Air Fryer basket with cooking oil. .

5. Put the tofu into the basket of the Air Fryer and cook for 10 minutes at 390°F Shake until midway.

6. Apply the mixture of cooked tofu and sauce to the pan and steam for 3–5 minutes over moderate flame.

7. Cherish and serve.

Nutrition: Calories: 225 | Fat: 12 g | Fiber: 5 g | Carbohydrates: 12 g | Protein: 27 g

## 452. Grilled Tomatoes
Ready in: 35 minutes | Servings: 2 | Difficulty: Normal

**Ingredients**
- Pepper to taste
- High-quality cooking spray
- 2 tomatoes, medium to large
- Herbs of your choice, to taste

**Directions**

1. Before cutting them in 2, wash and dry the tomatoes.

2. Spray them all over gently with cooking oil.

3. Dress each half with herbs as needed and black pepper (oregano, basil, parsley, rosemary, thyme, sage, etc.).

4. Place the halves in your Air Fryer tray At 320°F, cook for 20 minutes, or further if needed It can take longer for bigger tomatoes to roast.

Nutrition: Calories: 275 | Fat: 12 g | Fiber: 6 g | Carbohydrates: 12 g | Protein: 26 g

## 453. Veggie Pastries
Ready in: 47 minutes | Servings: 8 | Difficulty: Hard

**Ingredients**
- ½ c onion, chopped
- 2 garlic cloves, minced
- 2 tbsps. fresh ginger, minced
- 3 puff pastry sheets
- 2 large potatoes, peeled
- ½ c green peas shelled
- Salt and ground black pepper, as needed
- 1 tbsp. olive oil
- ½ c carrot, peeled and chopped

**Directions**

1. Place the potatoes in a pan of boiling water and cook for about 20 minutes.

2. Deplete the potatoes well and mash the potatoes with a potato masher.

3. Heat oil over a moderate flame in a skillet and sauté the carrot, onion, ginger, and garlic for approximately 4–5 minutes.

4. Drain all of the skillet fat.

5. Add the mashed potatoes, carrots, green peas, salt, and black pepper and mix well Cook for 1–2 minutes, roughly.

6. Drop the potato mixture from the heating until completed and put it aside to cool fully.

7. On a flat surface, put the puff pastry on.

8. Cut 4 pieces of every puff pastry sheet and then cut each slice into a circular shape.

9. Over every pastry round, add about 2 tablespoons of veggie filling.

10. To seal the filling, fold each pastry round in half and moisten the corners using your damp palms.

11. Push the sides tightly with a fork.

12. Set the Air Fryer to a temperature of 390°F.

13. Connect the pastries to the Air Fryer basket in 2 batches in a single layer.

14. Air fry for 5 minutes or so.

15. Just serve.

Nutrition: Calories: 308 | Fat: 7 g | Fiber: 4 g | Carbohydrates: 20 g | Protein: 40 g

## 454. Bacon-Filled Poppers
Ready in: 20 minutes | Servings: 4 | Difficulty: Easy

**Ingredients**
- 1 tbsp. bacon fat
- 1 tsp kosher salt
- Black pepper, ground, to taste
- ½ c jalapeño peppers, diced
- 2/3 c almond flour
- 4 strips crispy cooked bacon
- 3 tbsps. butter
- 2 oz. Cheddar cheese, white, shredded
- 1 pinch cayenne pepper

**Directions**

1. Preheat the Air Fryer to 390°F and oil the basket with the Air Fryer.

2. In a pan, mix the butter with salt and water over moderate flame.

3. Stir in the flour and fry for a few minutes or so.

4. Dish it out in a bowl and combine to form a dough with the rest of the ingredients.

5. Cover the dough with a plastic wrap and chill for about 30 minutes.

6. From this dough, make tiny popper balls and place them in the Air Fryer basket.

7. Heat and dish out for about 15 minutes to eat warmly.

Nutrition: **Calories: 308 | Fat: 7 g | Fiber: 4 g | Carbohydrates: 20 g | Protein: 40 g**

## 455. Pumpkin Seeds

Ready in: 1 hour and 5 minutes | Servings: 2 | Difficulty: Hard

**Ingredients**

• 1 ½ tsp salt
• 1 tsp smoked paprika
• 1 ½ c pumpkin seeds from a large whole pumpkin
• Olive oil

**Directions**

1. In a pot, simmer 2 quarts of well-salted water In the boiling water, roast the pumpkin seeds for 10 minutes.

2. Until at least 20 minutes, pour the contents of the container into a colander and dry the seeds on paper towels.

3. Preheat to 350°F with the Air Fryer.

4. Until putting them in the Air Fryer basket, coat the seeds with olive oil, salt, and smoked paprika.

5. Air fry for 35 minutes To guarantee the pumpkin seeds are crispy and gently golden brown, offer the basket a good shake many intervals during the cooking time.

6. Prior to serving, let the seeds cool Conversely, for munching or for use as a yogurt covering, you should store them in an airtight jar or jar.

Nutrition: **Calories: 210 | Fat: 4 g | Fiber: 4 g | Carbohydrates: 10 g | Protein: 14 g**

## 456. Mediterranean-Style Cocktail Meatballs

Ready in: 20 minutes | Servings: 4 | Difficulty: Easy

**Ingredients**

**For the meatballs:**

• 4 garlic cloves, finely minced
• 1 lb. ground pork
• 2 tbsps. capers
• 1 ½ tbsps. melted butter
• ½ tbsp. fresh cilantro, finely chopped

• 2 eggs
• 2 tsps. red pepper flakes, crushed
• 2 tbsps. fresh mint leaves, finely chopped
• 1 tsp kosher salt

**For the Mediterranean dipping sauce:**

• 1/3 c Greek-style yogurt
• 2 tbsps. fresh rosemary
• 1/3 c black olives, pitted and finely chopped
• 2 tbsps. fresh Italian parsley
• ½ tsp dill, fresh or dried, and chopped
• ½ tsp lemon zest

**Directions**

1. Begin by heating up to 395°F for your Air Fryer.

2. Put all of the items for the meatballs in a large mixing dish; blend to mix properly Form the blend into meatballs sized for golf balls.

3. Heat the meatballs, operating in groups, for about 10 minutes

4. Meanwhile, render the dipping sauce by tucking all the sauce ingredients extensively Use the ready Mediterranean dipping sauce to serve warm meatballs.

Nutrition: **Calories: 210 | Fat: 4 g | Fiber: 4 g | Carbohydrates: 10 g | Protein: 14 g**

## 457. Feta and Parsley Filo Triangles

Ready in: 15 minutes | Servings: 6 | Difficulty: Easy

**Ingredients**

• 2 frozen filo pastry sheets, thawed and cut into 3 strips
• 2 tbsps. olive oil
• Salt and black pepper, to taste
• 4 oz. Feta cheese, crumbled
• 1 egg yolk

• 1 scallion, chopped finely
• 2 tbsps. fresh parsley, chopped finely

**Directions**

1. Preheat the Air Fryer to 390°F and oil the basket with the Air Fryer.

2. In a large bowl, whisk the egg yolk and lb. it well.

3. Combine scallion, parsley, salt, and black pepper with the Feta cheese.

4. Place 1 tbsp. the Feta combination over one edge of the filo strip and spray the pastry with olive oil.

5. To make a triangle, fold diagonally and keep folding until the filling is fully wrapped.

6. Repeat and fill and cover the triangles with olive oil with the leftover strips.

7. In the Air Fryer Basket, position the triangles and cook for approximately 3 minutes.

8. Adjust the Air Fryer to 360°F, then cook for an additional 2 minutes.

9. Dish out, serve sweet.

Nutrition: **Calories: 190 | Fat: 4 g | Fiber: 2 g | Carbohydrates: 12 g | Protein: 9 g**

## 458. Cheddar Cheese Breadsticks

Ready in: 40 minutes | Servings: 4 | Difficulty: Hard

**Ingredients**

- 6 oz. mature Cheddar, cold, freshly grated
- Sea salt and ground black pepper, to taste
- 2 tbsps. cream cheese
- 2 tbsps. cold butter
- ½ c almond meal
- ¼ tsp smoked paprika
- ½ tsp celery seeds

**Directions**

1. Begin by heating up the air Fryer to 330°F Line the parchment paper Air Fryer basket.
2. Comb the almond meal, salt, black pepper, paprika, and celery seeds well in a mixing dish.
3. After which, in the tank of a stand mixer, mix the cream cheese and butter Mash in the almond meal combination gently and blend well to combine.
4. Later, pack the batter into a star disk-fitted cookie press Pipe through the parchment paper with the long ribbons of dough Split into 6-inch lengths, then.
5. Bake for 1 minute in the hot oven Air Fryer with the leftover dough, repeat On a shelf, let the cheese straws cold In an airtight jar, you can stack them between sheets of parchment Top with Cheddar cheese Bon appétit!

Nutrition: **Calories: 190 | Fat: 4 g | Fiber: 2 g | Carbohydrates: 12 g | Protein: 9 g**

# CHAPTER 7

## BAKERY AND DESSERTS

## 459. Fruit Tarts

Ready in: 15 minutes | Servings: 6 | Difficulty: Easy

**Ingredients**

- 1 tbsp. sliced cashew
- 2 c cold water
- 2 tbsps. powdered sugar
- 3 tbsps. unsalted butter
- ½ c cocoa powder
- 1 ½ c plain flour

**For the truffle filling:**
- 3 tbsps. butter
- 1 c fresh cream
- 2 c mixed sliced fruits

**Directions**

1. Combine all of the ingredients in soft dough by kneading them together with milk.

2. The dough should now be rolled out and cut into 2 circles Prick the dough on all sides with a fork before pressing it into the pie tins.

3. In a mixing bowl, combine the filling ingredients Make sure it's a little chunky Fill the pie with the filling and top it with the second round.

4. Preheat the fryer for 5 minutes at 300°F You'll need to cover the tin and place it in the basket.

5. Remove the tin from the oven when the pastry has turned golden brown and set aside to cool Slice and serve with a dollop of sour cream.

Nutrition: **Calories: 190 | Fat: 4 g | Fiber: 2 g | Carbohydrates: 12 g | Protein: 9 g**

## 460. Muffins and Jam

Ready in: 15 minutes | Servings: 6 | Difficulty: Easy

**Ingredients**

- Parchment paper
- 2 c buttermilk
- 1 tbsp. unsalted butter
- 2 tbsps. jam
- ½ tsps. baking soda
- 1 tsp baking powder
- 1 ½ c all-purpose flour, plus 2 tbsps.
- 1 c powdered sugar, plus 2 tbsps.

**Directions**

1. Combine the flour and buttermilk in a mixing bowl Using a spatula, fold the mixture together Whisk the ingredients together to ensure that the jam has thinned Continue to mix the ingredients in the bowl with the remaining ingredients Don't over-mix the ingredients.

2. Prepare the muffin molds by greasing them and filling them with parchment leaf Fill the cups halfway with the mixture and put them aside.

3. Preheat the fryer for 5 minutes at 300°F Reduce the temperature to 250°F and place the muffin molds in the basket Enable to cool in the basket before serving.

Nutrition: **Calories: 220 | Fat: 6 g | Fiber: 3 g | Carbohydrates: 8 g | Protein: 27 g**

## 461. Honey and Oats Cookie

Ready in: 15 minutes | Servings: 6 | Difficulty: Easy

**Ingredients**

- 2 tsps. honey
- 1 tbsp. unsalted butter
- ½ c oats
- 2 tbsps. powdered sugar
- 1 tbsp. liquid glucose
- ½ c milk
- 1 tsp baking powder
- 1 c flour
- 1 c all-purpose flour

**Directions**

1. In a big mixing cup, combine the dry ingredients and warm the glucose with a little water In a mixing bowl, combine the glucose, honey, and butter, then add the milk You'll need a rolling pin to roll out the dough.

2. Create cookies and place them on a baking tray that has been prepared.

3. Preheat the fryer for 5 minutes at 300°F.

4. Reduce the temperature to 250°F and place the baking tray in the basket To ensure that the cookies cook evenly, turn them in the tray.

5. Place the cookies in an airtight container once they have cooled.

Nutrition: **Calories: 220 | Fat: 6 g | Fiber: 3 g | Carbohydrates: 8 g | Protein: 27 g**

## 462. Oats Muffins

Ready in: 35 minutes | Servings: 6 | Difficulty: Normal

**Ingredients**

- ½ tsps. vanilla essence
- 1 c oats
- 3 tsps. vinegar
- 1 c sugar
- 2 tbsps. butter
- ½ tsps. baking soda
- ½ tsps. baking powder
- 1 ½ c milk
- 2 c all-purpose flour

**Directions**

1. To make a crumbly mixture, combine the ingredients and rub them together with your fingers.

2. Divide the milk in half and mix one half with the baking soda and the other half with the vinegar.

3. Mix the 2 milk mixtures and wait for the milk to foam up Add this to the crumbly mixture and whisk everything together quickly When you've made a smooth batter, pour it into a muffin mold and put it aside.

4. Preheat your fryer for 5 minutes at 300°F Place the muffin tins in the basket and wrap them with plastic wrap Cook the muffins for 15 minutes, and test them with a toothpick to see whether they're finished Remove the molds from the oven and serve immediately.

Nutrition: **Calories: 224 | Fat: 3 g | Fiber: 5 g | Carbohydrates: 10 g | Protein: 22 g**

## 463. Tapioca Pudding

Ready in: 25 minutes | Servings: 2 | Difficulty: Normal

### Ingredients
- 3 tbsps. unsalted butter
- 3 tbsps. powdered sugar
- 2 tbsps. custard powder
- 2 c milk
- 2 c tapioca pearls

### Directions
1. In a saucepan, bring the milk and sugar to a boil, combine the custard powder and tapioca pearls, and constantly stir until a thick mixture forms.
2. Preheat the fryer for 5 minutes at 300°F.
3. Reduce the temperature to 250°F and place the dish in the basket Cook for 10 minutes before removing from the heat and allowing it to cool.

Nutrition: Calories: 224 | Fat: 3 g | Fiber: 5 g | Carbohydrates: 10 g | Protein: 22 g

## 464. Banana Pancakes

Ready in: 15 minutes | Servings: 6 | Difficulty: Easy

### Ingredients
- 3 tbsps. butter
- Salt and pepper to taste
- 2 tsps. dried parsley
- 2 tsps. dried basil
- 3 eggs
- 1 ½ c almond flour
- 4 ripe bananas, shredded

### Directions
1. Preheat the oven to 250°F Combine the ingredients in a small bowl Make sure the mixture is smooth and evenly distributed.
2. Oil a pancake mold with butter and set aside Fill the mold with batter and place it in the Air Fryer basket.
3. Cook until the pancakes are golden brown on both sides and serve with maple syrup.

Nutrition: Calories: 300 | Fat: 6 g | Fiber: 3 g | Carbohydrates: 13 g | Protein: 15 g

## 465. Nan Khatai

Ready in: 15 minutes | Servings: 6 | Difficulty: Easy

### Ingredients
- 1 tsp cardamom powder
- 1 tsp baking soda
- 1 tsp baking powder
- 1 tbsp. unsalted Butter
- 1 c icing sugar, plus 3 tbsps.
- 1 c gram flour
- 1 ½ c all-purpose flour

### Directions
1. Using the ingredients, make a crumbly mixture and roll it into small balls, flattening them on a prepared baking tray.
2. Preheat the fryer for 5 minutes at 300°F Reduce the temperature to 250°F and put the baking tray in the basket Heat for 5 minutes on both sides of the ball to maintain consistent heating Store the nan khatai in an airtight jar until they have cooled.

Nutrition: Calories: 300 | Fat: 6 g | Fiber: 3 g | Carbohydrates: 13 g | Protein: 15 g

## 466. Baked Yogurt

Ready in: 25 minutes | Servings: 6 | Difficulty: Easy

### Ingredients
**For the yogurt:**
- 2 c fresh cream
- 2 c yogurt
- 2 c condensed milk

**For the garnishing:**
- 4 tsps. water
- 3 tsps. sugar
- 1 handful of mint leaves
- 1 c blackberries
- 1 c fresh blueberries
- 1 c fresh strawberries

### Directions
1. To make a thick paste, combine all of the ingredients of the yogurt in a mixing bowl.
2. Transfer to baking dishes, being careful not to overfill them.
3. Preheat the fryer for 5 minutes at 300°F Place the bowls in the basket and cover it with a cloth Cook for 15 minutes at 350°F .
4. The mixture should shake but not break when you shake the bowls Allow it to set in the refrigerator before arranging the fruits, garnishing, and serving.

Nutrition: Calories: 213 | Fat: 3 g | Fiber: 7 g | Carbohydrates: 14 g | Protein: 16 g

## 467. Pumpkin Pancakes

Ready in: 20 minutes | Servings: 4 | Difficulty: Easy

### Ingredients
- 3 tbsps. butter
- Salt and pepper to taste
- 2 tsps. dried parsley
- 2 tsps. dried basil
- 3 eggs
- 1 ½ c almond flour
- 1 large pumpkin, shredded

### Directions
1. Preheat the oven to 250°F Combine the products in a shallow dish Make sure the mixture is consistent and uniformly spread.
2. Oil a pancake mold with butter and set aside Fill the mold with batter and put it in the Air Fryer basket.
3. Cook until the pancakes are golden brown on all sides and serve with maple syrup.

Nutrition: Calories: 325 | Fat: 5 g | Fiber: 1 g | Carbohydrates: 15 g | Protein: 14 g

## 468. Chocolate Sponge Cake

Ready in: 25 minutes | Servings: 3 | Difficulty: Easy

### Ingredients
- Parchment or butter paper to line the tin
- 1 tsp vanilla essence
- ½ c soda
- 3 tbsps. powdered sugar
- ½ c oil
- ½ tsps. baking powder
- ½ tsps. baking soda
- ½ c cocoa powder
- 1 c all-purpose flour
- ½ c condensed milk

### Directions
1. To make a smooth and thick batter, combine all of the ingredients in a mixing bowl.

2. Butter a cake pan and line it with parchment paper or butter paper.

3. Load the flour into the muffin pan.

4. Preheat the fryer for 5 minutes at 300°F.

5. You'll need to cover the tin and put it in the basket.

6. Cook the cake for 15 minutes, and test it with a toothpick to see if it's finished.

7. Remove the cake from the pan and break it into slices to eat.

Nutrition: **Calories: 325 | Fat: 5 g | Fiber: 1 g | Carbohydrates: 15 g | Protein: 14 g**

## 469. Brownies

Ready in: 20 minutes | Servings: 3 | Difficulty: Easy

**Ingredients**

• ½ c condensed milk
• 1 c all-purpose flour
• 3 tbsps. melted dark chocolate
• ½ c chopped nuts
• 2 tbsps. water
• 1 tbsp. unsalted butter

**Directions**

1. Combine the ingredients in a mixing bowl and whisk until smooth.

2. Oil a baking pan with butter and set it aside Fill the tin halfway with the combination.

3. Preheat the fryer for 5 minutes at 300°F You'll need to cover the tin and put it in the basket Remove the tray and check if the brownies have been baked with a knife or a toothpick.

4. Break the brownies and serve with a dollop of ice cream after they have cooled.

Nutrition: **Calories: 325 | Fat: 5 g | Fiber: 1 g | Carbohydrates: 15 g | Protein: 14 g**

## 470. Cookie Custards

Ready in: 25 minutes | Servings: 4 | Difficulty: Easy

**Ingredients**

• 2 tbsps. margarine
• ½ c custard powder
• ½ c icing sugar
• 1 c all-purpose flour
• 1 pinch of baking soda and baking powder

**Directions**

1. Combine the margarine and sugar in a mixing cup Combine the remaining ingredients in a large mixing bowl and fold them together.

2. Oil a baking tray with butter and set it aside Shape dough into balls, cover them in flour, and put them in the tray.

3. Preheat the fryer for 5 minutes at 300°F The baking tray must be placed in the basket and covered Cook until the balls have turned a golden brown color.

4. Remove the tray from the oven and set it outside to cool for 30 minutes Keep the container airtight.

Nutrition: **Calories: 170 | Fat: 2 g | Fiber: 2 g | Carbohydrates: 12 g | Protein: 6 g**

## 471. Choco-Chip Muffins

Ready in: 35 minutes | Servings: 5 | Difficulty: Normal

**Ingredients**

• ½ tsps. vanilla essence
• ½ c chocolate chips
• 3 tsps. vinegar
• 1 c sugar
• 2 tbsps. butter
• ½ tsps. baking soda
• ½ tsps. baking powder
• 1 ½ c milk
• 2 c all-purpose flour

**Directions**

1. To make a crumbly paste, combine the ingredients and rub them together with your fingertips.

2. Continuously mix the baking soda and vinegar into the milk Add the milk to the mixture to make a batter that you'll need to pour into the muffin molds.

3. Preheat the fryer for 5 minutes at 300°F Place the muffin molds in the basket and cover them with plastic wrap.

4. Cook the muffins for 15 minutes, and test them with a toothpick to see whether they're finished.

5. Remove the molds from the oven and eat immediately.

Nutrition: **Calories: 200 | Fat: 2 g | Fiber: 6 g | Carbohydrates: 14 g | Protein: 12 g**

## 472. Blueberry Muffins

Ready in: 35 minutes | Servings: 5 | Difficulty: Normal

**Ingredients**

• ½ tsps. vanilla essence
• 2 c blueberries
• 3 tsps. vinegar
• 1 c sugar
• 2 tbsps. butter
• ½ tsps. baking soda
• ½ tsps. baking powder
• 1 ½ c milk
• 2 c all-purpose flour

**Directions**

1. To make a crumbly paste, combine the ingredients and rub them together with your fingertips

2. Continuously mix the baking soda and vinegar into the milk Add the milk to the mix to make a batter that you'll need to pour into the muffin tins

3. Preheat the fryer for 5 minutes at 300°F Place the muffin molds in the basket and cover them with plastic wrap Cook the muffins for 15 minutes, and test them with a toothpick to see whether they're finished

4. Remove the molds from the oven and eat immediately

Nutrition: **Calories: 200 | Fat: 2 g | Fiber: 6 g | Carbohydrates: 14 g | Protein: 12 g**

## 473. Vanilla and Oats Pudding

Ready in: 25 minutes | Servings: 5 | Difficulty: Easy

**Ingredients**

• 3 tbsps. unsalted butter
• 3 tbsps. powdered sugar
• 2 tbsps. custard powder
• 1 c oats
• 2 c milk
• 2 c vanilla powder

**Directions**

1. In a saucepan, carry the milk and sugar to a boil, then combine the custard powder, butter, vanilla powder, and oats, stirring continuously until the mixture thickens.

2. Preheat the fryer for 5 minutes at 300°F.

3. Reduce the temperature to 250°F and place the dish in the basket.

4. Cook for 10 minutes before removing from the heat and allowing it to cool.

Nutrition: **Calories: 190 | Fat: 2 g | Fiber: 2 g | Carbohydrates: 12 g | Protein: 6 g**

## 474. Chocolate Tarts

Ready in: 25 minutes | Servings: 5 | Difficulty: Easy

### Ingredients

- 1 tbsp. sliced cashew
- 2 c cold milk
- 2 tbsps. powdered sugar
- 3 tbsps. unsalted butter
- ½ c cocoa powder
- 1 ½ c plain flour

**For truffle filling:**
- 3 tbsps. butter
- 1 c fresh cream
- 1 ½ melted chocolate

### Directions

1. Mix the flour, cashew, cocoa powder, butter, and sugar with your fingertips in a big mixing cup.

2. Flour can be the consistency of the mixture Knead the dough with the cold milk, seal it in plastic wrap, and set it aside to cool for 10 minutes Prick the sides of the pie with a fork after rolling out the pastry.

3. In a mixing cup, combine the filling components Let sure it's a bit chunky Fill the pie with the filling and top it with the second round.

4. Preheat the fryer for 5 minutes at 300°F You'll need to cover the tin and put it in the basket Remove the tray from the oven. when the pastry has turned golden brown and set aside to cool

5. Slice and serve with a dollop of sour cream.

Nutrition: **Calories: 190 | Fat: 2 g | Fiber: 2 g | Carbohydrates: 12 g | Protein: 6 g**

## 475. Upside Down Pineapple Cake

Ready in: 35 minutes | Servings: 5 | Difficulty: Normal

### Ingredients

**For the batter:**
- ½ tbsps. powdered sugar
- Edible yellow food coloring
- 1 ½ c all-purpose flour, plus ½ c
- ¼ tsps. baking soda
- ¼ tsps. baking powder
- 2 tsps. pineapple essence
- ¼ c condensed milk
- 2 tbsps. butter (preferably unsalted butter)

**For the tin preparation:**
- 8 cherries
- 3 tbsps. sugar (this is to make the caramel)
- 6 slices pineapple

### Directions

1. To begin, you'll need to prepare the tin Butter the tin and use the butter paper to line it on both levels You'll need to sprinkle the tin with flour now.

2. Place the pineapple slices on the bottom of the tin, accompanied by the cherries To use the cherries, split them in half and put them in the cavities.

3. The sugar must now be melted and transformed into caramel Place the tin in the caramel and put it aside.

4. To create the batter, blend all of the ingredients in a big mixing bowl.

5. To start, sieve the flour, baking soda, and powder, and then add them to the mixing bowl.

6. Now apply the butter to the bowl and mix it In a mixing cup, combine the sugar and condensed milk and beat until smooth.

7. In a mixing cup, combine the essence and yellow food coloring, then add the dry ingredients Made sure the batter is consistent and clear of lumps.

8. Load the flour into the muffin pan Preheat the fryer for 5 minutes at 300°F You'll need to cover the tin and put it in the basket.

9. Cook the cake for 15 minutes, and test it with a toothpick to see if it's finished Remove the cake from the pan and break it into slices to eat.

Nutrition: **Calories: 190 | Fat: 2 g | Fiber: 2 g | Carbohydrates: 12 g | Protein: 6 g**

## 476. Zucchini Pancakes

Ready in: 20 minutes | Servings: 4 | Difficulty: Easy

### Ingredients

- 3 tbsps. butter
- Salt and pepper to taste
- 2 tsps. dried parsley
- 2 tsps. dried basil
- 3 eggs
- 1 ½ c almond flour
- 2 zucchinis, shredded

### Directions

1. Preheat the oven to 250°F.

2. Combine the products in a shallow dish Make sure the mixture is consistent and uniformly spread.

3. Oil a pancake mold with butter and set aside Fill the mold with batter and put it in the Air Fryer basket.

4. Cook until the pancakes are golden brown on all sides and serve with maple syrup.

Nutrition: **Calories: 210 | Fat: 7 g | Fiber: 4 g | Carbohydrates: 15 g | Protein: 12 g**

## 477. Saffron Pudding

Ready in: 25 minutes | Servings: 4 | Difficulty: Easy

### Ingredients

- 3 tbsps. unsalted butter
- 3 tbsps. powdered sugar
- 2 tbsps. custard powder
- 2 c almond flour
- 2 tbsps. saffron
- 2 c milk

### Directions

1. In a saucepan, bring the milk and sugar to a boil, combine butter, custard powder, and almond flour, and constantly stir until a thick mixture forms Mix in the saffron and whisk until the color is evenly distributed.

2. Preheat the fryer for 5 minutes at 300°F Reduce the temperature to 250°F and place the dish in the basket.

3. Cook for 10 minutes before removing from the heat and allowing it to cool.

Nutrition: Calories: 280 | Fat: 7 g | Fiber: 3 g | Carbohydrates: 12 g | Protein: 14 g

## 478. Chocolate Chip Waffles
Ready in: 20 minutes | Servings: 6 | Difficulty: Easy

**Ingredients**
- 1 c chocolate chips
- 3 tbsps. butter
- Salt and pepper to taste
- 2 tsps. dried parsley
- 2 tsps. dried basil
- 3 eggs
- 3 c cocoa powder

**Directions**
1. Preheat the oven to 250°F.
2. Combine all of the products, except the chocolate chips, in a shallow mixing cup Make sure the mixture is consistent and uniformly spread.
3. Butter a waffle model and use it to make waffles Fill the mold with batter and put it in the Air Fryer basket Cook until all sides are golden colored.
4. Serve with chips as a garnish.

Nutrition: Calories: 250 | Fat: 1 g | Fiber: 4 g | Carbohydrates: 14 g | Protein: 12 g

## 479. Vanilla Pudding
Ready in: 15 minutes | Servings: 3 | Difficulty: Easy

**Ingredients**
- 3 tbsps. unsalted butter
- 3 tbsps. powdered sugar
- 2 tbsps. custard powder
- 1 tbsp. vanilla essence
- 2 c almond flour
- 2 c milk

**Directions**
1. Boil your milk and the sugar in a pan and add in your custard powder accompanied by some almond flour, vanilla essence, and butter; now stir till you get a nice thick mix.
2. Preheat your fryer for 5 minutes at 300°F.
3. Reduce the temperature to 250°F and place the dish in the basket.
4. Cook for 10 minutes before removing from the heat and allowing it to cool.

Nutrition: Calories: 250 | Fat: 1 g | Fiber: 4 g | Carbohydrates: 14 g | Protein: 12 g

## 480. Cranberry Pancakes
Ready in: 15 minutes | Servings: 3 | Difficulty: Easy

**Ingredients**
- 3 tbsps. butter
- Salt and pepper to taste
- 2 tsps. dried parsley
- 2 tsps. dried basil
- 3 eggs
- 1 ½ c almond flour
- 2 c minced cranberry

**Directions**
1. Preheat the oven to 250°F.
2. Combine the products in a shallow dish Make sure the mixture is consistent and uniformly spread.
3. Oil a pancake mold with butter and set aside Fill the mold with batter and put it in the Air Fryer basket.
4. Cook until the pancakes are golden brown on all sides and serve with maple syrup.

Nutrition: Calories: 200 | Fat: 11 g | Fiber: 6 g | Carbohydrates: 14 g | Protein: 11 g

## 481. Cardamom Cakes
Ready in: 20 minutes | Servings: 4 | Difficulty: Easy

**Ingredients**
- Muffin molds
- 2 tbsps. sugar
- 2 tbsps. butter
- ½ tsps. baking soda
- ½ tsps. baking powder
- 1 tbsp. cardamom powder
- 1 ½ c milk
- 2 c all-purpose flour

**Directions**
1. To make a crumbly paste, combine the ingredients and rub them together with your fingertips.
2. Continuously mix the baking soda and vinegar into the milk.
3. Add the milk to the liquid to make a batter that you'll need to pour into the muffin molds.
4. Preheat the fryer for 5 minutes at 300°F.
5. Place the muffin molds in the basket and cover them with plastic wrap.
6. Cook the muffins for 15 minutes, and test them with a toothpick to see whether they're finished.
7. Remove the muffins from the oven and eat immediately.

Nutrition: Calories: 200 | Fat: 11 g | Fiber: 6 g | Carbohydrates: 14 g | Protein: 11 g

## 482. Sagu Payasam
Ready in: 15 minutes | Servings: 2 | Difficulty: Easy

**Ingredients**
- 3 tbsps. unsalted butter
- 3 tbsps. powdered sugar
- 2 tbsps. custard powder
- 2 c soaked sagu
- 2 c milk

**Directions**
1. Boil your milk and some sugar in a medium-sized pan and add in custard powder accompanied by the sagu and butter; stir till you get a thick mixture.
2. Preheat the fryer for 5 minutes at 300°F Reduce the temperature to 250°F and place the dish in the basket.
3. Cook for 10 minutes before removing from the heat and allowing it to cool.

Nutrition: Calories: 200 | Fat: 11 g | Fiber: 6 g | Carbohydrates: 14 g | Protein: 11 g

## 483. Mini Pancakes

Ready in: 10 minutes | Servings: 4 | Difficulty: Easy

**Ingredients**

- 3 tbsps. butter
- Salt and pepper to taste
- 2 tsps. dried parsley
- 2 tsps. dried basil
- 3 eggs
- 1 ½ c almond flour

**Directions**

1. Preheat the oven to 250°F.

2. Combine the products in a shallow dish Make sure the mixture is consistent and uniformly spread.

3. Oil a pancake mold with butter and set aside Fill the mold with batter and put it in the Air Fryer basket Cook until the pancakes are golden brown on all sides and serve with maple syrup.

Nutrition: **Calories: 170 | Fat: 3 g | Fiber: 2 g | Carbohydrates: 12 g | Protein: 8 g**

## 484. Po'e

Ready in: 15 minutes | Servings: 4 | Difficulty: Easy

**Ingredients**

- 1 c banana slices
- 1 c mango slices
- 1 c pineapple slices
- 3 tbsps. unsalted butter
- 3 tbsps. powdered sugar
- 2 tbsps. custard powder
- 1 c fresh cream
- 2 c coconut milk

**Directions**

1. Boil your milk and some sugar in a medium-sized pan now; add in your custard powder, followed by butter and some fresh cream Keep on stirring till you get a thick blend Add the chopped fruits to your mixture.

2. Preheat the fryer for 5 minutes at 300°F Reduce the temperature to 250°F and place the dish in the basket.

3. Cook for 10 minutes before removing from the heat and allowing it to cool.

Nutrition: **Calories: 170 | Fat: 3 g | Fiber: 2 g | Carbohydrates: 12 g | Protein: 8 g**

## 485. Blueberry Pudding

Ready in: 15 minutes | Servings: 2 | Difficulty: Easy

**Ingredients**

- 3 tbsps. unsalted butter
- 3 tbsps. powdered sugar
- 2 tbsps. custard powder
- 2 c milk
- 1 c blueberry juice

**Directions**

1. Boil your milk and some sugar in a medium-sized pan, then add the custard powder followed by the blueberry juice and the butter; now stir till you get a nice thick mixture.

2. Preheat the fryer for 5 minutes at 300°F.

3. Reduce the temperature to 250°F and place the dish in the basket Cook for 10 minutes before removing from the heat and allowing it to cool.

Nutrition: **Calories: 260 | Fat: 10 g | Fiber: 4 g | Carbohydrates: 12 g | Protein: 24 g**

## 486. Orange Citrus Blend

Ready in: 20 minutes | Servings: 4 | Difficulty: Easy

**Ingredients**

- 2 persimmons, sliced
- 2 oranges, sliced
- 3 tbsps. unsalted butter
- 3 tbsps. powdered sugar
- 2 tbsps. custard powder
- 2 c almond flour
- 2 c milk

**Directions**

1. In a saucepan, bring the milk and sugar to a boil, combine butter, custard powder, and almond flour, and constantly stir until a thick mixture forms Add the cut fruits to the mixture.

2. Preheat the fryer for 5 minutes at 300°F Reduce the temperature to 250°F and place the dish in the basket.

3. Cook for 10 minutes before removing from the heat and allowing it to cool.

Nutrition: **Calories: 252 | Fat: 4 g | Fiber: 2 g | Carbohydrates: 12 g | Protein: 8 g**

## 487. Pistachio Pudding

Ready in: 20 minutes | Servings: 2 | Difficulty: Easy

**Ingredients**

- 2 c finely chopped pistachio
- 3 tbsps. unsalted butter
- 3 tbsps. powdered sugar
- 2 tbsps. custard powder
- 2 c almond flour
- 2 c milk

**Directions**

1. In a saucepan, bring the milk and sugar to a boil, combine butter, custard powder, and almond flour, and constantly stir until a thick mixture forms Add the pistachio nuts to the mixture.

2. Preheat the fryer for 5 minutes at 300°F Reduce the temperature to 250°F and place the dish in the basket.

3. Cook for 10 minutes before removing from the heat and allowing it to cool.

Nutrition: **Calories: 320 | Fat: 4 g | Fiber: 3 g | Carbohydrates: 12 g | Protein: 15 g**

## 488. Baked Cream

Ready in: 20 minutes | Servings: 3 | Difficulty: Easy

**Ingredients**

- 2 c fresh cream
- 2 c condensed milk

**For the garnishing:**

- 4 tsps. water
- 3 tsps. sugar
- 1 handful of mint leaves
- 1 c blackberries
- 1 c fresh blueberries
- 1 c fresh strawberries

**Directions**

1. Blend the cream and apply the milk to it Whisk the ingredients well together and pass this mixture into tiny baking bowls, ensuring you do not overfill the bowls.

2. Preheat the fryer for 5 minutes at 300°F Place the bowls in the basket and cover them with a blanket Cook for 15 minutes at 350°F The mixture can shift but not crack as you shake the bowls.

3. Allow it to set in the refrigerator before arranging the fruits, garnishing, and serving.

Nutrition: Calories: 230 | Fat: 8 g | Fiber: 7 g | Carbohydrates: 13 g | Protein: 14 g

## 489. Apricot Pudding
Ready in: 25 minutes | Servings: 3 | Difficulty: Easy
**Ingredients**
- 2 c apricot
- 3 tbsps. unsalted butter
- 3 tbsps. powdered sugar
- 2 tbsps. custard powder
- 2 c milk
- 2 c almond flour

**Directions**
1. Boil the milk and the sugar in a pan and apply the custard powder accompanied by the almond flour and the butter and whisk until you have a thick mixture Finely chop the apricot and apply it to the mixture.
2. Preheat the fryer for 5 minutes at 300°F Reduce the temperature to 250°F and place the dish in the basket.
3. Cook for 10 minutes before removing from the heat and allowing it to cool.
4. Serve the fruits on top of the bread.

Nutrition: Calories: 230 | Fat: 8 g | Fiber: 7 g | Carbohydrates: 13 g | Protein: 14 g

## 490. Fig Pudding
Ready in: 20 minutes | Servings: 3 | Difficulty: Easy
**Ingredients**
- 2 c figs
- 3 tbsps. unsalted butter
- 3 tbsps. powdered sugar
- 2 tbsps. custard powder
- 2 c almond flour
- 2 c milk

**Directions**
1. In a saucepan, bring the milk and sugar to a boil, combine butter, custard powder, and almond flour, and constantly stir until a thick mixture forms Chop the figs finely and apply them to the mixture.
2. Preheat the fryer for 5 minutes at 300°F Reduce the temperature to 250°F and place the dish in the basket Cook for 10 minutes before removing from the heat and allowing it to cool.

Nutrition: Calories: 230 | Fat: 8 g | Fiber: 7 mg | Carbohydrates: 13 g | Protein: 14 g

## 491. Honey and Orange Pancakes
Ready in: 10 minutes | Servings: 1 | Difficulty: Easy
**Ingredients**
- 3 tbsps. butter
- Salt and pepper to taste
- 2 tsps. dried parsley
- 2 tsps. dried basil
- 1 tbsp. honey
- 3 eggs
- 1 ½ c almond flour
- 1 orange, zested

**Directions**
1. Preheat the oven to 250°F Combine the products in a shallow dish Make sure the mixture is consistent and uniformly spread.
2. Oil a pancake mold with butter and set aside Fill the mold with batter and put it in the Air Fryer basket.
3. Cook until the pancakes are golden brown on all sides and serve with maple syrup.

Nutrition: Calories: 230 | Fat: 8 g | Fiber: 7 g | Carbohydrates: 13 g | Protein: 14 g

## 492. Cream Caramel
Ready in: 15 minutes | Servings: 2 | Difficulty: Easy
**Ingredients**
- 4 tbsps. caramel
- 3 tbsps. unsalted butter
- 3 tbsps. powdered sugar
- 2 c custard powder
- 2 c milk

**Directions**
1. In a saucepan, bring the milk and sugar to a boil, then apply butter and custard powder and whisk until a thick mixture forms.
2. Preheat the fryer for 5 minutes at 300°F.
3. Reduce the temperature to 250°F and place the dish in the basket.
4. Cook for 10 minutes before removing from the heat and allowing it to cool.
5. Serve the caramel on top of the dish when it's still soft.

Nutrition: Calories: 200 | Fat: 8 g | Fiber: 8 g | Carbohydrates: 13 g | Protein: 9 g

## 493. Bebinca
Ready in: 15 minutes | Servings: 2 | Difficulty: Easy
**Ingredients**
- 3 tbsps. unsalted butter
- 3 tbsps. powdered sugar
- 2 tbsps. custard powder
- 2 c milk
- 1 c almond flour
- 1 c coconut milk

**Directions**
1. In a saucepan, bring the milk and sugar to a boil, then combine the custard powder, flour, butter, and coconut milk, constantly stirring until the mixture thickens.
2. Preheat the fryer for 5 minutes at 300°F Reduce the temperature to 250°F and place the dish in the basket.
3. Cook for 10 minutes before removing from the heat and allowing it to cool.

Nutrition: Calories: 200 | Fat: 8 g | Fiber: 8 g | Carbohydrates: 13 g | Protein: 9 g

## 494. Almond Milk
Ready in: 15 minutes | Servings: 3 | Difficulty: Easy
**Ingredients**
- 3 tbsps. unsalted butter
- 3 tbsps. powdered sugar
- 2 tbsps. custard powder
- 1 tsp gelatin

• 2 c milk                    • 2 c almond powder

**Directions**

1. In a saucepan, bring the milk and sugar to a boil, then combine the custard powder, accompanied by the almond powder, and whisk until a thick mixture forms Combine all of the products, including the gelatin, in a large mixing bowl.

2. Preheat the fryer for 5 minutes at 300°F Reduce the temperature to 250°F and place the dish in the basket.

3. Cook for 10 minutes before removing from the heat and allowing it to cool.

Nutrition: **Calories: 2 | Protein: 0 g | Carbohydrates: 1 g | Fat: 0 g | Fiber: 0 g**

## 495. Banana Pudding

Ready in: 15 minutes | Servings: 6 | Difficulty: Easy

**Ingredients**

• 3 tbsps. chopped mixed nuts      • 2 tbsps. custard powder
• 3 tbsps. unsalted butter         • 2 c milk
• 3 tbsps. powdered sugar          • 1 c banana juice

**Directions**

1. In a saucepan, bring the milk and sugar to a boil, combine butter, custard powder, and banana juice, and constantly stir until a thick mixture forms.

2. Preheat the fryer for 5 minutes at 300°F Reduce the temperature to 250°F and place the dish in the basket.

3. Cook for 10 minutes before removing from the heat and allowing it to cool.

4. Nuts may be used as a garnish.

Nutrition: **Calories: 220 | Fat: 2 g | Fiber: 5 g | Carbohydrates: 13 g | Protein: 15 g**

## 496. Strawberry Pudding

Ready in: 25 minutes | Servings: 3 | Difficulty: Easy

**Ingredients**

• 1 c strawberry slices
• 3 tbsps. unsalted butter
• 3 tbsps. powdered sugar
• 2 tbsps. custard powder
• 2 c milk
• 1 c strawberry juice or 2 c strawberry powder

**Directions**

1. In a saucepan, bring the milk and sugar to a boil, combine butter, custard powder, and strawberry juice or powder Constantly stir until the mixture thickens.

2. Preheat the fryer for 5 minutes at 300°F Reduce the temperature to 250°F and place the dish in the basket.

3. Cook for 10 minutes before removing from the heat and allowing it to cool.

4. Serve with cherry as a garnish.

Nutrition: **Calories: 240 | Fat: 3 g | Fiber: 5 g | Carbohydrates: 12 g | Protein: 17 g**

## 497. Strawberry Tart

Ready in: 20 minutes | Servings: 2 | Difficulty: Easy

**Ingredients**

• 2 c cold milk                **For the filling:**
• 2 tbsps. powdered sugar      • 3 tbsps. butter
• 3 tbsps. unsalted butter     • 1 c fresh cream
• 1 1/2 c plain flour          • 2 c sliced strawberries
• Cocoa powder

**Directions**

1. Mix the flour, cocoa powder, butter, and sugar with your fingertips in a big mixing cup.

2. Breadcrumbs can be the consistency of the mixture Knead the dough with the cold milk, seal it in plastic wrap, and set it aside to cool for 10 minutes Prick the sides of the pie with a fork after rolling out the pastry.

3. In a mixing cup, combine the filling components Let sure it's a bit chunky Preheat the fryer for 5 minutes at 300°F You'll need to cover the tin and put it in the basket.

4. Remove the tray from the oven when the pastry has turned golden brown and set aside to cool Slice and serve with a dollop of sour cream.

Nutrition: **Calories: 240 | Fat: 3 g | Fiber: 5 g | Carbohydrates: 12 g | Protein: 17 g**

## 498. Blackberry Pancakes

Ready in: 20 minutes | Servings: 5 | Difficulty: Easy

**Ingredients**

• 3 tbsps. butter              • 2 tsps. dried basil
• Salt and Pepper to taste     • 3 eggs
• 2 tsps. dried parsley        • 1 1/2 c almond flour
                               • 2 c minced blackberry

**Directions**

1. Preheat the oven to 250°F.

2. Combine the products in a shallow dish Ascertain that the mixture is homogeneous well-balanced, and smooth.

3. Oil a pancake mold with butter and set aside Fill the mold with batter and put it in the Air Fryer basket Cook until the pancakes are golden brown on all sides and serve with maple syrup.

Nutrition: **Calories: 240 | Fat: 3 g | Fiber: 5 g | Carbohydrates: 12 g | Protein: 17 g**

## 499. Persimmons Pudding

Ready in: 15 minutes | Servings: 2 | Difficulty: Easy

**Ingredients**

• 3 tbsps. unsalted butter     • 1 c persimmon slices
• 3 tbsps. powdered sugar
• 2 tbsps. custard powder
• 2 c milk

**Directions**

1. In a saucepan, bring the milk and sugar to a boil, add butter, custard powder, and persimmon slices, and constantly stir until the mixture thickens.

2. Preheat the fryer for 5 minutes at 300°F.

3. Reduce the temperature to 250°F and place the dish in the basket.

4. Cook for 10 minutes before removing from the heat and allowing it to cool.

**Nutrition: Calories: 280 | Fat: 7 g | Fiber: 2 g | Carbohydrates: 10 g | Protein: 13 g**

## 500. Orange Pudding

Ready in: 20 minutes | Servings: 1 | Difficulty: Easy

**Ingredients**
- 3 tbsps. unsalted butter
- 3 tbsps. powdered sugar
- 2 tbsps. custard powder
- 2 c milk
- 1 c orange juice

**Directions**

1. In a saucepan, bring the milk and sugar to a boil, add butter, custard powder, and orange juice, and constantly stir before the mixture thickens.

2. Preheat the fryer for 5 minutes at 300°F.

3. Reduce the temperature to 250°F and place the dish in the basket Cook for 10 minutes before removing from the heat and allowing it to cool.

**Nutrition: Calories: 280 | Fat: 7 g | Fiber: 2 g | Carbohydrates: 10 g | Protein: 13 g**

## 501. Green Citrus Pie

Ready in: 20 minutes | Servings: 2 | Difficulty: Easy

**Ingredients**
- 2 c cold milk
- 4 tsps. powdered sugar
- 1 tbsp. unsalted butter
- 1 c plain flour

**For the filling:**
- 4 tsps. lemon zest
- 2 tbsps. sugar
- 2 tsps. Lemon juice
- ½ tsp cinnamon
- 1 c sliced kiwi
- ½ c roasted nuts

**Directions**

1. To make a crumbly mixture, combine all of the ingredients in a mixing bowl Wrap the mixture in cold milk after kneading it.

2. Prick the pie tin sides with a fork and roll out the dough into 2 large circles Press the dough into the pie tin.

3. On low heat, combine the filling ingredients and pour them into the tin The second round should be used to cover the pie tin

4. Preheat the fryer for 5 minutes at 300°F You'll need to cover the tin and put it in the basket.

5. Remove the tray from the oven when the pastry has turned golden brown and set aside to cool Slice and serve with a dollop of sour cream.

**Nutrition: Calories: 250 | Fat: 3 g | Fiber: 6 g | Carbohydrates: 2 g | Protein: 9 g | Protein: 12 g**

## 502. Pineapple Pie

Ready in: 25 minutes | Servings: 5 | Difficulty: Easy

**Ingredients**
- 2 c cold milk
- 4 tsps. powdered sugar
- 1 tbsp. unsalted butter
- 1 c plain flour

**For the pineapple filling:**
- 2 tsps. lemon juice
- ½ tsp cinnamon
- 2 tbsps. sugar
- 1 pineapple
- ½ c roasted nuts

**Directions**

1. To make a crumbly paste, combine all of the ingredients in a mixing bowl Cover the paste in cold milk after kneading it.

2. Prick the pie tin's edges with a fork and roll out the dough into 2 wide circles Press the dough into the pie tin On low heat, combine the filling materials and add them into the tin.

3. The second round can be used to cover the pie tin.

4. Preheat the fryer for 5 minutes at 300°F You'll need to cover the tin and put it in the basket.

5. Remove the tray from the oven when the pastry has turned golden brown and set aside to cool Slice and serve with a dollop of sour cream.

**Nutrition: Calories: 261 | Fat: 7 g | Fiber: 2 g | Carbohydrates: 14 g | Protein: 17 g**

## 503. Butterscotch Muffins

Ready in: 30 minutes | Servings: 5 | Difficulty: Normal

**Ingredients**
- 1 tsp vanilla extract
- 2 tbsps. sugar
- 2 tbsps. butter
- 3 eggs
- 1 ½ c milk
- 2 c cornstarch
- ½ tsp baking soda

**Directions**

1. To make a crumbly paste, combine the ingredients and rub them together with your fingertips.

2. Continuously pour the baking soda into the milk Add the milk to the mix to make a batter that you'll need to pour into the muffin molds.

3. Preheat the fryer for 5 minutes at 300°F Place the muffin molds in the basket and cover them with plastic wrap.

4. Cook the muffins for 15 minutes, and test them with a toothpick to see whether they're finished.

5. Remove the cups from the oven and eat immediately.

**Nutrition: Calories: 261 | Fat: 7 g | Fiber: 2 g | Carbohydrates: 14 g | Protein: 17 g**

## 504. Bacon and Maple Muffins

Ready in: 30 minutes | Servings: 5 | Difficulty: Normal

**Ingredients**
- 2 tbsps. maple syrup
- 1 ½ c buttermilk
- 2 tbsps. butter
- ½ tsp baking soda
- 1 c finely sliced bacon
- ½ tsp baking powder
- 2 c all-purpose flour

**Directions**

1. To make a crumbly paste, combine the ingredients and rub them together with your fingertips Continuously pour the baking soda into the milk.

2. Add the milk to the mix to make a batter that you'll need to pour into the muffin molds.

3. Preheat the fryer for 5 minutes at 300°F Place the muffin molds in the basket and cover them with plastic wrap.

4. Cook the muffins for 15 minutes, and test them with a toothpick to see whether they're finished Remove the molds from the oven and eat immediately.

Nutrition: Calories: 213 | Fat: 2 g | Fiber: 2 g | Carbohydrates: 7 g | Protein: 14 g

## 505. Vanilla Cake

Ready in: 25 minutes | Servings: 5 | Difficulty: Normal

**Ingredients**

• ½ c condensed milk
• 1 c all-purpose flour
• 2 tsps. vanilla extract
• 2 tbsps. water
• 1 tbsp. unsalted butter

**Directions**

1. Combine the ingredients in a mixing bowl and whisk until smooth.

2. Oil a baking pan with butter and set it aside Fill the tin halfway with the combination.

3. Preheat the fryer for 5 minutes at 300°F You'll need to cover the tin and put it in the basket Test to see if the cake has risen properly.

4. Allow the cake to cool before serving.

Nutrition: Calories: 310 | Fat: 4 g | Fiber: 4 g | Carbohydrates: 13 g | Protein: 15 g

## 506. Raspberry Buttermilk Cupcakes

Ready in: 25 minutes | Servings: 6 | Difficulty: Easy

**Ingredients**

• 2 c sliced raspberries
• 1 ½ c buttermilk
• 2 tbsps. butter
• ½ tsp baking soda
• 2 tbsps. sugar
• ½ tsp baking powder
• 2 c all-purpose flour

**Directions**

1. To make a crumbly paste, combine the ingredients and rub them together with your fingertips.

2. Continuously pour the baking soda into the milk Add the milk to the mix to make a batter that you'll need to pour into the muffin molds.

3. Preheat the fryer for 5 minutes at 300°F Place the muffin molds in the basket and cover them with plastic wrap.

4. Cook the muffins for 15 minutes, and test them with a toothpick to see whether they're finished Remove the molds from the oven and eat immediately.

Nutrition: Calories: 314 | Fat: 4 g | Fiber: 4 g | Carbohydrates: 7 g | Protein: 17 g

## 507. Honey Banana Muffins

Ready in: 30 minutes | Servings: 6 | Difficulty: Normal

**Ingredients**

• 1 tbsp. honey
• 2 c mashed banana
• 2 tbsps. butter
• ½ tsp baking soda
• ½ tsp baking powder
• 1 ½ c milk
• 2 c wheat flour

**Directions**

1. To make a crumbly paste, combine the ingredients and rub them together with your fingertips.

2. Continuously pour the baking soda into the milk Add the milk to the liquid to make a batter that you'll need to pour into the muffin molds.

3. Preheat the fryer for 5 minutes at 300°F Place the muffin molds in the basket and cover them with plastic wrap.

4. Cook the muffins for 15 minutes, and test them with a toothpick to see whether they're finished.

5. Remove the molds from the oven and eat immediately.

Nutrition: Calories: 273 | Fat: 4 g | Fiber: 6 g | Carbohydrates: 12 g | Protein: 16 g

## 508. Cheddar Cheese Muffins

Ready in: 15 minutes | Servings: 2 | Difficulty: Easy

**Ingredients**

• 2 tsps. vinegar
• 1 tbsp. sugar
• 2 c melted Cheddar cheese
• 2 tbsps. butter
• ½ tsp baking soda
• ½ tsp baking powder
• 1 ½ c milk
• 2 c all-purpose flour

**Directions**

1. To make a crumbly paste, combine the ingredients and rub them together with your fingertips.

2. Continuously mix the baking soda and vinegar into the milk Add the milk to the mix to make a batter that you'll need to pour into the muffin molds.

3. Preheat the fryer for 5 minutes at 300°F Place the muffin molds in the basket and cover them with plastic wrap Cook the muffins for 15 minutes, and test them with a toothpick to see whether they're finished.

4. Remove the molds from the oven and eat immediately.

Nutrition: Calories: 256 | Fat: 6 g | Fiber: 8 g | Carbohydrates: 12 g | Protein: 24 g

## 509. Pumpkin Choco-Chip Muffins

Ready in: 25 minutes | Servings: 6 | Difficulty: Normal

**Ingredients**

• ½ c chocolate chips
• 2 tsps. vinegar
• 1 tbsp. sugar
• 2 c grated pumpkin
• 2 tbsps. butter
• ½ tsp baking soda
• ½ tsp baking powder
• 1 ½ c milk
• 2 c all-purpose flour

**Directions**

1. To make a crumbly paste, combine the ingredients and rub them together with your fingertips.

2. Continuously mix the baking soda and vinegar into the milk Add the milk to the mix to make a batter that you'll need to pour into the muffin molds.

3. Preheat the fryer for 5 minutes at 300°F Place the muffin molds in the basket and cover them with plastic wrap.

4. Cook the muffins for 15 minutes, and test them with a toothpick to see whether they're finished.

5. Remove the molds from the oven and eat immediately.

Nutrition: Calories: 235 | Fat: 4 g | Fiber: 4 g | Carbohydrates: 12 g | Protein: 17 g

## 510. Corn Muffins

Ready in: 15 minutes | Servings: 3 | Difficulty: Easy

**Ingredients**

- 1 c boiled corn
- 2 tsps. vinegar
- 1 tbsp. sugar
- 2 tbsps. butter
- ½ tsp baking soda
- ½ tsp baking powder
- 1 ½ c milk
- 2 c all-purpose flour

**Directions**

1. To make a crumbly paste, combine the ingredients and rub them together with your fingertips.

2. Continuously mix the baking soda and vinegar into the milk Add the milk to the liquid to make a batter that you'll need to pour into the muffin molds.

3. Preheat the fryer for 5 minutes at 300°F Place the muffin molds in the basket and cover them with plastic wrap.

4. Cook the muffins for 15 minutes, and test them with a toothpick to see whether they're finished.

5. Remove the molds from the oven and eat immediately.

Nutrition: Calories: 235 | Fat: 4 g | Fiber: 4 g | Carbohydrates: 12 g | Protein: 17 g

## 511. Jalapeño Waffles

Ready in: 20 minutes | Servings: 3 | Difficulty: Easy

**Ingredients**

- 1 c pickled jalapeños
- 3 tbsps. butter
- Salt and pepper to taste
- 2 tsps. dried parsley
- 2 tsps. dried basil
- 3 eggs
- 1 ½ c almond flour

**Directions**

1. Preheat the oven to 250°F Combine all of the products, except the jalapeños, in a shallow mixing cup.

2. Make sure the mixture is consistent and uniformly spread Butter a waffle model and use it to make waffles.

3. Fill the mold with batter and put it in the Air Fryer basket Cook until all sides are golden colored Make a cavity and fill it with jalapeños before serving.

Nutrition: Calories: 310 | Fat: 3 g | Fiber: 5 g | Carbohydrates: 12 g | Protein: 22 g

## 512. Lemon Poppy Cakes

Ready in: 15 minutes | Servings: 6 | Difficulty: Easy

**Ingredients**

- 1 tbsp. crushed poppy seeds
- 2 tsps. vinegar
- 2 tbsps. lemon juice
- 1 tbsp. sugar
- 2 tbsps. butter
- ½ tsp baking soda
- ½ tsp baking powder
- 1 ½ c milk
- 2 c all-purpose flour

**Directions**

1. To make a crumbly paste, combine the ingredients and rub them together with your fingertips.

2. Continuously mix the baking soda and vinegar into the milk Add the milk to the mix to make a batter that you'll need to pour into the muffin molds.

3. Preheat the fryer for 5 minutes at 300°F Place the muffin molds in the basket and cover them with plastic wrap.

4. Cook the muffins for 15 minutes, and test them with a toothpick to see whether they're finished.

5. Remove the molds from the oven and eat immediately.

Nutrition: Calories: 310 | Fat: 3 g | Fiber: 5 g | Carbohydrates: 12 g | Protein: 22 g

## 513. Chocolate Cake

Ready in: 25 minutes | Servings: 6 | Difficulty: Normal

**Ingredients**

- ½ c condensed milk
- 1 c all-purpose flour
- 3 tbsps. melted dark chocolate
- 2 tbsps. cocoa powder
- 2 tbsps. water
- 1 tbsp. unsalted butter

**Directions**

1. Combine the ingredients in a mixing bowl and whisk until smooth.

2. Oil a baking pan with butter and set it aside Fill the tin halfway with the combination.

3. Preheat the fryer for 5 minutes at 300°F You'll need to cover the tin and put it in the basket Test to see if the cake has risen properly.

4. Serve after the cake has cooled and been garnished with chocolate chips.

Nutrition: Calories: 310 | Fat: 4 g | Fiber: 6 g | Carbohydrates: 12 g | Protein: 14 g

## 514. Cinnamon Cakes

Ready in: 22 minutes | Servings: 6 | Difficulty: Normal

**Ingredients**

- 2 tbsps. sugar
- 2 tbsps. butter
- ½ tsp baking soda
- ½ tsp baking powder
- 1 tbsp. cinnamon powder
- 1 ½ c milk
- 2 c all-purpose flour

**Directions**

1. To make a crumbly paste, combine the ingredients and rub them together with your fingertips.

2. Continuously mix the baking soda and vinegar into the milk.

3. Add the milk to the mix to make a batter that you'll need to pour into the muffin molds.

4. Preheat the fryer for 5 minutes at 300°F Place the muffin molds in the basket and cover them with plastic wrap.

5. Cook the muffins for 15 minutes, and test them with a toothpick to see whether they're finished.

6. Remove the molds from the oven and eat immediately.

Nutrition: Calories: 321 | Fat: 6 g | Fiber: 4 g | Carbohydrates: 12 g | Protein: 18 g

## 515. Buttermilk and Blueberry Muffins

Ready in: 35 minutes | Servings: 4 | Difficulty: Normal

### Ingredients

• 2 c sliced blueberries
• 2 tsps. vinegar
• 2 tbsps. sugar
• 2 tbsps. butter
• ½ tsp baking soda
• ½ tsp baking powder
• 1 ½ c buttermilk
• 2 c all-purpose flour

### Directions

1. To make a crumbly paste, combine the ingredients and rub them together with your fingertips.

2. Continuously mix the baking soda and vinegar into the milk Add the milk to the mix to make a batter that you'll need to pour into the muffin molds.

3. Preheat the fryer for 5 minutes at 300°F Place the muffin molds in the basket and cover them with plastic wrap.

4. Cook the muffins for 15 minutes, and test them with a toothpick to see whether they're finished.

5. Remove the molds from the oven and eat immediately.

Nutrition: Calories: 321 | Fat: 6 g | Fiber: 4 g | Carbohydrates: 12 g | Protein: 18 g

## 516. Cranberry Muffins

Ready in: 20 minutes | Servings: 4 | Difficulty: Normal

### Ingredients

• 2 c grated cranberries
• 2 tsps. vinegar
• 2 tbsps. sugar
• 2 tbsps. butter
• ½ tsp baking soda
• ½ tsp baking powder
• 1 ½ c milk
• 2 c all-purpose flour

### Directions

1. To make a crumbly paste, combine the ingredients and rub them together with your fingertips

2. Continuously mix the baking soda and vinegar into the milk Add the milk to the mix to make a batter that you'll need to pour into the muffin molds

3. Preheat the fryer for 5 minutes at 300°F Place the muffin molds in the basket and cover them with plastic wrap

4. Cook the muffins for 15 minutes, and test them with a toothpick to see whether they're finished

5. Remove the molds from the oven and eat immediately

Nutrition: Calories: 263 | Fat: 4 g | Fiber: 2 g | Carbohydrates: 12 g | Protein: 22 g

## 517. Orange Muffins

Ready in: 30 minutes | Servings: 6 | Difficulty: Normal

### Ingredients

• 1 ½ c milk
• 2 tsps. vinegar
• ½ tsp baking soda
• 2 tbsps. sugar
• 2 tbsps. butter
• 3 tbsps. orange juice and zest
• ½ tsp baking powder
• 2 c all-purpose flour

### Directions

1. To make a crumbly paste, combine the ingredients and rub them together with your fingertips.

2. Continuously mix the baking soda and vinegar into the milk Add the milk to the mix to make a batter that you'll need to pour into the muffin molds.

3. Preheat the fryer for 5 minutes at 300°F Place the muffin molds in the basket and cover them with plastic wrap.

4. Cook the muffins for 15 minutes, and test them with a toothpick to see whether they're finished Remove the molds from the oven and eat immediately.

Nutrition: Calories: 263 | Fat: 4 g | Fiber: 2 g | Carbohydrates: 12 g | Protein: 22 g

## 518. Buko Pie

Ready in: 15 minutes | Servings: 3 | Difficulty: Easy

### Ingredients

• 1 tbsp. sliced cashew
• 2 c cold water
• 2 tbsps. powdered sugar
• 3 tbsps. unsalted butter
• 1 ½ c plain flour

**For the filling:**
• 3 tbsps. butter
• 1 c fresh cream
• 2 young coconuts (remove the flesh)
• 1 c shredded coconut

### Directions

1. To make a crumbly paste, combine all of the ingredients in a mixing bowl.

2. Cover the paste in cold milk after kneading it Prick the pie tin's edges with a fork and roll out the dough into 2 wide circles Press the dough into the pie tin.

3. On low heat, combine the filling materials and add them into the tin The second round can be used to cover the pie tin.

4. Preheat the fryer for 5 minutes at 300°F You'll need to cover the tin and put it in the basket.

5. Remove the tray from the oven when the pastry has turned golden brown and set aside to cool Slice and serve with a dollop of sour cream.

Nutrition: Calories: 286 | Fat: 8 g | Fiber: 7 g | Carbohydrates: 14 g | Protein: 17 g

## 519. Bougatsa

Ready in: 15 minutes | Servings: 6 | Difficulty: Easy

### Ingredients

• 1 tbsp. sliced cashew
• 2 tbsps. powdered sugar
• 3 tbsps. unsalted butter
• 2 tbsps. custard powder

- 2 c cold water
- 1 ½ c plain flour

**For the filling:**
- 3 tbsps. butter
- 1 c fresh cream
- 1 c Cheddar cheese, melted
- 2 c minced meat

## Directions

1. To make a crumbly paste, combine all of the ingredients in a mixing bowl.
2. Cover the paste in cold milk after kneading it.
3. Prick the pie tin's edges with a fork and roll out the dough into 2 wide circles Press the dough into the pie tin.
4. On low heat, combine the filling materials and add them into the tin.
5. The second round can be used to cover the pie tin.
6. Preheat the fryer for 5 minutes at 300°F You'll need to cover the tin and put it in the basket Remove the tray from the oven when the pastry has turned golden brown and set aside to cool Slice and serve with a dollop of sour cream.

Nutrition: **Calories: 286 | Fat: 8 g | Fiber: 7 g | Carbohydrates: 14 g | Protein: 17 g**

## 520. Blueberry Tarts

Ready in: 15 minutes | Servings: 2 | Difficulty: Easy

### Ingredients

- 1 tbsp. sliced cashew
- 2 c cold water
- 2 tbsps. powdered sugar
- 3 tbsps. unsalted butter
- 1 ½ c plain flour

**For the filling:**
- 3 tbsps. butter
- 1 c fresh cream
- 1 c fresh blueberries, sliced

## Directions

1. To make a crumbly paste, combine all of the ingredients in a mixing bowl.
2. Cover the paste in cold milk after kneading it.
3. Prick the pie tin's edges with a fork and roll out the dough into 2 wide circles Press the dough into the pie tin.
4. On low heat, combine the filling materials and add them into the tin The second round can be used to cover the pie tin.
5. Preheat the fryer for 5 minutes at 300°F You'll need to cover the tin and put it in the basket.
6. Remove the tray from the oven when the pastry has turned golden brown and set aside to cool Slice and serve with a dollop of sour cream.

Nutrition: **Calories: 286 | Fat: 8 g | Fiber: 7 g | Carbohydrates: 14 g | Protein: 17 g**

## 521. Bisteeya

Ready in: 20 minutes | Servings: 3 | Difficulty: Easy

### Ingredients

- 1 tbsp. sliced cashew
- 2 c cold water
- 2 tbsps. powdered sugar
- 3 tbsps. unsalted butter

- 1 ½ c almond flour

**For the filling:**
- 3 tbsps. butter
- 1 c sliced almonds
- 2 c minced chicken

## Directions

1. To make a crumbly paste, combine all of the ingredients in a mixing bowl.
2. Cover the paste in cold milk after kneading it.
3. Prick the pie tin's edges with a fork and roll out the dough into 2 wide circles Press the dough into the pie tin.
4. On low heat, combine the filling materials and add them into the tin.
5. The second round can be used to cover the pie tin.
6. Preheat the fryer for 5 minutes at 300°F You'll need to cover the tin and put it in the basket.
7. Remove the tray from the oven when the pastry has turned golden brown and set aside to cool Slice and serve with a dollop of sour cream.

Nutrition: **Calories: 286 | Fat: 8 g | Fiber: 7 g | Carbohydrates: 14 g | Protein: 17 g**

## 522. Kidney Bean Tart

Ready in: 25 minutes | Servings: 5 | Difficulty: Normal

### Ingredients

- 1 tbsp. sliced cashew
- 2 tbsps. powdered sugar
- 3 tbsps. unsalted butter
- 2 c cold water
- 1 ½ c plain flour

**For the filling:**
- 3 tbsps. butter
- 1 c fresh cream
- 2 c mashed kidney beans

## Directions

1. To make a crumbly paste, combine all of the ingredients in a mixing bowl.
2. Cover the paste in cold milk after kneading it Prick the pie tin's edges with a fork and roll out the dough into 2 wide circles Press the dough into the pie tin.
3. On low heat, combine the filling materials and add them into the tin.
4. The second round can be used to cover the pie tin.
5. Preheat the fryer for 5 minutes at 300°F You'll need to cover the tin and put it in the basket.
6. Remove the tray from the oven when the pastry has turned golden brown and set aside to cool Slice and serve with a dollop of sour cream.

Nutrition: **Calories: 263 | Fat: 4 g | Fiber: 6 g | Carbohydrates: 12 g | Protein: 16 g**

## 523. Strawberry Pancakes

Ready in: 20 minutes | Servings: 6 | Difficulty: Easy

### Ingredients

- 3 tbsps. butter
- Salt and pepper to taste
- 2 tsps. dried parsley
- 2 tsps. dried basil

- 3 eggs
- 1 ½ c almond flour
- 2 c minced strawberries

**Directions**

1. Preheat the oven to 250°F.
2. Combine the products in a shallow dish Make sure the mixture is consistent and uniformly spread.
3. Oil a pancake mold with butter and set aside Fill the mold with batter and put it in the Air Fryer basket.
4. Cook until the pancakes are golden brown on all sides and serve with maple syrup.

Nutrition: **Calories: 263 | Fat: 4 g | Fiber: 6 g | Carbohydrates: 12 g | Protein: 16 g**

## 524. Banana Cream Pie

Ready in: 20 minutes | Servings: 3 | Difficulty: Easy

**Ingredients**

- 1 tbsp. sliced cashew
- 2 c cold water
- 2 tbsps. powdered sugar
- 3 tbsps. unsalted butter
- 1 ½ c plain flour

**For the filling:**
- 3 tbsps. butter
- 1 c fresh cream
- 2 c sliced banana

**Directions**

1. To make a crumbly paste, combine all of the ingredients in a mixing bowl Cover the paste in cold milk after kneading it.
2. Prick the pie tin's edges with a fork and roll out the dough into 2 wide circles Press the dough into the pie tin On low heat, combine the filling materials and add them into the tin The second round can be used to cover the pie tin.
3. Preheat the fryer for 5 minutes at 300°F You'll need to cover the tin and put it in the basket.
4. Remove the tray from the oven when the pastry has turned golden brown and set aside to cool Slice and serve with a dollop of sour cream.

Nutrition: **Calories: 263 | Fat: 4 g | Fiber: 6 g | Carbohydrates: 12 g | Protein: 16 g**

## 525. Banoffee Pie

Ready in: 15 minutes | Servings: 6 | Difficulty: Easy

**Ingredients**

- 2 c cold water
- 2 tbsps. powdered sugar
- 3 tbsps. unsalted butter
- 1 tbsp. sliced cashew
- 1 ½ c plain flour

**For the filling:**
- 1 c fresh cream
- 1 c toffee
- 3 tbsps. butter
- 2 c sliced banana

**Directions**

1. To make a crumbly paste, combine all of the ingredients in a mixing bowl.
2. Cover the paste in cold milk after kneading it Prick the pie tin's edges with a fork and roll out the dough into 2 wide circles Press the dough into the pie tin.
3. On low heat, combine the filling materials and add them into the tin The second round can be used to cover the pie tin.

4. Preheat the fryer for 5 minutes at 300°F You'll need to cover the tin and put it in the basket Remove the tray from the oven when the pastry has turned golden brown and set aside to cool Slice and serve with a dollop of sour cream.

Nutrition: **Calories: 263 | Fat: 4 g | Fiber: 6 g | Carbohydrates: 12 g | Protein: 16 g**

## 526. Bacon and Egg Pie

Ready in: 20 minutes | Servings: 3 | Difficulty: Easy

**Ingredients**

- 1 tbsp. sliced cashew
- 2 c cold water
- 2 tbsps. powdered sugar
- 3 tbsps. unsalted butter
- 1 ½ c plain flour

**For the filling:**
- 3 tbsps. butter
- 8 slices bacon
- 1 c scrambled egg

**Directions**

1. To make a crumbly paste, combine all of the ingredients in a mixing bowl.
2. Cover the paste in cold milk after kneading it.
3. Prick the pie tin's edges with a fork and roll out the dough into 2 wide circles Press the dough into the pie tin.
4. On low heat, combine the filling materials and add them into the tin The second round can be used to cover the pie tin.
5. Preheat the fryer for 5 minutes at 300°F You'll need to cover the tin and put it in the basket.
6. Remove the tray from the oven when the pastry has turned golden brown and set aside to cool Slice and serve with a dollop of sour cream.

Nutrition: **Calories: 220 | Fat: 4 g | Fiber: 2 g | Carbohydrates: 8 g | Protein: 14 g**

## 527. Apricot Blackberry Crumble

Ready in: 30 minutes | Servings: 5 | Difficulty: Normal

**Ingredients**

- 1 ½ c flour
- 2 c fresh blackberries
- 3 tsps. lemon juice
- 1 c sugar
- 3 tbsps. unsalted butter
- 2 c fresh apricots

**Directions**

1. Preheat the oven to 350°F Break the fruits and mix them with half of the sugar and the lemon juice in a bowl.
2. Mix all of the ingredients well before scooping them into an oven dish and spreading them out.
3. In a separate dish, combine the flour, remaining sugar, butter, and 2 tablespoons of water Check to see if the mixture is crumbly.
4. Place the dish in the oven basket for 20 minutes or until the rings are golden brown Heat the dish before eating.

Nutrition: **Calories: 273 | Fat: 4 g | Fiber: 5 g | Carbohydrates: 12 g | Protein: 18 g**

## 528. Vegetable and Oats Muffins

Ready in: 25 minutes | Servings: 6 | Difficulty: Normal

### Ingredients

- ½ tsp vanilla essence (this is an optional ingredient)
- 1 c mixed vegetables
- ½ c oats
- 3 tsps. vinegar
- 1 c + 3 tsps. sugar
- 2 tbsps. butter
- ½ tsp baking soda
- ½ tsp baking powder
- 1 ½ c milk
- 1 c + 2 tbsps. whole wheat flour

### Directions

1. To make a crumbly paste, combine the ingredients and rub them together with your fingertips.
2. Continuously mix the baking soda and vinegar into the milk Add the milk to the mix to make a batter that you'll need to pour into the muffin molds.
3. Preheat the fryer for 5 minutes at 300°F Place the muffin molds in the basket and cover them with plastic wrap.
4. Cook the muffins for 15 minutes, and test them with a toothpick to see whether they're finished Remove the molds from the oven and eat immediately.

Nutrition: Calories: 231 | Fat: 3 g | Fiber: 5 g | Carbohydrates: 7 g | Protein: 17 g

## 529. Coconut and Plantain Pancakes

Ready in: 10 minutes | Servings: 2 | Difficulty: Easy

### Ingredients

- 3 tbsps. butter
- Salt and pepper to taste
- 2 tsps. dried parsley
- 2 tsps. dried basil
- 3 eggs
- 1 ½ c almond flour
- 1 c shredded coconut
- 2 fresh plantains, shredded

### Directions

1. Preheat the oven to 250°F.
2. Combine the products in a shallow dish Make sure the mixture is consistent and uniformly spread.
3. Oil a pancake mold with butter and set aside Fill the mold with batter and put it in the Air Fryer basket.
4. Cook until the pancakes are golden brown on all sides and serve with maple syrup

Nutrition: Calories: 253 | Fat: 3 g | Fiber: 2 g | Carbohydrates: 12 g | Protein: 14 g

## 530. Honey and Nut Pie

Ready in: 30 minutes | Servings: 5 | Difficulty: Normal

### Ingredients

- 2 tsps. lemon juice
- 2 tbsps. sugar
- 1 tbsp. unsalted butter
- 1 c roasted mixed nuts
- 2 c cold milk
- 3 tbsps. honey
- 4 tsps. powdered sugar
- ½ tsp cinnamon
- 1 c plain flour

### Directions

1. To make a crumbly paste, combine all of the ingredients in a mixing bowl Cover the paste in cold milk after kneading it.

2. Prick the pie tin's edges with a fork and roll out the dough into 2 wide circles Press the dough into the pie tin.
3. On low heat, combine the filling materials and add them into the tin The second round can be used to cover the pie tin.
4. Preheat the fryer for 5 minutes at 300°F You'll need to cover the tin and put it in the basket.
5. Remove the tray from the oven when the pastry has turned golden brown and set aside to cool Slice and serve with a dollop of sour cream.

Nutrition: Calories: 253 | Fat: 3 g | Fiber: 2 g | Carbohydrates: 12 g | Protein: 14 g

## 531. Strawberry Muffins

Ready in: 30 minutes | Servings: 4 | Difficulty: Normal

### Ingredients

- ½ tsp vanilla essence
- 3 tsps. vinegar
- ½ tsp baking powder
- 1 c sugar
- 2 tbsps. butter
- ½ tsp baking soda
- ½ c chocolate chips
- 1 ½ c milk
- 2 c all-purpose flour

### Directions

1. To make a crumbly paste, combine the ingredients and rub them together with your fingertips.
2. Continuously mix the baking soda and vinegar into the milk Add the milk to the mix to make a batter that you'll need to pour into the muffin molds.
3. Preheat the fryer for 5 minutes at 300°F Place the muffin molds in the basket and cover them with plastic wrap.
4. Cook the muffins for 15 minutes, and test them with a toothpick to see whether they're finished Remove the molds from the oven and eat immediately.

Nutrition: Calories: 284 | Fat: 6 g | Fiber: 6 g | Carbohydrates: 12 g | Protein: 24 g

## 532. Apple Pie

Ready in: 25 minutes | Servings: 2 | Difficulty: Normal

### Ingredients

- 2 c cold milk
- 4 tsps. powdered sugar
- 1 tbsp. unsalted butter
- 1 c plain flour

For the apple filling:
- 2 tsps. lemon juice
- ½ tsp cinnamon
- 2 tbsps. sugar
- 3 apples, peeled and chopped into slices
- ½ c roasted nuts

### Directions

1. To make a crumbly paste, combine all of the ingredients in a mixing bowl.
2. Cover the paste in cold milk after kneading it.
3. Prick the pie tin's edges with a fork and roll out the dough into 2 wide circles Press the dough into the pie tin.
4. On low heat, combine the filling materials and add them into the tin The second round can be used to cover the pie tin.

5. Preheat the fryer for 5 minutes at 300°F You'll need to cover the tin and put it in the basket.

6. Remove the tray from the oven when the pastry has turned golden brown and set aside to cool Slice and serve with a dollop of sour cream.

Nutrition: **Calories: 284 | Fat: 6 g | Fiber: 6 g | Carbohydrates: 12 g | Protein: 24 g**

## 533. Vanilla Brownies

Ready in: 15 minutes | Servings: 3 | Difficulty: Easy

**Ingredients**

- ½ c condensed milk
- 2 c all-purpose flour
- 3 tbsps. vanilla essence
- ½ c chopped nuts
- 2 tbsps. water
- 1 tbsp. unsalted butter

**Directions**

1. Combine the ingredients in a mixing bowl and whisk until smooth.

2. Oil a baking pan with butter and set it aside Fill the tin halfway with the combination.

3. Preheat the fryer for 5 minutes at 300°F You'll need to cover the tin and put it in the basket.

4. Remove the tray and check if the brownies have been baked with a knife or a toothpick Break the brownies and serve with a dollop of ice cream after they have cooled.

Nutrition: **Calories: 320 | Fat: 7 g | Fiber: 6 g | Carbohydrates: 12 g | Protein: 22 g**

## 534. Cucumber Pancakes

Ready in: 15 minutes | Servings: 3 | Difficulty: Easy

**Ingredients**

- 3 tbsps. butter
- Salt and pepper to taste
- 2 tsps. dried parsley
- 2 tsps. dried basil
- 3 eggs
- 1 ½ c almond flour
- 5 medium cucumbers, shredded

**Directions**

1. Preheat the oven to 250°F.

2. Combine the products in a shallow dish Make sure the mixture is consistent and uniformly spread.

3. Oil a pancake mold with butter and set aside Fill the mold with batter and put it in the Air Fryer basket.

4. Cook until the pancakes are golden brown on all sides and serve with maple syrup.

Nutrition: **Calories: 320 | Fat: 7 g | Fiber: 6 g | Carbohydrates: 12 g | Protein: 22 g**

## 535. Chocolate Pudding

Ready in: 15 minutes | Servings: 3 | Difficulty: Easy

**Ingredients**

- 3 tbsps. unsalted butter
- 3 tbsps. powdered sugar
- 2 tbsps. custard powder
- 2 c milk

- 2 c cocoa powder

**Directions**

1. In a saucepan, bring the milk and sugar to a boil, then combine butter and custard powder, accompanied by the cocoa powder, then whisk until a thick mixture forms.

2. Preheat the fryer for 5 minutes at 300°F.

3. Reduce the temperature to 250°F and place the dish in the basket Cook for 10 minutes before removing from the heat and allowing it to cool.

Nutrition: **Calories: 289 | Fat: 12 g | Fiber: 8 g | Carbohydrates: 12 g | Protein: 20 g**

## 536. Bread Pudding

Ready in: 20 minutes | Servings: 4 | Difficulty: Easy

**Ingredients**

- 3 tbsps. unsalted butter
- 3 tbsps. powdered sugar
- 2 tbsps. custard powder
- 2 c milk
- 6 slices bread
- Jam

**Directions**

1. Spread butter and jam on the bread slices and carve them into the desired shapes Put them in an oiled baking dish.

2. In a saucepan, bring the milk and sugar to a boil, then apply the custard powder and whisk until a thick mixture forms.

3. Preheat the fryer for 5 minutes at 300°F Reduce the temperature to 250°F and place the dish in the basket.

4. Cook for 10 minutes before removing from the heat and allowing it to cool.

Nutrition: **Calories: 289 | Fat: 12 g | Fiber: 8 g | Carbohydrates: 12 g | Protein: 20 g**

## 537. Chocolate Lava Cake

Ready in: 30 minutes | Servings: 4 | Difficulty: Normal

**Ingredients**

- 1 c dark cocoa chocolate melted
- 1 butter piece
- 2 eggs
- 4 tbsps. sugar-sugar
- 1 tbsp. honey
- 4 tbsps. flour
- Kosher salt touch
- Cloves ground
- ¼ tsps. nutmeg brushed
- ¼ tsps. powdered cinnamon

**Directions**

1. Spray the inside of 4 baking spray custard bowls.

2. Heat the melted chocolate candy and butter for 15–30 seconds in the microwave.

3. Mix the eggs, sugar, and honey in a large bowl with a fork till they get viscous Pour the molten blend of chocolate in.

4. Put in most of the components and blend them with a manual mixer or an electronic machine.

5. Shift equivalent amounts of the blend into the custard cups that have been made.

6. Put it in the Air Fryer and cook for 12 minutes at 350°F.

7. Pull from the Air Fryer and permit 4–5 minutes to settle.

8. On a pastry tray, put each bowl upside-down and then let the cake slip out Offer with berries or, if wanted, chocolate syrup.

Nutrition: Calories: 250 | Fat: 2 g | Fiber: 7 g | Carbohydrates: 14 g | Protein: 14 g

## 538. Chocolate Brownie
Ready in: 25 minutes | Servings: 4 | Difficulty: Normal
**Ingredients**
- 1 c bananas, overripe
- 1 protein powder scoop
- 2 tbsps. cocoa powder unsweetened
- ½ c butter with almond, softened

**Directions**
1. Set the temperature to 325°F of the Air Fryer.
2. Sprinkle the cooking pan of the Air Fryer using cooking spray.
3. In the mixer, combine all the ingredients and mix once fluffy.
4. Pour the mixture into a ready pan and place it in the Air Fryer's bucket.
5. Cook the brownie for 16 minutes.
6. Experience and start serving.

Nutrition: Calories: 250 | Fat: 2 g | Fiber: 7 g | Carbohydrates: 14 g | Protein: 14 g

## 539. Spanish-Style Doughnut Tejeringos
Ready in: 25 minutes | Servings: 4 | Difficulty: Normal
**Ingredients**
- ¾ c water
- 6 tbsps. butter
- ¾ c all-purpose flour
- 1 tbsp. sugar
- ¼ tsp sea salt
- ¼ tsp ground cloves
- ¼ tsp grated nutmeg
- Eggs

**Directions**
1. Warm the water in a skillet over medium-high heat to make bread; then add the sugar, salt, nutmeg, and cloves; bake once soluble.
2. Add the butter, and then lower the heat to a low level Mix the flour in steadily, constantly stirring, till the solution turns a ball.
3. Turn off the heat; roll one at a time into the eggs, shaking well to mix.
4. With just a large star cap, put the solution into a serving bowl Try squeezing the dough pieces into the oiled Air Fryer pan.
5. For 6 minutes, simmer at 410°F, working in stages Bon appétit!

Nutrition: Calories: 270 | Fat: 12 g | Fiber: 6 g | Carbohydrates: 12 g | Protein: 23 g

## 540. Father's Day Cranberry and Whiskey Brownies
Ready in: 1 hour | Servings: 9 | Difficulty: Hard
**Ingredients**
- ¾ c self-rising flour
- ¾ c white sugar
- ¼ tsp ground cardamom
- 1 tsp pure rum extract
- 3 tbsps. coconut flakes
- 1/3 c cranberries
- 3 tbsps. whiskey
- 8 oz. white chocolate
- ½ c coconut oil
- 2 eggs plus egg yolk, whisked

**Directions**
1. Microwave white chocolate with coconut oil until it is started to melt; allow the solution to cool down at room temperature.
2. Mix the eggs, sugar, rum concentrate, and cardamom completely afterward.
3. Apply the rum/egg combination to the chocolate mixture in the next stage Whisk in the flakes of coconut and the flour; blend to combine.
4. Stir the bourbon with the cranberries, and then let them simmer for 15 minutes—place in the batter for them Push the batter into a finely buttered cake.
5. Cook in the Air Fryer for 3 minutes at 340°F Before cutting and serving, let them cool a bit on a wire rack.

Nutrition: Calories: 270 | Fat: 12 g | Fiber: 6 g | Carbohydrates: 12 g | Protein: 23 g

## 541. Lemon Berries Stew
Ready in: 35 minutes | Servings: 4 | Difficulty: Normal
**Ingredients**
- 1 tbsp. lemon juice
- 1 ½ c water
- 1 lb. strawberries, halved
- 4 tbsps. Stevia

**Directions**
1. Place all the items in a pot that would be perfect for your Air Fryer, shake Place it in the Air Fryer and bake for 10 minutes at 340°F.
2. Break the stew into containers, and deliver it cold.

Nutrition: Calories: 240 | Fat: 5 g | Fiber: 4 g | Carbohydrates: 8 g | Protein: 15 g

## 542. Berry Pudding
Ready in: 25 minutes | Servings: 6 | Difficulty: Normal
**Ingredients**
- 1/3 c blueberries
- 2 c coconut cream
- 3 tbsps. Swerve
- Zest of 1 lime, grated
- 1/3 c blackberries

**Directions**
1. Mix all the ingredients in a mixer and pulse.
2. Split this into 6 tiny ramekins; place them in your Air Fryer, then bake for 10 minutes at 340°F.
3. Only serve it cold.

Nutrition: Calories: 265 | Fat: 7 g | Fiber: 6 g | Carbohydrates: 15 g | Protein: 32 g

## 543. Puffy Coconut and Pecan Cookies
Ready in: 25–35 minutes | Servings: 10 | Difficulty: Hard
**Ingredients**
- ½ tsp pure vanilla extract
- ½ tsp pure coconut extract

- ⅛ tsp fine sea salt
- ¾ c coconut oil, room temperature
- 1 ½ c coconut flour
- ¼ tsp freshly grated nutmeg
- 1/3 tsp ground cloves
- 1/3 tsp baking soda
- ½ tsp baking powder
- 1 c pecan nuts, unsalted and roughly chopped
- 3 eggs plus 1 egg yolk, whisked
- 1 ½ c extra-fine almond flour
- ¾ c Monk Fruit

## Directions

1. Mix all grades of flour, baking soda, and baking powder together in a dish Beat the egg whites with coconut oil in a different dish Integrate the flour mixture with the beaten egg.

2. Drop in the rest of the ingredients and blend properly Form into cookies with the combination.

3. Cook for approximately 25 minutes Bon appétit!

Nutrition: **Calories: 288 | Fat: 5 g | Fiber: 6 g | Carbohydrates: 12 g | Protein: 23 g**

## 544. Mixed Berries with Pecan Streusel

Ready in: 15-20 minutes | Servings: 3 | Difficulty: Normal

### Ingredients

- 1 egg
- 2 tbsps. cold salted butter, cut into pieces
- ½ c mixed berries
- 3 tbsps. pecans, chopped
- 3 tbsps. granulated Swerve
- ½ tsp ground cinnamon
- 3 tbsps. almonds, slivered
- 2 tbsps. walnuts, chopped

### Directions

1. Integrate the nuts, Swerve, cinnamon, butter, and egg till almost mixed.

2. Put the mixed berries on the base of a secure Air Fryer tray that is lightly oiled Cover with the coating that's been set.

3. Cook for 15 minutes At ambient temperature, serve Bon appétit!

Nutrition: **Calories: 288 | Fat: 5 g | Fiber: 6 g | Carbohydrates: 12 g | Protein: 23 g**

## 545. Soft Buttermilk Biscuits

Ready in: 30 minutes | Servings: 4 | Difficulty: Normal

### Ingredients

- ½ tsp baking powder
- ¾ c buttermilk
- 4 tbsps. butter, chopped
- 1 tsp sugar
- ½ tsp baking soda
- ½ c cake flour
- ¾ tsp salt

### Directions

1. Preheat the Air Fryer to 400°F and mix the ingredients in a cup Put the melted butter and roll it in the bowl's flour mix until it has been lightly breaded Whisk the buttermilk in.

2. Flour a flat, dried surface and roll it out to a dense ½-inch Using a tiny cookie cutter, cut out 10 rounds On a lined baking dish, prepare the biscuits for 10 minutes.

Nutrition; **Calories: 240 | Fat: 8 g | Fiber: 6 g | Carbohydrates: 10 g | Protein: 22 g**

## 546. Apple-Toffee Upside-Down Cake

Ready in: 40 minutes | Servings: 9 | Difficulty: Hard

### Ingredients

- ¾ c coconut sugar + 3 tbsps.
- 1 tsp baking soda
- 1 tsp vinegar
- ¾ c water
- 1 c plain flour
- 1 lemon, zest
- ¼ c almond butter
- 1 ½ tsp mixed spice
- ¼ c sunflower oil
- ½ c walnuts, chopped
- 3 baking apples, cored and sliced

### Directions

1. Preheat the Air Fryer to 390°F.

2. Dissolve the almond butter and 3 tablespoons of sugar in a pan Over a baking dish that would suit the Air Fryer, spoon the mixture Place the pieces of apples on top Just put aside.

3. Combine the flour, ¾ cup of sugar, including baking soda in a blending dish Add the spice mixture.

4. Place the oil, water, vinegar, and then lemon zest in another dish Whisk in the walnuts that have been sliced.

5. Add the wet ingredients until they have been sufficiently blended with the dry ingredients.

6. Spill over the tin with apple slices.

7. Bake for 30 minutes, just until the inserted toothpick comes out clean.

Nutrition: **Calories: 240 | Fat: 8 g | Fiber: 4 g | Carbohydrates: 13 g | Protein: 24 g**

## 547. Tangerine Cake Recipe

Ready in: 10-20 minutes | Servings: 8 | Difficulty: Hard

### Ingredients

- Juice and zest from 1 tangerine
- 2 c flour
- Tangerine segments for serving
- ¾ c sugar
- ¼ c olive oil
- ½ c milk
- ½ tsp vanilla extract
- 1 tsp cider vinegar
- Juice and zest from 2 lemons

### Directions

1. In a cup, combine the flour and sugar and whisk to blend.

2. Add the oil with the milk, vinegar, vanilla essence, lemon juice, zest, and the tangerine zest in another bowl and stir well enough.

3. Add flour; mix properly, put into a cake pan that suits your Air Fryer, attach to the fryer, and bake for 10 minutes Offer with tangerine pieces on top right away.

Nutrition: **Calories: 340 | Fat: 12 g | Fiber: 9 g | Carbohydrates: 14 g | Protein: 27 g**

## 548. Cheese Butter Cookies

Ready in: 19 minutes | Servings: 8 | Difficulty: Easy

### Ingredients

- 1/3 c Mozzarella cheese, shredded
- 2 eggs
- 5 tbsps. butter, melted
- ½ tsp baking powder
- ½ tsp salt
- 1/3 c sour cream
- 1 ¼ c almond flour

**Directions**

1. Heat the fryer to 370°F.
2. In a large bowl, mix all the ingredients and use a hand mixer to combine.
3. Through the mini silicone muffin molds, scoop the batter, then put it in the Air Fryer and cook for 10 minutes.
4. Experience and serve.

Nutrition: **Calories: 340 | Fat: 12 g | Fiber: 9 g | Carbohydrates: 14 g | Protein: 27 g**

## 549. Ricotta Cheese Cake

Ready in: 30–35 minutes | Servings: 8 | Difficulty: Normal

**Ingredients**

• 1 c almond flour
• 1 c Ricotta cheese, soft
• ½ c ghee, melted
• 3 eggs, lightly beaten
• 1/3 c Erythritol
• 1 tsp baking powder

**Directions**

1. Into the cup, combine all the ingredients and blend until well mixed.
2. Put the flour into the oiled Air Fryer's casserole tray and put it in the Air Fryer.
3. Cook for 30 minutes.
4. Slice and serve.

Nutrition: **Calories: 250 | Fat: 12 g | Fiber: 3 g | Carbohydrates: 7 g | Protein: 14 g**

## 550. Almond Chocolate Cupcakes

Ready in: 30 minutes | Servings: 6 | Difficulty: Normal

**Ingredients**

• ½ tsp vanilla extract
• 1 ½ oz. dark chocolate chunks
• ½ c almonds, chopped
• ¾ c self-rising flour
• 1 c powdered sugar
• 2 oz. butter, softened
• 1 egg, whisked
• ¼ tsp salt
• ¼ tsp nutmeg, preferably freshly grated
• 1 tbsp. cocoa powder
• 2 tbsps. almond milk

**Directions**

1. Combine flour mixture by mixing flour, sugar, salt, nutmeg, and cocoa powder in a mixing dish Match to blend properly.
2. Stir the butter, egg, almond milk, then vanilla together in another mixing dish.
3. Then, apply to the dry ingredients the wet egg mixture After which, shape the chocolate pieces and almonds cautiously; swirl to blend softly.
4. Scrap the paste into muffin molds with the batter For 12 minutes, bake the cupcakes at 350°F till a toothpick comes out clean.
5. Adorn if needed with chocolate frosting Serve and love!

Nutrition: **Calories: 250 | Fat: 12 g | Fiber: 3 g | Carbohydrates: 7 g | Protein: 14 g**

## 551. Classic Cake

Ready in: 45 minutes | Servings: 8 | Difficulty: Hard

**Ingredients**

• 1 ½ c coconut flour
• 1 pinch of ground star anise
• ½ c buttermilk
• 1 tsp vanilla essence
• ½ tsp baking powder
• 1 c Swerve
• 4 eggs
• ½ tsp baking soda
• 1 stick butter, at room temperature
• ¼ tsp salt
• 1 pinch of freshly grated nutmeg

**Directions**

1. Start by heating up to 320°F for your Air Fryer Spray with cooking spray on the bottom edge of a cooking pan.
2. Beat the butter and change direction until smooth with a hand mixer Later, fold one at a time into the eggs and blend well until soft.
3. Whisk in the flour together with the rest of the supplies Match to blend properly Into the ready baking pan, scrape the batter.
4. Bake for 15 minutes; turn the pan and bake for a further 15 minutes, until softly squeezed with your fingertips, the top of the cake springs up Bon appétit!

Nutrition: **Calories: 270 | Fat: 6 g | Fiber: 7 g | Carbohydrates: 12 g | Protein: 22 g**

## 552. Angel Food Cake

Ready in: 40 minutes | Servings: 12 | Difficulty: Hard

**Ingredients**

• 2 tsps. cream of tartar
• 1 pinch of salt
• 1 tsp strawberry extract
• ¼ c butter, melted
• 1 c powdered Erythritol
• 12 egg whites

**Directions**

1. Preheat the Air Fryer for 5 minutes.
2. Combine the egg whites with the tartar cream.
3. Using a stick blender and mix once soft and white.
4. Except for the butter, introduce the remaining ingredients and stir for the next minute.
5. Pour it into a bowl for baking.
6. Put in a basket of Air Fryer and cook at 400°F for 30 minutes or if a toothpick inserted in the middle comes out clean.
7. Sprinkle until cooled with melted butter.

Nutrition: **Calories: 261 | Fat: 11 g | Fiber: 1 g | Carbohydrates: 8 g | Protein: 22 g**

## 553. Easy Spanish Churros

Ready in: 32 minutes | Servings: 2 | Difficulty: Normal

**Ingredients**

• ¼ tsp sea salt
• ¼ tsp grated nutmeg
• ¾ c water
• 1 tbsp. Swerve
• 6 tbsps. butter
• ¾ c almond flour
• 2 eggs
• ¼ tsp ground cloves

## Directions

1. Boil the water in a pan over medium heat to make bread, then insert the Swerve, salt, nutmeg, and cloves; bake once soluble.
2. Insert the butter, and then turn the heat to a low level Mix in the almond flour steadily, constantly stirring, till the mixture forms a ball.
3. Turn off the heat; place one egg at a time into the mix, mixing well to combine.
4. With a large star tip, pour the combination into a piping bag Try squeezing the dough pieces into the oiled Air Fryer pan.
5. Working in batches for 6 minutes, simmer at 410°F Bon appétit!

Nutrition: **Calories: 240 | Fat: 7 g | Fiber: 2 g | Carbohydrates: 10 g | Protein: 17 g**

## 554. Fudge Cake with Pecans

Ready in: 40 minutes | Servings: 6 | Difficulty: Hard

### Ingredients

- ¼ tsp fine sea salt
- 1 oz. bakers' chocolate, unsweetened
- ¼ c pecans, finely chopped
- ½ tsp baking powder
- ¼ c cocoa powder
- ½ tsp ground cinnamon
- 1 egg
- ½ c almond flour
- ½ c butter, melted
- ½ c Swerve
- 1 tsp vanilla essence

### Directions

1. Begin by heating up to 350°F on your Air Fryer Now, oil 6 silicone molds gently.
2. Shake the melted butter with the Swerve in a blending dish once smooth After that, whisk in the egg and vanilla and proceed again.
3. Include the almond flour, baking powder, cocoa powder, cinnamon, and salt afterward Mix before it is combined properly.
4. Fold in the pecans and chocolate; blend to combine—Cook for 20–22 minutes in the hot oven Air Fryer Enjoy!

Nutrition: **Calories: 270 | Fat: 5 g | Fiber: 3 g | Carbohydrates: 10 g | Protein: 12 g**

## 555. Almond Coconut Lemon Cake

Ready in: 58 minutes | Servings: 8 | Difficulty: Hard

### Ingredients

- 4 eggs
- 2 tbsps. lemon zest
- ½ c butter softened
- 2 tsps. baking powder
- ½ c fresh lemon juice
- ¼ c Swerve
- 1 tbsp. vanilla
- ¼ c coconut flour
- 2 c almond flour
- 4 eggs
- 2 tbsps. lemon zest
- ½ c butter softened

### Directions

1. Preheat the fryer to 280°F.
2. Sprinkle the Air Fryer with cooking spray on the baking dish and put it aside.
3. Shake all ingredients in a bowl using a hand mixer once smooth.

4. In the prepared bowl, add the butter, put it in the Air Fryer, and cook for a few minutes.
5. Slice and serve.

Nutrition: **Calories: 270 | Fat: 5 g | Fiber: 3 g | Carbohydrates: 10 g | Protein: 12 g**

## 556. Coconut Chocolate

Ready in: 10 minutes | Servings: 2 | Difficulty: Easy

### Ingredients

- 1 tsp butter
- 1 tbsp. cocoa powder
- ¼ tsp vanilla extract
- 1/3 c coconut milk
- ½ oz. dark chocolate
- 1 tsp Monk Fruit

### Directions

1. Mix the coconut milk and cocoa powder in a large bowl Include the vanilla extract and the Monk Fruit whenever the liquid is smooth Slowly pour it.
2. Insert dark chocolate and butter, too.
3. Place the chocolate mixture in the fryer and bake it for 3 minutes at 375°F and mix and simmer the liquid for a further 4 minutes.
4. Detach the cups of hot chocolate gently from the Air Fryer Swirls the hot cocoa softly with the aid of a spoon.

Nutrition: **Calories: 310 | Fat: 5 g | Fiber: 4 g | Carbohydrates: 11 g | Protein: 17 g**

## 557. Pumpkin Bars

Ready in: 35 minutes | Servings: 6 | Difficulty: Normal

### Ingredients

- ¾ tsp baking soda
- ½ c dark sugar-free chocolate chips, divided
- 1 c canned sugar-free pumpkin puree
- ¼ c Swerve
- 1 tsp cinnamon
- ½ tsp ginger
- ⅛ tsp salt
- ¼ tsp nutmeg
- ⅛ tsp ground cloves
- 1 tsp vanilla extract
- ¼ c almond butter
- 1 tbsp. unsweetened almond milk
- ½ c coconut flour

### Directions

1. Preheat the Air Fryer to 360°F and spread the wax paper on a baking sheet.
2. In a pan, blend the pumpkin puree, Swerve, vanilla extract, milk, and butter.
3. In another bowl, mix the coconut flour, spices, salt, including baking soda.
4. Combine both blends once smooth and mix well.
5. Apply around 1/3 cup of chocolate chips without sugar and pass this mixture to the baking tray.
6. Switch to the basket with the Air Fryer and cook for about 25 minutes.

7. On low flame, microwave-free sugar-free chocolate pieces and dish the baked cake out of the pan.

8. Cover with chocolate and slice molten to serve.

Nutrition: **Calories: 270 | Fat: 7 g | Fiber: 9 g | Carbohydrates: 12 g | Protein: 17 g**

## 558. Milky Doughnuts

Ready in: 32 minutes | Servings: 12 | Difficulty: Normal

**Ingredients**

- 2 tbsps. condensed milk
- 1 tbsp. cocoa powder
- Salt, to taste
- ¾ c sugar
- 1 egg
- 1 tbsp. butter, softened

- 1 c all-purpose flour
- 1 c whole wheat flour
- 2 tsps. baking powder
- ½ c milk
- 2 tsps. vanilla extract

**For the glaze:**
- 2 tbsps. icing sugar

**Directions**

1. Start by heating up to 360°F for the Air Fryer.

2. Flour mixture thoroughly in a mixing dish with baking powder and salt.

3. Shake the butter and Swerve once pale and soft with a hand mixer; combine the whisked egg's flavors, vanilla, including butter rum; blend again to mix well Then, mix in the dry components.

4. To blend, add in the sliced walnuts and mix Divide the mixture into small balls; use a fork to straighten each ball and move them to a baking tray lined with foil.

5. Bake for 15 minutes in the hot oven Air Fryer Work in a few lots and move to cool fully to wire racks Bon appétit!

Nutrition: **Calories: 270 | Fat: 7 g | Fiber: 9 g | Carbohydrates: 12 g | Protein: 17 g**

## 559. Delicious Fall Clafoutis

Ready in: 35 minutes | Servings: 6 | Difficulty: Normal

**Ingredients**

- ¾ c coconut milk
- 3 eggs, whisked
- ½ c powdered sugar, for dusting
- ¾ c white sugar
- ½ tsp baking soda
- 1/3 tsp ground cinnamon
- ½ tsp crystallized ginger
- ¼ tsp grated nutmeg

- ½ tsp baking powder
- ¾ c extra-fine flour
- 1 ½ c plums, pitted
- 4 medium-sized pears, cored and sliced
- ½ c coconut cream

**Directions**

1. Gently oil 2 mini pie pans using nonstick cooking oil On top of the pie pans, put the plums and pears on the bottom.

2. Warm the cream together with coconut milk in a frying pan preheated over a low flame until fully cooked.

3. Lift the pan from the heat; whisk along with baking soda and baking powder in the flour.

4. Toss the eggs, white sugar, and spices in a moderate mixing bowl; whip until the combination is smooth.

5. Insert a blend of smooth milk Pour this paste over the fruits cautiously.

6. Bake for about 25 minutes at 320°F To serve, sprinkle with powdered sugar.

Nutrition: **Calories: 260 | Fat: 5 g | Fiber: 7 g | Carbohydrates: 12 g | Protein: 20 g**

## 560. Blueberry Caramel

Ready in: 25 minutes | Servings: 5 | Difficulty: Normal

**Ingredients**

- 4 tbsps. caramel
- 3 tbsps. unsalted butter
- 1 c sliced blueberry

- 3 tbsps. powdered sugar
- 2 c custard powder
- 2 c milk

**Directions**

1. In a saucepan, carry the milk and sugar to a boil, then whisk in the custard powder before the mixture thickens Combine the blueberry slices with the rest of the ingredients and whisk to combine.

2. For 5 minutes, preheat the fryer to 300°F Reduce the temperature to 250°F with the dish in the basket.

3. Cook for 10 minutes before removing it from the oven and allowing it to cool.

4. Serve soft with a layer of caramel on top.

Nutrition: **Calories: 260 | Fat: 5 g | Fiber: 7 g | Carbohydrates: 12 g | Protein: 20 g**

## 561. Barbadian Pudding

Ready in: 15 minutes | Servings: 4 | Difficulty: Easy

**Ingredients**

- 1 c strawberry slices
- 3 tbsps. unsalted butter
- 3 tbsps. powdered sugar

- 2 tbsps. custard powder
- 2 c milk
- 1 c Barbadian pulp

**Directions**

1. In a saucepan, carry the milk, butter, and sugar to a simmer, then whisk in the custard powder and Barbadian pulp until a thick mixture develops.

2. For 5 minutes, preheat the fryer to 300°F.

3. Reduce the temperature to 250°F with the dish in the basket.

4. Cook for 10 minutes before removing from the oven and enabling it to cool Add strawberry slices to the top as a garnish.

Nutrition: **Calories: 270 | Fat: 6 g | Fiber: 7 g | Carbohydrates: 10 g | Protein: 16 g**

## 562. Walnut Milk

Ready in: 20 minutes | Servings: 3 | Difficulty: Easy

**Ingredients**

- 3 tbsps. unsalted butter
- 3 tbsps. powdered sugar
- 2 tbsps. custard powder
- 1 tsp gelatin

- 2 c milk
- 2 c walnut powder

## Directions

1. In a saucepan, carry the milk, butter, and sugar to a simmer, then whisk in the custard powder and walnut powder until a thick mixture develops.
2. Combine all of the products, including the gelatin, and thoroughly blend them.
3. For 5 minutes, preheat the fryer to 300°F Reduce the temperature to 250°F with the dish in the basket Cook for 10 minutes before removing from the oven and enabling it to cool.

Nutrition: **Calories: 356 | Fat: 14 g | Fiber: 4 g | Carbohydrates: 10 g | Protein: 27 g**

## 563. Plum Pudding

Ready in: 15 minutes | Servings: 5 | Difficulty: Easy

### Ingredients

• 3 tbsps. unsalted butter
• 3 tbsps. powdered sugar
• 2 tbsps. custard powder
• 2 c milk
• 1 c plum pulp

### Directions

1. In a saucepan, bring the milk, butter, and sugar to a boil, then whisk in the custard powder and plump pulp until a thick mixture forms.
2. For 5 minutes, preheat the fryer to 300°F Reduce the temperature to 250°F with the dish in the basket Cook for 10 minutes before removing from the oven and enabling it to cool.

Nutrition: **Calories: 270 | Fat: 7 g | Fiber: 2 g | Carbohydrates: 8 g | Protein: 20 g**

## 564. Apple Pudding

Ready in: 20 minutes | Servings: 5 | Difficulty: Easy

### Ingredients

• 1 c strawberry slices
• 3 tbsps. unsalted butter
• 3 tbsps. powdered sugar
• 2 tbsps. custard powder
• 2 c milk
• 1 c apple pulp

### Directions

1. In a saucepan, heat the milk and sugar, then combine the custard powder and apple pulp, stirring rapidly until the mixture thickens
2. For 5 minutes, preheat the fryer to 300°F Reduce the temperature to 250°F with the dish in the basket
3. Cook for 10 minutes before removing from the oven and allowing it to cool
4. Add strawberry slices to the top as a garnish

Nutrition: **Calories: 260 | Fat: 10 g | Fiber: 6 g | Carbohydrates: 8 g | Protein: 22 g**

## 565. Strawberry Pancakes

Ready in: 20 minutes | Servings: 5 | Difficulty: Easy

### Ingredients

• 3 tbsps. butter
• Salt and pepper to taste
• 2 tsps. dried parsley
• 2 tsps. dried basil

• 3 eggs
• 1 ½ c almond flour
• 2 c minced strawberries

### Directions

1. Preheat the Air Fryer to 250°F.
2. Combine the ingredients in a shallow bowl and blend well Make sure the mixture is silky smooth and uniformly spread.
3. Butter the interior of a pancake mold Put the batter into the mold, then in the Air Fryer basket Cook until the pancakes are golden brown on all sides, then serve with maple syrup.

Nutrition: **Calories: 280 | Fat: 17 g | Fiber: 5 g | Carbohydrates: 12 g | Protein: 34 g**

## 566. Creamy Fig Pie

Ready in: 25 minutes | Servings: 5 | Difficulty: Easy

### Ingredients

• 1 tbsp. sliced cashew
• 2 c cold water
• 2 tbsps. powdered sugar
• 3 tbsps. unsalted butter
• 1 ½ c plain flour

**For the filling:**
• 3 tbsps. butter
• 1 c fresh cream
• 2 c sliced figs

### Directions

1. To make a crumbly paste, combine the ingredients in a bowl Place the pasta in plastic wrap and knead it with cold milk.
2. Prick the pie tin sides with a fork after turning out the dough into 2 wide circles Cover the tin with the filling materials that have been cooked on a low flame.
3. The second round should be placed on top of the first Preheat the fryer to 300°F for 5 minutes Cover the tin and drop it in the basket.
4. Remove the tin and cool the pastry until it has become golden brown Serve with a dollop of cream and cut into strips.

Nutrition: **Calories: 280 | Fat: 17 g | Fiber: 5 g | Carbohydrates: 12 g | Protein: 34 g**

## 567. Kidney Beans Waffles

Ready in: 20 minutes | Servings: 4 | Difficulty: Easy

### Ingredients

• 1 c mashed beans
• 3 tbsps. butter
• 2 tsps. dried basil
• Salt and pepper to taste
• 2 tsps. dried parsley
• 3 eggs
• 1 ½ c almond flour

### Directions

1. Preheat the Air Fryer to 250°F Except for the beans, add all of the ingredients in a shallow dish.
2. Make sure the mixture is silky smooth, and uniformly spread Using butter, oil a waffle mold In the Air Fryer basket, Put the batter into the mold.
3. Cook until browned on both sides Make a cavity in the middle and fill it with the beans before serving.

Nutrition: **Calories: 330 | Fat: 13 g | Fiber: 2 g | Carbohydrates: 13 g | Protein: 25 g**

## 568. Teen Mangos Pudding

Ready in: 20 minutes | Servings: 5 | Difficulty: Easy

### Ingredients
- 3 tbsps. unsalted butter
- 3 tbsps. powdered sugar
- 2 tbsps. custard powder
- 2 c milk
- 1 c teen mangos pulp

### Directions
1. In a saucepan, heat the milk, butter, and sugar Combine the custard powder and teen mangos pulp, and constantly stir until the mixture thickens.
2. Preheat the fryer to 300°F for 5 minutes Reduce the temperature to 250°F with the dish in the basket Cook for 10 minutes before removing from the oven and enabling it to cool.

Nutrition: Calories: 213 | Protein: 345 g | Carbohydrates: 05 g | Fat: 71 g | Fiber: 02 g

## 569. Custard Apple Cake

Ready in: 20 minutes | Servings: 4 | Difficulty: Easy

### Ingredients
- ½ c condensed milk
- 1 c custard apple juice
- 1 c corn flour
- 2 tsps. vanilla extract
- 2 tbsps. water
- 1 tbsp. unsalted butter

### Directions
1. To make a smooth paste, combine all of the ingredients and whisk them together.
2. Butter a baking pan Fill the muffin tin halfway with the combination.
3. Preheat the fryer to 300°F for 5 minutes Cover the tin and drop it in the basket Examine the cake and see if it has properly grown.
4. Remove the cake from the oven and allow it to cool completely before serving.

Nutrition: Calories: 247 | Protein: 214 g | Carbohydrates: 17 g | Fat: 171 g | Fiber: 05 g

## 570. Mango Custard

Ready in: 15 minutes | Servings: 6 | Difficulty: Easy

### Ingredients
- 3 tbsps. unsalted butter
- 3 tbsps. powdered sugar
- 2 tbsps. custard powder
- 2 c milk
- 2 c mango slices

### Directions
1. In a saucepan, carry the milk, butter, and sugar to a simmer, then whisk in the custard powder and mango slices until a thick mixture emerges.
2. Preheat the fryer to 300°F for 5 minutes Reduce the temperature to 250°F with the dish in the basket Cook for 10 minutes before removing from the oven and enabling it to cool.

Nutrition: Calories: 247 | Protein: 214 g | Carbohydrates: 17 g | Fat: 171 g | Fiber: 05 g

## 571. Citrus Custard

Ready in: 25 minutes | Servings: 5 | Difficulty: Normal

### Ingredients
- 3 tbsps. unsalted butter
- 3 tbsps. powdered sugar
- 2 tbsps. custard powder
- 2 c milk
- 1 tsp orange zest
- 1 tsp lemon zest
- 1 c kiwis

### Directions
1. In a saucepan, heat the milk, butter, and sugar Combine the custard powder and fruits, and constantly stir until a thick mixture forms.
2. Preheat the fryer to 300°F for 5 minutes Reduce the temperature to 250°F with the dish in the basket Cook for 10 minutes before removing from the oven and enabling it to cool.

Nutrition: Calories: 363 | Protein: 382 g | Carbohydrates: 08 g | Fat: 232 g | Fiber: 02 g

## 572. Persimmons Muffins

Ready in: 20 minutes | Servings: 2 | Difficulty: Easy

### Ingredients
- 1 tsp vanilla extract
- 2 c persimmons pulp
- 2 tbsps. sugar
- 2 tbsps. butter
- 3 eggs
- 1 ½ c milk
- 2 c cornstarch

### Directions
1. To make a crumbly paste, combine the ingredients and blend between your fingertips.
2. Continuously add in the baking soda with the sugar Mix in the milk to make a batter, which you'll need to pour into muffin molds.
3. Preheat the fryer to 300°F for 5 minutes The muffin molds should be placed in the basket and covered.
4. Cook for 15 minutes, and use a toothpick to determine whether the muffins are finished Serve immediately after removing the cups.

Nutrition: Calories: 220 | Protein: 183 g | Carbohydrates: 22 g | Fat: 67 g | Fiber: 61 g

## 573. Mango Muffins

Ready in: 20 minutes | Servings: 4 | Difficulty: Easy

### Ingredients
- 2 tbsps. maple syrup
- ½ tsp baking powder
- 2 tbsps. butter
- ½ tsp baking soda
- 2 c mango pulp
- 1 ½ c buttermilk
- 2 c all-purpose flour

### Directions
1. To make a crumbly paste, combine the ingredients and blend between your fingertips.
2. Continuously add in the baking soda with the sugar Mix in the milk to make a batter, which you'll need to pour into muffin molds.

3. Preheat the fryer to 300°F for 5 minutes The muffin molds should be placed in the basket and covered.

4. Cook for 15 minutes, and use a toothpick to determine whether the muffins are finished Serve immediately after removing the cups.

Nutrition: **Calories: 150 | Protein: 146 g | Carbohydrates: 46 g | Fat: 79 g | Fiber: 12 g**

## 574. Blackberry Buttermilk Cupcakes

Ready in: 15 minutes | Servings: 5 | Difficulty: Easy

### Ingredients
- 2 c sliced blackberries
- 2 tbsps. sugar
- 2 tbsps. butter
- ½ tsp baking soda
- ½ tsp baking powder
- 1 ½ c buttermilk
- 2 c all-purpose flour

### Directions
1. To make a crumbly paste, combine the ingredients and blend between your fingertips.

2. Continuously pour in the baking soda with the sugar Mix in the milk to produce a batter, which you'll need to put into muffin molds.

3. Preheat the fryer to 300°F for 5 minutes The muffin molds should be put in the basket and sealed.

4. Cook for 15 minutes, and use a toothpick to determine whether the muffins are finished Serve immediately after removing the cups.

Nutrition: **Calories: 231 | Protein: 225 g | Carbohydrates: 21 g | Fat: 146 g | Fiber: 1 g**

## 575. Apricot and Fig Muffins

Ready in: 27 minutes | Servings: 3 | Difficulty: Easy

### Ingredients
- 2 tsps. vinegar
- 2 c sliced figs
- 2 c sliced apricots
- 1 tbsp. honey
- 2 tbsps. butter
- ½ tsp baking soda
- ½ tsp baking powder
- 1 ½ c milk
- 2 c wheat flour

### Directions
1. To make a crumbly paste, combine the ingredients and blend between your fingertips.

2. In a large mixing cup, add the baking soda and vinegar Mix in the milk to make a batter, which you'll need to pour into muffin molds.

3. Preheat the fryer to 300°F for 5 minutes The muffin molds should be placed in the basket and covered.

4. Cook for 15 minutes, and use a toothpick to determine whether the muffins are finished Serve shortly after extracting the cups.

Nutrition: **Calories: 352 | Protein: 274 g | Carbohydrates: 442 g | Fat: 94 g | Fiber: 104 g**

## 576. Jackfruit Pudding

Ready in: 27 minutes | Servings: 4 | Difficulty: Normal

### Ingredients
- 3 tbsps. unsalted butter
- 3 tbsps. powdered sugar
- 2 tbsps. custard powder
- 2 c milk
- 2 c grated jackfruit

## Directions
1. In a saucepan, bring the milk, butter, and sugar to a boil, then whisk in the custard powder and jackfruit juice before the mixture thickens.

2. Preheat the fryer to 300°F for 5 minutes Reduce the temperature to 250°F with the dish in the basket Cook for 10 minutes before removing from the oven and enabling it to cool.

Nutrition: **Calories: 134 | Protein: 76 g | Carbohydrates: 87 g | Fat: 77 g | Fiber: 19 g**

## 577. Papaya and Pineapple Pie

Ready in: 15 minutes | Servings: 4 | Difficulty: Easy

### Ingredients
- 2 c cold milk
- 4 tsps. powdered sugar
- 1 tbsp. unsalted butter
- 1 c plain flour

**For the filling:**
- 2 tsps. lemon juice
- ½ tsp cinnamon
- 2 tbsps. sugar
- 1 c sliced papaya
- 1 c sliced pineapple

## Directions
1. To make a crumbly paste, combine the ingredients in a bowl Place the pasta in plastic wrap and knead it with cold milk.

2. Prick the pie tin sides with a fork after turning out the dough into 2 wide circles.

3. Cover the tin with the filling materials that have been cooked on a low flame The second round should be placed on top of the first.

4. Preheat the fryer to 300°F for 5 minutes Cover the tin and drop it in the basket.

5. Remove the tin and cool the pastry until it has become golden brown

6. Serve with a dollop of cream and cut into strips.

Nutrition: **Calories: 136 | Protein: 165 g | Carbohydrates: 44 g | Fat: 55 g | Fiber: 04 g**

## 578. Lamb Muffins

Ready in: 30 minutes | Servings: 4 | Difficulty: Normal

### Ingredients
- 2 c minced lamb
- 2 tbsps. sugar
- 2 tbsps. butter
- 3 eggs
- 1 ½ c milk
- 2 c cornstarch

## Directions
1. To produce a crumbly paste, combine the ingredients and blend between your fingertips.

2. Continuously pour in the baking soda with the sugar Mix in the milk to produce a batter, which you'll need to put into the muffin molds.

3. Preheat the fryer to 300°F for 5 minutes The muffin molds should be put in the basket and sealed Cook for 15 minutes, and use a toothpick to determine whether the muffins are finished.
4. Serve shortly after extracting the molds.

Nutrition: **Calories: 164 | Protein: 189 g | Carbohydrates: 56 g | Fat: 8 g | Fiber: 16 g**

## 579. Chicken and Honey Muffins
Ready in: 30 minutes | Servings: 6 | Difficulty: Normal
### Ingredients
• 2 tbsps. honey
• 2 c minced chicken
• 2 tbsps. Butter
• ½ tsp Baking soda
• ½ tsp baking powder
• 1 ½ c buttermilk
• 2 c all-purpose flour

### Directions
1. To make a crumbly paste, combine the ingredients and blend between your fingertips.
2. Continuously pour in the baking soda with the sugar Mix in the milk to produce a batter, which you'll need to put into the muffin molds.
3. Preheat the fryer to 300°F for 5 minutes The muffin molds should be put in the basket and sealed.
4. Cook for 15 minutes, and use a toothpick to verify whether the muffins are finished Serve shortly after extracting the molds.

Nutrition: **Calories: 221 | Protein: 259 g | Carbohydrates: 05 g | Fat: 123 g | Fiber: 0 g**

## 580. Mixed Fruit Cupcake
Ready in: 20 minutes | Servings: 4 | Difficulty: Easy
### Ingredients
• ½ c condensed milk
• 1 c all-purpose flour
• 2 c mixed fruit
• 2 tbsps. water
• 1 tbsp. unsalted butter

### Directions
1. Add all of the ingredients and whisk them together to produce a smooth paste.
2. Butter a baking pan Fill the muffin tin halfway with the combination.
3. Preheat the fryer to 300°F for 5 minutes Cover the tin and drop it in the basket Examine the cake and see if it has properly grown Take the cake from the oven and allow it to cool fully before serving.

Nutrition: **Calories: 221 | Protein: 259 g | Carbohydrates: 05 g | Fat: 123 g | Fiber: 0 g**

## 581. Pear Muffins
Ready in: 20 minutes | Servings: 6 | Difficulty: Easy
### Ingredients
• 2 c sliced pears
• 2 tbsps. sugar
• 2 tbsps. butter
• ½ tsp baking soda

• ½ tsp baking powder
• 1 ½ c buttermilk
• 2 c all-purpose flour

### Directions
1. To make a crumbly paste, combine the ingredients and blend between your fingertips.
2. Continuously pour in the baking soda with the sugar Mix in the milk to produce a batter, which you'll need to put into the muffin molds.
3. Preheat the fryer to 300°F for 5 minutes The muffin molds should be put in the basket and sealed.
4. Cook for 15 minutes, and use a toothpick to verify whether the muffins are finished Serve shortly after extracting the molds.

Nutrition: **Calories: 117 | Protein: 101 g | Carbohydrates: 164 g | Fat: 12 g | Fiber: 37 g**

## 582. Vanilla Cupcakes
Ready in: 21 minutes | Servings: 4 | Difficulty: Easy
### Ingredients
• 2 tsps. vinegar
• 3 tbsps. vanilla extract
• 1 tbsp. honey
• 2 tbsps. butter
• ½ tsp baking soda
• ½ tsp baking powder
• 1 ½ c milk
• 2 c wheat flour

### Directions
1. To make a crumbly paste, combine all of the ingredients in a mixing bowl and crumble with your fingertips.
2. Continuously mix the baking soda and vinegar into the milk Add the milk to the liquid to make a batter that you'll need to pour into the muffin molds.
3. Preheat the fryer for 5 minutes at 300°F Place the muffin molds in the basket and cover them with plastic wrap.
4. Cook the muffins for 15 minutes, and measure them with a toothpick to see whether they're finished Remove the molds from the oven and eat immediately.

Nutrition: **Calories: 117 | Protein: 101 g | Carbohydrates: 164 g | Fat: 12 g | Fiber: 37 g**

## 583. Mixed Vegetable Muffins
Ready in: 24 minutes | Servings: 4 | Difficulty: Easy
### Ingredients
• 1 tbsp. sugar
• 2 c mixed vegetables
• 2 tbsps. butter
• ½ tsp baking soda
• ½ tsp baking powder
• 1 ½ c milk
• 2 c all-purpose flour

### Directions
1. To make a crumbly paste, combine all of the ingredients in a mixing bowl and crumble with your fingertips.
2. Continuously pour the baking soda into the milk Add the milk to the mix to make a batter that you'll need to pour into the muffin molds.
3. Preheat the fryer for 5 minutes at 300°F Place the muffin molds in the basket and cover them with plastic wrap.

4. Cook the muffins for 15 minutes, and check them with a too-thpick to see whether they're finished Remove the molds from the oven and eat immediately.

Nutrition: Calories: 465 | Protein: 232 g | Carbohydrates: 355 g | Fat: 25 g | Fiber: 42 g

## 584. Blueberry Cake

Ready in: 21 minutes | Servings: 2 | Difficulty: Easy

**Ingredients**
- ½ c condensed milk
- 1 c all-purpose flour
- 2 c sliced blueberries
- 2 tbsps. water
- 1 tbsp. unsalted butter

**Directions**

1. Combine the ingredients in a mixing bowl and whisk until smooth

2. Oil a baking pan with butter and set it aside Fill the tin halfway with the combination

3. Preheat the fryer for 5 minutes at 300°F You'll need to cover the tin and drop it in the basket Check to see if the cake has risen properly Serve after the cake has cooled and been garnished with chocolate chips

Nutrition: Calories: 465 | Protein: 232 g | Carbohydrates: 355 g | Fat: 25 g | Fiber: 42 g

## 585. Corn Waffles

Ready in: 20 minutes | Servings: 3 | Difficulty: Easy

**Ingredients**
- 2 c boiled corn and mayonnaise
- 3 tbsps. butter
- Salt and pepper to taste
- 2 tsps. dried parsley
- 2 tsps. dried basil
- 3 eggs
- 1 ½ c almond flour

**Directions**

1. Preheat the oven to 250°F.

2. Combine all of the products in a little bowl, except the corn and mayonnaise Make sure the mixture is consistent and evenly distributed.

3. Butter a waffle model and use it to make waffles Fill the mold with batter and put it in the Air Fryer basket.

4. Cook until all sides are golden colored Make a cavity and cover it with corn and mayonnaise before serving.

Nutrition: Calories: 180 | Protein: 277 g | Carbohydrates: 1 g | Fat: 65 g | Fiber: 03 g

## 586. Mexican Waffles

Ready in: 15 minutes | Servings: 4 | Difficulty: Easy

**Ingredients**
- 2 tbsps. salsa
- 1 c black olives
- 1 c green olives
- 1 c pickled jalapeños
- 3 tbsps. butter
- Salt and pepper to taste
- 2 tsps. dried parsley
- 2 tsps. dried basil

- 3 eggs
- 1 ½ c almond flour

**Directions**

1. Preheat the oven to 250°F.

2. Combine all of the ingredients in a shallow bowl, except the jalapeños, olives, and salsa Make sure the mixture is consistent and evenly distributed.

3. Butter a waffle model and use it to make waffles Fill the mold with batter and put it in the Air Fryer basket.

4. Cook until all sides are golden colored Make a cavity and fill it with the jalapeños, olives, and salsa before serving.

Nutrition: Calories: 180 | Protein: 277 g | Carbohydrates: 1 g | Fat: 65 g | Fiber: 03 g

## 587. Honey and Blackberry Cake

Ready in: 20 minutes | Servings: 6 | Difficulty: Easy

**Ingredients**
- 2 tsps. vinegar
- 2 c sliced blackberry
- 2 tbsps. honey
- 2 tbsps. butter
- ½ tsp Baking soda
- ½ tsp baking powder
- 1 ½ c milk
- 2 c all-purpose flour

**Directions**

1. To make a crumbly paste, combine all of the ingredients in a mixing bowl and crumble with your fingertips.

2. Continuously mix the baking soda and vinegar into the milk Add the milk to the mix to make a batter that you'll need to pour into the muffin molds.

3. Preheat the fryer for 5 minutes at 300°F Place the muffin molds in the basket and cover them with plastic wrap.

4. Cook the muffins for 15 minutes, and check them with a too-thpick to see whether they're finished Remove the molds from the oven and eat immediately.

Nutrition: Calories: 298 | Protein: 349 g | Carbohydrates: 131 g | Fat: 117 g | Fiber: 31 g

## 588. Dark Chocolate Muffins

Ready in: 25 minutes | Servings: 4 | Difficulty: Easy

**Ingredients**
- 1 tbsp. sugar
- 2 tbsps. butter
- ½ tsp baking soda
- ½ tsp baking powder
- 3 tbsps. dark cocoa powder
- 1 ½ c milk
- 2 c all-purpose flour

**Directions**

1. To make a crumbly paste, combine all of the ingredients in a mixing bowl and crumble with your fingertips.

2. Continuously pour the baking soda into the milk Add the milk to the mix to make a batter that you'll need to pour into the muffin molds.

3. Preheat the fryer for 5 minutes at 300°F Place the muffin molds in the basket and cover them with plastic wrap.

4. Cook the muffins for 15 minutes Check them with a toothpick to see whether they're finished Remove the molds from the oven and eat immediately.

Nutrition: **Calories: 298 | Protein: 349 g | Carbohydrates: 131 g | Fat: 117 g | Fiber: 31 g**

## 589. Raspberry Cake

Ready in: 25 minutes | Servings: 5 | Difficulty: Easy

**Ingredients**

• ½ c condensed milk
• 1 c all-purpose flour
• 2 c sliced raspberries
• 2 tbsps. water
• 1 tbsp. unsalted butter

**Directions**

1. Combine the ingredients in a mixing bowl and whisk until smooth.

2. Oil a baking pan with butter and set it aside Fill the tin halfway with the combination.

3. Preheat the fryer for 5 minutes at 300°F You'll need to cover the tin and drop it in the basket.

4. Check to see if the cake has risen properly Serve after the cake has cooled and been garnished with chocolate chips.

Nutrition: **Calories: 139 | Protein: 139 g | Carbohydrates: 102 g | Fat: 45 g | Fiber: 21 g**

## 590. Cardamom Cheese Cake

Ready in: 20 minutes | Servings: 6 | Difficulty: Easy

**Ingredients**

• 2 tbsps. sugar
• 2 tbsps. butter
• ½ tsp baking soda
• 1 c cheese
• ½ tsp baking powder
• 1 tbsp. cardamom powder
• 1 ½ c milk
• 2 c all-purpose flour

**Directions**

1. To make a crumbly paste, combine all of the ingredients in a mixing bowl and crumble with your fingertips.

2. Continuously pour the baking soda into the milk Add the milk to the mix to make a batter that you'll need to pour into the muffin molds.

3. Preheat the fryer for 5 minutes at 300°F Place the muffin molds in the basket and cover them with plastic wrap.

4. Cook the muffins for 15 minutes, and check them with a toothpick to see whether they're finished Remove the molds from the oven and eat immediately.

Nutrition: **Calories: 139 | Protein: 139 g | Carbohydrates: 102 g | Fat: 45 g | Fiber: 21 g**

## 591. Mediterranean Waffles

Ready in: 15 minutes | Servings: 4 | Difficulty: Easy

**Ingredients**

• 1 c coleslaw
• 3 tbsps. butter
• Salt and pepper to taste
• 2 tsps. dried parsley
• 2 tsps. dried basil
• 3 eggs
• 1 ½ c almond flour

**Directions**

1. Preheat the oven to 250°F Combine all of the products, except the coleslaw, in a shallow mixing cup.

2. Be sure the mixture is consistent and well-balanced before proceeding Butter a waffle model and use it to make waffles.

3. Fill the mold with batter and put it in the Air Fryer basket Cook until all sides are golden colored Make a cavity and cover it with coleslaw before serving.

Nutrition: **Calories: 269 | Protein: 221 g | Carbohydrates: 68 g | Fat: 162 g | Fiber: 06 g**

## 592. Cranberry Pudding

Ready in: 20 minutes | Servings: 4 | Difficulty: Easy

**Ingredients**

• 3 tbsps. unsalted butter
• 3 tbsps. powdered sugar
• 2 tbsps. custard powder
• 2 c milk
• 1 c cranberry juice

**Directions**

1. In a saucepan, bring the milk, butter, and sugar to a boil, then add custard powder and cranberry juice, and constantly stir until the mixture thickens.

2. Preheat the fryer for 5 minutes at 300°F Reduce the temperature to 250°F and put the dish in the basket.

3. Cook for 10 minutes before removing from the heat and allowing it to cool.

Nutrition: **Calories: 269 | Protein: 221 g | Carbohydrates: 68 g | Fat: 162 g | Fiber: 06 g**

## 593. Butterscotch Cake

Ready in: 15 minutes | Servings: 6 | Difficulty: Easy

**Ingredients**

• ½ c condensed milk
• 1 c corn flour
• 2 tbsps. brown sugar
• 2 tsps. vanilla extract
• 2 tbsps. water
• 1 tbsp. unsalted butter

**Directions**

1. Combine the ingredients in a mixing bowl and whisk until smooth.

2. Oil a baking pan with butter and set it aside Fill the tin halfway with the combination.

3. Preheat the fryer for 5 minutes at 300°F You'll need to cover the tin and drop it in the basket.

4. Check to see if the cake has risen properly Allow the cake to cool before serving.

Nutrition: **Calories: 398 | Protein: 428 g | Carbohydrates: 102 g | Fat: 204 g | Fiber: 18 g**

## 594. Kiwi Custard

Ready in: 20 minutes | Servings: 4 | Difficulty: Easy

**Ingredients**
- 3 tbsps. unsalted butter
- 3 tbsps. powdered sugar
- 2 tbsps. custard powder
- 2 c milk
- 1 c kiwi slices

**Directions**

1. In a saucepan, bring the milk, butter, and sugar to a boil; add the custard powder and kiwi pieces, and stir, until the mixture thickens.

2. Preheat the fryer for 5 minutes at 300°F Reduce the temperature to 250°F and put the dish in the basket.

3. Cook for 10 minutes before removing from the heat and allowing it to cool.

Nutrition: **Calories: 398 | Protein: 428 g | Carbohydrates: 102 g | Fat: 204 g | Fiber: 18 g**

## 595. Fruit Custard

Ready in: 25 minutes | Servings: 4 | Difficulty: Easy

**Ingredients**
- 3 tbsps. unsalted butter
- 3 tbsps. powdered sugar
- 2 tbsps. custard powder
- 2 c milk
- 1 c mixed fruits

**Directions**

1. In a saucepan, carry the milk, butter, and sugar to a simmer, combine the custard powder and mixed fruits, and stir rapidly until the mixture thickens.

2. Preheat the fryer for 5 minutes at 300°F.

3. Reduce the temperature to 250°F and put the dish in the basket Cook for 10 minutes before removing from the heat and allowing it to cool.

Nutrition: **Calories: 398 | Protein: 428 g | Carbohydrates: 102 g | Fat: 204 g | Fiber: 18 g**

## 596. Butter Cake

Ready in: 20 minutes | Servings: 4 | Difficulty: Normal

**Ingredients**
- a pinch of salt
- 7 tbsp. butter, at room temperature
- 1 egg
- 2 tbsp. white sugar
- 1 2/3 c all-purpose flour
- ¼ c white sugar
- 6 tbsp. milk
- cooking spray

**Directions**

1. Preheat your air fryer to about 350°F (180 degrees C) Using cooking spray, coat a small flared tube pan.

2. In a mixing bowl, whisk together the butter and 1/4 cup plus 2 tablespoons sugar with an electric blender until the mixture is light and fluffy.

3. Mix in the egg until it is smooth and frothy Combine flour and salt in a mixing bowl.

4. Add the milk and completely combine the batter Pour the mixture into the prepared pan and smooth the top with the backside of a spoon.

5. In the air fryer basket, put the pan Make a 15-minute timer on your clock Cook until a knife put into the center of the pan pulls out clean Remove the cake from the pan and set it aside to cool for around 5 minutes.

Nutrition: **Calories: 347 | Protein: 52 g | Carbohydrates: 569 g | Fat: 117 g | Fiber: 732 mg**

## 597. Beignets

Ready in: 15 minutes | Servings: 4 | Difficulty: Normal

**Ingredients**
- a pinch of salt
- ½ c all-purpose flour
- ½ tsp baking powder
- ⅛ c water
- 1 ½ tsp melted butter
- 1 large egg, separated
- ½ tsp vanilla extract
- ¼ c white sugar
- 2 tbsp. icing sugar
- cooking spray

**Directions**

1. Preheat the air fryer to about 370°F (185 degrees C) Using nonstick cooking spray, coat a silicone egg-bite mold.

2. In a large mixing bowl, combine sugar, flour, egg yolk, water, butter, vanilla essence, baking powder, and salt To mix, stir everything together.

3. In a small mixing bowl, beat egg whites on medium speed with an electric food processor until stiff peaks form Toss into the batter Using a tiny hinged ice cream scoop, spoon batter into the prepared mold.

4. Fill the silicone mold and place it in the air fryer basket Cook for 10 minutes in a preheated air fryer Carefully remove the mold from the basket; pop the beignets out and turn them over onto a parchment paper ring.

5. Return the beignets to the air fryer basket on the parchment circle Cook for a further 4 minutes Dust the beignets with confectioners' sugar after removing them from the air fryer basket.

Nutrition: **Calories: 88 | Protein: 18 g | Carbohydrates: 163 g | Fat: 17 g | Fiber: 735 mg**

## 598. Triple-Chocolate Oatmeal Cookies

Ready in: 10 minutes | Servings: 2 | Difficulty: Easy

**Ingredients**
- 1 c chopped walnuts (Optional)
- 1 ½ c all-purpose flour
- 1 tsp vanilla extract
- 1 (34 ounces) package instant chocolate pudding mix
- ¾ c white sugar
- 1 tsp salt
- ¾ c brown sugar
- 1 c butter, softened
- 2 eggs
- 1 tsp baking soda
- 2 c chocolate chips
- ¼ c cocoa powder
- nonstick cooking spray
- 3 c quick-cooking oatmeal

**Directions**

1. Preheat your air fryer to about 350 degrees F (175 degrees C), as the manufacturer directs Using nonstick cooking spray, coat the air fryer basket.

2. In a mixing dish, combine the flour, oatmeal, pudding mix, cocoa powder, baking soda, and salt Let it rest.

3. Using an electric blender, beat together brown sugar, butter, and white sugar in a separate dish Combine the eggs and vanilla essence in a mixing bowl Mix in the oatmeal mixture well Combine the chocolate chips and walnuts in a mixing bowl.

4. Using a big cookie spoon, put the dough into the air fryer; smooth out and allow approximately 1 inch between each biscuit Cook for 6 to 10 minutes, or until gently browned Before serving, cool on a wire rack.

Nutrition: **Calories: 199 | Protein: 29 g | Carbohydrates: 247 g | Fat: 107 g | Fiber: 180 mg**

## 599. Roasted Bananas
Ready in: 10 minutes | Servings: 2 | Difficulty: Easy
**Ingredients**
• avocado oil or some other cooking spray
• 1 banana, peeled sliced into 1/8-inch thick diagonals

**Directions**
1. Using some parchment paper, line the air fryer basket Preheat your air fryer to about 375°F (190 degrees C)
2. Put banana pieces in the basket, ensuring they don't touch; if required, cook in groups Avocado oil should be sprayed over banana slices
3. Cook for 5 minutes in the air fryer Retrieve the banana slices from the basket and gently turn them (they will be soft)
4. Cook for another 2 to 3 minutes, or until the banana pieces are browning and caramelized Remove from the basket with care

Nutrition: **Calories: 107 | Protein: 13 g | Carbohydrates: 27 g | Fat: 07 g | Fiber: 84 mg**

## 600. Apple Fritters
Ready in: 10 minutes | Servings: 2 | Difficulty: Easy
**Ingredients**
• 2 tbsp. white sugar
• ½ tsp ground cinnamon
• 1 c all-purpose flour
• a pinch of salt
• 1 ½ tsp baking powder
• 1 egg
• ¼ c milk
• ¼ c white sugar
• 1 apple - peeled, cored, and chopped
• cooking spray
**Glaze:**
• ½ tsp caramel extract (such as Watkins™)
• 1 tbsp. Milk
• ¼ tsp ground cinnamon
• ½ c confectioners' sugar

**Directions**
1. Preheat your air fryer to 350°F (175 degrees C) In the base of the air fryer, place a circle of parchment paper Using nonstick frying spray, coat the pan.
2. In a small mixing bowl, combine 1/4 cup sugar, flour, egg, milk, baking powder, and salt Stir until everything is well mixed
3. In a separate dish, combine 2 tablespoons sugar and cinnamon; sprinkle over apples until evenly covered Mix the apples into the flour mixture until everything is well mixed.
4. Using a cookie scoop, put fritters into the air fryer basket's base Air-fry for 5 minutes in a prepared fryer Cook for another 5 minutes after flipping the patties.

5. In a separate dish, combine caramel extract, milk, sugar, and cinnamon Pour glaze over fritters and place on a cooling rack.

Nutrition: **Calories: 173 | Protein: 39 g | Carbohydrates: 175 g | Fat: 98 g | Fiber: 84 mg**

## 601. Churros
Ready in: 12-15 minutes | Servings: 2 | Difficulty: Normal
**Ingredients**
• ½ tsp ground cinnamon
• 2 eggs
• ½ c all-purpose flour
• a pinch of salt
• ¼ c white sugar
• ½ c milk

**Directions**
1. In a small saucepan, melt the butter Stir in the milk and season with salt Reduce the heat to moderate and bring to a simmer, constantly stirring with a wooden spoon Add the flour all at once Stir the dough until it comes together.
2. Turn off the heat and set it aside to cool for 5–7 minutes With a wooden spoon, stir in the eggs till the dough joins together Fill a pastry bag with the dough and a big star tip directly into the air fryer basket, pipe dough into rectangles.
3. Air fried churros for 5 minutes at about 340 degrees F (175 degrees C) Next, in a separate dish, mix the sugar and cinnamon and pour over a flat plate Take the cooked churros out of the air fryer and roll them in the cinnamon-sugar mix.

Nutrition: **Calories: 173 | Protein: 39 g | Carbohydrates: 175 g | Fat: 21 g | Fiber: 112 mg**

## 602. Fried Oreos
Ready in: 10 minutes | Servings: 4 | Difficulty: Easy
**Ingredients**
• 1 tbsp. sugar
• 9 any chocolate sandwich cookies
• cooking spray
• 1/3 c of water
• ½ c of pancake mix

**Directions**
1. Combine the pancake mix and water in a large mixing bowl Using parchment paper, line an air fryer basket.
2. Using nonstick cooking spray, coat parchment paper Place each cookie in the basket after dipping it in the pancake batter Make sure they're not touching and, if required, cook them in batches.
3. Preheat the air fryer to 400 degrees Fahrenheit (200 degrees Celsius) (200 degrees C) Fry for 4 to 5 minutes with the basket in place; turn and cook for another 2 to 3 minutes until golden brown Lastly, dust with powdered sugar.

Nutrition: **Calories: 77 | Protein: 12 g | Carbohydrates: 137 g | Fat: 21 g | Fiber: 156 mg**

## CONCLUSION

These times, air frying is one of the most common cooking techniques, and Air Fryers have become one of the chef's most impressive devices In no time, Air Fryers can help you prepare nutritious and tasty meals! You do not need to be a master in the kitchen to prepare unique dishes for you and your family members

Everything you have to do is buy an Air Fryer and this wonderful cookbook for your device! Soon, you can make the greatest dishes ever and inspire those around you.

Cooked meals at home by you! Believe us! Get your hands on an Air Fryer and this handy set of recipes for Air Fryers and begin your new cooking experience! Have fun!

# A SPECIAL GIFT FOR YOU!

Thank you for reading this book.
If you enjoyed it, please visit the site where you purchased it and write a brief review. Your feedback is important to me and will help other readers decide whether to read the book too.

I have an extraordinary gift ready for you!

You can either click on the link,
**https://BookHip.com/TBCVDJL**

or use the QR Code with your smartphone, or alternatively send an email to **rachel89dash@gmail.com** and you will receive for free a colour copy of : Instant Vortex air Fryer Cookbook full of images !!!

You got it right! This Gift contains all the recipes of the cookbook that you have already purchased in a beautiful graphic design and with a color image for every single recipe!
**What are you waiting for?**

**Thank you! — Rachel Dash**

Made in United States
North Haven, CT
19 March 2022

17325815R00083